Investigation

CHILD VICTIMS,
CHILD WITNESSES

CHILD VICTIMS, CHILD WITNESSES

Understanding and Improving Testimony

Edited by

Gail S. Goodman
Bette L. Bottoms

The Guilford Press
New York   London

Printed in the United States of America

This book is printed on acid-free paper.

Last digit is print number: 9 8 7 6 5 4 3 2

Library of Congress Cataloging-in-Publication Data

Child victims, child witnesses : understanding and improving testimony
/ edited by Gail S. Goodman, Bette L. Bottoms.
     p.   cm.
  Includes bibliographical references and index.
  ISBN 0-89862-789-3
  1. Children as witnesses—United States.   2. Interviewing in child
abuse—United States. 3. Child molesting—United States—
Psychology. 5. Psychology, Forensic.   I. Goodman, Gail S.
II. Bottoms, Bette L.
KF9672.A75C48   1993
347.73′66′083—dc20
[347.30766083]   92-30072
                                                   CIP

Contributors

JENNIFER MARIE BATTERMAN-FAUNCE, M.A., is a graduate student in Clinical Psychology at the State University of New York at Buffalo.

BARBARA W. BOAT, Ph.D., is an Associate Professor of Psychiatry in the Department of Psychiatry, University of North Carolina at Chapel Hill, and a Codirector of the Program on Childhood Trauma and Maltreatment.

GAIL K. BORNSTEIN, B.S., is a graduate of the University of California, Los Angeles.

BETTE L. BOTTOMS, Ph.D., is an Assistant Professor of Psychology at the University of Illinois at Chicago.

KAY BUSSEY, Ph.D., is a Senior Lecturer in Psychology at Macquarie University.

MARK D. EVERSON, Ph.D., is a Clinical Associate Professor of Psychiatry, University of North Carolina at Chapel Hill, and a Codirector of the Program on Childhood Trauma and Maltreatment.

ROBYN FIVUSH, Ph.D., is an Associate Professor of Psychology at Emory University.

RHONA H. FLIN, Ph.D., is Reader in Applied Psychology at The Robert Gordon University, Aberdeen, Scotland.

SUSAN GEE, B.A. (Honors), is a Ph.D. student in the Psychology Department at the University of Otago, Dunedin, New Zealand.

R. EDWARD GEISELMAN, Ph.D., is a Professor of Psychology at the University of California, Los Angeles.

GAIL S. GOODMAN, Ph.D., is Professor of Psychology at the University of California at Davis.

ELIZABETH J. GRIMBEEK, B.A., is a graduate student in Women's Studies at the University of New South Wales.

ROBIN HUNTER, B.A., is a former Research Assistant at the University of British Columbia.

PETER K. ISQUITH, Ph.D., is a Fellow in Psychology at Harvard Medical School and Children's Hospital, Boston.

RISHA JOFFE, M.A., is pursuing doctoral work in psychology at the University of British Columbia.

KERRY LEE, B.A. (Honors), is a graduate student in Psychology at Macquarie University.

MICHAEL R. LEIPPE, Ph.D., is an Associate Professor of Psychology at Adelphi University.

MURRAY LEVINE, J.D., Ph.D., is a Professor of Psychology in the Department of Psychology and an Adjunct Professor of Law in the School of Law at the State University of New York at Buffalo; he is also Codirector of the Research Center for Children and Youth at the State University of New York at Buffalo.

ANDREW P. MANION, Ph.D., is an Assistant Professor of Psychology at St. Mary's College of Minnesota.

MARGARET-ELLEN PIPE, Ph.D., is on the faculty of the Psychology Department at the University of Otago, Dunedin, New Zealand.

ANN ROMANCZYK, M.A., is an Assistant Professor of Psychology at Slippery Rock University and is currently completing her doctorate at Adelphi University.

DESMOND K. RUNYAN, M.D., Dr.P.H., is Associate Professor of Social Medicine and Pediatrics at the University of North Carolina School of Medicine at Chapel Hill.

KAREN J. SAYWITZ, Ph.D., is an Assistant Professor of Psychiatry at the UCLA School of Medicine, Harbor–UCLA Medical Center.

JANINE SCHEINER, Ph.D., is the Director of Child and Family Services of Sullivan County for West Central Services, New Hampshire.

LYNN SNYDER, Ph.D., is a Professor of Communicative Disorders at California State University, Long Beach.

CLARE WILSON, B.Sc. (Honors), is a Ph.D. student in the Psychology Department at the University of Otago, Dunedin, New Zealand.

JOHN C. YUILLE, Ph.D., is a Professor of Psychology at the University of British Columbia.

JUDY ZAPARNIUK, M.A., is a Psychology Ph.D. student at the University of British Columbia.

Preface

Our intention in this book is to provide a set of stimulating, scholarly, up-to-date chapters on children's testimony—chapters that are research based but clinically relevant. That's a tall order, but one we feel the contributors have skillfully met. Our second goal in conceiving this book was to stimulate research and thinking about how to optimize children's performance as accurate witnesses. Although debates about children's abilities in this domain are likely to continue for years, researchers can make substantial contributions to society by exploring techniques that help children communicate their experiences accurately and completely.

As readers will quickly see, most of the chapters of this book concern forensic issues related to child victims of sexual abuse. This is no accident. Although children are interviewed by authorities about other criminal acts, the surge in reporting and prosecution of child sexual abuse has brought children's testimony to the forefront of public and scientific concern. We encourage researchers interested in children's memory, as well as professionals interested in social policy, to study children's testimony regarding other stressful events; at present, however, it's clear that children's role as victim-witnesses in child sexual abuse cases demands the attention of legal and psychological scholars.

Although this book is focused on forensic issues, it also makes a contribution to basic science. Research on child witnesses has received considerable attention in recent years, not only because it contributes to the solution of an important social problem but also because it advances our understanding of the human mind. For example, research on children's eyewitness testimony has motivated memory-development researchers to expand their studies to include children's memory for real-life events and to consider the effects of social and motivational factors on children's reports. Scientists are learning a great deal from such research.

The book contains chapters by top researchers in the field, each reporting exciting and novel empirical findings. Several themes run throughout the book, reflecting major topics of concern in the field of children's testimony:

1. Do children have the cognitive capacity to recall and report past events accurately and to resist false suggestions? How can knowledge about children's memory improve our understanding of their ability to testify in forensic settings?
2. How do socioemotional and motivational factors influence the accuracy of children's reports? Are children likely to conceal or fabricate information about past events?
3. Are there ways to enhance the likelihood of obtaining accurate information from child witnesses?
4. Can jurors accurately evaluate children's testimony? Are jurors biased in ways that might hinder the fair adjudication of trials involving child witnesses?
5. What is the emotional impact on child witnesses of involvement in legal proceedings?
6. What special precautions or techniques can be used by courts to accommodate the special needs of child witnesses? How do such techniques affect the accuracy of children's testimony?

In this book, we provide empirically based answers to these questions. To preview, the authors of the first two chapters focus on research concerning children's memory abilities and the implications of such research for children's testimony. Specifically, Robyn Fivush provides a cognitive developmental perspective on children's basic abilities to remember past events of importance to them. Margaret-Ellen Pipe and her colleagues extend this theme in discussing the role played by verbal and physical cues in improving children's recall of events. In the third chapter, Barbara Boat and Mark Everson focus on current investigations of the effectiveness of a specific type of cue—anatomically detailed dolls—often used in child sexual abuse investigations.

Applying what we know from research directly to forensic interviews, both R. Edward Geiselman and his colleagues and John Yuille and his coworkers describe methods for conducting interviews with alleged child abuse victims. In Chapters 4 and 5, they outline empirically derived interview techniques designed to obtain the most complete reports from children with the minimal amount of suggestion.

Following initial interviews, children who allege abuse may have to testify about their experiences in a court of law. Karen J. Saywitz and Lynn Snyder's work, presented in Chapter 6, gives special consideration to the demands and problems encountered by children who testify in court. These authors discuss techniques to improve children's testimony by preparing children both for what to expect and how to react to the unnatural context of a courtroom, including how to use strategies to report information accurately and completely and how to recognize and respond to developmentally inappropriate and suggestive questions.

When evaluating children's abilities to provide accurate reports of past events, not only are purely cognitive factors of interest but so too are motivational factors. In Chapter 7, Kay Bussey and her coauthors provide a thorough examination of research addressing the likelihood that children will purposely make false reports, whether by omitting or fabricating information.

The next three chapters, by Michael R. Leippe and colleagues, Peter K. Isquith and colleagues, and Bette L. Bottoms, shift attention from children's abilities to give accurate testimony to jurors' perceptions of children's reports. No matter how accurate children's statements may actually be, justice depends on how judges and jurors evaluate that testimony. Leippe and colleagues report a set of studies of both the actual and perceived accuracy of child witnesses. Jurors, they find, may be quite fallible in their evaluations and judgments of child witnesses. Given this finding, it is important to explore factors other than children's actual accuracy that contribute to case decisions. To this end, Peter K. Isquith, Murray Levine, and Janine Scheiner investigate factors affecting mock jurors' perceptions of child witnesses in child sexual abuse cases. The authors note that perceivers are sensitive to such factors as the age of child witnesses, assigning blame prejudicially to older versus younger minors who allege sexual abuse. Bette L. Bottoms continues inquiry into the perceived credibility of child victims with a chapter exploring the underlying determinants of individual differences in jurors' perceptions of child sexual abuse victims. From a social psychological perspective, she explores the effects of jurors' attitudes and empathy on judgments made in cases of child sexual assault.

In Chapter 11, Desmond Runyan considers the emotional effects on children of legal involvement. When children are victims of familial abuse, do attempts by the legal system to improve their lives succeed or fail? Is there an emotional toll associated with testifying in a courtroom? Runyan provides empirical answers to these questions and discusses policy implications.

The authors of Chapters 12 and 13 discuss responses by the courts to placing child witnesses into a legal system designed for adults. Rhona H. Flin brings an international perspective to the discussion of children's testimony; she assesses the psychological merits of innovative techniques for children in British and Scottish courts. Although her perspective is British, the techniques and issues she discusses parallel those of concern in U.S. courts. Jennifer Batterman-Faunce and Gail S. Goodman consider use of special techniques in U.S. courts and present research on the impact of these techniques on the accuracy of child witnesses in sexual abuse cases.

We hope that the study of children's testimony, as presented in these chapters, will be as intrinsically interesting to our readers as it is to us. We feel fortunate to work on research that contributes simultaneously to science, social policy, children's welfare, and justice.

This book benefited from the advice and guidance of our editor at The Guilford Press, Sharon Panulla. We wish to thank her. We also thank Phillip R. Shaver for professional and personal encouragement and our families for their unwavering support.

Creation of this book was greatly facilitated by grants from the National Center on Child Abuse and Neglect of the United States Department of Health and Human Services.

Contents

CHILD VICTIMS, CHILD WITNESSES

1

Developmental Perspectives on Autobiographical Recall

Robyn Fivush
Emory University

Over the last decade there has been increasing controversy over children's ability to give credible eyewitness testimony. As demonstrated by the chapters in this volume, researchers have been concerned with factors affecting the accuracy, suggestibility, and malleability of children's memory. But these questions must be placed in the context of children's developing memory abilities. Children's eyewitness testimony can be understood only in terms of how much children are able to remember about experienced events, how long they can retain this information, and how accurate their memories are. Most important, these abilities must be placed in developmental perspective; children of different ages have different memory skills, and we need to understand how these skills develop in order to be able to effectively evaluate children's testimony.

I have been investigating the development of children's memory for personally experienced events in a series of studies of children ranging in age from 2½ through 11 years. Different studies have examined different influences on autobiographical recall, including age of the child, time since the experience, who is asking the child for recall, and what kinds of memory questions and cues are asked. Each of these factors has important effects on what information is remembered on any given recall occasion. In this chapter, I review this research, as well as related research on autobiographical memory, both with adults and children, with an emphasis on issues relevant to children's ability to give credible testimony. It is important to emphasize at the outset that the research reviewed here focuses on the recall of unique, single-occurrence events under conditions where no misleading or suggestive information is introduced. I return to these issues at the end of the chapter. In the first section, I discuss the amount and accuracy of recall; in the second section I focus on the consistency of information recalled across time and social contexts. In the third section, I try to integrate the developmental findings on accuracy and consistency, and present a model of the development of autobiographical memory. Finally, in the last section, I discuss the implications of this model for issues surrounding children's testimony.

AMOUNT AND ACCURACY OF AUTOBIOGRAPHICAL RECALL

The issue of how to conceptualize accuracy in autobiographical recall has a long and controversial history in psychology. Given the widespread acceptance that memory is at least partly reconstructive (Bartlett, 1932; Neisser, 1967), it becomes difficult to determine whether an individual is recalling the actual details of a particular experience or reconstructing what must have occurred based on general event knowledge. Moreover, an individual can be accurate as to the details of what occurred, but may interpret those events differently than other participants, or even than they themselves interpreted those events on previous recall occasions (Spence, 1988). A full discussion of these issues is well beyond the scope of this chapter. For purposes of this review, I operationally define accuracy of memory as agreement between the individual's recall and either an objective record of the event or social consensus from other participants of the event as to what occurred.

Using this definition, there is growing evidence in the literature that under certain conditions, adults can be remarkably accurate in what they recall about personally experienced events over extremely long periods of time (but see Barclay & DeCooke, 1988, for alternative interpretations). For example, both Linton (1982) and Wagenaar (1986) conducted diary studies of their own memories over several years. Essentially, these researchers kept written records of events in their lives and then tested their recall of these events at various retention intervals. Linton focused on recall of when particular events occurred, whereas Wagenaar would cue himself with one or more facts, such as a person who was present, the time of the event, the location of the event, etc., to determine if, and if so, how much, he could recall about particular events. Not surprisingly, both researchers found that recall of events diminished over time but that what was recalled was quite accurate. These results indicate that exhaustiveness of recall and accuracy of recall are separable dimensions; although the overall amount of information recalled decreased over time, what information was recalled seemed to be recalled quite accurately. Moreover, as time since the event occurred increased, more memory cues were needed in order to recall any information about the event at all. Most intriguing, Wagenaar found that with enough cues, he was able to recall at least some information about every event tested over a 6-year period.[1]

In a unique study examining autobiographical memory over several decades, Wagenaar and Groeneweg (1990) were able to compare concentration camp survivors' recall of their experiences within a few years of release to their recall 40 years later. Overall, the authors conclude that "[t]here is no doubt that almost all witnesses remember Camp Erika in great detail, even after 40 years. The accounts of the conditions of the camp, the horrible treatment, the daily routine, the forced labor, the housing, the food, the main characters of the guards, are remarkably consistent. Also the recall of smaller details were remarkably accurate in many instances" (p. 84). However, many survivors had difficulty recalling certain aspects of the event, especially the names of guards and fellow prisoners. Overall, then, research with adults indicates that as the time since experience increases, the amount of information recalled about an event decreases, and the number of specific memory cues needed to retrieve the memory increases. Nevertheless the accuracy of information recalled remains quite high.

A similar pattern emerges when we examine the developmental research. Gold and Neisser (1980) asked fifth, seventh, and ninth graders to recall various kindergarten experiences and checked the children's responses against the kindergarten teacher's records. Although only a small subset of kindergarten activities were recalled by fifth graders, what was recalled was accurate. Moreover, there was no further decrease in memory from fifth grade through ninth grade. These results suggest that several years after an experience, children's memories are accurate and stable, but they do not address how much information is forgotten during the first few years after an experience or whether more information could have been recalled if children had been provided with additional appropriate memory cues.

We investigated these issues in a study of children's memories for a kindergarten class trip to a museum of archeology (Hudson & Fivush, 1987). The trip was special in that children learned about archeology and archaeological tools, they dug for "artifacts" in a large sandbox, and they made clay models of what they had found. Thus, this was an unusual and fun outing for the children. We asked children for recall immediately after the event, 6 weeks later, 1 year later, and 6 years later. This study was unique in that we had detailed knowledge of the event to be recalled and we had photographs of the event to use as memory cues. Moreover, we were able to compare children's memories immediately after the event to their memories at various retention intervals.

Not surprisingly, children were quite good at recalling the event immediately after the experience. They recalled an average of about nine main activities that had occurred, and their recall was quite detailed and completely accurate. Six weeks later, children recalled as much information in as much detail, and their recall was just as accurate as on immediate recall. After a year, however, children began to have more difficulty recalling the event. Only one child was able to recall this event when asked, "Tell me what happened at the Jewish Museum (the name of the museum)." But when given more specific cues ("Remember it was a museum of archeology?" and "Remember you dug in a big sandbox?"), all the children were able to recall accurate information about the event. Most interesting, with the introduction of these cues, children were able to recall as much information in as much detail as they had on the first two interviews. Six years after the event, children needed even more specific cues in order to recall the event (a few children did not recall anything until shown the photographs); moreover, children recalled significantly less information about the event after 6 years (about three of the major activities) but what they did recall was recalled as accurately and in as much detail as on the previous interviews.

These findings are consistent with the adult literature. First, children's memories for a personally experienced event remain accurate over an extended period of time. However, the amount of recall decreases. But with specific memory cues, children can recall as much even a year after the event occurred as they had immediately after the event. After six years, children need even more specific cues to recall the event at all, and even with these more specific cues, they may not recall as much information. The comparability of findings suggest that recall processes are similar in school-age children and adults, but they do not address whether children and adults recall equal amounts of information to begin with.

In a study directly comparing children's and adults' memories, Sheingold and Tenney (1982) asked subjects ranging in age from 4 years old through adulthood to recall the birth of their sibling. For all subjects, the sibling was born when the subjects were 4 years old. Thus the retention interval ranged from a few months for the youngest subjects to many years for the oldest subjects. Somewhat surprisingly, neither age nor retention interval affected how much information subjects were able to recall about this event; all subjects were able to recall "an impressive amount" (p. 209) of information, and, again, most of the information recalled was accurate, as determined by mothers.

These results suggest that school-age children can recall as much about personally experienced events as do adults; note, however, that Sheingold and Tenney (1982) used a standardized interview with 20 specific questions concerning the experience. Thus, this is a highly cued memory task. Subjects of different ages would most likely have recalled different amounts of information if simply asked an open-ended free-recall question. A great deal of research indicates that younger children recall less information to open-ended requests for recall than do older children or adults (see Pillemer & White, 1989, for a review). In addition, Sheingold and Tenney only counted the number of questions responded to but did not consider how much information was recalled in response to each question. It seems possible that age or retention interval effects might have emerged if more sensitive measures of recall had been used. Even so, the data from this and the previously reviewed studies indicate remarkable continuity of memory from school-age children through adulthood. But what of even younger children? Are preschoolers able to retain and report accurate information about personally experienced events?

Todd and Perlmutter (1980) examined personal memories of 3- and 4-year-old children; memory was elicited during a play session in which the investigator queried the child about various types of events that many preschoolers have experienced, such as going to the circus or the zoo. Note that using this methodology, the investigators did not know beforehand whether the child had actually experienced any of these events, or, if the child had experienced these events, when they had occurred. Four year olds recalled somewhat more information on the average than did 3 year olds, but there were no age differences in accuracy; just over 70% of the information children recalled was accurate, as determined by parents.[2] This figure may actually underestimate preschool children's accuracy. Because the memory interview took place in the context of a play session, and children were not asked to "only tell what really happened," it is quite likely that children thought it was acceptable to include some fantasy material even if they knew that this did not actually occur. Moreover, children seemed to respond to questions about events they had not actually experienced by drawing on general knowledge learned from books and television (e.g., the child knows that one sees lions and tigers at the zoo, even if the child had never been to the zoo), and this material appears to have been coded as inaccurate recall. Given these considerations, preschoolers' autobiographical memory appears to be quite accurate. Interestingly, amount of recall did not differ as a function of time since experiencing the event. However, because retention interval was not systematically varied in this study, it is difficult to draw any conclusions from this finding.

In a similar study, we asked 29- through 35-month-old children to recall personally experienced events (Fivush, Gray, & Fromhoff, 1987). But we asked children to report these events in a more formal interview situation and we explicitly asked children to recall events that they had experienced in the recent past (within the previous 3 months) and the distant past (more than 3 months ago). Events to ask each child about were determined in conversation with the mother immediately before the child interview. We examined both how much information children recalled as a function of time since experience and whether children needed more questions and prompts in order to recall more distantly experienced events.

As in the Todd and Perlmutter (1980) study, children in this study recalled as much information about distantly experienced events as about more recently experienced events. However, it should be noted that children only recalled information about approximately half of the events asked about overall. For those events for which children did recall information, children recalled an average of 12.89 units of information about more recently experienced events, and 12.30 units of information about more distantly experienced events. In fact, all the children recalled at least one event that occurred more than 6 months in the past. Most interesting, children did not need more specific questions in order to recall the more distantly experienced events. However, this result needs to be interpreted within the finding that children generally needed many questions and prompts in order to recall both recently and distantly experienced events. The interviewer asked an average of 13.8 questions about recently experienced events, and a mean of 11.73 questions about distantly experienced events, in order to elicit children's recall. Not quite half (44%) of the information children recalled was in response to the very first open-ended question asked, and the remaining recall tended to be drawn out in bits and pieces over the remaining series of questions. Finally, approximately 90% of the information that children recalled was deemed accurate by parents.

These findings demonstrate, first, that even quite young children are able to recall accurate information about personally experienced events over a considerable period of time. It is important to emphasize that in a situation in which preschool children understand that they are being asked to recall what "really happened," they include very little inaccurate information. Moreover, even the figure of 90% accuracy may underestimate children's accuracy because information that the mother could not understand was deemed inaccurate for purposes of these analyses, and it is not clear whether this information was actually wrong. Second, it seems that preschool children need much more support from the adult, in the form of questions and prompts, in order to recall events than do older children and adults. However, because we studied such a restricted age range, developmental differences in recall could not be examined. Further, all children were asked about different events, and so amount of recall across children and retention interval was difficult to interpret.

In order to more fully explore these issues, we interviewed children about a family trip to Disneyworld (Hamond & Fivush, 1991). Children who went to Disneyworld when they were approximately 2½ years old were compared to children who went to Disneyworld when they were approximately 4½ years old. Half of the children in each of these age groups were interviewed 6 months after their Disneyworld experience and half were interviewed 18 months after the experience, using a structured interview format. Surprisingly, there were no effects of age or retention interval on how much children recalled. Children who were approximately 4 years old at the time of the interview and went to Disneyworld when they were 2½ years old recalled as much information as children who were 5 years old at the time of the interview, and 4½ years old at the time of their trip. On average, children recalled about 40 units of information, and virtually everything children recalled was accurate, as determined by parents.

However, there were two intriguing developmental differences. First, although younger children recalled as many propositional units as did the older children, older children's recall was significantly more detailed than the younger children's. Detail was operationalized as adjectives, adverbs, and adjective and adverb phrases (e.g., "I went on the cars *that were way high up in the sky.*"). Older children included an average of 0.31 details per proposition, whereas younger children included only 0.23 details per proposition. Of course, it is not clear whether older children's recounts are more detailed because their memory representations are more elaborate or because they are linguistically more sophisticated than the younger children at time of interview. More fine-grained analyses of the data suggest that children who were older at the time of their trip to Disneyworld are recounting more details than children who visited Disneyworld when they were younger, regardless of age at time of the interview. Thus, the amount of detail in children's reports seems to be more a function of age at time of experience than age at time of interview. This is a critically important finding because it begins to disentangle effects of age at time of experience, age at time of interview, and retention interval, which are obviously complexly intertwined in any study of children's autobiographical memory.

A second developmental finding was that older children recalled more information spontaneously than did younger children. That is, although younger children recalled as much information as did older children, they tended to recall only that information directly asked for, whereas older children would often provide additional information not directly queried for. Twenty-five percent of propositional units recalled by older children were recalled spontaneously, compared to 19% of the propositional units for the younger children. Note, however, that the majority of information reported even by the older children was recalled in response to a direct question.

In contrast to studies demonstrating the remarkable accuracy of preschoolers' autobiographical memories, Pillemer (as discussed in Pillemer & White, 1989) found that 3-year-old children did not recall a fire drill at school as well as 5-year-old children did. More specifically, 3 year olds seemed to confuse the temporal order of events such that they reported leaving the building and then hearing the alarm. Pillemer argues that because 3-year-old children did not understand the connection between the alarm and leaving the building, they were unable to comprehend the event as it was occurring and were therefore unable to recall it coherently. Obviously, events that are incomprehensible are difficult to recall even for adults (Bransford & McCarrell, 1977), but it must certainly be the case that younger children find more of the world incomprehensible than do older children and adults, and this may be a crucial limitation on their ability to recall certain events. Clearly, this is a question that deserves serious research consideration. It should be stressed, however, that younger children did not include inaccurate information in their reports of the fire drill; they simply reported the events that occurred in an incorrect temporal sequence.

Overall, the research indicates that even quite young preschoolers are remarkably accurate in their autobiographical recall. Moreover, preschool children retain information about personally experienced events over extremely long periods of time. A few studies even suggest that preschool children may recall as much information as older children in very structured interview situations (Hamond & Fivush, 1990; Sheingold & Tenney, 1982), although it is doubtful that preschoolers' recall is as detailed or as exhaustive as older children's recall. Moreover, preschool children do not recall as much information spontaneously as do older children and adults, and this seems to hold regardless of how recently the event being recalled was experienced. Older children and adults can usually recall a great deal of information in response to a general free recall question about a recent event, but they need additional cues as time since the event increases. Preschool children, in contrast, need many questions and cues even about recently experienced events. It seems they need as many questions and cues about recently experienced events as about distantly experienced events. Thus, preschoolers might be able to recall a great deal of information about personally experienced events but they clearly need a great deal of external support, in the form of questions and cues, in order to retrieve this information.

The fact that young children do not report much information spontaneously, but rather are recalling information in response to specific questions, is particularly relevant to considerations of children's credibility as witnesses. The more specific the questions needed to elicit recall, the less credible the child witness appears; specific questions are often assumed to be suggestive, or even misleading, and are often contested forms of questioning for legal testimony. Yet relying solely on preschoolers' responses to open-ended questions about what happened may seriously underestimate their event memories. In order to most accurately and fairly assess the credibility of young witnesses, the legal system must consider both the strengths and the limitations of preschoolers' memories.

CONSISTENCY OF AUTOBIOGRAPHICAL RECALL

Consistency of recall refers to the extent to which subjects' recall is stable over time. This can be conceptualized in at least two ways. One conceptualization originates with psychotherapeutic concerns and evaluates the consistency of the affective and evaluative aspects of recall, as well as whether the same events are seen as significant in defining one's life over time (Adler, 1956). The focus is often on how recalled events form a life theme or narrative (Bruner, 1987; Spence, 1982), and whether the narrative is stable over time.

A second way of conceptualizing consistency is more circumscribed; the focus is on whether or not the same units and details of information are recalled across multiple occasions of recalling the same event. This is really the more critical conceptualization of consistency for issues concerning eyewitness testimony, in which people are required to report the details of the same target event when interviewed on different occasions, by different people, and in different contexts. In this situation, consistency of recalled information is often taken as an index of accuracy of recall. That is, although no one expects perfectly consistent recall from one occasion to another, a great deal of inconsistency in recall is often taken as evidence of inaccurate or even fabricated recall (see Lieppe, Manion & Romanczyk, Chapter 8, this volume, for a fuller discussion and empirical evidence on this issue). Unfortunately, very little research has explored this aspect of consistency of autobiographical recall. However, what little is known provides some provocative insights into the relation between accuracy and consistency and may contribute to understanding how autobiographical memory develops.

In Wagenaar and Groeneweg's (1990) study of concentration camp survivors' memories, they claim that victims' memories were "remarkably consistent" (p. 84), although they do not present any analyses of this issue. Similarly, in a study examining adults' memory for the space shuttle Challenger disaster, McCloskey, Wible, and Cohen (1988) assessed the consistency of recall 1 week after the disaster to recall 9 months later. Although recall decreased over this period, subjects were highly consistent in their recall; approximately 80% of the information each subject recalled was the same across recall occasions. In contrast, Harsch and Neisser (1989) found little consistency in adults' recall of the space shuttle Challenger disaster. Subjects were asked to recall how they heard the news of the disaster the day after the event and then again 3 years later. Assuming that subjects were accurate on the first interview, they computed a weighted accuracy score for information recalled 3 years later that ranged from 0 (no information recalled was accurate as compared to the first interview) to 7 (all the information was accurate as compared to the first interview). The mean weighted accuracy score was only 2.9; 11 of 44 subjects scored 0.

Reasons for the discrepant findings are not clear. A detailed comparison of the way in which recall was coded as accurate or inaccurate might clarify some of the differences. Also, the two studies assessed memory at very different retention intervals. However, given the research reviewed earlier on accuracy of recall across long retention intervals, it is not clear exactly how this may have affected the results. Another possible explanation concerns which aspects of the event were being recalled. Harsch and Neisser (1989) did not include recall of the explosion itself in their measures, but McCloskey et al. (1988) did. Thus, many of the inaccuracies in memory documented by Harsch and Neisser surrounded what may be considered more peripheral details of the event, such as what subjects were wearing when they learned of the news. Even so, these findings indicate that under certain circumstances, adults might be highly inconsistent in their recall. They further indicate, in contrast to the research reviewed in the previous section, that adults might be highly inaccurate in their recall under certain conditions. One difference between the Challenger studies and the previously reviewed studies concerns the personal significance of the events being recalled. In the diary studies with adults and the interview studies with children, events were chosen to be salient life events, whereas the research on memory for the Challenger disaster preselects the event to be remembered. This event may or may not have any personal significance for the subjects. Still the discrepancy between the Harsch and Neisser findings and other research on adults' autobiographical recall is intriguing. Clearly, more research is needed that delineates the conditions under which adults are likely to be accurate and consistent in their recall.

Only one study has examined consistency of recall in school-age children. In the study of sixth graders' recall of a kindergarten trip to a museum discussed earlier (Hudson & Fivush, 1987), we examined whether children reported the same information at each of the recall trials. One year after the experience, about 62% of what children recalled had been recalled previously. Six years after the experience, 87% of what was recalled had been recalled previously. Looking only at the central activities occurring during the museum trip, these percentages rise to about 89% at the 1-year recall and 97% at the 6 year recall. These findings suggest that central aspects of an event are consistently recalled by school-age children, but recall of idiosyncratic or peripheral details may be more variable. Moreover, as time since the experience increases, recall of the more peripheral details drops out, but recall of the central aspects remains high, accurate, and consistent.

When we examine the data on preschool children, however, a very different pattern emerges. In one study, we examined consistency of preschool children's autobiographical recall over a 1-year period (Fivush & Hamond, 1990). Children were asked to recall several novel events that they had experienced, such as an airplane trip, a family outing to the circus, etc., on three occasions. During the first interview, conducted when the children were between 30 and 35 months of age, mothers were asked to discuss these events with their child. During the second interview, conducted 6 weeks later, a naive female experimenter asked children to recall the same events that they had previously discussed with their mothers. Approximately 14 months later, a different female experimenter asked the child to recall some of the same events that had been recalled on the previous interviews. Only those events that had not recurred in the interim were included; thus, Christmas and birthdays were eliminated, but events such as an airplane trip were included if the child had not flown an another airplane during the previous year. All interviews were conducted in the child's home.

First and foremost, children at the third interview, who were now almost 4 years old, were able to recall as much information about events that had occurred before they were 2½ years old as they had recalled 14 months earlier. Again, this is strong evidence that young children are able to retain information about personally experienced events over extended periods of time. Moreover, about 90% of what children recalled at all three interviews was accurate, as determined by parents. However, and perhaps most interesting, children were remarkably inconsistent in what they recalled at each interview. A mere 10% of the information children recalled on the second interview was the same as information the children had recalled on the first interview 6 weeks earlier. About 1 year later, on the third interview, 26% of what children recalled about these events was information that had been recalled on either of the first two interviews. Again, it is important to emphasize that virtually all of the information children recalled was accurate, as determined by parents. In other words, children are recalling different, but still accurate, information each time they are asked to recall an event.

Why might preschool children be so much more inconsistent in their recall than are older children and adults? One possibility is that the type of information that children are recalling changes as a function of development. Nelson (1988) and Hudson (1986) have both argued that young preschoolers focus on routine and general information; that is, on information that is similar across events, and thus allows the most predictability for future occurrences. As children build up their general knowledge about events, they begin to focus more on the special and distinctive aspects of events, aspects that make a specific event different and unusual. In fact, we found that children during the first two interviews, occurring when the children were 30 to 35 months of age, recalled as much information about the routine or typical components of these unusual events, such as information about eating and sleeping routines, as about the more distinctive components of the events. At the third interview, however, when the children were almost 4 years old, they reported significantly more distinctive information than they had on the previous interviews, and significantly more distinctive information than typical information. Thus, there is some suggestion in these data that there is a shift from recalling routine, typical information to recalling more distinctive information about events across the preschool years.

A developmental shift, however, cannot account for the high inconsistency between the first two interviews, which were only 6 weeks apart. One of the major differences between these two interview situations is that children were asked about these events by their mothers during the first interview and by a stranger during the second interview. This changes the social context of recall in several interesting and potentially important ways. On the one hand, mothers have usually experienced these events with their child and thus they are able to ask quite specific questions and provide specific memory cues. On the other hand, because the mother has experienced these events with the child, the child may view this situation as a memory "test." When the stranger asks the child what happened, however, the child may view this as a real and legitimate request for information.

This distinction rests on the assumption that it is some aspect of the social demands of the situation that vary between mothers' and strangers' conversations that lead to children's inconsistent recall. However, there is another aspect to what is happening in these conversations that is important to consider. Adults, in questioning children about past events, are also providing a good deal of information about what occurred during those events. This is especially true in the case of mothers, who experienced the events with their children. For example, in questioning her child about visiting her grandparents, one mother asked, "Remember when we went to visit Grandma and Grandpa and we took a long drive in the car and you looked out the window and what did you see?" Clearly, mothers are not only questioning their children; they are also informing their children about what occurred. Even strangers do this to some extent. For example, in questioning a child about last Christmas, the stranger might ask, "Did you get any presents under the tree?" This question provides information that there were probably presents and even that there was a tree. It is possible that children are incorporating adult-provided information into their subsequent recall of the event. That is, children may be learning *what* to remember. If this is the case, inconsistent recall can be attributed to children changing the information "recalled" from what they themselves remember to what the adult has highlighted about the event.

This is obviously a critical issue when children are being asked to testify. Legal testimony invariably involves multiple interviews, and if children are incorporating information provided by the interviewer during one session into their own subsequent recall of the event, then their ability to give accurate testimony must be seriously questioned. Further, in many cases in which children are being asked to testify, it is the mother who initially questions the child. It is imperative to determine if the kinds of questions the mother asks and, especially, the kind of information she provides, alter the child's subsequent recall.

Hudson (1990) examined some of these issues in a study of mothers conversing about past events with their 24- to 30-month-old children. Mothers asked about the same four events during four different sessions, a week apart. Two weeks after the fourth session, a stranger asked the child to recall the same four events. Hudson examined both how much consistent information mothers provided over time and how much consistent information children recalled. At the second mother–child session, 54% of the information provided by mothers was new information; by the fourth session, only 32% of information provided by mothers was different from what they had provided on previous interviews. For children, just over 50% of the information they recalled on each interview was different from information recalled on previous interviews. When the children then recalled these events with the stranger, 36% of the information they recalled had not been reported by either the mother or the child in the previous four interviews, but this figure was not broken down into whether the information had been previously provided by the mother or the child. These results support the previous finding of high inconsistency in preschool children's recall. They further suggest that mothers may be asking children about different aspects of an event at each interview, accounting for the low consistency across interviews for mothers' contributions as well as the low consistency for children's recall. Thus, children may be inconsistent in what they recall because mothers are inconsistent in what they ask for. However, this was not directly examined in these data. Moreover, these data do not directly address the issue of whether children are incorporating information provided by the adult into their subsequent recall.

In order to explore these possibilities in more depth, we examined differences in children's recall as a function of conversational partner (Fivush, Hamond, Harsch, Singer, & Wolf, 1991). Thirty- to 35-month-old children were asked to recall the same personally experienced events on two occasions, 6 weeks apart. Children were either interviewed by their mother on both occasions (mother–mother condition), by the same female stranger on both occasions (stranger–stranger condition), or by their mother on the first occasion and by a female stranger on the second occasion (mother–stranger condition). Again, all interviews were conducted in the child's home. We were interested in examining two questions. First, are adults consistent in the questions they ask about the same events across interviews? If so, are children consistent in their responses to these questions? Second, do children incorporate information provided by the adult during one recall occasion into their own recall of the event on a subsequent recall occasion?

As in all other studies of preschool children's recall, the information recalled was quite accurate across all interviews. But again, children's recall was quite inconsistent from the first to the second interview. Overall, about two thirds of the information that children recalled on the second interview was new and different information than had been recalled on the first interview. Only about 20% of information that children recalled on the second interview was the same information that they themselves had recalled on the first interview, and about 12% of what children recalled on the second interview was information that the adult had provided on the first interview. These patterns were virtually identical across the three conversational partner conditions. These results indicate two things. First, preschoolers' inconsistency in recall is just as high when recalling the event with the same person over time as when recalling the event with different people over time. Second, children show little tendency to incorporate information provided by adults into their own subsequent recall of events.

In order to examine the effects of consistent questioning in more depth, we first classified all questions that adults asked as either general, open-ended questions (e.g., Can you tell me about last Christmas?) or specific questions (e.g., What did you eat that was special last Christmas?). Overall, adults asked many more specific questions (a mean of 34.63 per event) than general questions (a mean of 15.40 per event). Further, children were significantly more likely to recall information in response to a specific question than in response to a general question. We next examined whether children were likely to give the same response if the same question was asked on both interviews. Children tended to give the same answer to the same question in the mother–mother interviews but not in either the stranger–stranger or the mother–stranger interviews. But this was because the most likely occurrence was for the child to respond to a question on one of the interviews but not respond to that same question on the other interview.

Overall, this research suggests, first, that children are recalling information in response to specific questions, and, second, that there may be some tendency for young children to recall the same information when asked the same question if they respond to that question on both recall occasions. Because children are recalling information in response to specific questions, if the same questions are not asked on different recall occasions, their recall will appear quite inconsistent. At the same time, it is important to emphasize that children are not incorporating very much information provided by the adult during questioning into their subsequent recall of the event.

INTEGRATING ACCURACY AND CONSISTENCY: A MODEL OF THE DEVELOPMENT OF AUTOBIOGRAPHICAL MEMORY

Several conclusions can be drawn from the research on children's autobiographical recall. First, even quite young children recall accurate details about personally experienced events over extended periods of time. Second, younger children need more social support, in the form of specific questions, prompts, and cues from adults in order to recall information than do older children and adults. Third, young children can be surprisingly inconsistent in the information they recall about any given event on different recall occasions. Together, these findings suggest that young children are encoding a great deal of information about events, but they have difficulty retrieving that information in an interview situation.

Recalling an event requires more than simply reporting details of what occurred. In order to provide a coherent account, one must report the "who, what, where, and when" of an event (Neisser, 1982); that is, one must tell the event in a culturally conventionalized narrative form. The research reviewed here suggests that children may recall accurate information about personally experienced events, but they are not yet able to recount that information in a canonical narrative. But note that the narrative form provides more than coherence for the listener; it provides a structure to guide retrieval of information as well. Thus, one begins a narrative with setting information (where and when the event occurred) and character introduction (who participated), continues with referential information (the component activities) usually leading to a climax, followed by an evaluation (the affective meaning of the event) or resolution (Labov, 1982; Peterson & McCabe, 1983). Older children and adults are able to use the canonical categories and sequence of an event narrative to cue themselves as to what information they should report in what order in their recall. But younger children do not. How might this skill develop?

In contrast to the research reviewed here indicating that young children are not learning *what* to remember in conversation with adults, there is a growing body of research suggesting that children are learning *how* to remember in these adult-guided conversations (Eisenberg, 1985; Fivush, 1991; Hudson, 1990; McCabe & Peterson, 1991). More specifically, adults are implicitly modeling the canonical narrative forms in the structure of their questions and statements during conversations about past events. Children of mothers who use more sophisticated narrative forms in these early conversations become better narrators than do children of mothers using less sophisticated narrative forms. However, regardless of individual differences in mothers and children, children are developing narrative skills across the preschool years, and by the age of 5 or 6 are able to recount a fairly coherent narrative about a personally experienced event (Hudson & Shapiro, 1991; Peterson & McCabe, 1983). Notice that by this age, children also need fewer questions and prompts from the adult in order to recall.

What these findings suggest is that preschool children, who do not yet have control over canonical narrative forms for recounting the past, are dependent on the adult's questions to cue their recall. Because they have only rudimentary structures available for retrieving the information on their own, they rely on the structure provided by the adult. Thus, preschool children will recall the information asked for but little more. Moreover, because they are relying on external cues to guide their recall, their recall will be inconsistent if the external structure is inconsistent. This explains how children can be accurate and yet so largely inconsistent in their recall.

But there are two additional developmental differences that need to be considered. First, preschool children probably do not recall as much information as older children and adults. Although a couple of studies have found that preschool children may recall as much as older children under very structured interview situations (Hamond & Fivush, 1990; Sheingold & Tenney, 1982), there is a great deal of research indicating that preschool children simply do not recall as much information as do older children (see Pillemer & White, 1989, for a review). Again, this may be due to lack of external support for recall. If preschoolers are dependent on external guidance for retrieval, they will be at a disadvantage in situations that do not provide such assistance. This is clearly an important memory limitation for younger children; however, if provided with enough external support, it is possible that preschoolers can recall as much information as older children. Additional research is needed to clarify the locus of the developmental differences in amount of recall.

Second, preschool children may focus on, and therefore recall, different aspects of an event than do older children or adults. As discussed briefly above, preschool children tend to report as much information about the typical or routine aspects of events as about the unique or distinctive aspects of events. It should be noted that even adults recall a good deal about routine aspects of novel events (e.g., Barsalou, 1988), but preschool children seem to focus on routines to a greater extent. Again, this may be a function of the available structures for recall. Young children are in the process of building up knowledge about how the world usually works. These generalized event representations, or scripts, allow children to anticipate and predict future events, but they also provide a framework for recalling past events (Nelson, 1986). Younger children seem to be more "script-dependent" than older children; that is they seem to place even unusual and distinctive events in the context of more familiar routines.

As children become older and accumulate more experience with the world, they begin to focus more on the distinctive aspects of events, those aspects that make the event interesting and ultimately reportable. Note, however, that scripts continue to provide the background structure for comprehending and reporting events (Hudson & Shapiro, 1991). That is, scripts provide the shared cultural knowledge necessary for understanding and interpreting events, both as experienced and as recounted.

Thus, the development of autobiographical memory across the preschool years seems to involve two complementary processes. First, children are learning the canonical narrative structures for recounting an event. These structures allow children to give a coherent account of a past event, and also provide an internal retrieval guide. Thus, children become less and less dependent on adults' questions and prompts in order to recall information about personally experienced events. Second, children are shifting focus from typical to distinctive aspects of events. Thus, the first narrative form they have available conforms to a script; they report what usually happens. With increasing experience, the script fades into the background, and children begin to focus on the unusual aspects of events. They can now report a more interesting story about past experiences, focusing on what was unusual, distinctive, and ultimately memorable about each event.

IMPLICATIONS FOR CHILDREN'S TESTIMONY

The single most important finding to emerge from the research on children's autobiographical memory is that children's recall can be quite accurate. Moreover, preschoolers seem to be as accurate as older children and accuracy does not appear to diminish over a period of years. These are clearly important considerations for assessing children's abilities as credible witnesses because legal cases often stretch over long periods of time. Moreover, children' s recall remains accurate over multiple recall interviews, again suggesting that children are able to give accurate testimony in legal situations that involve the telling and retelling of events. An intriguing wrinkle to this finding, however, is the high degree of inconsistency in preschoolers' recall.

Thus, it is imperative to keep in mind that inconsistent recall does not necessarily mean inaccurate recall, especially for very young children. Because young children are dependent on adults' questions to guide their retrieval, they will often not recall information not asked for directly. Thus the questions asked will largely determine the information recalled when interviewing preschoolers about personally experienced events.

Moreover, preschool children seem to need fairly specific questions in order to recall information. Yet the research further indicates that preschool children do not tend to incorporate information provided in adults' questions into their own recall of the event. Thus, although interviewers may need to ask specific questions in order to elicit recall from young children, the specificity of the questions asked does not seem to compromise subsequent recall. These are important qualifications to bear in mind for two reasons. First, as mentioned earlier, inconsistency in recall is often taken as an index of inaccuracy. Yet the results reported here suggest that this is simply not true in evaluating young children's recall. Inconsistency seems to be more a function of the questions that young children are asked rather than the inability of young children to recall accurately. Second, specific questions are often assumed to be suggestive or misleading. But while the research indicates that young children need reasonably specific questions to recall, it does not seem to be the case that they incorporate information provided in these specific questions into their subsequent recall. Thus, the research suggests that preschoolers may indeed be able to give quite accurate reports of personally experienced events over multiple recall interviews and long periods of time.

However, there are two important limitations to these conclusions. First, only recall of unique, single-occurrence events was examined. As already mentioned, there is overwhelming evidence that young children and adults form generalized event representations, or scripts, for recurring events (see Nelson, 1986, for a review). One of the consistent findings in this literature is that recall of single instances of a scripted event can be extremely difficult. This is related to but different from the argument presented earlier about preschoolers' tendency to focus on routine aspects of events. That argument stated that even unique, single-occurrence events will be understood in terms of their similarities to scripted events. Here, the argument is that when trying to recall a specific instance of an event that has been experienced many times, both children and adults have difficulty distinguishing any one occurrence from all other occurrences.

Moreover, there appear to be developmental differences in how easily one can differentiate a single instance from the script. Preschool children are more likely to simply give a script report when asked about a single instance than are older children or adults (Hudson, 1986; Hudson & Nelson, 1986). This is not so much a question of accuracy; the script is accurate with reference to the specific instance. Rather it is a question of differentiation and detail. Preschool children seem to have more difficulty distinguishing what happened during any one instance of a recurring event from what usually happens during this event (see Farrar & Goodman, 1990, for an extended discussion of this issue). This has obvious implications for children's testimony, especially in cases of abuse that often recur and become scripted events. In these situations, young children may be able to recall what usually happens, but may have particular difficulty recounting a single instance of the event.

The second major limitation has to do with the social context of recall. In the research reviewed in this chapter, the interviewers did not present any suggestive or misleading information to the children, nor did they have any personal stake in what the children recalled. Clearly, in cases of testimony, the way in which these factors affect children's recall needs to be considered. Preschool children seem to be more sensitive to suggested and misleading information than are older children and adults (see Ceci, Toglia, & Ross, 1987, for a review). This may seem somewhat surprising given the findings reviewed here that preschoolers do not incorporate information provided by others into their own recall. One possible explanation of this discrepancy concerns the types of events children are asked to recall. Experiments in which children are given misleading information about personally experienced events, as opposed to misinformation about stories, tend to find less of an effect of misleading information. A second possible explanation concerns the significance of the event to the child. Events that are extremely personally important are probably less prone to suggestion than are less important events, and the real events of a child's life are probably more significant than story events and events constructed for the laboratory. Finally, misleading information is more likely to influence future recall when it is about the peripheral details of an event rather than more central aspects; in the studies reviewed here, children were rarely asked about peripheral details of the events (see Goodman, Rudy, Bottoms, & Aman, 1990, for a discussion of these issues). All of these reasons need to be considered when evaluating possible effects of misleading information on children's testimony.

Finally, the motivations of the interviewer need to be considered. In the studies reviewed in this chapter, children were certainly encouraged to recall events but they were not cajoled. If they could not recall anything about a given event, the interviewer, whether mother or researcher, simply went on to ask about a different event. There was obviously wide individual variability in how many events asked about were recalled, but on average, young preschoolers seem to recall information about approximately half of the events requested.[3] This is clearly a very different situation than eliciting recall in a testimony situation, in which interviewers may pressure children to recall information about a specific event. In this situation, it is conceivable that young children may fabricate information in order to appease an insistent adult.

Even given these limitations, it is important to stress the mnemonic competencies of preschool children. There is widespread belief that preschoolers are incapable of recalling their experiences accurately, and also that they cannot recall these experiences over long periods of time. The research indicates that this is simply not so. Although there are probably developmental differences in the amount of information recalled, and certainly in the control of the retrieval process, preschool children can and do recall accurate details about personally experienced events over a period of years. Under what circumstances and to what extent memory can be distorted or misled are certainly important questions. But these questions must be placed in the context of young children's remarkable abilities to recall accurate information about personally experienced events over extended periods of time.

ACKNOWLEDGMENTS

I am grateful to Dick Neisser and Craig Barclay for their comments on an earlier version of this chapter.

NOTES

1. Note that in these studies all of the provided cues were accurate to the events being recalled. The ability to provide such cues may be critical for accurate long-term recall of personally experienced events. This issue is well beyond the scope of this chapter, but see Barclay and DeCooke (1988) for a discussion.
2. Having parents determine whether their child's recall is accurate is similar to a recognition test of memory rather than a recall test. That is, the parent need only give a "yes" or "no" response to the information that had been provided by the child. It is entirely possible (in fact quite likely) that if asked to recall the event, parents and children would report different information.
3. The exception to this pattern is the study on children's memories for their trip

to Disneyworld. In this study, all the children were easily able to respond to questions about this one experience, although they varied in the specificity of questions needed to elicit recall. Reasons why this event may have been so easy to remember are discussed in Hamond and Fivush (1990).

REFERENCES

Adler, A. (1956). Science of Living. In H. L. Ansbacher & R. R. Ansbacher (Eds.), *The individual psychology of Alfred Adler* (pp. 350–365). New York: Harper & Row. (Original work published 1929)

Barclay, C. R., & DeCooke, P. A. (1988). Ordinary everyday memories: Some of the things of which selves are made. In U. Neisser & E. Winograd (Eds.), *Remembering reconsidered: Ecological and traditional approaches to the study of memory* (pp. 91–125). New York: Cambridge University Press.

Barsalou, L. (1988). The organization of autobiographical memory. In U. Neisser & E. Winograd (Eds.), *Remembering reconsidered: Ecological and traditional approaches to the study of memory* (pp. 193–244). New York: Cambridge University Press.

Bartlett, F. C. (1932). *Remembering: A study in experimental and social psychology.* New York: Cambridge University Press.

Bransford, J. D., & McCarrell, N. S. (1977). A sketch of a cognitive approach to comprehension: Some thoughts about understanding what it means to comprehend. In P. N. Johnson-Laird & P. C. Watson (Eds.), *Thinking: Reading in cognitive science* (pp. 377–399). Cambridge, MA: Cambridge University Press.

Bruner, J. (1987). Life as narrative. *Social Research, 54,* 11–32.

Ceci, S. J., Toglia, M. P., & Ross, D. F. (1987). *Children's eyewitness memory.* New York: Springer-Verlag.

Eisenberg, A. R. (1985). Learning to describe past experience in conversation. *Discourse Processes, 8,* 177–204.

Farrar, M. J., & Goodman, G. S. (1990). Developmental differences in the relation between scripts and episodes: Do they exist? In R. Fivush & J. A. Hudson (Eds.), *Knowing and remembering in young children* (pp. 30–64). New York: Cambridge University Press.

Fivush, R. (1991). The social construction of personal narratives. *Merrill-Palmer Quarterly, 37,* 59–82.

Fivush, R., Gray, J. T., & Fromhoff, F. A. (1987). Two year olds talk about the past. *Cognitive Development, 2,* 393–410.

Fivush, R., & Hamond, N. R. (1990). Autobiographical memory across the preschool years. In R. Fivush & J. A. Hudson (Eds.), *Knowing and remembering in young children* (pp. 223–248). New York: Cambridge University Press.

Fivush, R., Hamond, N.R., Harsch, N., Singer, N., & Wolf, A. (1991). Content and consistency in early autobiographical recall. *Discourse Processes, 14,* 373–388.

Gold, E., & Neisser, U. (1980). Recollections of kindergarten. *The Quarterly Newsletter of the Laboratory of Comparative Human Cognition, 2,* 77-80.

Goodman, G.S., Rudy, L., Bottoms, B.L., & Aman, C. (1990). Children's concerns and memory: Ecological issues in the study of children's eyewitness testimony. In R. Fivush & J.A. Hudson (Eds.) *Knowing and remembering in young children* (pp. 249-284). NY: Cambridge University Press.

Hamond, N.R., & Fivush, R. (1990). *Memories of Mickey Mouse: Young children recount their trip to Disneyworld. Cognitive Developpment, 6,* 433–448.

Harsch, N., & Neisser, U. (1989). *Substantial and irreversible errors in flashbulb memories of the Challenger explosion.* Paper presented at the Psychonomic Society Meetings, Atlanta, GA.

Hudson, J. A. (1986). Memories are made of this: General event knowledge and the development of autobiographic memory. In K. Nelson (Ed.), *Event knowledge: Structure and function in development* (pp. 97-118). Hillsdale, NJ: Erlbaum.

Hudson, J. A. (1990). The emergence of autobiographic memory in mother–child conversations. In R. Fivush & J.A. Hudson (Eds.), *Knowing and remembering in young children* (pp. 166-196). New York: Cambridge University Press.

Hudson, J. A., & Fivush, R. (1987). As time goes by: Sixth graders remember a kindergarten experience. *Emory Cognition Project Report #13,* Emory University, Atlanta.

Hudson, J.A., & Nelson, K. (1986). Repeated encounters of a similar kind: Effects of familiarity on children's autobiographic recall. *Cognitive Development, 1,* 253–271.

Hudson, J.A., & Shapiro, L. (1991). Effects of task and topic on children's narratives. In A. McCabe & C. Peterson (Eds.), *New directions in developing narrative structure* (pp. 59–136). Hillsdale, NJ: Erlbaum.

Labov, W. (1982). Speech actions and reaction in personal narrative. In D. Tannen (Ed.), *Analyzing discourse: Text and talk* (pp. 219–247). Washington, DC: Georgetown University Press.

Linton, M. (1982). Transformations of memory in everyday life. In U. Neisser (Ed.), *Memory observed* (pp.77-92). San Francisco: Freeman.

McCabe, A., & Peterson, C. (1991). Getting the story: A longitudinal study of parental styles in eliciting narratives and developing narrative skill. In A. McCabe & C. Peterson (Eds.), *New directions in developing narrative structure* (pp. 217–293). Hillsdale, NJ: Erlbaum.

McCloskey, M., Wible, C. G., & Cohen, N. J. (1988). Is there a special flashbulb memory mechanism? *Journal of Experimental Psychology: General, 117,* 171–181.

Neisser, U. (1967). *Cognitive psychology.* New York: Appleton Century Crofts

Neisser, U. (1982). Snapshots or benchmarks? In U. Neisser (Ed.), *Memory observed* (pp. 43–48). San Francisco: Freeman.

Nelson, K. (1986). *Event knowledge: Structure and function in development.* Hillsdale, NJ: Erlbaum.

Nelson, K. (1988). The ontogeny of memory for real events. In U. Neisser & E. Winograd (Eds.), *Remembering reconsidered: Traditional and ecological approaches to the study of memory* (pp. 244-277). New York: Cambridge University Press.

Peterson, C., & McCabe, A. (1983). *Developmental psycholinguistics: Three ways of looking at a narrative.* New York: Plenum.

Pillemer, D., & White, S.H. (1989). Childhood events recalled by children and adults. In H.W. Reese (Ed.), *Advances in child development and behavior,* (Vol. 22, pp. 297-346). New York: Academic.

Sheingold, K., & Tenney, Y. J. (1982). Memory for a salient childhood event. In U. Neisser (Ed.), *Memory observed* (pp. 201-212). San Francisco: W. H. Freeman & Co.

Spence, D. P. (1982). *Narrative truth and historical truth.* New York: W. W. Norton.

Spence, D.P. (1988). Passive remembering. In U. Neisser & E. Winograd (Eds.), *Remembering reconsidered: Traditional and ecological approaches to the study of memory* (pp. 311-325). New York: Cambridge University Press.

Todd, C., & Perlmutter, M. (1980). Reality recalled by preschool children. In M. Perlmutter (Ed.), *New directions for child development, No 10: Children's memory* (pp. 69-86). San Francisco: Jossey-Bass.

Wagenaar, W. A. (1986). My memory: A study of autobiographic memory over six years. *Cognitive Psychology, 18,* 225-252.

Wagenaar, W.A., & Groeneweg, J. (1990). The memory of concentration camp survivors. *Applied Cognitive Psychology, 4,* 77-87.

2

Cues, Props, and Context: Do They Facilitate Children's Event Reports?

Margaret-Ellen Pipe, Susan Gee,
and Clare Wilson
University of Otago, Dunedin, New Zealand

> INTERVIEWER: A couple of weeks ago you came and saw a magic
> show. Well, I'd like you to tell me all about it. Let's start at
> the beginning . . . someone came to get you out of your class.
> What happened then?
> JR: We did a magic show.

W hen children are simply asked to describe something that has
happened, their accounts are frequently very brief (Goodman, Aman &
Hirschman, 1987; King & Yuille, 1987; Marin, Holmes, Guth & Kovac,
1979; Wilkinson, 1988). The above example from a 6-year-old child in
one of our studies illustrates just how little information may be
spontaneously offered when an interviewer asks a general question.
The advantage of such free-recall accounts is, however, that the
information provided is typically very accurate (e.g., Cole & Loftus,
1987; Goodman & Reed, 1986; Marin et al., 1979). In legal contexts there
is a premium on accuracy, and, accordingly, concern about the
reliability of children as witnesses has focused on whether they are
susceptible to suggestion or misleading questioning (e.g., Ceci, Ross &
Toglia, 1987; Goodman et al., 1987; King & Yuille, 1987; Zaragoza,
1987). But the omission of significant details from children's reports,
whether intentional (Pipe & Goodman, 1991) or as the result of

difficulty in retrieving the appropriate information, will also hinder the legal process. Free recall alone is therefore seldom likely to be a satisfactory basis for obtaining children's testimony.

Traditionally, ways of increasing the amount of information children report have focused on questioning. More recently, however, attention has turned to nonverbal procedures for enhancing recall, such as taking children back into the situation in which an event occurred (context reinstatement) or providing props for children to reenact the event (e.g., Goodman & Aman, 1990; King & Yuille, 1987; Price & Goodman, 1990; Wilson & Pipe, 1989). In the legal context, props and "exhibits" may already be used in evidential interviews and court proceedings, although little is known about their effects. Anatomically detailed dolls are the most common (and controversial) examples (see Boat & Everson, Chapter 3, this volume) but they are not the only cues and props likely to be of use. For example, context cues have been found to be effective in prompting children's recall in natural environments (Nelson & Ross, 1980; Todd & Perlmutter, 1980) and may be especially important for very young children, for whom memory may be strongly tied to context (e.g., Daehler & Greco, 1985; White & Pillemer, 1979). Taking children back into the situation in which an event occurred or providing very specific physical cues related to the event may therefore provide stimulus support for children's recall of it. Props may also enable children to demonstrate their knowledge of routine events such as going to bed or bathing, or details of specific episodes of these routines, which they might otherwise find difficult to describe because of limitations on language. Further, Jones and McQuiston (1988) recommend toys and scale models, presented in the context of play, as a means of structuring and guiding interviews with children. These procedures will not, of course, always be appropriate; rather, they extend the range of techniques available to the investigative interviewer.

Despite the potential benefits of cues and props, there may also be disadvantages when they are used to obtain testimony from children. In particular, there is the danger that irrelevant cues will have a suggestive function and mislead children into making errors in their reports (King & Yuille, 1987). Even relevant cues and props could introduce errors, for example by prompting children to describe activities that, although associated with the prop items, are irrelevant to the event of interest (Piaget & Inhelder, 1973). A main issue, therefore, is whether retrieval techniques that increase the amount of information recalled do so at the expense of accuracy. The effectiveness as well as the limitations of cues and props needs to be considered before the cues and props are adopted as aids for gathering children's testimony.

In the present chapter we examine the potential of physical cues and props for enhancing children's reports. In the first section we argue from Tulving's (1983) principle of encoding specificity that physical cues should provide more effective retrieval cues than standard free-recall instructions and that as props they may reduce the verbal skills required of young children. In the second section we review studies in which physical cues have been used to facilitate children's recall. These studies provide preliminary evidence that retrieval cues may be useful for enhancing children's event reports, particularly when actual items and objects from the event are used. In the third section we report the results of three studies in which we examine the effects of reinstating different contextual cues, such as the environmental context or specific relevant and irrelevant items, on children's event descriptions over periods as long as 2 months since the event. These studies suggest that both the nature of the cues and the methods of presenting them are important determinants of their influence on the content and accuracy of children's reports. Finally, we draw conclusions about the use of cues to facilitate children's recall and consider the implications in the context of children's eyewitness testimony.

THEORETICAL CONSIDERATIONS

Both theoretical and practical considerations suggest that cues and props at the time of recall should be useful in facilitating the reports of young children. Compared to older children, young children are less efficient at freely recalling not only events but also word lists (e.g. Ackerman, 1986), pictures (Kobasigawa, 1974), objects (Perlmutter & Ricks, 1979), stories (e.g. Saywitz, 1987), and even autobiographical information (Nelson, 1986). We assume that the problem is partly one of retrieving information that has been encoded and stored. Although children's accumulating knowledge base and efficiency of encoding are also significant factors in determining the amount of information children recall (Chi, 1976), encoding is not amenable to modification for the investigative interviewer. Retrieval cues are therefore of particular interest because they are used at the time children are interviewed about past events.

Retrieval cues are those particular aspects of the physical or cognitive environment that "initiate or influence the process of retrieval" (Tulving, 1983). Tulving has likened retrieval cues to a key: If the key fits the lock, the memory becomes accessible. To extend this analogy further, the shape of the lock is determined by encoding. This interaction has been entitled the "encoding specificity principle": The specific encoding operations performed will determine which retrieval cues will later be effective in accessing the memory. A recollection of an event occurs if, and only if, the properties of the memory trace for the event are sufficiently similar to the properties of the retrieval cues.

One rationale of contextual reinstatement is, therefore, that retrieval cues replicate the encoding context and maximize the overlap between retrieval cues and features encoded. Physical cues typically replicate more of the features that were available at encoding than verbal cues such as questions. This replication of physical features may be especially significant for young children for whom cross-modal cues such as a word for an object may be ineffective (e.g., Turtle & Wells, 1987). Indeed, young children are generally not as flexible as older children and adults in their use of retrieval cues (Ceci & Howe, 1978) and are less likely to spontaneously use internally generated cues such as imagery (see Zaragoza, 1987).

A second potential advantage of context reinstatement is that the availability of cue items as props decreases verbal demands on young children. Young children's free-recall accounts of events will be circumscribed by their ability to express the details of the event (Mertin, 1989). Even when told that they are not making themselves clear, children often find it difficult to improve their communication (Cashmore, 1990). Further, verbal encoding of events by young children is likely to be less efficient than that of adults (Bruner, 1964) and information that has been encoded may remain verbally inaccessible, even when visual cues are available (Smith, Ratner & Hobart, 1987). Reenactment using cues and props offers children a means to demonstrate knowledge not verbally accessible by showing or acting out what happened (Piaget & Inhelder, 1973; Wilkinson, 1988).

The theoretical and practical considerations outlined above implicate a special role for nonverbal cues in enhancing children's memory. In the remainder of the chapter, we consider relevant empirical evidence.

EXPERIMENTAL STUDIES

Nonverbal cues have been examined in a variety of laboratory-based studies of, for example, infant memory (Rovee-Collier & Hayne, 1987), memory for location and hidden objects (Ratner & Myers, 1980; Schneider & Sodian, 1988), and picture (Kobasigawa, 1974) and story recall (Brown, 1975; Ruch & Levin, 1979). Infants as young as 3 months are more likely to remember a past event when the environmental context is reinstated (Rovee-Collier & Hayne, 1987), and children as young as 3 years may have a basic awareness of the potential use of cues when searching for hidden objects (e.g., Ratner & Myers, 1980). However, children's use of cues, as well as their awareness of when cues are likely to be effective in facilitating memory, undergo marked developmental changes throughout childhood (e.g., Fabricius & Wellman, 1983; Schneider & Sodian, 1988).

Studies of children's memory for pictures or stories indicate that although context cues may be effective in enhancing recall, context effects depend on age, the instructions relating to cue use, and the nature of the cues themselves. In a now classic study, Kobasigawa (1974) found that 8- and 11-year-old children were not only more likely to spontaneously use context cues to facilitate recall of picture lists than were 6-year-old children, they were also more likely to use them more efficiently. When younger children were specifically directed to use the cues, however, age differences in the amount of information recalled disappeared. Instructing children to use the cues was, therefore, particularly useful for the youngest age group. Even younger children may be able to effectively use cues to facilitate list recall when explicitly prompted to do so (Ritter, Kaprove, Fitch, & Flavell, 1973).

Consistent with the encoding specificity hypothesis, the effectiveness of cues in prompting recall depends on their specific relation to the to-be-recalled information. In a series of studies with children ages between 3 and 4 and a half years, Perlmutter, Sophian, Mitchell and Cavanaugh (1981) found that cues that were meaningfully related to pictures children were asked to remember were effective, particularly for the older children. However, unrelated pictures were effective as retrieval cues only if they had been physically integrated with the to-be-remembered pictures (see also Ruch & Levin, 1979).

Recently studies have begun to examine whether cues are useful in prompting children's event memory. In these studies children have either observed or participated in an event, and the cues and props have included both scale models and reinstatement of the actual environmental context or items from the event. These studies are more directly relevant to the use of cues in legal contexts than studies of picture or story recall not only in terms of the information to be recalled, but also in terms of the time over which the information is remembered. In legal contexts children are likely to be asked to recall events that happened weeks, months, and even years earlier, and the question of whether cues and props are effective in facilitating recall over such long periods is particularly important.

Several studies suggest that reinstatement of the entire context of an event may be useful in enhancing children's descriptions of it (Price & Goodman, 1990; Smith et al., 1987; Wilkinson, 1988). In the study by

Smith et al. (1987) kindergarten children were shown how to make clay and immediately afterwards were asked to describe what they had done, first in free recall and then in one of three cue conditions. In one condition, children were simply asked to describe again what had happened. In the second condition the ingredients and utensils used in making clay were on display and the children were again asked to report everything that happened, and in the third condition the children were asked to remake the clay and to describe verbally everything as they did so. Children interviewed with the object cues without reenactment reported more new information than those interviewed with standard free recall instructions. However, children who had the opportunity to reenact the event recalled more actions than children in either of the other retrieval conditions. Over half of the information recalled was communicated through reenactment without description. Accuracy was high overall, although in a free-recall account 2 weeks later those children who had previously reenacted the event were less accurate than the other two groups.

Context cues may also enhance children's reports of a series of activities (Wilkinson, 1988). In Wilkinson's study, pairs of 4-year-old children from a nursery school were taken for a walk through a park. During the walk, various activities took place, such as finding a ball and singing a song. The next day the children were either taken back along the path and asked to describe as they went what had happened the previous day, or were interviewed in a room at the nursery school. Children interviewed in the context of the walk recalled significantly more information than those interviewed in the nursery, even when nonverbal information was excluded from the analysis.

Scale models and toys, including anatomically detailed dolls, are already in use in the legal context and their effects on children's reports are therefore of particular interest. O'Callaghan and D'Arcy (1989) examined the effects of model props on 4-year-olds' accounts of a "whodunnit" video when interviewed immediately after the video. Reenactment with model props significantly increased the amount of information reported in both free recall and in response to questions, compared to interviews without the props. However, increased free recall was associated with decreased accuracy. O'Callaghan and D'Arcy therefore concluded that although props facilitated the report of detail "such use of props may increase the likelihood of embellishment or distortion in free recall" (p. 194).

Goodman and Aman (1990) also found that scale models enhanced children's event reports but in contrast to O'Callaghan and D'Arcy, they found no effect on accuracy. In their study, children ages 3 and 5 years were asked to recall an interaction with an unfamiliar male adult a week after it had taken place. The children were interviewed under one of four cue conditions: with anatomically detailed dolls and props, regular dolls and props, dolls and props visible but out of reach, or without dolls or props. Props included scale-model replicas of the items used in the interaction as well as distractor items, and children in the reenactment conditions were encouraged to use the props to act out as well as verbally recount what had happened. Although props as visual cues only did not improve recall, reenactment added to the verbal accounts, especially of the older children.

Saywitz, Goodman, Nicholas, and Moan (1991) recently examined the effects of model cues and props on children's reports of activities more closely analogous to sexual abuse than in previous studies. Five- and 7-year-olds were interviewed about a medical checkup which, for half of the children, had included genital and anal examination. Interviews were conducted either 1 week or 1 month after the examination. Reenactment using anatomically detailed dolls and scale models of doctor instruments (including distractor items) resulted in a twofold increase in the amount of information reported compared to free recall without the props. Interestingly, props did not increase the frequency of reports of activities most closely analogous to those likely to be involved in sexual abuse (genital and anal touching). Props increased errors in general, many of which involved the distractor toys. However, accuracy was overall high in reenactment and it is worthy of note that none of the errors in free recall and reenactment were of the kind that would lead to a suspicion of sexual abuse.

Although preliminary, the evidence to date suggests that model props, such as toys or scale models, may be less effective as cues than actual objects from an event or reinstatement of the original event context (Price & Goodman, 1990). In Price and Goodman's (1990) study, children ages 3 and 5 years took part in a recurring event, "visiting the wizard," which comprised a series of activities. Price and Goodman found that although model props significantly increased recall, reenactment in the actual context produced better recall of the component actions than did either reenactment with the model or free recall alone.

It is possible that scale models and toys pose particular problems when used as cues or props, especially with young children. As Goodman and Aman (1990) point out, children may have difficulty in recognizing the relation between a model and an event they have witnessed or experienced. Indeed, DeLoache and colleagues have recently shown that the larger the discrepancy between a scale model and the real-life equivalent, the less likely young children are to make the connection, even in quite simple tasks (DeLoache, 1990; DeLoache,

Kolstad, & Anderson, 1991). For example, in one study DeLoache et al. (1991) asked 2- and 3-year-old-children to find a small Snoopy dog hidden in a scale model after watching an experimenter hide a large Snoopy dog in the room on which the model was based. The children had to be taught to use model replicas, and the younger children required a greater degree of similarity between the scale models and the original room than did older children in order to successfully find the toy. Such difficulties may have contributed to the relatively small effects of models and toys in facilitating recall compared to reinstatement of the actual context (Price & Goodman, 1990) and possibly also to their effects on the accuracy of children's reports (O'Callaghan & D'Arcy, 1989).

THE PRESENT STUDIES

The studies reviewed above provide preliminary evidence that stimulus support at the time of interview may indeed enhance children's event recall (e.g., Price & Goodman, 1990; Smith et al., 1987; Wilkinson, 1988). Reinstating the actual context of the event appears to be particularly effective compared to model props and standard verbal recall instructions. These findings are encouraging. However, there are a number of questions that need to be addressed if physical cues are to be used when children give testimony.

One important question in the context of children's testimony is whether irrelevant cues have a suggestive effect on children's reports. In real-life situations, an interviewer will often not know which items and objects are relevant to the events being recalled. At issue is whether the irrelevant items mislead children and contaminate their reports. The effects of relevant cues, also, remain poorly understood. Questions relating to, for example, which cues and props are most effective in facilitating recall, how they should be presented in interviews, the effects of using cues repeatedly, and developmental changes in the influence of cues and props on children's reports have received little attention to date. We examine aspects of these questions in the studies described below.

In each of our studies, children took part either individually or in pairs in a contrived interaction with an unfamiliar adult who was "practicing" to become a magician. She dressed the child (or one of the children) as an assistant in hat, cape, and gloves and asked him or her to help with the magic tricks. The general script was the same in all three studies although there were variations in the specific "incidents" occurring, for example, whether the show was interrupted and whether there was an ink spill. The magic show had the advantages that it could be standardized across children and was novel and interesting. We also wanted the event to include activities that children might find difficult to describe in detail, and the magic tricks satisfied these criteria. The interactions, which lasted about 10 minutes, took place in a room at the child's school. Children were interviewed 10 days and 10 weeks after the interaction, delays that are realistic in the context of children's testimony.

Object and Verbal Cues: Study 1

In the first study (Wilson & Pipe, 1989), we examined whether having object cues in view is more effective than presentation of verbal cues as a means of facilitating young children's reports of an event in which they had participated. Twenty-four children between 5 and 6 years individually took part in the interaction with the unfamiliar adult "magician." Approximately 10 days later, the children were interviewed about what had happened. The interviewer explained that she did not know what the magician had done and she wanted the child to tell her everything. Children initially gave a free-recall account, then cues were introduced and the child was again asked to describe what had happened. For half the children, cues were items and objects from the interaction; for example, objects used in the magic tricks and items of clothing. For the remaining children, verbal labels of the same items were read aloud several times. To see whether cues were more effective following a long delay we reinterviewed all children following a further delay of 2 months.

When children were interviewed after 10 days, most of the information reported about the event was in free recall prior to the introduction of cues. Table 2.1 shows that cues prompted relatively little information at this early interview. However, at the 10-week delay cues had quite a substantial effect. Although children recalled less during free recall than they had in the earlier interview, they recalled more during cued recall. This interaction between type of recall (free vs. cued) and delay (short vs. long) was significant, F (1,20) = 51.35, $p < .001$. Object cues were more effective than were the verbal cues in cued recall, t (20) = 3.58, $p < .001$, with the result that at the long delay children interviewed with object cues recalled more information in total than those interviewed with verbal cues, t (20) = 3.57, $p < .001$. These results show that physical cues did facilitate children's free-recall reports of an event in which they had participated. Moreover, actual items and objects were superior to their verbal labels and the cues were particularly effective at the 10-week delay when free recall had declined.

TABLE 2.1. Items of Information Recalled (Study 1)

	Interview					
	10-day			10-week		
	Free recall	Cued recall	Total recall	Free recall	Cued recall	Total recall
Group						
Object cues	7.1	3.0	**10.1**	3.7	10.0	**13.7**
Verbal cues	7.8	1.8	**9.6**	4.3	4.9	**9.2**

Environmental, Relevant, and Irrelevant Cues: Study 2

Items and objects involved in activities comprising an event, as used in the above study and also in that of Smith et al. (1987), clearly facilitate event recall, even without reenactment. However, the effects of different kinds of cues, such as general environmental cues or distractor items have received little attention to date. In our second study we examined the influence of irrelevant (distractor) items on children's reports and, in particular, whether their presence during the interview misled children into making errors (King & Yuille, 1987). We also examined the role of general environmental context cues (or "distal" context cues) in facilitating children's reports compared to more specific activity-related (or "proximal") cues. Environmental cues might be expected to be less effective than cue items specifically involved in the event and integrated with it (Perlmutter et al., 1981; Rovee-Collier & Hayne, 1987). Finally, in this study we included a group of 10-year-olds in addition to the 6-year-old children to determine whether cues attenuated age differences in amount recalled (Kobasigawa, 1974) and whether distractor items differentially affected the accuracy of the two age groups (King & Yuille, 1987).

The 88 children in each age group took part in pairs in the magic show, with only one child dressing up as the magician's assistant. As in study 1, each child was interviewed both shortly (10 days) after the event and then again following a longer (10-week) delay. Children were interviewed under one of four conditions of stimulus support. In the *context* cues (only) condition, children were interviewed back in the room in which the interaction had taken place. Distinctive features that had been present during the interaction were still in the room, such as the backdrop curtains, boxes, and the table on which the tricks had been performed, but there were no objects specifically related to the tricks or incidents occurring during the interaction. Children in the *specific* cues condition were also interviewed in the same room, but in addition, cues relating to the specific activities, for example, objects used in the magic tricks, were in view on a table beside the child throughout the interview. In the *irrelevant* cues condition, context and specific cues were again present, and additionally there were "irrelevant" cues that were consistent with the magic show, such as items from magic tricks, which had not in fact been used. Finally, in the *control* condition, children were interviewed in a different room from that in which the interaction had taken place, without specific or irrelevant cues.

Children were first asked for a free-recall account of the event. Figure 2.1 shows the total number of items of information (correct + incorrect) recalled by children interviewed in each condition. Children interviewed with specific cues (children in both the specific and the irrelevant cues groups) recalled significantly more items of information than those interviewed without cues or with only the context cues, F (3, 160) = 13.61, $p < .001$. Context cues alone did not enhance children's reports compared to the control condition. Specific cues facilitated reports of both age groups and did not attenuate the highly significant difference in the amount of information recalled by the 6- and 10-year-olds respectively, F (1,160) = 41.97, $p < .001$.

Although the children reported more when interviewed soon after the event than following the 10-week delay, F (1,160) = 35.04, $p < .001$, we did not find a greater effect of cues when children were interviewed at the long delay. Based on the results of our first study we expected that cues would be more effective following the longer delay. However, in study 1 cues were introduced following free recall, and information prompted by cues could be examined separately. In the present study, cues were present throughout the period of free recall,

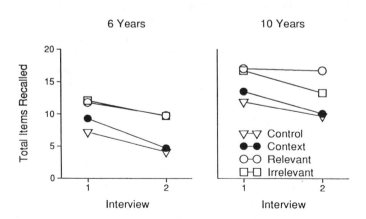

FIGURE 2.1. Number of items recalled in free recall (study 2).

and information freely recalled and prompted by cues was combined, attenuating differences due to the cues. Looking at the loss of information between the 10-day and 10-week interviews, there is the same trend for the present study as for study 1. For younger children interviewed with the specific cues (children in the relevant and irrelevant cues conditions combined), there was an 18% loss of information between the interviews, whereas for children interviewed without cues (children in the context and control conditions combined), information reported at the 10-day interview had been reduced by nearly 46% 2 months later. For the older children the comparable figures were 11% and 22%. Clearly, then, children interviewed with the specific cues reported considerably more information over the 2-month period than those interviewed without.

Although cues increased the amount children recalled about the event, the increase in total recall may have been at the expense of accuracy; however, this was not the case. To examine the accuracy of children's reports, the number of items of information correctly recalled (correct items) were expressed as a proportion of the total number of items recalled (correct + incorrect items). Table 2.2 shows that although overall accuracy was higher for the older children (M = 92%) than for the younger (M = 87%), both age groups were generally very accurate. There was a small but significant decline in accuracy over the 2-month period between the interviews for both age groups (M = 6% for 6-year-olds, 2% for 10-year-olds), F (1,44) = 8.73, $p < .01$. However, proportions of items correctly recalled were remarkably similar for children interviewed in the different cues conditions, F (3,44) = < 1. The enhanced recall of the children interviewed with either relevant items or a mixture of relevant and irrelevant items was not, therefore, associated with a decrease in the accuracy of the information recalled.

We also examined the effects of cues on the accuracy of children's responses to questions. Following free recall, each child was asked ten specific questions, five leading questions and five misleading questions. The questions related to various aspects of the interaction,

TABLE 2.2. Proportion of Items Correctly Recalled (Study 2)

	6 years		10 years	
Cues condition	Interview 1	Interview 2	Interview 1	Interview 2
No cues	.90	.84	.93	.92
Context	.91	.87	.93	.90
Relevant	.87	.86	.91	.92
Irrelevant	.91	.80	.92	.87

including questions about roles, the magician's clothing, and the time and place of the interaction. Overall, older children were more accurate than younger children. Means (percent correct) for specific, leading, and misleading questions were 71%, 90%, and 50% for the 6-year-olds, and 87%, 92%, and 75% for the 10-year-olds, respectively. However, the presence of cues during interviews did not influence accuracy of responses overall or for any of the question types when analyzed separately.

In summary, the findings of our second study confirm earlier reports that having cues in view is indeed a useful means for increasing the amount of information children report about an event in free recall. We found that generally cues did not influence the accuracy of children's reports whether obtained by free recall or by questioning. In particular, there was little evidence that irrelevant cues misled children into making more errors. These results suggest that cues may not only be useful, they may also be a safe means of facilitating recall. This finding has potentially important implications in the context of children's testimony. However, its generality needs to be established.

Directed and Repeated Cue Use: Study 3

In evidential interviews it is likely that the child will be asked directly whether cue items or props represent things that were in the actual event, and the child may even be invited to demonstrate what happened by using them. Laboratory-based studies suggest that it is under such conditions that retrieval cues are most effective for young children, and hence most likely to attenuate age differences in recall (Kobasigawa, 1974). It is also possible that irrelevant cues will be more likely to lead to errors in children's reports when children are invited to interact with them (Piaget & Inhelder, 1973). In study 2, the physical cues were present throughout the interview but no attempt was made to direct the child's attention to them. In our third study, therefore, we directed children to attend to relevant and irrelevant cue items and examined the effects on both the amount and the accuracy of the information prompted by the cues. Further, in this study we explicitly examined the effects of repeatedly interviewing children with cues.

A total of 95 children between 5 and 6 years of age or 9 and 10 years interacted with the magician, in pairs. Half of the children were interviewed 10 days after the interaction and then again following a further delay of 2 months (repeated-interview group), as in the earlier studies, while the remaining children were interviewed only once following the long delay (nonrepeated group). This manipulation enabled us to assess the effects of presenting irrelevant cues in one interview on children's reports in a subsequent interview. Children were interviewed either in a control condition or with both specific and irrelevant cues. The items and objects in the cues condition were not introduced until prompted recall, after children had completed free recall. Children in the cues condition were shown a group of objects and given the general directive "What can you tell me about these things?" followed by open-ended questions such as "What did the magician wear?" Children interviewed with no cues were asked the same questions but without the general directives.

Table 2.3 shows that the amount of information reported in prompted recall was greater for children interviewed with cues than for those interviewed without. The overall analysis at the long delay showed that this difference was significant, F (1,87) = 12.52, p < .001, and did not depend on whether children had been interviewed previously or were interviewed for the first time at the long delay. The older children gave more information than the younger children, F (1,87) = 15.38, p < .001. However, the interaction between age and condition did not reach significance. This was in contrast to our prediction that cues would help the younger children to a greater extent than the older children. To examine this prediction further, we compared children interviewed with cues and those in the control condition separately for each age group and each interview. The F-ratios are shown in Table 2.3. Younger children with cues provided at least 50% more information than those interviewed without cues in each interview, whereas for the older children the difference between the cues and no-cues groups was always smaller and nonsignificant.

Cues would be of limited value in prompting recall if they merely encouraged the children to repeat more of the information they had

TABLE 2.3. Items of Information Recalled during Prompted Recall (Study 3)

	Interview					
	10-day			10-week		
	Control	Cues	F[a]	Control	Cues	F[a]
6 years						
Repeated group	8.7	14.0	NS	7.5	14.9	9.46
Nonrepeated group	—	—		8.5	13.0	8.18**
10 years						
Repeated group	16.7	19.0	NS	15.5	17.0	NS
Nonrepeated group	—	—		13.3	15.7	NS

[a] F value for control vs. cues comparison.
* p <.05. ** p <.01.

already mentioned in free recall. With this in mind, we compared the number of items in prompted recall that were repeated from free recall and the number of new items, separately. Children interviewed with cues did not differ from those interviewed without in the number of items repeated in prompted recall. In contrast, children interviewed with cues recalled more new information (information not previously reported in free recall) in prompted recall than those without cues, at the short delay F (1,38) = 4.05, p < 0.05 for the repeated group; at the long delay F (1,38) = 12.53, p < .001 for the repeated group; at the long delay F (1,49) = 12.98, p < .001 for the nonrepeated group. Clearly cues were useful in generating additional information.

Although the cues increased the amount of information reported, they may also have compromised the accuracy of children's reports. We therefore analyzed the accuracy of prompted recall (that is, the number of correct items as a proportion of the total correct + incorrect items recalled). At the long delay the older children were more accurate than the younger, F (1,81) = 7.11, p < .01, and children interviewed in the control condition were more accurate than those interviewed with cues, F (1,81) = 4.55, p < .05. There were no significant interactions. However, comparisons of the cues and control groups for the 10-day and 10-week interviews for the repeated group and the 10-week interview for the nonrepeated group, separately, showed that the only significant difference was for the second interview of the repeated group; children interviewed with cues were less accurate than those interviewed without cues (M = 75% vs. 83%), F (1,40) = 4.05, p < .05. The comparison of these same children in their first interview failed to reveal a significant difference between the cues and control conditions (M = 84% for cues and 88% for control). For children interviewed only after the 10-week delay the difference also failed to reach significance (M = 79% and 83%, respectively). These data suggest that repeated interviewing with cues may have had a detrimental effect on the accuracy of prompted recall.

Any effects of cues on accuracy when children were interviewed the second time were, however, specific to the prompted recall with the cues present. When we compared the accuracy of free recall in the second interview there was no evidence that prior exposure to the cues "contaminated" children's reports. The effect of cues on children's accuracy in response to questions was also examined (see Table 2.4). Following free and prompted recall, children were asked four leading, four misleading, and four specific questions. Results showed that for all questions (combined), the 9- to 10-year-olds were more accurate than the 5- to 6-year-olds. As can be seen in Table 2.4, younger children

TABLE 2.4. Percentage Correct Responses to Questions (Study 3)

	Interview					
	10-day			10-week		
	Control	Cues	F^a	Control	Cues	F^a
6 years						
Repeated group	56	65	NS	51	62	7.30*
Nonrepeated group	—	—		48	58	5.51*
10 years						
Repeated group	73	73	NS	68	65	NS
Nonrepeated group	—	—		61	66	NS

[a] F value for control vs. cues comparison.
* $p < .05.$ ** $p < .01.$

interviewed with cues answered more questions correctly than those interviewed without cues, particularly following the long delay, whereas cues had little impact on the accuracy of the older children.

In summary, the data from this study suggest that when children are directed to attend to cues, the cues facilitate the recall of younger children in particular. In prompted recall, children interviewed with cues were less accurate than those interviewed in the control condition although the difference was significant only for the children interviewed a second time. Further, this effect on accuracy was specific to prompted recall; children did not include more erroneous information in free recall as a result of prior exposure to the cues and children interviewed with cues were more accurate in response to questions than those interviewed without cues.

CONCLUSIONS

Both theoretical and practical considerations suggest that reinstating the context of an event should facilitate children's event recall. Laboratory studies support this prediction, in particular when the context is closely related to the target information (e.g., Perlmutter et al., 1981) and when children are directed to the cues (Kobasigawa, 1974; Ritter et al., 1973). Our studies together with other recent studies (Price & Goodman, 1990; Saywitz et al., 1991; Smith et al., 1987; Wilkinson, 1988) extend these findings to children's event memory and support the conclusion that reinstatement of actual items and objects leads to more complete reports of events in which children have participated. As in the laboratory-based studies, however, the particular cues used and the method of presenting them are important determinants of both the amount and the accuracy of the information reported, as discussed below.

We found that reinstating cues relating to specific activities is more likely to facilitate recall than reinstating only the environmental context cues. Simply taking children back into the environment in which an event occurred was not sufficient to enhance children's recall. It is, of course, possible that under some conditions environmental cues will help children to remember and report details. The environmental context in our studies, although distinctive, was not integrated with the activities comprising the event and integration may be necessary if cues are to be useful (Perlmutter et al., 1981). Moreover, all children were interviewed in a room at school, and therefore had some contextual information available at the time of the interview. Reinstatement of environmental context may be maximally effective when there would otherwise be very marked differences between the context of the event and that of the interview (Baddeley, 1986). This may be the case when children are interviewed in legal contexts when, for example, the event of interest has occurred in a very unfamiliar environment.

Consistent with Tulving's principle of encoding specificity, evidence to date suggests that reinstating the actual context and objects from an event has a greater effect than more abstract cues such as verbal labels (Wilson & Pipe, 1989) or toy models (Goodman & Aman, 1990; Price & Goodman,1990). Price and Goodman (1990) found that when children reenacted activities in context they recalled more than when they reenacted them with model replicas. Similarly, we found that simply having items and objects from an event present was sufficient to increase recall, whereas Goodman and Aman (1990) found no effect of model props under comparable conditions. That models are less effective than actual items is probably due to the difficulty children have in making the connection between the model items and the event (DeLoache, 1990). Very young children, especially, may fail to appreciate the relevance of the model items, even in quite simple situations, if there is no prior training and considerable physical similarity between the toys and the items they represent (DeLoache et al., 1991). In real-life situations, of course, it may be difficult to ensure a good match between the models and the represented items. Further, there is some evidence that model cues and props may decrease the accuracy of children's reports, perhaps especially when used in the relatively unstructured context of free recall (O'Callaghan & D'Arcy, 1989; Saywitz et al., 1991). Models or toys may prompt children to enact activities other than those from the particular event of interest (Goodman & Aman, 1990; Piaget & Inhelder, 1973). Although this is a problem with real objects also, it is likely to be exacerbated with models and toys.

The results of our studies have implications regarding the way in which cue items should be presented during interviews. We found that simply having the cues in view, without inviting the children to reenact the event with them, was sufficient to facilitate event reports. The facilitative effect of cues was comparable for both younger and older children, and under these conditions there was no evidence to suggest that prior exposure to cues contaminated children's reports at a later date. Even children who had been interviewed with irrelevant cues were as accurate as the other children. When children were directed to the cues and asked about them, the reports of the younger children in particular were enhanced, so that age differences were attenuated. However, under these conditions cues also had some detrimental effect on accuracy, particularly when children were interviewed with them a second time. This effect on accuracy was specific to prompted recall, in which children were asked general open-ended questions relating to the cues. There was no effect of prior exposure to cues on the accuracy of either their free-recall reports or responses to specific questions. Indeed, to the contrary, for the younger children the combination of cues with specific questions increased accuracy, perhaps because the actual items were less ambiguous than the questions alone. Additionally, the combination of questions with physical cues might have constrained the children's responses to the event of interest (see also O'Callaghan & D'Arcy, 1989).

Further work on how best to instruct children to use cues to facilitate remembering is clearly needed. Simply having cues available visually may help children recall information without adversely affecting the accuracy of their reports. Younger children may benefit to a greater extent, however, when their attention is directed to the cues and they can interact with them. Directing children's attention to the cues with much more explicit instructions may be maximally advantageous, as suggested by our finding that children responded more accurately to questions accompanied by cues than to questions alone. Future research will need to investigate ways of introducing cues that minimize potential confusion, for example, practice lineups of both familiar and novel items. We are currently examining children's responses to the not unrealistic scenario in which they are confronted with an array of irrelevant items that the interviewer assumes to be relevant.

In conclusion, there is now clear evidence that cues and props can help children to provide more complete event reports than they would normally provide in a free-recall account. Cues and props may also help when children are questioned quite specifically if the questions relate directly to the cue items. Interviewers must, of course, always be aware of the risk that these retrieval techniques might reduce the accuracy of reports. The effect on accuracy appears to depend on the nature of the cues and props, the way they are presented, and how children are instructed to use them. We are cautiously optimistic that there will be few adverse effects on accuracy when children are interviewed with props in view or when props are used in conjunction with specific questions.

ACKNOWLEDGMENTS

We are indebted to the many Dunedin schools that supported these studies: We would like to thank Jocelyn Burke, Jan Egerton, Megan Gollop, Shyamala Nada Raja, Kate Paulin, and Tushar Robins who gave valuable assistance to the research studies described in this chapter. Thanks also to Jan Egerton and Megan Gollop for their help in the preparation of this chapter. This research was supported in part by grants to the first author from the Social Sciences Research Fund Committee and from the New Zealand National Children's Health Research Foundation.

REFERENCES

Ackerman, B. P. (1986). The relation between attention to the incidental context and memory for words in children and adults. *Journal of Experimental Child Psychology, 41*, 149–163.

Baddeley, A. D. (1986). *Working memory.* Oxford: Oxford University Press.

Brown, A. L. (1975). Recognition, reconstruction and recall of narrative sequences by preoperational children. *Child Development, 46*, 156–166.

Bruner, J. S. (1964). The course of cognitive growth. *American Psychologist, 19*, 1–15.

Cashmore, J. (1990). Problems and solutions in lawyer–child communication. *Criminal Law Journal, 15.* 193–202.

Ceci, S. J., & Howe, M. J. (1978). Semantic knowledge as a determinant of developmental differences in recall. *Journal of Experimental Child Psychology, 26*, 230–245.

Ceci, S. J., Ross, D. F., & Toglia, M.P. (1987). Suggestibility of children's memory: Psycholegal implications. *Journal of Experimental Psychology: General, 116*, 38–49.

Chi, M. T. H. (1976). Short-term memory limitations in children: Capacity or processing deficits? *Memory & Cognition, 4*, 599–572.

Cole, C. B., & Loftus, E. F. (1987). The memory of children. In S. J. Ceci, M. P. Toglia, & D. F. Ross (Eds.), *Children's eyewitness memory* (pp. 178–208). New York: Springer-Verlag.

Daehler, M. W., & Greco, C. (1985). Memory in very young children. In M.

Pressley & C. J. Brainerd (Eds.), *Cognitive learning and memory in children. Progress in cognitive development research* (pp. 49–79). New York: Springer-Verlag.

DeLoache, J. S. (1990). Young children's understanding of models. In R. Fivush & J. A. Hudson (Eds.), *Knowing and remembering in young children* (pp. 94–126). Cambridge: Cambridge University Press.

DeLoache, J. S., Kolstad, V., & Anderson, K. N. (1991). Physical similarity and young children's understanding of scale models. *Child Development, 62,* 111–126.

Fabricius, W. V., & Wellman, H. M. (1983). Children's understanding of retrieval cue utilization. *Developmental Psychology, 19,* 15–21.

Goodman, G. S., & Aman, C. (1990). Children's use of anatomically detailed dolls to recount an event. *Child Development, 61,* 1859–1871.

Goodman, G. S., Aman, C., & Hirschman, J. (1987). Child sexual and physical abuse: Children's testimony. In S. J. Ceci, M. P. Toglia, & D. F. Ross (Eds.), *Children's eyewitness memory* (pp. 1–23). New York: Springer-Verlag.

Goodman, G. S., & Reed, R. S. (1986). Age differences in eyewitness testimony. *Law and Human Behavior, 10,* 317–332.

Jones, D. P. H., & McQuiston, M. G. (1988). *Interviewing the sexually abused child.* London: Gaskell.

King, M. A., & Yuille, J. C. (1987). Suggestibility and the child witness. In S. J. Ceci, M. P. Toglia, & D. F. Ross (Eds.), *Children's eyewitness memory* (pp. 24–35). New York: Springer-Verlag.

Kobasigawa, A. (1974). Utilization of retrieval cues by children in recall. *Child Development, 45,* 127–134.

Marin, B. V., Holmes, D. L., Guth, M., & Kovac, P. (1979). The potential of children as eyewitnesses. *Law and Human Behavior, 3,* 295–305.

Mertin, P. (1989). The memory of young children for eyewitness events. *Australian Journal of Social Issues, 24,* 23–32.

Nelson, K. (1986). *Event knowledge: Structure and function in development.* Hillsdale, NJ: Erlbaum.

Nelson, K., & Ross, G. (1980). The generalities and specifics of long-term memory in infants and young children. In M. Perlmutter (Ed.), *Children's memory. New directions for child development, No. 10* (pp. 87–107). San Francisco: Jossey-Bass.

O'Callaghan, G., & D'Arcy, H. (1989). Use of props in questioning preschool witnesses. *Australian Journal of Psychology, 41,* 187–195.

Perlmutter, M., & Ricks, M. (1979). Recall in preschool children. *Journal of Experimental Child Psychology, 27,* 423–436.

Perlmutter, M., Sophian, C., Mitchell, D. B., & Cavanaugh, J. C. (1981). Semantic and contextual cuing of preschool children's recall. *Child Development, 52,* 873–881.

Piaget, J., & Inhelder, B. (1973). *Memory and intelligence.* London: Routledge & Kegan Paul.

Pipe, M.-E., & Goodman, G. S. (1991). Elements of secrecy: Implications for children's testimony. *Behavioral Sciences and the Law, 9,* 33–41.

Price, D. W. W., & Goodman, G. S. (1990). Visiting the wizard: Children's memory for a recurring event. *Child Development, 61,* 664–680.

Ratner, H. H., & Myers, N. A. (1980). Related picture cues and memory for hidden-object locations at age two. *Child Development, 51,* 561–564.

Ritter, K., Kaprove, B. H., Fitch, J. P., & Flavell, J. (1973). The development of retrieval strategies in young children. *Cognitive Psychology, 5,* 310–321.

Rovee-Collier, C., & Hayne, H. (1987). Reactivation of infant memory: Implications for cognitive development. *Advances in Child Development and Behavior, 20,* 185–238.

Ruch, M. D., & Levin, J. R. (1979). Partial pictures as imagery-retrieval cues in young children's prose recall. *Journal of Experimental Child Psychology, 28,* 268–279.

Saywitz, K. J. (1987). Children's testimony: Age-related patterns of memory errors. In S.J. Ceci, M.P. Toglia, & D.F. Ross (Eds.), *Children's eyewitness memory* (pp. 36–52). New York: Springer-Verlag.

Saywitz, K. J., Goodman, G. S., Nicholas, E., & Moan, S. (1991). Children's memories of physical examinations involving genital touch: Implications for reports of child sexual abuse. *Journal of Consulting and Clinical Psychology, 59,* 682–691.

Schneider, W., & Sodian, B. (1988). Metamemory behaviour relationships in young children: Evidence from a memory-for-location task. *Journal of Experimental Child Psychology, 45,* 209–233.

Smith, B. S., Ratner, H. H., & Hobart, C. J. (1987). The role of cuing and organization in children's memory for events. *Journal of Experimental Child Psychology, 44,* 1–24.

Todd, C. M., & Perlmutter, M. (1980). Reality recalled by preschool children. In M. Perlmutter (Ed.), *Children's memory. New directions for child development, No. 10* (pp. 69–85). San Francisco: Jossey-Bass.

Tulving, E. (1983). *Elements of episodic memory.* Oxford: Oxford University Press.

Turtle, J. W., & Wells, G. L. (1987). Setting the stage for psychological research on the child eyewitness. In S. J. Ceci, M. P. Toglia, & D. F. Ross (Eds.), *Children's eyewitness memory* (pp. 230–248). New York: Springer-Verlag.

White, S. H., & Pillemer, D. B. (1979). Childhood amnesia and the development of a socially accessible memory system. In J. F. Kihlstrom and F. J. Evans (Eds.), *Functional disorders of memory* (pp. 29–73). Hillsdale, NJ: Erlbaum.

Wilkinson, J. (1988). Context in children's event memory. In M. M. Gruneberg, P. E. Morris, & R. N. Sykes (Eds.), *Practical aspects of memory: Current research and issues (Vol.1,* pp. 107–111). Chichester: Wiley.

Wilson, J. C., & Pipe, M.-E. (1989). The effects of cues on young children's recall of real events. *New Zealand Journal of Psychology, 18,* 65–70.

Zaragoza, M. (1987). Memory, suggestibility and eyewitness testimony in children and adults. In S. J. Ceci, M. P. Toglia, & D. F. Ross (Eds.), *Children's eyewitness memory* (pp. 53–78). New York: Springer-Verlag.

3

The Use of Anatomical Dolls in Sexual Abuse Evaluations: Current Research and Practice

Barbara W. Boat and
Mark D. Everson
University of North Carolina

T he fact that child sexual abuse has been the focus of attention of clinicians and researchers for only about 15 years is sobering. Sexual activity between adults and children has been noted for centuries, but the high incidence of sexual abuse of children remained unacknowledged until the seminal research by Finkelhor (1979) and others. Research and clinical professionals were also unaware of the startling fact that up to one third of sexually abused children had been molested before the age of 7 years (Finkelhor, 1984, 1986). The inclusion of such a large percentage of young children garnered concerned attention.

As the decade progressed, the research focus shifted from documenting the incidence of abused children to facilitating their disclosures in order to intervene and protect the victims. The reality that concrete interviewing props would need to be employed with pre-school-aged children was taken for granted by many interviewers. To this end, professionals from as diverse settings as social services, medicine, mental health, and law sought props and techniques to help the children accurately describe sexual abuse.

Although puppets, anatomical drawings, Playdough people, nonanatomical dolls, and other props limited only by the creativity of the interviewer have been employed (Conte, Sorenson, Fogarty, &

Rosa, 1991), no tool quite captured the interest of professionals as did anatomical dolls. Such interest may have been enhanced because of the variety of useful functions the dolls could serve when interviewing the child witness (see Everson & Boat, in press, for a review).

First, the dolls could be used as an "icebreaker" to help focus the child on broad sexual issues. For example, several writers of interview guidelines (Boat & Everson, 1986; Friedemann, & Morgan, 1985; White, Strom, Santilli, & Quinn, 1987) recommend questioning the child about gender differences when introducing the clothed dolls (e.g., "Does this doll look like a boy or a girl?"). The assumption is that the interviewer is focusing the child's attention in a gentle, non-leading manner on sexual topics and on parts of the body that the child may be reluctant to discuss.

Second, the dolls could be used as an "anatomical model" to visually cue the child when assessing his or her knowledge of sexuality and especially the child's names and understanding of the function of various body parts.

Third, the dolls could be used as a "memory stimulus" to trigger the child's memory and/or serve as a "demonstration aid" to enable the child to show what happened and clarify alleged abusive acts.

Finally, there was a perception that the dolls might be useful as a "diagnostic test" in that abused children might interact with the dolls in ways that would definitively differentiate them from their non-abused counterparts.

Each type of doll usage raises concerns about influencing or misinterpreting behaviors or statements of the child witness. The purpose of this chapter is to present the research that addresses these four functional uses of the dolls (i.e., icebreaker use, anatomical model use, memory stimulus/demonstration aid use, and diagnostic test use) as they are related to the suggestiveness of the dolls and the suggestibility of the child witness. This discussion is preceded by a brief presentation of a historical perspective on the dolls, the features of the dolls, and the professionals who use the dolls.

HISTORICAL PERSPECTIVE ON THE ANATOMICAL DOLLS

The Anatomical Dolls from 1978–1990

The first anatomical dolls to be marketed in the public domain were probably made in Oregon by Migima Designs and Analeka Industries in about 1978. The simple cloth dolls had vaginal openings and penises and scrotums. Their expressions were somber, befitting a somber topic. Their stated purpose (Friedemann & Morgan, 1985) was to enable children to identify body parts and functions (anatomical model use) and to demonstrate and/or clarify what had happened to them (demonstration aid use). Few anticipated that 10 years later the anatomical dolls would become the focus of heated controversies on the suggestiveness of the dolls to stimulate sexualized fantasies in children and the suggestibility of young children to be so influenced. Such controversies culminated in the California courts banning information obtained when anatomical dolls are used as interview aids (e.g., *In re Amber B.* and *In re Christine C.,* [1987]) as well as unfavorable judgments concerning the dolls' suitability as aids in diagnostic interviews in England (see *Family Law Reports,* 1987) and The Netherlands (*Nederlands Juristen Blad,* 1988).

Why Such Furor over the Anatomical Dolls?

The emotional climate in which the dolls were conceived and nurtured is unique. It has long been recognized that communication with young children is enhanced through the use of nonverbal techniques, and it is universally accepted that in working with children a variety of tools are indicated. As Berliner (1988) writes, "It makes sense that children might find it easier to show rather than tell about experiences that are out of the ordinary, for which they might not have words and that are embarrassing or shameful." Why, then, has so much attention been focused on the use of the anatomical dolls as a tool for communicating with children? We speculate that there are several reasons.

First, the dolls were a novel tool that immediately captivated many interviewers. Some interviewers, publicly and privately, nourished a covert hope that the dolls would be a test of child sexual abuse. That is, they hoped research would demonstrate that abused children interacted with the dolls in such a reliably different manner from nonabused children that the dolls would be a litmus test of abuse. The genesis of this hope is easily understandable—child sexual abuse is an abhorrent crime, secret and difficult to detect. There also exists the realistic but extraordinarily difficult mandate that professionals neither disbelieve an abused child nor falsely accuse an alleged perpetrator. Any "test" that would diminish the probability of false positives would greatly enhance the skills and comfort level of the professionals involved in such important detection.

The issue of elevating anatomical dolls to the status of a test was complicated by a report from the American Psychological Association's Committee on Psychological Testing and Assessment (Landers,

1988). The Committee pronounced that the dolls "are considered to be a psychological test and are subject to the [psychological test] standards when used to assess individuals and make inferences about their behavior" (Landers, 1988, p. 25). This statement was inherently misleading unless the definition of a "psychological test" was also included:

> The Committee on Psychological Testing and Assessment considers any procedure of arriving at inferences concerning psychological characteristics (whether covert responses, current states or stable dispositions) to be forms of psychological assessment, irrespective of the basis of such inferences or their scientific soundness. For example, psychological inferences based on horoscope readings, conformation of the skull, behavior ratings or IQ test results are all forms of psychological assessment. (Landers, 1988, p. 25)

This overinclusive definition of a test rendered the committee's statement fairly meaningless in the debate over the proper role of anatomical dolls in evaluations. However, the committee's statement served the purpose of focusing the debate on the dolls as a test and provided fuel for defense attorneys to attack child interviewers: "The American Psychological Association states anatomical dolls are a psychological test. Only licensed psychologists can administer psychological tests. You are not a licensed psychologist. Therefore, you are guilty of malpractice." (Fortunately, the American Psychological Association Council of Representatives adopted a more reasonable position on February 8, 1991, supporting the usefulness of anatomical dolls as interview tools by a range of professionals.)

Once the use of the dolls was construed as a test of sexual abuse, the dolls became justifiable targets for criticisms as well as judicial actions. In California, evidence obtained using the anatomical dolls was ruled inadmissible because the dolls did not meet the standards of the Frye Test (*Frye v. United States*, 1923). Commonly known as the "general acceptance test," the Frye Test stipulated that evidence must be based on techniques that have general acceptance in the relevant scientific community (see Meyers, 1989, for discussion).

A second reason that undue attention has been focused on anatomical dolls is a continuing belief in our society that children are predisposed to lie about sexual activity in general and, specifically, about sexual abuse (Boat & Everson, 1990; Meyers, 1989). Despite accumulated evidence that false reports of sexual abuse by children are relatively uncommon (Everson & Boat, 1989; Jones & McGraw, 1987), a pervasive concern persists that simply questioning children about an abusive experience carries substantial risk of eliciting false reports. This risk is believed to increase when a prop as sexually explicit as an anatomical doll is added. At the heart of this controversy is the belief that anatomical dolls may be overly suggestive to young children (e.g., Terr in Yates & Terr, 1988a, 1988b; Yuille, 1988). According to this position, the anatomical novelty and sexual explicitness of the dolls are likely to induce even normal, nonabused children to have sexual fantasies and to act out in sexually explicit ways that might then be misinterpreted as evidence of sexual abuse. This problem can be exacerbated by certain interviewer errors such as asking highly leading questions, posing the dolls in sexual positions, or verbally reinforcing sexualized play (Underwager, Wakefield, Legrand, & Bartz, 1986; White, 1986).

A third reason for garnering attention is that the anatomical dolls are the most flagrant reminder that the abuse we are evaluating is sexual and, thus, the dolls tend to evoke a wide range of emotional reactions. Berliner (1988) writes that it is revealing that in our society there is substantial concern that simply seeing genitals would be a dramatic and new experience for children. She questions, "Why should children be shocked or frightened or stimulated by dolls that look more like people than the usual ones?" (p. 469). The dolls may be more likely than other interviewing aids to elicit adults' attitudes about sexuality, and these adult issues may be projected onto the dolls. For example, some interviewers will not use dolls with pubic hair because they find the hair to be personally "disgusting." Such projections may explain the surprisingly intense reaction of some doll critics. For example, anatomical dolls have been described as "dirty" and "ugly" (Tylden, 1987) and characterized as "voodoo" dolls (Naumann, 1985), and professionals who use anatomical dolls have been accused of being "guilty of medical malpractice and unethical conduct" (McIver & Wakefield, 1987).

Despite, or perhaps due to, the furor and attention that anatomical dolls have elicited, they have become the focus for a number of research studies that have added to our knowledge of children as witnesses and the use of anatomical dolls as an interview aid in evaluating child sexual abuse.

Features of the Anatomical Dolls

Historically there has not been, nor is there today, a uniform set of standards governing the features of anatomical dolls. The original dolls were lacking in many features considered important by professionals, including manageable size, separated fingers, mouth and anal openings, and pleasant facial expressions. Although several manufacturers make and sell anatomical dolls commercially, many dolls continue to be crafted by local individuals. During the past 12 years, professionals' input has created several changes in the dolls. Certain features are now considered standard (e.g., vaginal, anal, and mouth openings; fingers; and pubic hair to designate sexually mature dolls), and the use of dolls with these features is increasing among professionals. In a 1986 survey of 198 professionals in North Carolina who were using anatomical dolls, fewer than half reported using dolls with mouth openings or finger digits whereas the majority had dolls with vaginal and anal openings and pubic hair (Boat & Everson, 1988). In a 1989 survey of Boston-area professionals who evaluated alleged sexually abused children, 71% of 147 doll users had dolls with finger digits and 92% of their dolls had mouth openings (Kendall-Tackett & Watson, 1992). The dolls are a relatively expensive purchase and although many professionals are aware that their dolls are outdated, they lack the resources to buy new dolls.

One criticism leveled at the dolls is that their genitalia appear disproportionately large, resulting in their being labeled "anatomically grotesque dolls." Bays (1990) measured the genitalia and breasts of 17 doll sets and extrapolated her findings to human adult sizes to determine whether the dolls' sexual parts were exaggerated in size. The vulval slit, penis, scrotum, and breasts of the dolls were not found to be exaggerated. Indeed, the author noted that some manufacturers needed to enlarge the genitalia and breasts to make them more anatomically accurate.

Incidence of Doll Usage

The use of anatomical dolls has increased and proliferated among a range of professionals, and their widespread use mandates that careful attention be paid to the area of training and updating professionals on relevant research. As Boat and Everson (1988) wrote, "perhaps no current area of social concern has drawn together such a disparate group of professionals to perform a similar task as has child sexual abuse and the use of the anatomical dolls" (p. 171). In their 1985 survey, professionals representing protective services, mental health, law enforcement, and medicine were using the dolls. Child protection workers had the highest number of doll users (63/92 respondents, 68%), and respondents anticipated that within the year, 95% of the child protection agencies would be using anatomical dolls. A survey conducted in 1989 among 201 Boston-area mental health and legal professionals who were likely to use the dolls (Kendall-Tackett &

Watson, 1992) found that 73% used the dolls at least some of the time when talking to children. A 1988 survey (Conte et al., 1991) noted that 92% of 212 professionals (86% were in child protective services or mental health) used anatomical dolls. Furthermore, the anatomical dolls were the most frequently endorsed tool, followed by free drawings (88%) and anatomical drawings (66%).

This extraordinarily widespread use of anatomical dolls led Meyers and White (1989) to suggest a set of guidelines to prevent their misuse by ill-informed evaluators. Specifically, Meyers and White recommended that doll users be prepared to describe how and why the dolls were used in a particular case, be familiar with the research and acceptable practice in the field, and be aware of the limits in the use of anatomical dolls, acknowledging that they are interview aids rather than a litmus test for sexual abuse.

Training

Not only has the use of the dolls proliferated, relevant training in using the dolls as an interview aid has also kept pace. In the 1986 survey (Boat & Everson, 1988), fewer than half of the doll users had any training (defined as written or taped instructions, attendance at workshops, or teaching from colleagues or supervisors), only 15% followed a protocol and 34% had less than one year of experience with the dolls. The 1989 survey by Kendall-Tackett and Watson revealed that 98% of doll users had received some training, 78% followed a protocol, and 97% had at least one year of experience using the dolls as an interview aid (Kendall-Tackett & Watson, 1992).

USES OF ANATOMICAL DOLLS

Presenting the Dolls in the Interview:
The Icebreaker Use

The manner in which the dolls are introduced during the interview has been debated in the clinical realm and surveyed among practitioners, but has not been subjected to empirical research in terms of impact on the child's response to the dolls. One question, which is discussed in reviews by Wescott, Davies, and Clifford (1989) and White and Santilli (1988), is whether the dolls should be presented clothed or unclothed. The rationale for this concern appears to be that presenting the child with unclothed dolls may predispose the child to sexualized play, setting up such an expectation at the beginning of the interview. Terr (Yates & Terr, 1988a) is sharply critical of presenting unclothed dolls to the children and argues: "They (these dolls) seem to have no clothes so you can't play school with them, set them up for tea, or even undress them to take a bath. There is one main thing you can see on these dolls—their sex . . . there is just about one game to play with these dolls—'sex' " (p. 256).

Although Terr implies that the dolls are usually presented unclothed, this is not the common practice according to available research on doll users. In the Boat and Everson survey (1988) all 109 professionals who used the dolls, including child protection workers, mental health practitioners, physicians, and law enforcement officers, presented them clothed. In the more recent survey of Boston-area professionals, (Kendall-Tackett & Watson, 1992) only one doll user out of 147 respondents presented the dolls unclothed. An earlier survey of doll purchasers by Harnest and Chavern (1986) indicated that "most" of their 374 clients who responded introduced the dolls fully dressed.

In addition, most written guidelines on interviewing children and using the dolls recommend presenting the dolls clothed (Boat & Everson, 1988; MacFarlane & Krebs, 1986; Vizard, Bentovim & Tranter, 1987; White et al., 1987). Friedemann and Morgan (1985) suggest that the dolls may be presented clothed or unclothed. Professionals appear to endorse a view that the dolls' bodies ordinarily have some form of cover and presenting the dolls clothed enables the child to make an initial decision whether or not to remove the clothing.

What proportion of young children can be expected to spontaneously undress the dolls? Three normative studies provide some information on this question. Glaser and Collins (1989) analyzed data on 78 nonreferred children, ages 3–6 years in a play setting in England. The majority of children (74%) undressed the dolls spontaneously or with little encouragement from an adult. Twenty-two children (28%) redressed the dolls spontaneously. The authors noted that the dolls were incorporated into the usual wide range of imaginative play, including feeding, bathing, and putting them to bed. In another study of 209 racially and socially diverse preschoolers, ages 2 to 5 years, fewer than half of the 2-year-olds and fewer than one third of the 3-, 4-, and 5-year-olds spontaneously undressed the dolls in a setting where no other toys were available (Boat & Everson, 1992). Finally, Sivan, Schor, Koeppl and Noble (1988) did not offer specific data on the rate of undressing the dolls among 144 3- to 8-year-olds, but they observed that the dolls occupied little of the children's interest relative to the other toys in the room. Feeding was the most popular role-taking activity. When the dolls were undressed by the interviewer, girls engaged in more dressing behaviors than did boys.

Naming of Body Parts and Body Functions:
The Anatomical Model Use

The decision as to when and how the dolls should be introduced into the interview structure appears to be largely clinical or personal in nature. However, there is agreement among professionals who have developed interviewing protocols that an initial rapport building with the child is necessary and that if the dolls are introduced, part of the introduction generally includes identification of the doll's gender and naming of the body parts (American Professional Society on the Abuse of Children [APSAC] Guidelines, 1990; Boat & Everson, 1988; Friedemann & Morgan, 1985; Vizard et al., 1987; White et al., 1987). Most interview guidelines caution against giving the children names for body parts or suggesting functions to the children.

One approach to assessing the anatomical model use is to question young children about their names for the doll's sex-related body parts and understanding of their functions. Only one study has described children's names for body parts and no published study has inquired about body functions. Schor and Sivan (1989) asked 144 nonreferred children ages 3 through 8 years to label the sex-related body parts on the anatomical dolls. The children used over 100 different words for the specified body parts. More than half the parents of children in each age group did not have separate names for the sex-related body parts. For example, the term "bottom" referred collectively to anus, buttocks, and vagina. Children's names for breast, buttock, and penis were more precise than for other body parts (anus, scrotum, and vagina). Fewer than half the respondents had labels for anus and scrotum. Older children had more accurate terminology than younger children for sex-related parts except penis and anus. The penis was clearly identified by children of younger as well as older ages; the anus was difficult to label for children across the age spectrum. The authors suggest that there is a sharp increase in children's ability to communicate about sexual body parts around the age of 5 years. When asked if they could think of another name for a specific body part, investigators found that that younger children offered significantly more labels per body part. Their additional labels were often incorrect, suggesting that younger children were more prone to providing responses to a request for possible additional information, even when they had no meaningful answers. The children also offered many labels for body parts that differed from those offered by their parents. Schor and Sivan also comment that there was no evidence in verbal or behavioral responses of the subjects when naming body parts that raised a suspicion as to whether the child might have been sexually abused.

Using the Dolls to Aid Recall and Demonstration: Memory Stimulus/ Demonstration Aid Use

Exposing the genitalia may occasionally trigger a spontaneous disclosure statement from a child. For example, Joanie was a 4-year-old twin with expressive speech delays, although she appeared to comprehend questions accurately. During the earlier stages of the interview, when no anatomical dolls were present, Joanie acknowledged that she had "worries" about being "bothered" but did not elaborate. The interviewer introduced the female child anatomical doll and proceeded to ask Joanie names for the doll's body parts and their functions. Joanie poked the vulva of the doll with her index finger and said, "That's what Bob did to me." The experienced interviewer proceeded to clarify who Bob was and sought verbal descriptive details from the child to corroborate her demonstration.

Raskin and Yuille (1989) believe that this use of anatomical dolls is highly problematic and contend that the introduction of any prop into the questioning of a young child can influence that child's suggestibility. While the spontaneous statement of the child may be unarguably the "most accurate" or "least contaminated" version of what happened to the child, such critics of the dolls are concerned that mere exposure to the dolls' genitalia will induce young children to fantasize, confabulate, or, in other ways, inadvertently misrepresent the truth. Professionals and researchers are themselves polarized. The major criticism of the dolls focuses on their alleged suggestiveness. Terr (Yates & Terr, 1988b, p. 387) states that "the demand inherent in asking a child to play with these explicit toys makes the techniques . . . far too vulnerable to suggestion to be regularly used in the courts." Yuille (1988) has commented, "Perhaps the major problem associated with the dolls is their suggestibility" (p. 256). He believes that exposure to the dolls encourages children to act out behaviors they have seen in the media or heard about during suggestive questioning. McIver and Wakefield (1987) demand that "[a]ny information obtained from such (doll) interviews should be discarded. There is nothing to support their use as diagnostic or assessment tools." Use of the dolls has also been described as "unethical" (McIver & Wakefield, 1987) and abusive to the child (*Family Law Reports*, 1987).

Once again we must look to laboratory studies to address the issue of suggestiveness of the dolls as a memory stimulus and demonstration aid. Countering the criticisms is a growing body of literature that argues that the dolls, in and of themselves, are not suggestive to young, sexually naive children. Researchers in children's memory have made significant contributions with greater attention to the issue of ecological validity in order to enhance the generalizability of the results. This research can be cited under three main questions on the suggestiveness of the dolls and the suggestibility of young children.

1. *Does the use of anatomical dolls as demonstration/memory aids lead young children to make false allegations of sexual abuse?* Goodman and Aman (1990) and Saywitz, Goodman, Nicholas, and Moan (1991) have addressed this question directly in two studies of the impact of anatomical dolls on children's recall. In the first study, 80 3- and 5-year-old children experienced a brief individual play session with a man. During the session they played a series of games including a version of "Simon Says" in which the man asked the child to touch parts of the child's own body (e.g., ear, toes) and also to touch the man's knee while the man touched the child's knee. A week later the child was questioned by a woman about the play session under one of four experimental conditions: with anatomical dolls as props, with regular (nonanatomical) dolls as props, with anatomical dolls out of reach but in view, and with no dolls as props. In the two doll conditions, the dolls were available during the questioning and the child was encouraged to use the dolls to show what had happened in the play session.

The children were asked a series of specific questions about possible "abuse" that might have occurred during the play session, modeled after direct questions that might be used in a sexual abuse investigation. The questions were: "Show me where he touched you," "Did he keep his clothes on?" "Did he touch your private parts?" "Did he ask you to keep a secret about your private parts?" and "Did he put anything in your mouth?" In addition, the children were asked three misleading questions about possible abuse: "He took your clothes off, didn't he?" "He kissed you, didn't he?" and "How many times did he spank you?"

The use of anatomical dolls as interview props was not found to decrease the accuracy of the children's responses to the abuse questions. Regardless of their age, the children interviewed with anatomical dolls did not make any more errors on the specific or misleading abuse questions than did the children interviewed either with regular dolls or with no dolls. The 3-year-olds, on average, did prove to be less accurate in all four interview conditions than the 5-year-olds. However, the vast majority of errors they made on the abuse questions occurred in response to the two "private parts" questions, a term many 3-year-olds did not understand. When asked the clearer question, "Show me where he touched you," none of the children indicated their genitals. In addition, none of the children provided spontaneous comments or elaborations that would suggest that sexual abuse had occurred. However, critics claim that the children had no motivation to mislead the interviewers (e.g., there was not a component of shame or attempting to protect a perpetrator by alleging that another person had committed abuse, or issues of secondary gain). Thus, critics contend that the results cannot be generalized to evaluations of allegedly sexually abused children.

Saywitz and her colleagues (Saywitz et al., 1991) looked at nonreferred children's memories for examinations involving genital touch. Seventy-two 5- and 7-year-old girls experienced a medical checkup performed by a pediatrician. Half of the children received a genital examination as part of the checkup (genital condition) and half received an identical checkup except that a scoliosis examination replaced the genital component (nongenital condition). After 1 week or 1 month, the children's memories of the physical were solicited first through free recall, then by demonstration with anatomical dolls and props (doctor kit items), and finally by direct and misleading questions. In the doll demonstration phase of the interview, the child was presented with several anatomical dolls (one of which had been undressed to show the genitalia) and asked to use the dolls and toys to show and tell what happened at the doctor's office. After the child demonstrated what happened, the direct and misleading questions were asked. For several of the questions, including the ones concerning genital touch, the interviewer held up an undressed anatomical doll and pointed to the relevant body parts while asking the question. According to the authors, past studies indicate that stimulus supports (dolls, toys, pictures) aid children's recall by supplying retrieval cues, allowing reenactment and compensating for limited language abilities.

Only 22% of the children in the genital condition reported genital or anal touch in free recall. There were no false reports of genital or anal touch by children in the nongenital condition in free recall and the doll demonstration. In addition, using the dolls and props elicited twice as much accurate information as did free recall alone. However, the error rate also rose from 8.09% in free recall to 12.89% in the demonstration task. When the "seriousness" of the errors was examined, it was found that about half of children indicated that tongue depressors had been used as part of the examination when, in fact, they had not. None of the errors involved demonstration of sexually explicit behaviors.

Without direction questioning, 78% of the children in the genital condition failed to spontaneously report or demonstrate genital touching and 89% failed to report or demonstrate anal touching. All of these errors were errors of omission (failing to report touching when it had occurred). There were no errors of commission on this task (reporting genital touch when it had not occurred). Errors of commission were made by three children in the nongenital condition in response to direct questioning but not in response to demonstrations with the anatomical dolls. One child reported vaginal touching that did not occur and two reported anal touching that did not occur. Two children were unable to provide any further details about the touching; one child, upon further questioning, said that the anal touch had "tickled" and "the doctor used a long stick." Interestingly, the rates of false reports of genital touch are comparable to those reported clinical samples of children referred to agencies or emergency rooms for evaluations of child abuse (2–8%) (see review by Everson & Boat, 1989). The children showed high resistance to misleading abuse questions with near-perfect performance. Errors tended to be made by the younger children.

The authors discussed their results in a social–motivational model of remembering. They argue that direct questions about genital touch may provide not only memory cues but also social cues. The nature of the questions may have given the children implicit permission to talk about parts of the body they are socialized not to discuss with strangers. The use of anatomical dolls to point to the genital area eliminated potential confusion regarding children's idiosyncratic names for vagina and anus. It also eliminated the need to say the names of these body parts aloud, a potentially emotional (embarrassing) or value-laden activity.

Conclusions from this study support that the use of dolls does not stimulate false reports of genital contact, and by using stimulus supports (the anatomical dolls and props) twice as much accurate information was obtained as the initial free recall.

Additional evidence that children referred for sexual abuse evaluations may provide more information when anatomical dolls are used as props is found in a study by Leventhal, Hamilton, Rekedal, Tebano-Micci, and Eyster (1989). The authors conducted a retrospective review of case records of 83 children under the age of 7 who were referred for evaluation of possible sexual abuse. The dolls were employed in 72% of the cases. When the dolls were used, children provided significantly more information than by interview alone about what had happened and about the identity of the suspected perpetrator. Only 8 children (13%) provided a detailed description without the dolls, whereas 29 (48%) provided details when the dolls were used. When the dolls were used, twice as many children were able to indicate a suspected perpetrator. It should be noted, however, that the *accuracy* of the children's reports was not assessed.

2. *When exposed to anatomical dolls, are normal, sexually naive young children prone to demonstrate explicit sexual play with the dolls?* The answer to this question depends on one's definition of "explicit sexual play." One concern expressed is that exposing sexually naive children (children in whom there is no reason to suspect sexual abuse or exposure to overt sexualized behaviors such as intercourse) to the anatomical dolls will induce children to casually "put the stick in the hole." It is appropriate to document the extent to which this and other behaviors that could be misinterpreted as indicators of abuse occur in a presumably nonabused population.

The largest relevant study looked at over 200 nonreferred, presumably nonabused, children drawn from a general pediatric clinic population (Everson & Boat, 1990). The children ranged in age from 2 years through 5 years and represented a wide socioeconomic distribution. The children were seen in a structured videotaped interview that included review of the body parts and functions and free exploration of the dolls both in the presence and absence of the adult interviewer.

Touching and exploration of the doll genitalia were common behaviors, occurring in over 50% of the children at each age level. However, explicit sexual play in the form of apparent demonstrations of vaginal, oral, or anal intercourse (i.e., penile insertion, sexual placement with "humping motions, mouthing a doll's genitals) occurred in only 6% of the total sample (12 out of 209 children).

This low incidence rate of explicit sexual play is consistent with the findings of seven prior studies in which nonreferred, presumably nonabused children were observed with anatomical dolls. The studies include those by: August and Forman (1989); Cohn (1988); Gabriel (1985); Glaser and Collins (1989); Jampole and Weber (1987), Sivan et al. (1988); and White, Strom, Santilli, and Halpin (1986). The studies varied in format from free play to highly structured interviews with an adult. The children ranged in age from 2 to 8 years. Summarizing across all seven studies, exploration of doll genitalia was fairly commonly observed, but less than 2% of the nonreferred children in these studies enacted apparent sexual intercourse between dolls or between a doll and themselves (5 of 332 children). Such play was rare even though four of the studies included conditions in which the child was left alone with the dolls, minimizing the likelihood of the presence of the adult inhibiting sexualized play.

Although 6% of the Everson and Boat sample demonstrated explicit sexual play, the frequency of such play was significantly related to the child's age, socioeconomic status (SES), and race and somewhat to the child's gender. In fact, over 20% of the 4- and

5-year-old, low SES, black males in this sample demonstrated clear sexual intercourse of some type during our sessions.

Interestingly, the display of sexualized behaviors with the dolls appeared to have a socialization component that became apparent when the children who were "demonstrators" were followed up 18 months later in a similar doll interview (Boat & Everson, 1989). At this time, none of the 10 prior "demonstrators" seen in the follow-up showed clear intercourse positionings when the interviewer was present. Two (20%) demonstrated sexualized interactions when the interviewer was absent from the room, and the same rate of sexualized demonstrations was noted in the control group—children who were matched on age, SES, and race but had not demonstrated sexual knowledge during the initial doll interview. The results support the sociomotivational model described by Saywitz et al. (1991). The children at followup were 6 and 7 years old, subject to the socialization norms of the school system, and better able to censor and inhibit responses. As one child said, "My momma would whup me if I did anything with these dolls!"

The research to date offers substantial evidence that anatomical dolls do not induce young, nonabused, sexually naive children to engage in explicit sexual play. However, it should be noted that the dolls may provide sexually knowledgeable children with at least implicit permission as well as an easy vehicle for demonstrating their sexual knowledge.

3. *Following exposure to anatomical dolls, do young children engage in more sexualized behavior or play?* Another concern is that nonreferred, and presumably nonabused young children who are exposed to the unclothed anatomical dolls may not react in the constraints of the interview setting but will reveal their sexual suggestibility in their behaviors and interactions with others and their toys when they are in the more familiar, comfortable setting of their home. This delayed reaction could result in caregivers misinterpreting the children's sexualized behaviors as symptoms of possible sexual abuse.

The question of whether anatomical dolls might have a delayed impact on the behavior of children was addressed in follow-up interviews of 30 mothers whose children had been exposed to anatomical dolls (Boat, Everson, & Holland, 1990). The children ranged in age from 3 to 5 years and had been subjects in the normative study of 209 children described above (Everson & Boat, 1990). The interview occurred about 2 weeks after the doll session. Mothers were asked in general terms about any changes in their child's behavior that they attributed to their child's having participated in the doll session as well as specific questions about changes in sexual curiosity and sexual play since the session.

Twenty-three percent of the children were reported as displaying a heightened awareness of sexual body parts (e.g., a 4-year-old boy asked how boys and girls differ; a 4-year-old girl asked when she would get pubic hair). None of the children were reported to have begun playing with toys or regular dolls in a sexual way or to add genitals to their drawings of people. Only one child was described in any way as "acting out sexually"—a 3-year-old boy who took his clothes off while playing with a little girl his age. As his mother explained, "He thought since he took the dolls' clothes off, it was okay to take his own clothes off." Neither this child's mother nor any of the other mothers had any concerns about the behavior of their children after exposure to the dolls, and they did not report any behavior that might be misconstrued as an indication that sexual abuse had occurred.

Another study included a follow-up of 16 nonreferred children, ages 3–6, who were exposed to anatomical dolls (Vaughn, Dawson, & Wagner, 1989; Dawson, Vaughn, & Wagner, 1990). None of the children's parents reported observing sexualized behaviors or questions after the doll interview. In fact, most of the children reportedly did not recall their play with the dolls until prompted by the parent.

The research to date offers evidence that the anatomical dolls are not likely to induce young, sexually naive children to demonstrate sexual acts. The one study (McIver & Wakefield, 1987) that is sometimes cited as proof of the suggestiveness of the dolls is methodologically flawed and difficult to interpret. For example, the authors used a combined sexual and aggressive play category in coding child behavior and failed to distinguish among different types of sexualized behaviors (e.g., placement of dolls on top of each other vs. penile insertion in a doll's anus, vagina, or mouth), aggression toward the dolls (e.g., hitting, spanking), and other forms of role playing (e.g., wrestling).

However, as always, it remains incumbent upon an evaluator to rule out that a demonstration of sexualized behaviors with the dolls does not reflect the child's sexual knowledge (e.g., exposure to sexually explicit videos) rather than an abusive sexual experience.

Finally, Britton and O'Keefe (1991) recently addressed the issue of the suggestiveness of the dolls as demonstration aids in an interesting study that needs to be replicated with stricter methodology. They compared the doll interaction behaviors of 136 children, age 10 and under, who were referred for sexual abuse evaluations. Half of the children were interviewed using anatomical dolls as props and half were interviewed with nonanatomical dolls. The children demonstrated a similar frequency of sexually explicit behaviors with both types of dolls. The author concluded that dolls may be useful when interviewing children, not because of their genital organs but because the dolls—any dolls—are props that assist children in communicating their experiences. It should be noted that the accuracy of the children's communications was not reported.

The Use of Anatomical Dolls as a Diagnostic Tool: The Diagnostic Test Use

Although much of the research discussed to date has focused on the suggestibility of children exposed to anatomical dolls and the inherent suggestiveness of the dolls as a prop or memory stimulus, another area of concern is whether sexually abused and nonabused children interact differently with anatomical dolls in a manner that is diagnostically significant. This line of questioning is problematic because it is often based on a naive conceptualization of the dolls as a diagnostic tool and because of the difficulties inherent in identifying and matching truly abused and nonabused subjects. We have reviewed 20 different sets of written guidelines on the use of anatomical dolls in interviewing young children in sexual abuse evaluations and found *none* that advocated using the dolls as a diagnostic test (Everson & Boat, in press). There is also little evidence thus far that abused and nonabused children can be reliably differentiated on the basis of their *behavior* with the dolls alone, to the exclusion of their verbal statements. Indeed, *"there is no behavioral test for child abuse"* (Melton & Limber, 1989, p. 1231, emphasis in original). Despite this fact, some authors still insist that the difference between abused and nonabused children's responses to anatomical dolls "is the basis for the use of the dolls in child sexual abuse evaluations . . . " (Realmuto, Jensen, & Wescoe, 1990, p. 743).

One of the earliest studies to compare the responses of children referred and not referred for suspected sexual abuse is that of White et al. (1986). Fifty children (25 in each group), ages 2–6 years, were interviewed using a structured format. The referred children demonstrated significantly more sexually related behaviors with the dolls such as "excessive interest" in the dolls' "private parts" and demonstrations of sexual acts with the dolls.

August and Forman (1989) rated the behaviors of 16 abused and 16 nonabused girls, ages 5–8 years, under two conditions: (1) when the girls were left alone with the dressed dolls and told to change the dolls' clothes; and (2) when the girls were asked to tell the interviewer a story involving the dolls. In the "alone" condition, the nonabused girls played more with the dolls but displayed significantly fewer aggressive behaviors and made less reference to the dolls' genitalia than did the abused girls. Neither group spontaneously included reference to the dolls' genitalia during the storytelling condition when the interviewer was present, and the abused children showed significantly more avoidance of the dolls in this condition. Sexual activity with the dolls was demonstrated by 25% of abused girls and 0% of the nonreferred girls.

Jampole and Weber (1987) likewise reported significant differences between abused and nonabused children in demonstrating sexualized behaviors with the dolls. Twenty children (10 abused, 10 nonabused), ages 3 to 8 years, were observed interacting with the dolls when interviewers were present in the room and when the child was alone. Sexual behaviors with the dolls were demonstrated by 90% of the abused children relative to 20% of the nonabused children. With the exception of one boy, sexualized interactions occurred only when the interviewer was out of the room.

Cohn (1988) matched 35 children, age 2–6 years, who were suspected of being sexually abused, with 35 nonreferred children on age, sex, and race. Cohn reported no difference among the groups in sexualized behaviors. One child (3%) in each group demonstrated clear sexual intercourse with the dolls.

Abused children, by definition, can be assumed to have greater exposure to sexual behaviors, and three of the comparative studies are consistent in reporting that this knowledge is demonstrated with anatomical dolls at a rate that is significantly different from that of their nonabused counterparts. However, presumably nonabused children in two of the comparative studies also displayed sexual knowledge in their interactions with the dolls.

Thus, the available research indicates that explicit sexualized play with anatomical dolls, including enactment of sexual intercourse, cannot be considered a *definitive* marker of sexual abuse in the absence of a clear verbal account of abuse by the child. However, the fact that anatomical dolls are not a definitive diagnostic test for sexual abuse does not negate their clinical usefulness as a tool in sexual abuse evaluations (Maan, 1991). Evidence of explicit sexual knowledge in a young child warrants careful evaluation of the source of such knowledge. This is especially true for children under approximately 4 years of age (Everson & Boat, 1990; Gordon, Schroeder, & Abrams, 1990). Demonstrations of oral and anal intercourse with the dolls are also relatively uncommon and therefore raise clinical concern.

Two final issues remain to be addressed. Some professionals (e.g., Yates & Terr, 1988a, 1988b) advocate that by merely observing children playing with the dolls in a relatively unstructured environment, the interviewer will gather evidence as to the likelihood of abuse having occurred based on the children's responses to the dolls. The comparative studies described above suggest that this approach is unlikely to yield more useful data than structured interviews. Other professionals (Wescott et al., 1989) note that children are reluctant to display sexual knowledge in front of adults. Therefore, they suggest that the child at some stage in the interview be left alone with the dolls and observed. The problems inherent in this approach may outweigh the benefits. For example, the interviewer would need an observation facility and have to deal with the problem of "spying" on the child and asking for clarification of behaviors the child may believe were not being observed. More important, this approach removes the focus from gathering information through the use of skillfully worded questions and may erroneously imply that the dolls will elicit behaviors that are, themselves, definitive proof of sexual abuse.

CONCLUSION

Anatomical dolls are a legacy of professionals' acknowledgment of the high incidence of sexual abuse involving young children and the need for tools to assist the young child witness in relating the abuse.

The compelling challenges in the controversies raised by critics of the anatomical dolls is for the "scientist–practitioner" to make sure that clinical judgment is well informed by continuing empirical work. The preponderance of research supports the use of anatomical dolls as an interview tool but not as a litmus test for sexual abuse. It is important that we remember that the effectiveness of any tool is contingent upon the skill of its user.

REFERENCES

American Professional Society on the Abuse of Children. (1990). *Guidelines for psychosocial evaluation of suspected sexual abuse in young children.* Unpublished manuscript.

August, R. L., & Forman, B. D. (1989). A comparison of sexually and nonsexually abused children's behavioral responses to anatomically correct dolls. *Child Psychiatry and Human Development, 20,* 39–47.

Bays, J. (1990). Are the genitalia of anatomical dolls distorted? *Child Abuse and Neglect, 14,* 171–175.

Berliner, L. (1988). Anatomical dolls commentary. *Journal of Interpersonal Violence, 3,* 468–470.

Boat, B. W., & Everson, M. D. (1986). *Using anatomical dolls: Guidelines for interviewing young children in sexual abuse investigations.* Unpublished manuscript. University of North Carolina School of Medicine, Chapel Hill.

Boat, B. W., & Everson, M. D. (1988). Use of anatomical dolls among professionals in sexual abuse evaluations. *Child Abuse and Neglect, 12,* 171–179.

Boat, B. W., & Everson, M. D. (1989). Anatomical doll play among young children: A follow-up of sexual demonstrators and doll avoiders. In G. S. Goodman (Chair), *Understanding and improving children's testimony: Implications for child sexual abuse.* Symposium conducted at the 97th annual meeting of the American Psychological Association, New Orleans, LA.

Boat, B. W., & Everson, M. D. (1990). When the tail wags the dog: The response to legal challenges of the credibility of children's allegations of sexual abuse. *Child, Youth and Family Services Quarterly (American Psychological Association [APA] Division 37), 13,* 2–3.

Boat, B. W., & Everson, M. D. (in press). Exploration of anatomical dolls by nonreferred preschool-aged: Comparisons by age, gender, race, and socioeconomic status. *Child Abuse and Neglect.*

Boat, B. W., Everson, M. D., & Holland, J. (1990). Maternal perceptions of young children's behavior following exposure to anatomical dolls. *Child Welfare, 69,* 389–400.

Britton, H., & O'Keefe, M. A. (1991). Use of non-anatomically correct dolls in the sexual abuse interview. *Child Abuse and Neglect, 15,* 567–573.

Cohn, D. (1988). *Play activity with anatomically correct dolls: Is there a difference between preschool age children referred for sexual abuse and those not referred?* Paper presented at the National Symposium on Child Victimization, Anaheim, CA.

Conte, J.R., Sorenson, E., Fogarty, L., & Rosa, J.D. (1991). Evaluating children's reports of sexual abuse: Results from a survey of professionals. *American Journal of Orthopsychiatry, 61,* 428–437.

Dawson B., Vaughn, A. R., & Wagner, W. G. (in press). Normal responses to sexually anatomically detailed dolls. *Journal of Family Violence.*

Everson, M. D., & Boat, B. W. (1989). False allegations of sexual abuse by children and adolescents. *Journal of the American Academy of Child and Adolescent Psychiatry, 28,* 230–235.

Everson, M. D., & Boat, B. W. (1990). Sexualized doll play among young children: Implications for the use of anatomical dolls in sexual abuse evaluations. *Journal of the American Academy of Child and Adolescent Psychiatry, 29,* 736–742.

Everson, M. D., & Boat, B. W. (in press). Putting the anatomical doll controversy perspective: An examination of the major doll uses and related criticisms. *Child Abuse and Neglect.*

Family Law Reports. (1987). Special Issue, 4.

Finkelhor, D. (1984). *Child sexual abuse, new theory and research.* New York: Free Press.

Finkelhor, D. (1979). *Sexually victimized children*. New York: Free Press.

Finkelhor, D. (Ed.). (1986). *Sourcebook on child sexual abuse*. Beverly Hills, CA: Sage.

Friedemann, V., & Morgan, M. (1985). *Interviewing sexual abuse victims using anatomical dolls: The professional's guidebook*. Eugene, OR: Shamrock Press.

Frye v. United States 293 F. 1013 (1923).

Gabriel, R.M. (1985). Anatomically correct dolls in the diagnosis of sexual abuse of children. *Journal of the Melanie Klein Society, 3*, 40–51.

Glaser, D., & Collins, C. (1989). The response of young, non-sexually abused children to anatomically correct dolls. *Journal of Child Psychology and Psychiatry, 30*, 547–560.

Goodman, G. S., & Aman, C. J. (1990). Children's use of anatomically detailed dolls to recount an event. *Child Development, 61*, 1859–1871.

Gordon, B. N., Schroeder, C. S., & Abrams, J.M. (1990). Age and social class differences in children's knowledge of sexuality. *Journal of Clinical Child Psychology, 19*, 33–43.

Harnest, J., & Chavern, H.E. (1986). A survey of the use of anatomically correct dolls in sex education, investigation, therapy and courtroom testimony. *Family Professional, 1*, 13.

In re Amber B. & Teela B. 191 Cal. App. 3d 682 (1987).

In re Christine C. & Michael C. 191 Cal App. 3d 676 (1987).

Jampole, L., & Weber, M. K. (1987). An assessment of the behavior of sexually abused and non-sexually abused children with anatomically correct dolls. *Child Abuse and Neglect, 11*, 187-192.

Jones, D. P. H., & McGraw, J. M. (1987). Reliable and fictitious accounts of sexual abuse of children. *Journal of Interpersonal Violence, 2*, 27–45.

Kendall-Tackett, K. A., & Watson, M. W. (1992). Use of anatomical dolls by Boston-area professionals. *Child Abuse and Neglect, 61*, 423–428.

Landers, S. (1988). Use of "detailed dolls" questioned. *APA Monitor, 19*, 24–25.

Leventhal, J. M., Hamilton, J., Rekedal, S., Tebano-Micci, A., & Eyster, C. (1989). Anatomically correct dolls used in interviews of young children suspected of having been sexually abused. *Pediatrics, 84*, 900–906.

Maan, C. (1991). Assessment of sexually abused children with anatomically detailed dolls: A critical review. *Behavioral Sciences and the Law 9*, 43–51.

MacFarlane, K., & Krebs, S. (1986). Techniques of interviewing and evidence gathering. In K. MacFarlane & J. Waterman (Eds.), *Sexual abuse of young children: Evaluation and treatment* (pp. 67–100). New York: Guilford Press.

McIver, W., & Wakefield, H. G. (1987). *Behavior of abused and non-abused children with anatomically correct dolls*. Unpublished manuscript.

Melton, G. B., & Limber, S. (1989). Psychologists' involvement in cases of maltreatment. *American Psychologist, 44*, 1225–1233.

Meyers, J. E. B. (1989). Allegations of child sexual abuse in custody and visitation litigation: Recommendations for improved fact finding and child protection. *Journal of Family Law, 28*(1), 1–41

Meyers, J. E. B., & White, S. (1989). Dolls in court? *The Advisor* (Newsletter of the American Professional Society on the Abuse of Children), 2(3), 5–6.

Naumann, T. F. (1985). *The case of the indecent dolls or can voodoo be professional?* Unpublished manuscript.

Nederlands Juristen Blad (1988 September) *32*, 1173–1177.

Raskin, D. C., & Yuille, J. C. (1989). Problems in evaluating interviews of children in sexual abuse cases. In S. Ceci, D. Ross, & M. Toglia (Eds.), *Perspectives on children's testimony* (pp. 184–207). New York: Springer-Verlag.

Realmuto, G. M., Jensen, J. B., & Wescoe, S. (1990). Specificity and sensitivity of sexually anatomically correct dolls in substantiating abuse: a pilot study. *Journal of the American Academy of Child and Adolescent Psychiatry, 29,* 743–745.

Saywitz, K. J., Goodman, G. S., Nicholas, E., & Moan, S. (1991). Children's memories of physical examinations involving genital touch: Implications for reports of child sexual abuse. *Journal of Consulting and Clinical Psychology, 59,* 682–691.

Schor, D. P., & Sivan, A. B. (1989). Interpreting children's labels for sex-related body parts of anatomically explicit dolls. *Child Abuse and Neglect, 13,* 523–531.

Sivan, A. B., Schor, D. P., Koeppl, G. K., & Noble, L. D. (1988). Interaction of normal children with anatomical dolls. *Child Abuse and Neglect, 12,* 295–304.

Tylden, E. (1987). Child sexual abuse. *The Lancet, 2,* 1017.

Underwager, R. Wakefield, H., Legrand, R., & Bartz, C. (1986). *The role of the psychologist in cases of alleged sexual abuse of children.* Paper presented at the American Psychological Association Annual Convention, Washington, DC.

Vaughn, A.R., Dawson, B., & Wagner, W.G. (1989). *The use of anatomically detailed dolls in the investigation of child sexual abuse.* Paper presented at Association for Advancement of Behavior Therapy, Washington, DC.

Vizard, E., Bentovim, A., & Tranter, M. (1987). Interviewing sexually abused children. *Adoption and Fostering, 11,* 20-25.

Wescott, H., Davies, G., & Clifford, B. (1989). The use of anatomical dolls in child witness interviews. *Adoption and Fostering, 13,* 6–14.

White, S. (1986). Uses and abuses of the sexually anatomically correct dolls. *Division of Child, Youth and Family Services Newsletter* (APA Division 37), *9,* 3–6.

White, S., & Santilli, G. (1988). A review of clinical practices and research data on anatomical dolls. *Journal of Interpersonal Violence, 3,* 430–442.

White, S., Strom, G., Santilli, G., & Halpin, B. (1986). Interviewing young children with anatomically correct dolls. *Child Abuse and Neglect, 10,* 519–529.

White, S., Strom, G., Santilli, G., & Quinn, K.M. (1987). *Clinical guidelines for interviewing young children with anatomically correct dolls.* Unpublished manuscript, Case Western Reserve University School of Medicine, Cleveland.

Yates, A., & Terr, L. (1988a). Anatomically correct dolls: Should they be used as a basis for expert testimony? *Journal of the American Academy of Child and Adolescent Psychiatry, 27,* 254–257.

Yates, A., & Terr, L. (1988b). Issue continued: Anatomically correct dolls: Should they be used as a basis for expert testimony? *Journal of the American Academy of Child and Adolescent Psychiatry, 27,* 387–388.

Yuille, J.C. (1988). The systematic assessment of children's testimony. *Canadian Psychology, 29,* 247–262.

4

Effects of Cognitive Questioning Techniques on Children's Recall Performance

R. Edward Geiselman
University of California, Los Angeles

Karen J. Saywitz
UCLA School of Medicine,
Harbor–UCLA Medical Center

Gail K. Bornstein
University of California, Los Angeles

Both research and debate concerning the use and credibility of children as witnesses in a court of law have been expanding not only in frequency but also in scope. The issues of primary concern revolve around three domains: (1) the mismatch between the current legal system and the capabilities of children; (2) children's memory recall abilities and performance; and (3) concerns surrounding various forms of miscommunication between children and interviewers. As a reflection of the growing interest in children's testimony, many scholarly volumes have been published in recent years in which these important issues are discussed (Ceci, Toglia, & Ross, 1987; Ceci, Ross, & Toglia, 1989; Fivush & Hudson, 1990). This chapter focuses on the second and third issues.

Extensive investigation into the completeness and accuracy of children's memory performance has produced a complex network of outcomes, none of which allows for a sweeping, general conclusion regarding the veracity of children's memory as witnesses. Aside from the usual individual differences observed in any population of observers, factors affecting children's recollection of experiences have included the memory-testing procedure (Goodman & Reed, 1986), wording of questions (Dale, Loftus, & Rathbun, 1978), type of information requested (Goodman, Aman, & Hirshman, 1987), children's participation in the event (Geiselman, Saywitz, & Bornstein, 1990; Goodman, Rudy, Bottoms, & Aman, 1990), rapport development (Dent, 1982; Saywitz, 1988), suggestibility (Ceci, Ross, & Toglia, 1987; King & Yuille, 1987), and children's understanding of the legal process (Saywitz, 1989; Saywitz, Jaenicke, & Camparo, 1990).

As part of the body of literature on interview techniques with children, work by the current authors and colleagues has applied, evaluated, and refined the cognitive interview for use with children (Geiselman & Padilla, 1988; Geiselman et al., 1990). The elaboration and modification of standard interview techniques to include cognitive retrieval methods have, thus far, resulted in encouraging results, with a 21% improvement in correct recall of facts from a film (Geiselman & Padilla, 1988); and a 26% improvement in correct recall of facts from a live event (Geiselman et al., 1990). These improvements were obtained in comparison to standard police interview procedures without an accompanying increase in incorrect details.

Similar success with the cognitive interview procedure has been obtained with adults (Geiselman, Fisher, MacKinnon, & Holland, 1985), nonstudent adults (Geiselman, Fisher, MacKinnon, & Holland, 1986), educable mental retardates (Brown & Geiselman, 1990); and adult rape survivors (Latts & Geiselman, 1990). Across eight experiments conducted by Geiselman and colleagues on cognitive interviewing with a variety of subject populations and stimulus materials, the average accuracy rate for information recalled with cognitive interviewing was 87%.

The adult version of the cognitive interview was applied to a sample of 7- to 12-year-olds in the Geiselman and Padilla (1988) study. Based on both quantitative and qualitative analyses of the taped interviews, modifications were made to better match the individual techniques with the capabilities and limitations of children. One purpose of the Geiselman et al. (1990) study, which focused on 7- to 11-year-olds, was to perform an evaluation and further refinement of the revised procedures from Geiselman and Padilla (1988), using a live, staged event. A second purpose of the Geiselman et al. (1990) study was to derive and evaluate measures for avoiding potential miscommunication between the child and interviewer, which could lead to errors, confabulations, and misinterpretations of the child's recall. This examination of dyadic misconceptions between the child and the interviewer further established the importance of children's understanding of what is expected of them in an interview as witnesses or victims (Saywitz, 1987, 1989; Saywitz et al., 1990).

THE COGNITIVE INTERVIEW

The theoretical considerations that underlie the questioning techniques developed and evaluated by Geiselman et al. (1984) and revised by Fisher, Geiselman, Raymond, Jurkevich, and Warhafrig (1987) are based on two factors that are integrally involved in the retrieval of memories. First, a memory is composed of several features (Bower, 1967; Underwood, 1969; Wickens, 1970), and the effectiveness of any technique to access a memory is related to the extent to which the features of the context created by the retrieval technique overlap with the features comprising the memory for the information that is sought (Flexser & Tulving, 1978). Second, there may be several retrieval paths to a memory for an event, so that information not accessible with one memory-retrieval technique may be accessible with a different technique that creates a different memory cue (Tulving, 1974).

Based on this theoretical framework, a memory-retrieval procedure was developed for witnesses called the cognitive interview. This label was selected because, for the most part, the techniques comprising the procedure were borrowed from research in cognitive psychology. The cognitive interview consists of four general retrieval methods plus additional, more specific techniques. Of the four general methods, two attempt to increase the feature overlap between the memory for the event and the memory-retrieval mnemonic: (1) mentally reconstructing the environmental and personal context that existed at the time of the crime (Bower, Gilligan, & Monteiro, 1984; Malpass & Devine, 1981; Smith, 1979), and (2) reporting everything (being complete), even partial information, regardless of the perceived *importance* of the information (Smith, 1983). The other two methods encourage using multiple retrieval paths: (3) recounting the events in a variety of orders (Burns, 1981; Geiselman et al., 1986; Geiselman & Callot, 1989; Whitten & Leonard, 1981), and (4) reporting the events from a variety of perspectives (Anderson & Pichert, 1978; Firstenberg, 1983).

In addition to these general instructions, the cognitive interview contains several specific suggestions to facilitate the recall of appearance, speech characteristics, conversation, names, and numbers. For example, "Did the person (or voice) remind you of anyone (or any voice) you know. If so, why?" or, "Think about your reactions to what was said and the reactions of others who were there." Furthermore, if the witness is blocking on a name, he or she is asked to go through the alphabet searching for the first letter of the name. In laboratory experiments, the first-letter technique has been found to be successful roughly two thirds of the time (Gruneberg & Monks, 1976).

As noted by Geiselman et al. (1990), the literature on child development provides some reason to believe that some form of the cognitive interview would be useful with child witnesses. With respect to reconstructing the circumstances, Pressley and Levin (1980) have observed that imagery instructions enhance recall performance of children. With respect to reporting everything, children's spontaneous reports often are found to be less complete than those of adults (Chi & Ceci, 1986; King & Yuille, 1987; Marin, Holmes, Guth, & Kovac, 1979). In addition, children do not have a good idea of what has investigative value because they have limited knowledge of the legal system and many misconceptions about the forensic context (Saywitz, 1989). With respect to varied recall orders, the ability to order recall chronologically has been shown to develop gradually with age (Brown, 1975; Piaget, 1969). With respect to varied perspectives, the ability to take on the perspectives of others also has been shown to develop gradually with age (Flavell, 1986).

RATIONALE FOR THE PRESENT RESEARCH

The purposes for the present research were threefold. First, this work was designed to provide a further replication of the usefulness of cognitive interview procedures with a larger sample of children and with a different staged scenario than used by Geiselman and Padilla (1988) or Geiselman et al. (1990).

Second, the recorded interviews were used to refine all phases and segments of the cognitive interview process for children, including rapport development, interview preparation instructions (i.e., "rules of the game" for the interview), the narrative report, and the specific questions phase.

Third, the primary purpose for the present study was to evaluate the effects of a "practice" interview with children about an innocuous staged event prior to their being interviewed about the event targeted for investigation. Such a procedure would have the potential for at least three positive effects on the recollections of children as witnesses:

1. It would familiarize children with the process of being interviewed, thereby affecting their willingness to speak freely and reducing their feelings of anxiety.

2. It could identify specific misconceptions that a given child may have about being interviewed, such as what it means to say, "I don't know."

3. It would familiarize children with the cognitive interview techniques, both giving them practice and correcting any misconceptions that need to be addressed before a formal interview.

If successful, practice interviewing could be included in the current legal system's protocol for obtaining reports from children as witnesses without any apparent negative effects on due process for either the defense or the prosecution. Encouragement for the potential usefulness of practice can be taken from the results of a study with children conducted by Goodman, Bottoms, Schwartz-Kenney, and Rudy (1991). In their experiment, children who were given practice on lineup tasks with feedback improved their ability to perform accurately in subsequent lineup tasks.

METHOD

Staged Events

To preserve the ecological validity of the present investigation, both of the staged events used in this research for the practice and target interviews were live events, carried out by experienced actors.

Staged Event for the Detectives' Interviews

The scenario for the target staged event closely followed that used successfully by Geiselman et al. (1984). This incident is sufficiently rich in quantifiable information such that significant differences were obtained between cognitive and standard interview conditions. Two research assistants with acting experience served as the actors. A 31-year-old female played the role of a teacher who was introduced by the second author to show slides of landmarks in California to the group. Three or four children were assembled for each staging of the event, and the event was staged three or four times on any given day.

After seven slides were presented, along with short stories about the landmarks, a 40-year-old male entered the room waving a stick and throwing down a backpack, such that sufficient noise was made to gain the children's attention. A somewhat heated verbal exchange ensued between the intruder and the teacher over the scheduled use of the slide projector, in which several bits of key information were presented. This information included items about persons (physical descriptions, clothing, names), objects (backpack, ring of keys attached to a 12-inch stick wrapped in black tape, slide projector), and events (actions, dialogue). The dispute over the use of the slide projector was resolved in a socially acceptable manner and the intruder exited the room. The slide show was resumed and two additional landmarks were presented.

Waiting-Room Incident for the Practice Interviews

At the completion of the slide show, the third author returned to greet the children and to take them to a "waiting room." The third author left the waiting room and, after a brief delay, a male portraying a "surfer dude" entered. This character was played by another research assistant, a 21-year-old UCLA undergraduate. He informed the children that his name was Andrew and that he was waiting for a Mr. Henderson. He then asked the children if it would be okay if he waited in the room with them. As with the slide-show event, the waiting-room incident was rich in detail about persons (physical description, clothing, names), objects (skate board, stuffed animal, pencils as gifts), and events (actions, dialogue). This scenario included a discussion of the upcoming birthday party for the "surfer dude's" sister. After approximately 5 minutes, the "surfer dude" gave up waiting for Mr. Henderson and left the waiting room.

Subjects

The subjects who participated in this study were 34 third graders between the ages of 8 and 9 years (18 females, 16 males), and 58 sixth graders between the ages of 11 and 12 years (29 females, 29 males). They were recruited from two schools within the Inglewood, California, School District (Daniel Freeman Elementary School and Oak Street Elementary School) and from the University Elementary School at UCLA.

Design

Each child was randomly assigned to one of three interview format conditions: cognitive interviewing with practice = practice cognitive, target cognitive; cognitive interviewing without practice = practice rapport only, target cognitive; standard interviewing = practice rapport only, target standard. All practice sessions were conducted for the waiting-room incident and all target sessions were conducted for the slide-show incident. Thus, the general data matrix formed a 2 x 3 array, with the factors being grade level (third, sixth) and interview-format condition (cognitive interviewing with practice, cognitive interviewing without practice, standard interviewing). Comparisons were made between the target interviews in the cognitive interviewing without practice and standard interviewing conditions to assess effects of cognitive versus standard interviewing; and comparisons were made between the target interviews in the cognitive interviewing with practice and cognitive interviewing without practice conditions to assess effects of practice with cognitive interviewing.

Interviewers

The interviewers for the waiting-room incident were seven advanced undergraduate psychology majors from UCLA. Each interviewer was given written instructions on how to conduct the cognitive interview with children, and participated 1 week later in a 2-hour training session. The training session covered each phase of the interview format (rapport development, the narrative report, specific questions, and the cognitive memory-retrieval methods). In addition, a training videotape of a cognitive interview was shown, followed by a live demonstration and critique of a cognitive interview by the authors.

Each student interviewer was assigned at least one child from each of the three interview-format conditions. Thus, each student interviewer conducted some full cognitive interviews and some sessions of rapport development only.

The interviewers for the slide show were recruited from the Los Angeles County Sheriff's Department. Each of the 11 off-duty detectives who volunteered for this study had completed formal instruction from the Sheriff's Department on interviewing child witness/victims, and had a minimum of 4 years of experience in the field. Each interviewer was offered a $125 honorarium per day for his or her participation.

Each detective was assigned randomly to one of two interview conditions: cognitive or standard. None of the detectives was given prior knowledge of the contents of the staged scenario, and none was told the purpose of the experiment other than that it was a study of interview methods for children. Prior to participating in the experiment, the two groups of interviewers were provided with written instructions on how to conduct the type of interview to which they were assigned, and all but one of the interviewers attended a 2-hour training session conducted by the authors.

Procedure

The experimental procedure for each child was carried out over 2 days. On the first day, the children witnessed the slide-show incident followed by the waiting-room incident followed by an interview about the waiting-room incident with one of the UCLA students. All three components of the procedure were conducted on the school grounds at separate locations. The interviews conducted by the UCLA students consisted of either the full cognitive interview or rapport development only, and each child was interviewed individually.

Two days later, each child was introduced to one of the sheriff's deputies, who wore plain clothes and interviewed the child about the slide-show incident. This interview consisted of either the full cognitive interview or a full standard interview.

Interview Conditions

The student interviewers were told that a group of balloons had been placed in the room where the waiting-room event took place. The presence of the balloons was to be used by the student interviewers as an anchor to direct the children back in time to the appropriate episode targeted for the practice cognitive interviews. The sheriffs were told to question the children about "[t]he time when they were taken from their classroom to the stage in the cafeteria," and to tactfully refrain from discussing anything with them that may have happened once they were taken from the cafeteria.

Each of the interviews conducted by the students and the detectives began with the development of rapport with the child. For those sessions that were carried out in either the full cognitive or standard format, rapport development was followed immediately by the interviewer informing the child,"I am going to ask you some questions today."

The Narrative Report

The first phase of the questioning portion of the cognitive and standard interviews consisted of the child's narrative account of "what happened." The interviewers who conducted the cognitive sessions were given the following guidelines: Just prior to asking for the narrative report in the child's own words, the child was told to "[p]icture that time when you were taken from your classroom to the stage in the cafeteria, as if you were there right now." The procedure for reconstructing the circumstances was then carried out with the child responding to the environmental and personal context queries *aloud*.

To carry out the second cognitive interview technique prior to the narrative (to be complete), the interviewer instructed the child: "Now I want you to start at the beginning and tell me what happened, from the beginning to the middle, to the end. Tell me everything you remember, even little parts that you don't think are very important. Sometimes people leave out little things because they think little things are not important. Tell me everything that happened."

General Format for the Specific-Questions Phase

The second phase of the questioning portion of both the cognitive and standard interviews consisted of specific questions necessary to clarify and expand on what the child reported in the narrative. The interviewers were asked to gather as much information as possible about any persons and objects that were present and the events that occurred. All interviewers who conducted the cognitive and standard sessions were given the following guidelines:

1. Do not interrupt the child when he or she is answering a question. Deal with any inconsistencies in the story later on, near the end of the interview.

2. Try to ask the questions in an open-ended format, such as, "Can you tell me about the clothes that the man was wearing?" Save most of the direct questions for near the end of the interview, such as, "Did he have any scars or tatoos?" (Dent [1982] found that interviewers who obtained the most accurate descriptions relied on unprompted recall and general, open-ended questions.)

3. Do not ask the child a string of questions without waiting for a response.

4. Change to easier topics if the child says, "I don't remember" to three questions in a row. Do not become overly persistent or verbally abusive in response to your frustration about the child's inability to remember certain facts. Instead, change topics and return for the missing facts later in the interview.

5. Use language that is simple and appropriate for the child's level; use short sentences and one- or two-syllable words. To promote the team effort, phrase your questions using the child's own words whenever possible. Use your interaction with the child during rapport development to evaluate the child's level of speech, language, and vocabulary, and then use these observations to structure the questions addressed to the child in a style that is developmentally appropriate. (It

is well documented that there are age-related trends in children's knowledge of legal terminology [Saywitz et al., 1990].)

6. Use positive phrasing, such as, "Do you remember the color of the car?" rather than negative phrasing, such as, "You don't remember the color of the car, do you?"

7. Pay attention to the child's answers to your questions. Avoid giving the child information that was given to you by another child interviewed previously. (This guideline was given as a safeguard although previous research has indicated no order effects [Geiselman et al., 1986].)

8. It is a good idea to praise children for their effort (for "working so hard," for "helping you out," for "doing such a good job"). It is *not* a good idea to praise them for the content of what they report, as this may cause them to "report more of the same" whether they are certain about the information or not.

Cognitive Methods in the Specific-Questions Phase

The interviewers who conducted cognitive interviews were given guidelines pertaining to the reverse-order and change-perspectives techniques for use during the specific-questions phase of the interviews. To prevent the child from making grand leaps backward in time, the child was prompted continually, after each of his or her responses, with the question, "Then what happened *right before that?*" The specific memory-jogging techniques were described and were to be used where appropriate. When the child appeared to have exhausted memory for the event, he or she was to be asked to take on the perspective of a prominent person who was present in the child's report: "Put yourself in the body of _____, and tell me what you would have seen or heard if you had been that person."

Analysis

Each tape-recorded interview about the slide-show incident was transcribed by research assistants trained by the authors. This catalog of information then was used to score each child's transcribed report for the number of correct items of information recalled and the number of incorrect items of information generated.

Because an advantage for the cognitive questioning format could be found due simply to the number of questions asked or questioning time, those two variables were computed from each tape-recorded interview for analysis. The protocols also were examined to isolate instances in which the individual components of the cognitive questioning appeared to be successful or to create problems.

RESULTS

The transcriptions of the taped interviews were quantified in terms of six dependent variables: number of correct facts, number of incorrect facts, accuracy rate (number correct divided by the total number of facts recalled), number of questions asked about the staged event, the time taken to conduct the investigative portion of the interview, and the frequency of usage of the cognitive techniques (in the cognitive interviews). The results were examined as a function of grade level (third or sixth) and the interview-format condition (cognitive interviewing with practice, cognitive interviewing without practice, or standard interviewing). The results are presented in Table 4.1.

Number of Correct Facts Recalled

Overall, the older children recalled significantly more correct facts than did the younger children (50.81 vs. 34.39), with $F(1,86) = 8.46$, $MSe = 90.47$, $p < .01$. The number of correct items remembered also differed as a function of the type of interview format combination (cognitive interviewing with practice = 50.42, cognitive interviewing without

TABLE 4.1. Performance in Sheriffs' Interviews as a Function of Interview-Format Condition and Grade of Child Witness

| | Interview-format condition | | | | | |
| | Cognitive with practice | | Cognitive without practice | | Standard | |
Performance variable	Grade: 3rd n: 11	6th 20	3rd 11	6th 19	3rd 12	6th 19
Number correct items	38.64	64.00	32.00	48.00	26.83	38.53
Number incorrect items	6.09	6.20	5.18	5.00	6.58	5.79
Accuracy rate	.86	.91	.86	.91	.80	.87
Total questions asked	75.55	71.00	76.45	65.52	63.42	72.47
Length of interviews (min)	21.54	22.55	13.55	18.26	19.00	25.53

practice = 42.13, standard interviewing = 34.00), with $F(2,86)$ = 3.71, MSe = 90.47, $p < .05$. A Tukey's posttest showed that all conditions were significantly different from one another (all $ps < .05$). Cognitive interviews led to more correct facts recalled, and "practice" with the cognitive interview techniques further improved performance.

The interaction between grade level and interview-format condition was marginally nonsignificant statistically, with $F(2,86)$ = 3.00, MSe = 90.47, $p > .05$. A formal power analysis revealed sufficient power to detect a significant interaction (with effect size .40 and alpha = .05, power = .93). Inspection of the means in Table 4.1 indicated that there were trends for the number of correct items recalled to be affected more by practice and cognitive interviewing for the sixth graders than for the third graders.

Number of Incorrect Items Generated

The difference in the number of incorrect items generated by the two age groups was not significant (5.67 = sixth; 5.97 = third), with $F(1,86)$ < 1.00. This outcome is not consistent with the results of Geiselman et al. (1990) where somewhat fewer errors were committed by fifth graders than by second graders. The age-related difference in number of errors observed by Geiselman et al. while reliable statistically, was only 1.65 items (constituting less than 10% of the children's recall). Therefore, that difference in number of incorrect recall must be taken as unreliable given the current failure to replicate with children and interviewers from similar populations.

Also, the differences in incorrect item recall among the interview-format conditions were not significant (cognitive interviewing with practice = 6.16; cognitive interviewing without practice = 5.07; standard interviewing = 6.10), with $[F(2,86)$ = 2.08, $p > .05$, power = .63]; and this pattern held for both grade levels, with $[F(2,86)$ < 1.00 (power = .78)].

Accuracy Rates

As in the experiment conducted by Geiselman et al. (1990), the accuracy rates of the children's recall with the sheriffs were remarkably high, with cognitive interviewing with practice = 88%, cognitive interviewing without practice = 89%, and standard interviewing = 84%. These average absolute levels of accuracy provide another illustration of the capability of recollection by young children who are interviewed by experienced law-enforcement personnel. (Geiselman &

Padilla [1988] found 86% accuracy; Geiselman et al. [1990] found 93% accuracy.)

Number of Questions Asked

The average number of questions asked did not differ significantly as a function of grade level (71.81 = third, 69.66 = sixth), with [$F(1,86)$ = 2.49, $p > .05$]. The number of questions asked also did not differ significantly as a function of the interview-format condition, with cognitive interviewing with practice = 72.61, cognitive interviewing without practice = 69.53, and standard interviewing = 68.97; nor did grade level interact significantly with interview format (both $Fs < 1.00$). Thus, as in previous studies with adults (Geiselman et al., 1985; Geiselman et al., 1986) and with children (Geiselman et al., 1990), the greater number of correct facts remembered by the children with cognitive interviewing cannot be attributed simply to a greater number of questions asked.

Length of Interviews

Length of interview was computed as the total amount of time (in minutes) that the interviewer spent actually questioning the child about the slide-show event. The average amount of time taken to complete an interview was statistically the same for the sixth graders and the third graders (sixth = 22.11 min; third = 18.03 min, with $F(1,86)$ = 2.97, MSe = 17.92, $p < .05$), as was the case for the three interview-format conditions (cognitive interviewing with practice = 22.19 min, cognitive interviewing without practice = 16.00 min, and standard interviewing = 23.05 min, with $F < 1.0$). The interaction between grade level and interview-format condition also was not significant, with $F < 1.0$. Thus, as with the number of questions asked, a greater amount of time spent questioning the children cannot explain the effects of cognitive interviewing or practice with cognitive interviewing on recall performance.

Evaluation of the Individual Cognitive Techniques

It is apparent from the results of all three studies conducted in this laboratory with children that a special form of cognitive interviewing is required for use with children. The differences pertain both to the manner in which the techniques are presented and monitored by the interviewer and to the interpretation of the information obtained from the child.

First, however, an analysis was conducted on the frequency with which the interviewers in the present study made use of each of the four general cognitive techniques. The average percentage of usage values are presented in Table 4.2. This analysis showed that the student interviewers carried out a greater percentage of the components of the cognitive interview during the "practice sessions" (about the waiting room) than did the sheriffs during the target cognitive interviews (about the slide show), with cognitive interviewing with practice/ students = 88.75%, cognitive interviewing with practice/sheriffs = 62.25%, and cognitive interviewing without practice/sheriffs = 45.75%. Thus, while it is acknowledged that the students interviewed the children about a different event than did the sheriffs, a major concern continues to be the lack of use of the cognitive techniques by some experienced detectives.

The difference between the cognitive interviewing with practice and cognitive interviewing without practice conditions with the sheriffs suggests that the children were more likely to elicit the sheriff's use of the cognitive techniques or that the children were more likely to spontaneously use the techniques when they had received prior practice with the students. Evidence for the latter possibility was apparent in one sheriff's interview of a sixth grader in the cognitive interviewing with practice condition, where the child spontaneously said, "And now we will go backwards, right?"

The lack of uniformity in the use of the cognitive methods by the sheriffs provided us with a unique opportunity to establish further support for the claim of Geiselman et al. (1986) that each of the four general methods has the potential for making contributions to the

TABLE 4.2. Percentage Usage of the Four General Cognitive Interview Techniques as a Function of Interview-Format Condition

Interview technique	Interview-format condition		
	Students "practice"	Sheriffs NP	Sheriffs P
Reinstate context	90	71	52
Be complete	81	60	41
Reverse order	90	68	64
Change perspectives	94	50	26

Note. Sheriffs NP = cognitive interviews without prior practice; Sheriffs P = cognitive interviews with prior practice.

overall success of the cognitive interview method for interviewing witnesses. A chi-square was computed for each of the four cognitive methods, between whether that method was used during the interview and whether the number of correct facts obtained was above or below the average score (39.5). Data from the sheriffs' interviews in both the cognitive interviewing with practice and cognitive interviewing without practice conditions were combined to increase the sample size to 58 subjects per analysis. The use of the cognitive methods was consistently associated with higher memory performance scores. The chi-square results are as follows: reinstate context [$X^2(2)$ = 6.42, $p < .05$], be complete [$X^2(2)$ = 7.08, $p < .05$], reverse recall order [$X^2(2)$ = 3.95, $p < .05$], and change perspectives [$X^2(2)$ = 3.53, $p < .07$]. Thus, as concluded by Geiselman et al. (1986), the available evidence suggests that each of the four general cognitive methods exhibits the potential for increasing the amount of correct information gained from a witness.

An evaluation of the success of each component of the cognitive interview was conducted both in terms of the child's understanding or willingness to carry out the technique, and in terms of any traceable effect of the technique on recall performance. This evaluation was conducted to provide guidance toward refining the suggested instructions for using the cognitive procedures that were presented in the present method section. While some modifications are suggested, the authors wish to remind the reader that the cognitive interview for children used in the present experiment led to significant improvements in the number of correct items recalled in comparison to standard procedures. Collapsing across grade levels, the percentage of improvement over standard procedures was 18% with cognitive interviewing without practice, and was 45% with cognitive interviewing with practice. These figures probably are underestimates of the potential of the full cognitive interview, given that most of the sheriffs did not routinely utilize all of the techniques that comprise the cognitive interview procedure.

Reconstruction of the Circumstances

The reinstate-context technique was used in 90% of the practice cognitive interviews conducted by the students, but it was used in only 62% of the cognitive interviews conducted by the sheriffs. Its use was significantly associated with the number of correct facts obtained from the children in the sheriffs' cognitive interviews. Otherwise, the effect of this procedure on recall is not immediately identifiable in the protocols, given that it applies throughout the interview format where other cognitive methods were employed.

The language used by both the student interviewers and the sheriffs to present this technique was comparable to that suggested in the present *method* section, and this language was used with the children from both grade levels. However, most of the sheriffs who used the reconstruct-the-circumstances technique asked the children to close their eyes; whereas only one of the student interviewers routinely asked the children to close their eyes. No research has been conducted, to our knowledge, to determine whether closing the eyes has any effect on the success of the technique, either with adults or with children.

Be Complete

The be-complete technique was used in 81% of the practice cognitive interviews conducted by the students, but was used in only about 50% of the cognitive interviews conducted by the sheriffs. When it was used by the sheriffs, it was presented in language identical to or similar to that suggested in the experimenters' guidelines. As noted above, its use was significantly associated with the number of correct facts generated in the sheriffs' cognitive interviews; just as important, its use was not associated with more incorrect items generated.

Reverse Order

This technique was used in 90% of the practice cognitive interviews conducted by the students, and it was used in about 66% of the cognitive interviews conducted by the sheriffs. Its use was significantly associated with the number of correct facts generated in the sheriffs' cognitive interviews. In cases where the reverse-order technique was used, 44% resulted in new information, 79% of which was correct. As instructed, most of the sheriffs followed the instruction to continually prompt the child with "what happened right before that," so as to avoid any grand leaps backward in time by the child, as reported by Geiselman and Padilla (1988).

Change Perspectives

This technique was used in 94% of the practice cognitive interviews conducted by the students, but it was used in only 38% of the cognitive interviews conducted by the sheriffs. Its use was significantly associated with the number of correct facts generated in the sheriffs' cognitive interviews. In cases where the change-perspectives technique was used, 75% resulted in new information, 86% of which was correct.

Specific Retrieval Techniques

Only two of the specific cognitive techniques were utilized in the sheriffs' cognitive interviews: the first-letter name mnemonic and the technique of asking the children if one of the people mentioned reminded them of someone they know. Each of these specific techniques appeared in approximately 50% of the sheriffs' cognitive interviews, and, as with the general cognitive procedures, most typically these techniques either led to the retrieval of new, correct information or had no effect on recall performance. While the design of the present study did not include a formal experiment on name recall with children, recall for the names of the actors who participated in the slide-show scenario followed the same pattern as recall for other information from the scenario. More sixth graders recalled a name than did third graders (59% vs. 32%), more children remembered a name with cognitive interviewing than with standard interviewing (cognitive interviewing without practice = 30% vs. standard interviewing = 8%), and more children remembered a name when the cognitive interviewing was preceded by practice than when there was no practice (cognitive interviewing with practice = 67% vs. cognitive interviewing without practice = 30%). An incorrect name was given during 21% of the interviews, and the frequency of name-recall errors was unrelated to grade level or the interview-format condition.

The name-recall mnemonic became problematic when the interviewer failed to explain to the child, in a developmentally appropriate manner, that going through the alphabet is a unitary process, not a series of questions requiring an answer for each letter. When each letter was presented as a separate question, the child appeared to become frustrated and demoralized, or made up any name to end the process.

The other specific technique that was used in approximately 50% of the sheriffs' cognitive interviews was, "Did he/she remind you of anyone you know?" One sixth-grade child remarked: "He reminded me of this surfer guy I knew: He did weird things like being hyper; he moved around all the time. He wore ear rings, two of them in the same ear; and he had a scar on his arm." All of this information was correct. No instances appeared in the interview transcripts in which the generation of incorrect information could be linked directly to this procedure. When the procedure was used, 67% of the children responded that the person in question did not remind them of anyone they know.

Inappropriate Questioning

At a qualitative level of analysis, there were some methods used in the interviews that were logically inappropriate. These include interruptions by the interviewer, use of developmentally inappropriate language (Saywitz, 1989), overly persistent questioning, "rapid-fire" questioning (not allowing the child to answer one question before asking another), building unrealistic expectations for the child, and not attending carefully to the child's answers.

As one example, there were several instances where three or four questions were clustered together prior to allowing the child to respond to any one of them, such as, "Did you see some pictures on California? Did you see any pictures? Do you remember the lady that just came into the room that brought you here? Did she have an opportunity to talk with some other children?" In the worst scenario, some children eventually offered a seemingly random response to one of the embedded questions simply to stop the onslaught of questions.

Overly persistent questioning when the child has claimed and reaffirmed that he or she does not know the answer to a question also can be demoralizing. As a general rule of thumb, we suggest dropping a topic after receiving three "I don't know" responses in a row, and going on to something that the interviewer feels the child definitely can answer with confidence.

Suggesting that the child should know the answer to a question, when he or she may in fact not know the answer is also inappropriate for children. In one interview, for example, the child was told, "Girls usually remember a lot about hair styles. What kind was hers?" This approach creates a no-win situation: If a response is obtained, the answer is questionable due to the demand characteristics created, and if no response is obtained, the child likely is led to feel "different" than other girls.

Finally, on some occasions, the interviewers failed to listen carefully to the children's answers. In one case, the interviewer inadvertently altered the current child's report so that it was consistent with the reports of children interviewed previously. The child referred to one of his fellow students as "Fred," but the interviewer repeated and recorded the name as "Frankie," which was correctly obtained from a child interviewed previously.

CONCLUSIONS

The major conclusions that can be drawn from this research are that (1) cognitive questioning techniques can enhance the completeness of recollections by children, and (2) it is advantageous for children to have practice with the cognitive questioning procedures prior to receiving a cognitive interview about the event of legal importance. Practice, as well as cognitive interviewing without practice, was particularly effective for the 11- to 12-year-olds studied here. The 8- to 9-year-olds also showed a significant increase in correct recall with cognitive interviewing and practice, but the effects were somewhat less pronounced. Goodman et al. (1991) reported a similar positive effect of practice on subsequent lineup identification performance by children, where an age-related trend also was observed.

Practice can serve any of three purposes: It potentially clarifies the methods to be used in the later interview; it encourages the children to use the techniques spontaneously, so that more of the techniques are used; and it gives the children experience with the usually unfamiliar task of being interviewed about their episodic memories for an event by an unfamiliar adult.

In the field, the practice interview can concern some staged event in a waiting room, so that the interviewer knows the approximate facts as they actually happened. Alternatively, the practice interview can concern some standard aspect of the day's activities, such as what transpired at school on an earlier day. The advantage of using a staged event is that the interviewer will have prior knowledge of the event; and this knowledge can be used to identify when a child reports information that is in error. At such a point, the interviewer can pursue the possible source of the error, so as to clarify what is expected of the child during an interview. For example, the interviewer might need to further explain the meaning of saying "I don't know" for a certain child.

At first glance, the recommendation in favor of practice interviewing creates a dilemma. It has been emphasized elsewhere that victims and witnesses of child abuse must undergo several interview sessions regarding the alleged criminal act, and that this opens the door for numerous psychological and legal complications. Cody (1989), for example, has estimated that some victims of child abuse are asked to retell their story to as many as 15 different parties. Hence, the "practice" interview can be seen as just another interview session for the child.

On the other hand, with a more complete report from the child early on in the process (due to more effective interview techniques), less time should be required for interviewing the child overall. In the present study, the most complete reports about the target event were obtained from children who were given practice cognitive interviews about an unrelated event. The practical implication is that children who are witness/victims could receive practice at being interviewed without necessitating the child to retell frightening or anxiety-producing experiences for the currently required (or accepted) number of times (Cody, 1989). Minimal additional time and personnel would be necessary to carry out a "practice interview" phase by any agency connected with interviewing children, and the apparent positive impact on the target interview seems well worth the expense.

A second practical implication to be drawn from the present results concerns the training of interviewers in the use of the cognitive methods. As reported by Dent (1982) and Geiselman et al. (1990), even experienced investigators do not always use optimal or productive interviewing strategies. The present performance data show that for most interviews, all of the cognitive methods should be tried at least once (Geiselman et al., 1986). Few detectives in our sample used all of the cognitive methods. Furthermore, the detectives, as a group, were more likely to exhibit inappropriate interview tactics with the younger children. Experience and classroom-style training apparently are not sufficiently individualized to produce an interviewer who is reliably effective when questioning children. One possibility is to include in the training regimen an individualized role-playing exercise, which could be videotaped and critiqued by personnel proficient in cognitive interviewing (Fisher et al., 1987). It is hoped that our qualitative analyses of the present interviews will aid the instructor and practitioner alike in the development of more effective interview procedures for use with children.

NOTE

This document was developed under a grant from the National Institute of Justice (88-IJ-CX-0033). Points of view expressed herein are those of the authors and do not necessarily represent the official position or policies of the National Institute of Justice.

The authors extend their appreciation to the Inglewood School District, to the Seeds University Elementary School, and to all those involved in the implementation of this research, including the students and sheriffs who served as the interviewers and the research team that coordinated, transcribed, and analyzed the interviews.

REFERENCES

Anderson, R. C., & Pichert, J. W. (1978). Recall of previously unrecallable information following a shift in perspective. *Journal of Verbal Learning and Verbal Behavior, 17*, 1–12.

Bower, G. H. (1967). A multicomponent theory of the memory trace. In K. W.

Spence & J. T. Spence (Eds.), *The psychology of learning and motivation* (Vol. 1, pp. 299–325). New York: Academic Press.

Bower, G. H., Gilligan, S. C., & Monteiro, K. P. (1984). Selectivity of learning caused by affective states. *Journal of Experimental Psychology: General, 110,* 451–472.

Brown, A. (1975). The development of memory: Knowing, knowing about knowing, and knowing how to know. In H. W. Reese (Ed.), *Advances in child and behavior* (Vol. 10, pp. 104–153). New York: Academic Press.

Brown, C., & Geiselman, R. E. (1990, October). Eyewitness testimony of mentally retarded: Effects of the cognitive interview. *Journal of Police and criminal psychology, 6,* 14–22.

Burns, M. J. (1981). *The mental retracing of prior activities: Evidence for reminiscence in ordered retrieval.* Doctoral Dissertation, University of California, Los Angeles. *Dissertation Abstracts International, 42,* 2108B.

Ceci, S. J., Ross, D. F., & Toglia, M. P. (1987). Suggestibility of children's memory: Psycholegal implications. *Journal of Experimental Psychology: General, 116,* 38–49.

Ceci, S. J., Ross, D. F., & Toglia, M. P. (1989). *Perspectives on children's testimony.* New York: Springer-Verlag.

Ceci, S. J., Toglia, M. P., & Ross, D. F. (Eds.). (1987). *Children's eyewitness memory.* New York: Springer-Verlag.

Chi, M. T. H., & Ceci, S. J. (1986). Content knowledge and the reorganization of memory. *Advances in Child Development and Behavior, 20,* 1–37.

Cody, K. (1989). The McMartin question: The "no-maybe-sometimes-yes" syndrome. *Easy Reader, 19,* 16–25.

Dale, P. S., Loftus, E. F., & Rathbun, E. (1978). The influence of the form of the question on the eyewitness testimony of preschool children. *Journal of Psycholinguistic Research, 7,* 269–277.

Dent, H. R. (1982). The effects of interviewing strategies on the results of interviews with child witnesses. In A. Trankell (Ed.), *Reconstructing the past* (pp. 279–297). Netherlands: K.H. Aver.

Firstenberg, I. (1983). *The role of retrieval variability in the interrogation of human memory.* Doctoral Dissertation, University of California, Los Angeles. *Dissertation Abstracts International, 44,* 1623B.

Fisher, R. P., Geiselman, R. E., Raymond, D. S., Jurkevich, L. M., & Warhaftig, M. L. (1987). Critical analysis of police interview techniques. *Journal of Police Science and Administration, 15,* 177–185.

Fivush, R. & Hudson, J. (1990). *Knowing and remembering in young children.* New York: Cambridge University Press.

Flavell, J. H. (1986). The development of children's knowledge about the appearance-reality distinction. *American Psychologist, 41,* 418–425.

Flexser, A., & Tulving, E. (1978). Retrieval independence in recognition and recall. *Psychological Review, 85,* 153–171.

Geiselman, R. E., & Callot, R. (1989). Reverse versus forward recall of script-based texts. *Applied Cognitive Psychology, 3,* 141–144.

Geiselman, R. E., Fisher, R. P., Firstenberg, I., Hutton, L. A., Sullivan, S., Avetissian, I., & Prosk, A. (1984). Enhancement of eyewitness memory:

An empirical evaluation of the cognitive interview. *Journal of Police Science and Administration, 12,* 74–80.

Geiselman, R. E., Fisher, R. P., MacKinnon, D. P., & Holland, H. L. (1985). Eyewitness memory enhancement in the police interview: Cognitive retrieval mnemonics versus hypnosis. *Journal of Applied Psychology, 70,* 401–412.

Geiselman, R. E., Fisher, R. P., MacKinnon, D. P., & Holland, H. L. (1986). Enhancement of eyewitness memory with the cognitive interview. *American Journal of Psychology, 99,* 385–401.

Geiselman, R. E., & Padilla, J. (1988). Interviewing child witnesses with the cognitive interview. *Journal of Police Science and Administration, 16,* 236–242.

Geiselman, R. E., Saywitz, K., & Bornstein, G. K. (1990). *Cognitive questioning techniques for child victims and witnesses of crime* (unpublished technical report, SJI-88-11J-D-016). State Justice Institute.

Goodman, G. S., Aman, C., & Hirschman, J. (1987). Child sexual and physical abuse: Children's testimony. In S. J. Ceci, D. F., Ross, & M. P. Toglia (Eds.), *Children's eyewitness memory* (pp. 1–23). New York: Springer-Verlag.

Goodman, G. S., Bottoms, B. L., Schwartz-Kenney, B. M., & Rudy, L. (1991). Children's testimony about a stressful event: Improving children's reports. *Journal of Narrative and Life History, 1,* 69–99.

Goodman, G. S., & Reed, R. S. (1986). Age differences in eyewitness testimony. *Law and Human Behavior, 10,* 317–332.

Goodman, G. S., Rudy, L., Bottoms, B. L., & Aman, C. (1990). Children's concerns and memory: Issues of ecological validity in children's testimony. In R. Fivush & J. A. Hudson (Eds.), *Knowing and remembering in young children.* New York: Cambridge University Press.

Gruneberg, M. M., & Monks, J. (1976). The first letter search strategy. *IRCS Medical Science: Psychology and Psychiatry, 4,* 307.

King, M. A., & Yuille, J. C. (1987). Suggestibility and the child witness. In S. J. Ceci, D. F. Ross, & M. P. Toglia (Eds.), *Children's eyewitness memory* (pp. 24-35). New York: Springer-Verlag.

Latts, M., & Geiselman, R. E. (1990). Interviewing survivors of rape. *Journal of Police and Criminal Psychology, 7,* 8–17.

Malpass, R. S. & Devine, P. G. (1981). Guided memory in eyewitness identification. *Journal of Applied Psychology, 66,* 343–350.

Marin, C., Holmes, D., Guth, M., & Kovac, P. (1979). The potential of children as eyewitnesses. *Law and Human Behavior, 3,* 295–305.

Piaget, J. (1969). *The child's conception of time.* London: Rutledge & Kegan Paul.

Pressley, M., & Levin, J. (1980). The development of mental imagery retrieval. *Child Development, 51,* 558–560.

Rudy, L., & Goodman, G. S. (1991). Effects of participation on children's reports: Implications for children's testimony. *Developmental Psychology, 27,* 527–538.

Saywitz, K. J. (1987). Children's testimony: Age-related patterns of memory errors. In S. J. Ceci, M. P. Toglia, & D. F. Ross (Eds.), *Children's eyewitness memory* (pp. 36–52). New York: Springer-Verlag.

Saywitz, K. J. (1988). Interviewing children: A psychological perspective. *Family Advocate, 10,* 16–20.

Saywitz, K. J. (1989). Children's conceptions of the legal system: "Court is a place to play basketball." In S. Ceci, D. Ross, & M. Toglia (Eds.), *Perspectives on children's testimony* (pp. 131–157). New York: Springer-Verlag.

Saywitz, K. J., Jaenicke, C., & Camparo, L. (1990). Children's knowledge of legal terminology. *Law and Human Behavior, 14,* 523–535.

Smith, M. (1983). Hypnotic memory enhancement of witnesses: Does it work? *Psychological Bulletin, 94,* 384–407.

Smith, S. (1979). Remembering in and out of context. *Journal of Experiment Psychology: Human Learning and Memory, 5,* 460–471.

Tulving, E. (1974). Cue-dependent forgetting. *American Scientist, 62,* 74–82.

Underwood, B. J. (1969). Attributes of memory. *Psychological Review, 76,* 559–573.

Whitten, W., & Leonard, J. (1981). Directed search through autobiographical memory. *Memory and Cognition, 9,* 566–579.

Wickens, D. (1970). Encoding categories of words: An empirical approach to meaning. *Psychological Review, 77,* 1–15.

5

Interviewing Children in Sexual Abuse Cases

John C. Yuille, Robin Hunter,
Risha Joffe, and Judy Zaparniuk
University of British Columbia

THE PROBLEM OF CHILD ABUSE

Over the past 15 years, rapidly escalating rates of reported child sexual abuse have changed our perspective on what was once considered a minor social problem. Surveys of child protection services (e.g., Suski, 1986) and individuals (e.g., Russell, 1983) have revealed that the sexual abuse of children is pervasive. In one retrospective U.S. national survey of 1,145 men and 1,481 women, Finkelhor, Hotaling, Lewis, and Smith (1990) found that 27% of the women and 16 percent of the men reported sexual abuse as children. Because disclosure of abuse has a variety of consequences, it is likely that these reported rates underestimate the actual rates and, in fact, "may represent only a tip of an unfathomable iceberg" (Finkelhor, 1984, p. 19). Indisputably, the sexual exploitation of children is a major social problem.

Responding to child sexual abuse is a complex matter. The investigation of allegations of abuse depends on obtaining reliable information from the victim. Physical evidence corroborating the allegations is rare and, even when present, seldom identifies the abuser. Typically, there are only two witnesses to the abuse: the victim and the offender, and because the abuser usually denies the abuse, knowledge of what has happened depends on information the child provides during the victim interview. The fundamental importance of the victim interview has led to two different problems in the investigation of abuse: high rates of labeling allegations as unfounded and false allegations.

ERRORS IN CHILD ABUSE INVESTIGATIONS

The dependence on interviews with the child has led to a high rate of labeling valid disclosures as unfounded. Most surveys have estimated that at least 90% of all allegations are valid, yet as many as 47% are classified as "unfounded" (e.g., Jones & McGraw, 1987). The use of the word "unfounded" is most unfortunate; these are generally not false allegations but investigations in which insufficient information is obtained to prompt action. The reasons for the high rate of inaction range from adults' reluctance to believe children to inadequate training of investigators in methods of interviewing children.

Coinciding with the increasing rates of reported child sexual abuse are increasing problems with false allegations. Estimating the rate of false allegations is fraught with even more difficulties than is estimating the rate of abuse itself. As noted above, the child and the alleged offender are often the only source of evidence in a case. Determining ground truth criteria of guilt or innocence is particularly problematic, thus the figures cited must be viewed as estimates only. In the most thorough study to date, Jones and McGraw (1987) studied the 576 reports of sexual abuse received by the Denver Department of Social Services during 1983. Although the agency labeled 47% of the cases "unfounded," the researchers believed that less than 8% of the allegations were actually false. Most disturbing is the fact that false allegations seem to be increasing in the context of custody and visitation disputes. While less than 2% of contested custody and visitation cases involve sexual abuse allegations (Thoennes & Tjaden, 1990), false allegations may be as high as 35% in this specific context (Benedek & Schetky, 1985; Brant & Sink, 1984; Jones & Seig, 1988; Kaplan & Kaplan, 1981).

The senior author's experience in interviewing children suggests that false allegations can take a variety of forms. An adolescent could deliberately make a false allegation in order to obtain some control in a situation (e.g., a foster home) or to exact revenge on an adult. Given the difficulties of maintaining a false allegation of this type, the incidence is probably low, although there are no available statistics on the rates of such allegations. Sometimes children will honestly disclose abuse but, out of fear or concern about the consequences, will not name the actual perpetrator. This may lead to a false allegation against an innocent party, although the details of the abuse are correct. The incidence of "perpetrator substitution" is not known.

A false allegation can also occur without the deliberate complicity of the child. For example, a parent, caught up in a custody dispute, could deliberately generate a false allegation of abuse that a child might come to believe. Alternatively, both parent and child may make an allegation of abuse based on their misinterpretation of some behavior of the other parent. For example, the custodial parent might learn that, during a visit, the other parent had touched the daughter's genital area while bathing her. Although the touching was for hygienic reasons the custodial parent misinterprets it as sexual in nature. Over time, both the custodial parent and the child come to believe this misinterpretation and, in the context of a custody/visitation dispute, use this "evidence" against the other parent.

Poor interview procedures also can lead to false allegations. The highly publicized McMartin trial, concerning allegations of sexual abuse at a preschool center in Manhattan Beach, California, illustrates the grave consequences of inadequate training and biased interview procedures. The trial of Peggy McMartin Buckey and her son Ray Buckey lasted for 6 years and cost $15 million, yet, at its conclusion, the defendants were acquitted (and other charges were not pursued). Although the jury had mixed feelings about whether abuse had occurred, they agreed that the original interviews were so poorly conducted that conviction was not possible. In fact, it was apparently the investigative interviews of the children that "proved to be the undoing of the prosecutor's case" (Carlson, 1990, p. 32).

PROBLEMS INTERVIEWING CHILDREN

The need to reduce the number of cases wrongly labeled unfounded, coupled with the need to detect false allegations, emphasizes the importance of conducting adequate interviews of children. The investigative interview, that is, the interview to determine both what has happened to a child and who appears to be responsible, is of paramount importance. Unfortunately, lack of training has led professionals to commit a number of errors during the interview process. In doing so, they fail to obtain reliable and valid information for assessing the credibility of an allegation of sexual abuse. Not only can such errors lead to a failure to substantiate valid allegations or to an endorsement of false ones, they can also have a negative impact on a variety of decisions. On the basis of the investigative interview, child protection decisions are often made by social workers, psychologists may make decisions about therapeutic interventions, and police and prosecutors may make decisions about criminal charges. In all of these cases, the decisions can only be as good as the information obtained during the investigative interview.

Interview problems can arise if the interviewer is unaware of developmental changes in language ability and cognition. An untrained interviewer may misinterpret a child's words or may use age-inappropriate language that will confuse the child. Further, an untrained interviewer may not understand that children often conceptualize events in a different manner from adults. This can lead to a misunderstanding or misinterpretation of the child's description of the events. In addition, interviewers may unwittingly use suggestive or leading questions, yet children, particularly preschool children, are vulnerable to the misleading effects of such questions (for a review of the problems associated with suggestibility in children, see Doris, 1991; King & Yuille, 1987; Yuille, 1988; Yuille & Farr, 1987). The use of anatomical dolls in the investigative interview represents a special form of suggestion that can also be problematic (for a review of the issues related to the use of these dolls and other interview aids, see Boat & Everson, Chapter 3, this volume; Raskin & Yuille, 1989).

Professional biases are another source of problems in the investigation of an allegation of abuse. For example, our criminal justice systems have a long history of incorrectly doubting the eyewitness abilities of children. As a result, children have become victimized by "a discriminatory legal system which . . . [has] regarded children as inherently unreliable witnesses whose testimony must be specially scrutinized" (Bala, 1989, p. 2). Alternatively, some professionals believe that children, essentially, never lie about abuse (e.g., Giaretto, in Summit, 1983). Both of these biases interfere with determining what has happened to a child and deciding a course of action that is in the child's best interests.

An interviewer needs some basic knowledge of sexual development, and knowledge about the forms and nature of the sexual abuse of children. In addition, anyone who interviews special-needs children (e.g., hearing impaired, mentally handicapped) will require special knowledge to interact appropriately and sensitively with them. Similarly, special knowledge is required by those who interview children from different cultures.

A number of methods for interviewing children in cases of alleged sexual abuse have been introduced in recent years (e.g., Boat & Everson, 1986; Jones & McQuiston, 1985; Sgroi, 1978; White, Santilli, & Quinn, 1986). In the remainder of this chapter we present one interview method—the Step-Wise Interview—which is intended to overcome many potential problems associated with interviewing. Much of the following information outlining this interview method has been taken from the writings of Yuille and colleagues (e.g. Raskin & Yuille, 1989; Yuille, 1988; Yuille, 1991; Yuille & Farr, 1987).

The core of the Step-Wise Interview is the organization of the steps of the interview to maximize recall while minimizing contamination. The term "step-wise" refers to the use of a set of steps during the interview. These steps begin with the most open, least leading form of questioning and proceed to more specific forms of questioning as circumstances require. The initial goal is to give the child every opportunity to provide a free narrative before other forms of questioning are used. The next step is to use open, general questions to prompt more recall without leading the child in any way. Following this, the child is prompted for more specific recall, but only by requesting an elaboration on details already described or introduced in the child's earlier free narrative report (see Table 5.1).

The Step-Wise Interview is an attempt to combine our current knowledge of child development with memory techniques that can aid children in recalling episodic details from abusive events. The interview method is nonleading and nonsuggestive, and yet maximizes the information obtained from the child. The Step-Wise method was developed in combination with Statement Validity Analysis (SVA), a method for assessing the credibility of a child's evidence (for details on SVA, see Steller & Koehnken, 1989; Undeutsch, 1989; Yuille, 1988). Used together, the Step-Wise Interview and SVA represent useful aids in investigating allegations of child sexual abuse.

In the following section we elaborate on the goals of effective interviewing with children, and we indicate some necessary background knowledge that will enable professionals to work more effectively with children. The subsequent section outlines the interview

---

TABLE 5.1. The Principal Steps of the Step-Wise Interview

1. Rapport building
2. Requesting recall of two specific events
3. Telling the truth
4. Introducing the topic of concern
5. Free narrative
6. General questions
7. Specific questions (if necessary)
8. Interview aids (if necessary)
9. Concluding the interview

procedure. In a final section, we briefly discuss the results of a field study of the Step-Wise method.

THE GOALS OF AN EFFECTIVE INTERVIEW

There are four primary goals of an investigative interview:

1. Minimizing the trauma of the investigation for the child.
2. Maximizing the information obtained from the child about the alleged event(s).
3. Minimizing the contaminating effects of the interview on the child's memory for the event(s).
4. Maintaining the integrity of the investigative process.

In the following sections we discuss each of these goals.

Minimizing Trauma

Children who disclose sexual abuse are often subjected to repeated interviews during the investigative process. For example, Van de Kamp (1986) reported that the average number of interviews by police for 19 alleged child victims was seven per child, with one child having to suffer through 24 police interviews. Since children are also interviewed by other professionals, typically social workers, physicians, psychologists, and lawyers, Van de Kamp's figures represent only part of the systemic abuse (that is, problems for children that are the consequence of investigations by systems or agencies which deal with abuse) these children suffered. Without doubt, repeated interviews do represent a form of abuse by the systems charged with responding to child abuse (Bala, 1989). Because the child must talk with strangers and must describe intimate details during the interview, each interview is potentially upsetting for the child.

The Step-Wise Interview aims to minimize the trauma of an interview by minimizing the number of interviews. Also, the trauma of the interview can be minimized through training the interviewer; a knowledgeable and sensitive interviewer is equipped to help the child through the interviews.

The number of interviews can be minimized by recording the interview. Preferably, the interview will be videotaped but, in the absence of video equipment, an audiotape will suffice. If no electronic equipment is available, a verbatim record must be kept. There are many advantages to recording an interview, although having such an objective record of their interview performance may be intimidating for some professionals. It has come to our attention that, in the wake of the McMartin case, a number of professionals have decided not to record interviews. Since poor interview quality was a central feature of the McMartin case, many have decided that it is better not to have a record of an interview. It would seem that such a decision is based on the fear of having one's work publicly scrutinized. This is a most unfortunate development. Our goal should not be to hide poor interviews, for it is important that the adequacy of the methods used to obtain children's evidence be assessed. A more appropriate goal would be to educate interviewers in order to enable them to conduct interviews that can withstand public scrutiny.

It is in the best interests of the child to reduce the number of interviews and only recordings can accomplish this goal.

The reasons for recording the interview include:

1. Providing an accurate record of the interview.
2. Having a tape to show the nonoffending parent(s). It is a difficult task for a parent to deal with his or her child's abuse, especially if the offender is his or her spouse. Since the parent should not be present during the interview, the videotape can be an effective way of helping the parent(s) to learn the details of the events and can aid in informing the parent of the abuse. There may be circumstances, however, where this is inappropriate, depending on the child's wishes.
3. Police have reported to the first author that a videotape of the interview of the child is an effective aid in obtaining a confession by the perpetrator. The tape is shown to the suspect and, perhaps, his or her lawyer. Through viewing the tape, the abuser may come face to face with the nature and consequences of his or her actions for the first time. Furthermore, if the interview was well conducted, this may be the first time the suspect is aware of the child's ability to provide competent testimony.
4. The videotape can be admitted as evidence in some jurisdictions.
5. The videotape can assist the child in preparing for his or her court appearance.
6. The videotape can be useful in therapy.
7. A videotape is an important form of ongoing training for the interviewer and provides professional protection for him or her.

Maximizing Recall

The second goal of the interview is to maximize the amount of accurate information the child provides. To attain this goal the interviewer must be sensitive to the qualitative and quantitative developmental changes in memory. Regardless of age, children, if carefully interviewed, can recall as accurately as adults (e.g., Goodman, 1984; King & Yuille, 1987). However, younger children generally recall less about an event than older children do (cf. Doris, 1991). In order to maximize the amount of recall of an event, an interviewer needs a rough estimate of the amount of information that can be expected from the child. Although age guidelines are of some use, individual differences at each age in amount of recall are considerable (Kail, 1979). As a result, the Step-Wise Interview includes a procedure to give a rough estimate of the amount and type of detail the child provides in recalling a specific episode. Before discussing the event(s) of concern, the child is asked to provide two descriptions of past events (e.g., birthdays, school trips, etc.). These descriptions can furnish the interviewer with a rough gauge of the kind of recall the child provides for specific events.

There must also be an appreciation for the varying narrative forms children use at different ages. Preschool children typically provide an idiosyncratic organization when describing a specific episode (Liberty & Ornstein, 1973; Moely, 1977). In contrast, primary school children have usually acquired the narrative organizational skills necessary to tell an event from beginning to end. The interviewer must be both sensitive to and tolerant of these differences.

Although preschool children do not spontaneously employ retrieval strategies (e.g., Paivio & Yuille, 1966), they can benefit from such strategies if they are supplied (Geiselman, Saywitz, & Bornstein, 1989). In this latter study, children recalled more details with no loss in accuracy, compared to uninstructed children, when they were instructed to:

1. Mentally reconstruct the circumstances surrounding the event before recalling the details (context reinstatement).
2. Leave nothing out of their recall, no matter how trivial it seems (exhaust memory).
3. Try to recall the event from a different perspective.

These three components of the cognitive interview (Geiselman, Fisher, MacKinnon, & Holland, 1986) can play a valuable role in enhancing recall obtained with the Step-Wise Interview.

Minimizing Contamination

The amount of information a child provides about an event depends, in part, on the form of questioning used. It may be possible to evoke greater detail by using a series of specific questions. The problem with this approach, however, is that children are susceptible to being mislead (for a current review of the issues associated with children's susceptibility to suggestion, see Doris, 1991). It is not simply that a child may acquiesce to a leading question—the dangers are more subtle. For example, if a child is simply asked a specific question, such as, "What was the color of the man's hair?" the child may provide an answer despite lack of knowledge regarding that detail (e.g., King & Yuille, 1986). The younger the child, the more this pattern holds (Ceci, Ross, & Toglia, 1987; Varendonck, 1911). Younger children can operate with a belief that they are supposed to answer questions even if they must invent the response.

The problem facing the interviewer is to maximize the information the child provides without using techniques that will elicit incorrect information. The interviewer must be skilled in providing every opportunity, and memory aid, to help the child recall as many details as possible. At the same time, the interviewer must know how to avoid leading, suggesting, or influencing the child in any way that could change or contaminate the child's memory for the event. Furthermore, the interviewer must try to maintain a correspondence between intended and received tasks (McGarrigle, Grieve, & Hughes, 1978). That is, the interviewer may intend one thing with a question or line of questioning while the child may receive a different message. The interviewer needs enough knowledge about the language, cognition, and memory of children to maintain the correspondence between the intentions of the interview and the child's perceptions of the interview.

Maintaining Integrity

The fourth and final goal of the Step-Wise procedure is to achieve the first three goals while maintaining the investigative integrity of the interview. As noted earlier, all investigative interviews have certain systemic goals: a social worker will interview a child in order to make a child protection decision; a police officer, to determine (perhaps together with a prosecutor) if criminal charges should be laid; and a therapist, to determine what type of intervention or support the child requires. Also, different systems have different needs in terms of the nature or form of permissible questioning. The interview procedure must be flexible and able to meet these different goals.

THE STEP-WISE INTERVIEW

General Considerations

Ideally, the interview is conducted in a room specifically designed for interviewing children. Such a room is quiet and free of distractions. Any toys or interview aids are kept out of sight until needed. The furniture is comfortable and suited to the size and needs of children (furniture on wheels should be avoided). The room is equipped with nonintrusive video and audio recording equipment. Any equipment used must be shown and explained to the child. If a designated interview room is not available, the interviewer should try to arrange the circumstances to approximate these goals. Every effort must be made to avoid conducting the interview in the same location as the alleged abuse.

The interview situation should include only one adult and the child. However, it is often the case that interagency cooperation requires that both a police officer and a social worker witness the interview (Yuille, Hunter, & Harvey, 1990). In such cases, two options are available. The first option involves having one professional interview the child while the other observes and records the interview via video monitor or one-way screen. The second option, and the one we prefer, is that both adults are present; one adult serving as active interviewer and the other as recorder. The recorder makes notes of both significant developments during the interview and of any questions that should be pursued, although he or she does not verbally participate in the interview until the active interviewer has finished his or her questions. At the end of his or her interview, the active interviewer invites the recorder to present any additional questions to the child. In this fashion, various agency mandates can be met, and the two professionals can assist one another. At the same time, the sequential questioning (active interviewer first, recorder later) assures that the two adults will not interupt each other or confuse the child.

The active interviewer sits either facing or side by side with the child at a close but comfortable distance. No objects, such as tables, should be between the interviewer and child. The recorder is seated apart from the interviewer and child.

Every effort should be made to discourage other concerned adults (e.g., school personnel, therapists, parents, guardians) from sitting in on the interview since their presence may compromise the integrity of the process and may make it difficult for the child to openly elaborate on details. If the child insists that another adult be present, this adult must sit out of the child's view and not participate in the interview.

In order to achieve the goals of an effective interview, the interview should be recorded. A video recording is preferred, together with an audio duplicate, as it is easier to make a transcript from an audio recording. Furthermore, the audio portion of a videotape is not always of the best quality. In the absence of video equipment, an audio recording is made. If no equipment is available, a written verbatim record is kept (a role for the recorder). Whatever the method of recording, the child should be made aware of its existence and purpose.

The major steps of the interview are outlined in Table 5.1. These steps are generally followed in the order listed in the table. Within each step there may be one or more substeps.

Beginning the Interview

Rapport Building

The first aim of the interview is to establish rapport with the child. The interviewer needs to spend sufficient time discussing neutral topics until the child has relaxed as much as circumstances permit. The method employed here will vary with the individual needs of each child, and may involve discussing school interests with an adolescent or playing with a coloring book with a preschool child. During this phase, the interviewer makes informal observations of the child's linguistic, cognitive, behavioral, and social skills.

Describing Two Events

At some point during the rapport-building phase, the child is asked to describe two specific past experiences. These may include a description of a birthday party, a Christmas celebration, a school outing, and so forth. Each episode should be memorable in some fashion, but independent of any of the abuse allegations. There are three purposes for this step:

1. The description of these two episodes provides a rough basis to assess the amount and quality of detail this child provides for a specific experience. This can be used as a basis by which to assess the amount and quality of detail in the child's later recall of the abuse event(s).
2. The request to describe these events aids in establishing rapport with the child and affords the interviewer an opportunity to display interest in the child's experience.

3. This step provides an opportunity to model the form of the interview for the child. As the child describes each event, the interviewer encourages detailed recall by asking nonleading, open-ended questions—a pattern that will hold throughout the entire interview. It is more effective to introduce this pattern during the rapport-building phase than when the child is describing the events of concern.

In some cases, more than one meeting may be needed to establish rapport adequate for continuation of the interview.

Telling the Truth

The next step of the interview involves establishing the need to tell the truth. This aim is also approached in a step-wise manner. The topic of truth and falsehood is introduced in a very general fashion (e.g., "Do you know what it means to tell the truth?"). If a child cannot answer general questions about truth and lies, more specific questions are asked to introduce the topic (e.g., "If I said you had green hair, would that be the truth or a lie?"). In some cases, this discussion is assisted by telling the child a story containing a character who tells a lie. The child can then be questioned about the significance and consequences of the lie (see Yuille, Menard, & Marxsen, 1992). An agreement is made between interviewer and child that only the truth be discussed throughout the interview. For younger children, this point may be clarified by a reminder that elements of "pretend" or "make-believe" are not to be included.

The meaning of truth and the consequences of lying are discussed early on in the interview in order to maintain the integrity of the interview process (interview goal number 4) and to assure that the child is oriented to the serious nature of the investigative interview.

Introducing the Topic of Concern

The purpose of the interview is introduced in a step-wise fashion. General, open-ended questions are attempted first (e.g., "Do you know why you are talking with me today?"), proceeding to somewhat more specific questions as required (e.g., "Has anything happened to you which you would like to tell me about?" or even "Has anyone done something to you?"). If these questions do not lead to a disclosure, the interviewer may move on to ask the child, "Who are the people you like to be with?" and "Who are the people you don't like to be with?" and may ask about the child's reasons. Under no circumstances should the interviewer name the suspect or suggest what happened during the alleged acts.

If general questions have not introduced the topic of abuse, the use of drawings may be helpful. The child is asked to make an outline of a man or a woman (the interviewer may provide the outline if the child cannot do so). Then the child is asked to add each body part (e.g., from head to toe). For each body part, the child is asked to name it and describe its function. When the genitals (or anus) are described, the interviewer can ask if the child has seen this part of another person, and/or who has seen or touched this part of the child. The same procedure is then repeated for the drawing of the other gender.

Free Narrative

Once the topic of sexual abuse has been introduced, the interviewer encourages the child to provide a free narrative account of the event(s). The child is asked to describe each event from the beginning and without leaving out any details. During this phase, the interviewer's role is to act as facilitator, not interrogator. The interviewer does not interrupt, correct, or challenge the child's report. The child is allowed to proceed at his or her own pace. Patience and a tolerance for pauses and elaborations of even irrelevant details are essential. In order to maintain the free narrative, the child's pauses may be followed with gentle prompts (e.g., "Then what happened?" "Tell me about that").

If the allegations concern repeated abuse over a period of time, it is best to ask first for a description of the general pattern of the abuse—what Nelson and Gruendel (1986) have called script memory (e.g., "Can you tell me how it usually happens?"). Once the script has been obtained, it can be used to help the child recall specific episodes. For example, the child can be asked if the type of event in question ever happened in a different place or in a different fashion than usual (script violations). Departures from the typical script often constitute the specific events that the child will remember. If multiple incidents have been described, it is advisable to label the incidents (e.g., "You said it happened in the kitchen. Let's call it the kitchen time"). The child may take part in the labeling process. Such labeling is useful for helping the child organize his or her recall and for ensuring that the interviewer can clarify which incident is being discussed at any particular time.

General Questions

The next step in the interview is the use of general questions in order to allow the child to recall further details of the things and events described in the free narrative. Questions should be based only on the information provided by the child and should use the child's own terminology. Further, these questions must not be leading and must not suggest an answer. Questions are to be phrased in a manner that implies that an inability to recall, or a lack of knowledge, is acceptable (e.g., "You mentioned _____, do you remember anything more about that?"). It is up to the interviewer to make it clear that the child can say "I don't know."

If the child seems to be finding it difficult to talk about certain aspects of the event (e.g., repeatedly gives "I don't know" responses to every question on a specific topic), the interviewer may be able to distinguish lack of memory/knowledge from other difficulties by suggesting that the child use a signal (e.g., raise hand) to indicate when he or she knows something but isn't ready to talk about it. The topic can then be raised at a later point in the interview.

In situations in which the child becomes distressed while talking about a certain topic, the interviewer can shift the focus to aspects of the child's recall that are less stressful. When the child has regained his or her composure, the interviewer can attempt to return to the distressing topic. It may be necessary to shift from, then back to, a difficult topic several times before the child is able to talk about it.

Specific Questions

Ideally, the free-narrative and open-questions phases of the interview will exhaust the children's memory for the event. However, the specific-questions phase is helpful for obtaining clarification and extension of previous answers. At this stage, components of the cognitive interview (Geiselman et al., 1986; see Geiselman, Saywitz, & Bornstein, Chapter 4 this volume) may be useful. The child may be asked to mentally reinstate the context of an event (e.g., "Do you remember what you were doing before _____?" "Do you remember what the weather was like that day?"), and to take a different perspective (e.g., "What would a TV camera on the ceiling have seen that day?"). For the sake of maintaining the integrity of the interview it is important not to use words like "pretend" or "imagine" when presenting these questions to the child.

The interviewer should avoid the use of multiple-choice questions as much as possible. If they must be used, more than two alternatives should be included (e.g., "Did it happen when it was dark, light, or do you remember?"). When a multiple-choice question has been asked, the interviewer should repeat it at a later time with the alternatives in a different order to assess whether the child's earlier answer was due to a favored response bias (e.g., always agreeing to the last alternative presented).

During the specific-questions phase, the interviewer can follow up on inconsistencies in the child's account. Such inconsistencies should be probed in a gentle, nonthreatening manner (e.g., "I'm kind of confused. You said that he was touching your private parts but you said you had your clothes on. Can you tell me how that happened? Can you help me understand that?"). As well, the interviewer can investigate the origins of language or knowledge that appears inappropriate for a child of that age (e.g., "You said 'erection,' do you remember where you learned that word?").

When the child has exhausted his or her memory for the event, the interviewer asks the child once again to give his or her recall for the event. It is important that the interviewer convey that the purpose of the repetition is to help him or her understand the event, rather than that the child's report is being called into question (e.g., "I think I understand most of what you told me, but my memory's not so hot. Will you help me by telling me once more everything you remember about the time in the kitchen?").

Interview Aids

With young children or children with language or emotional difficulties, it may be necessary to use interview aids such as dolls and drawings. These are also used in a step-wise fashion and are not presented as part of any play activity. When drawings are used, the first step is to ask the child to make the drawing. If the child cannot or will not draw, a drawing without anatomical details may be provided (so that the child can supply the details). Similarly, when dolls are used, those without genital details are presented first. In short, every attempt is made, even when using interview aids, to have the information come from the child rather than from the interviewer.

Anatomically detailed dolls (those with genitals and an anal opening) are used only as a last resort (Yuille, 1988). These dolls can be useful in obtaining an understanding of exactly what sort of sex act occurred, but are to be used only *after* the child has disclosed details of the abuse. The dolls should never be used to obtain the disclosure, only to clarify it.

Finally, on some occasions, the interviewer may have concerns about the child's susceptibility to suggestion. In such cases, the interviewer may, prior to concluding the interview, ask a few leading questions about irrelevant issues (e.g., "You came here by taxi, didn't you?" "You wore a green shirt yesterday, didn't you?"). If the child demonstrates susceptibility to the suggestions, the information obtained through the interview will have to be scrutinized for possible contamination from suggestion.

Concluding the Interview

The interviewer can now ask the recorder if he or she has any questions. The recorder will then move into the role of active interviewer and can ask any questions that remain. The child is then thanked for participating, regardless of any conclusions the interviewers have drawn. The interviewer also explains to the child what will happen next in the investigative procedure. Interviewers must be cautious not to make any promises about future developments that they cannot keep (e.g., "We will make sure this never happens to you again"). Finally, any questions the child has are answered.

Field Research

The Step-Wise Interview provides a framework for professionals who conduct investigative interviews with children. It has been developed with the assistance of psychologists, social workers, police, and prosecutors, and it contains many components that have been tested in both field and laboratory settings. In fact, the entire procedure is currently being field-tested in British Columbia. The project involves child protection workers, police, and prosecutors in three districts, two of whom received an intensive 4-day training workshop on the Step-Wise Interview and SVA. The third district is initially serving as the control group. Since the completion of training, each reported case of suspected child sexual abuse has been documented for the project. In addition, when a taped interview (either audio or video) occurred, and when consent was obtained, a copy of the interview was supplied to the project.

Approximately 6 months after the initial workshop, the control district was trained, thus serving as a "before and after" comparison for itself. In order to accommodate the large number of trainees and assure a continuation of agency service during training, all three districts received the training program twice ($n = 131$).

To date, the training has been evaluated in three ways.

1. Anonymous evaluations provided by the trainees at the conclusion of the 4-day workshop.
2. A 6-month follow-up session with the two districts that received the initial training.

3. Ratings of the quality of the taped interviews of trained and untrained workers.

Seventy-one percent of the trainees completed the initial evaluations. The first question dealt with participants' overall view of the course content, and it netted very positive responses. The next question asked if there was adequate information supplied. Generally, participants felt that sufficient information was received, with a few people indicating that more of one aspect or another would have been helpful; for example, "perhaps there could have been more information on the characteristics of abuse; however, many experienced workers would already have that knowledge." The final question in the initial evaluation asked what suggestions participants could offer in order to improve future training sessions. A number of useful ideas were proposed, such as "more emphasis and practise of non-leading interview techniques. . . ."

Thirty-nine of the 62 people present at the 6-month follow-up completed evaluation questionnaires. The first question asked participants how often they used the Step-Wise method. While the majority of respondents indicated "sometimes to always," those not using it cited the child's age or lack of attentiveness as the reasons. When asked what benefits were found using the Step-Wise procedure, many individuals indicated that it helped them to better organize their interview.

The final evaluation method, rating interview quality, has shown exciting preliminary results. The experimental and control districts differed markedly in the extent to which the interviews obtained could be assessed for credibility. In the control group, 30% of the interviews defied adequate analysis because of either scant or contaminated information, whereas in the experimental group this figure drops to 5%.

The final results of this field study, which is being conducted by the senior author, should be available in 1992.

CONCLUSIONS

Training professionals in proper investigative interview techniques is only effective if the techniques have the support of the agencies within which those professionals are employed. Not only is agency support essential, but interagency cooperation is a prerequisite for an effective response to child sexual abuse. Child protection agencies, the police, the prosecution, and medical personnel must cooperate, and they must also receive similar training. The issues related to interagency cooperation in this area are explored in depth by Yuille, Hunter, and Harvey (1990).

The Step-Wise Interview has received enthusiastic support in anonymous evaluations of those who have been trained in the procedure. The recent report of the Pigot (1989) inquiry in the United Kingdom, into issues concerning children's evidence, recommended the adoption of the Step-Wise Interview as the national standard for the United Kingdom.

Although the emphasis in this chapter has been on interviews in child sexual abuse cases, the Step-Wise Interview is intended for any investigative interview conducted with children. The same principles hold regardless of the content of the event. In fact, most of the procedures also serve as the foundation for an investigative interview of an adult.

ACKNOWLEDGMENTS

The preparation of this chapter was supported by a grant to the first author from the Social Sciences and Humanities Research Council of Canada and from the Killam Foundation.

The development of the Step-Wise Interview was assisted by many individuals and sources. The authors wish to thank the advice of Udo Undeutsch, Max Steller, Nancy Frederick, Wendy Harvey, and Hunter MacDonald.

REFERENCES

Bala, N. (1989, February). *Double victims: Child sexual abuse and the criminal justice system.* Paper presented at the Canadian Bar Association—Ontario, Annual Education Institute, Criminal Law Program, Toronto, ON.

Benedek, E. P., & Schetky, D. H. (1985). Allegations of sexual abuse in child custody and visitation disputes. In D. H. Schetky & E. P. Benedek (Eds.), *Emerging issues in child psychiatry and the law* (pp. 145–156). New York: Brunner/Mazel.

Boat, B. W., & Everson, M. D. (1986). *Using anatomical dolls: Guidelines for interviewing young children in sexual abuse investigations.* Unpublished manuscript. University of North Carolina, School of Medecine.

Brant, R. S., & Sink, F. (1984, October). *Dilemmas in court ordered evaluations of sexual abuse charges during custody and visitation proceedings.* Paper presented at the 31st Annual Meeting of the American Academy of Child Psychiatry, Toronto, ON.

Carlson, M. (1990, January 29). Six years of trial by torture. *Time*, 32–33.

Ceci, S. J., Ross, D. F., & Toglia, M. P. (1987). Age differences in suggestibility: Narrowing the uncertainties. In S. J. Ceci, D. F. Ross, & M. P. Toglia (Eds.), *Children's eyewitness memory* (pp. 79–91). New York: Springer-Verlag.

Doris, J. L. (1991). *The suggestibility of children's memory*. Washington, DC: American Psychological Association.

Finkelhor, D. (1984). How widespread is child sexual abuse? *Children Today, 3*, 18–20.

Finkelhor, D., Hotaling, G., Lewis, I. A., & Smith, C. (1990). Sexual abuse in a national survey of adult men and women: Prevalence, characteristics, and risk factors. *Child Abuse and Neglect, 14*, 385–401.

Geiselman, R. E., Fisher, R. P., MacKinnon, D. P., & Holland, H. L. (1986). Enhancement of eyewitness memory with the cognitive interview. *American Journal of Psychology, 99*, 385–401.

Geiselman, R. E., Saywitz, K. J., & Bornstein, G. K. (1989). *Cognitive questioning techniques for child victims and witnesses of crime*. Unpublished manuscript. University of California, Department of Psychology, Los Angeles.

Goodman, G. S. (1984). The accuracies of children's eyewitness reports. In D. Bross (Ed.), *Multidisciplinary advocacy for mistreated children* (pp. 182–194). Denver: The National Association of Counsel for Children.

Jones, D. P. H., & McGraw, J. M. (1987). Reliable and fictitious accounts of sexual abuse to children. *Journal of Interpersonal Violence, 2*(1), 27–45.

Jones, D. P. H., & McQuiston, M. (1985). *Interviewing the sexually abused child*. Denver, CO: The C. Henry Kempe National Center for the Prevention and Treatment of Child Abuse and Neglect.

Jones, D. P. H., & Seig, A. (1988). Child sexual abuse in custody and visitations disputes. In E. B. Nicholson & J. Bulkley (Eds.), *Sexual abuse allegations in custody and visitation cases: A resource book for judges and court personnel* (pp. 22–36). Washington, DC: American Bar Association.

Kail, R. (1979). *The development of memory in children*. San Francisco: W. H. Freeman.

Kaplan, S. L., & Kaplan, S. J. (1981). The child's accusation of sexual abuse during a divorce and custody struggle. *Hillside Journal of Clinical Psychiatry, 3*(1), 81–95.

King, M. A., & Yuille, J. C. (1986). The child witness. *Canadian Psychological Association Highlights, 8*, 25–27.

King, M. A., & Yuille, J. C. (1987). Suggestibility and the child witness. In S. J. Ceci, M. P. Toglia, & D. F. Ross (Eds.), *Children's eyewitness memory* (pp. 24–35). New York: Springer-Verlag.

Liberty, C., & Ornstein, P. A. (1973). Age differences in organization and recall: The effects of training in categorization. *Journal of Experimental Child Psychology, 15*, 169–186.

McGarrigle, J., Grieve, R., & Hughes, M. (1978). Interpreting inclusion: A contribution to the study of the child's cognitive and linguistic development. *Journal of Experimental Child Psychology, 26*, 528–550.

Moely, B. E. (1977). Organizational factors in the development of memory. In R. V. Kail & J. W. Hagen (Eds.), *Perspectives on the development of memory and cognition* (pp. 203–236). Hillsdale, NJ: Erlbaum.

Nelson, K., & Gruendel, J. (1986). Children's scripts. In K. Nelson, (Ed.), *Event knowledge: Structure and function in development* (pp. 21–46). Hillsdale, NJ: Erlbaum.

Paivio, A., & Yuille, J. C. (1966). Word abstractness and meaningfulness of nouns in paired-associate learning in children. *Journal of Experimental Psychology, 4,* 81–89.

Pigot, His Honour Judge. (1989, December). *Report of the national advisory group on video evidence.* London: Home Office.

Raskin, D. C., & Yuille, J. C. (1989). Problems in evaluating interviews of children in child sexual abuse cases. In S. J. Ceci, M. P. Toglia, & D. F. Ross (Eds.), *Perspectives on children's testimony* (pp. 184–207). New York: Springer-Verlag.

Russell, D. (1983). The incidence and prevalence of intrafamiliar and extrafamiliar sexual abuse of female children. *Child Abuse & Neglect, 71,* 133–146.

Sgroi, S. M. (1978). Child sexual assault: Some guidelines for intervention and assessment. In A. W. Burgess, A. N. Groth, L. L. Holmstrom, & S. M. Sgroi (Eds.), *Sexual assault of children and adolescents* (pp. 129–142). Lexington, MA: D. C. Heath.

Sgroi, S. M., Porter, F. S., & Blick, L. C. (1982). Validation of child sexual abuse. In S. M. Sgroi (Ed.), *Handbook of clinical intervention child sexual abuse* (pp. 39–79). Lexington, MA: D.C. Heath.

Steller, M., & Koehnken, G. (1989). Criteria-based content analysis. In D. C. Raskin (Ed.), *Psychological methods in criminal investigation and evidence* (pp. 317–245). New York: Springer-Verlag.

Summit, R. C. (1983). The child sexual abuse accommodation syndrome. *Child Abuse and Neglect, 7,* 177–193.

Suski, L. B. (1986). Child sexual abuse—An increasingly important part of child protective service practice. *Protecting Children, 3*(1), 3–7.

Thoennes, N., & Tjaden, P. G. (1990). The extent, nature, and validity of sexual abuse allegations in custody/visitation disputes. *Child Abuse & Neglect, 14,* 151–163.

Undeutsch, U. (1989). The development of statement reality analysis. In J. C. Yuille (Ed.), *Credibility assessment* (pp. 101–117). Dordrecht, The Netherlands: Kluwer Academic.

Van De Kamp, J. K. (1986). *Report on the Kern County child abuse investigation.* Office of the Attorney General, Division of Law Enforcement Bureau of Investigation, Kern County, California.

Varendonck, J. (1911). Les termoignages d'enfants dans un process retentissant. *Archives de Psychologie, 11,* 129–171.

White, S., Santilli, G., & Quinn, K. (1986, August). *Child evaluator's roles in child sexual abuse assessments.* Paper presented at the American Psychological Association Annual Convention, Washington, DC.

Yuille, J. C. (1988). The systematic assessment of children's testimony. *Canadian Psychology, 19*(3), 247–261.

Yuille, J.C. (1991). *The Step-Wise Interview: A protocol for interviewing children.* Unpublished manuscript, University of British Columbia.

Yuille, J. C., & Farr, V. (1987, Fall). Statement validity analysis: A systematic approach to the assessment of children's allegations of child sexual abuse. *British Columbia Psychologist,* 19–27.

Yuille, J. C., Hunter, R., & Harvey, W. (1990). A coordinated approach to interviewing in child sexual abuse investigations. *Canada's Mental Health, 38*(2/3), 14–18.

Yuille, J. C., Menard, K. C., & Marxsen, D. P. (1992). *A manual for training investigative interviewers in child sexual abuse cases.* Manuscript in preparation.

6

Improving Children's Testimony with Preparation

Karen J. Saywitz
UCLA School of Medicine,
Harbor–UCLA Medical Center

Lynn Snyder
California State University, Long Beach

A 4-year-old witness is asked during questioning: "On the evening of January third, you did, didn't you, visit your grandmother's sister's house and didn't you see the defendant leave the house at 7:30, after which you stayed the night?" The child sat in silence and became tearful. Despite the fact that this question is linguistically complex, with embedded clauses, and unfamiliar terminology, all beyond a 4-year-old's stage of language acquisition; despite the fact that it requires an ability to tell time that 4-year-olds have not mastered; and despite the fact that it asks several questions under the guise of one question that must be answered yes or no, this child's inability to announce that she neither understood the question nor possessed the ability to verify times and dates was misinterpreted as a lack of both competence and credibility.

At times, child witnesses appear to be confused and inconsistent. In many instances, this has more to do with the competence of adults to relate to and communicate with children than with children's abilities to accurately relate their experiences. The problem is a function of the discrepancy between the typical process by which evidence is elicited and the developmentally sensitive process that is needed to elicit accurate information from young children. Consequently, children may not testify at the optimal level of which they are capable, and they may experience higher levels of system-related stress than is necessary.

The present chapter focuses on efforts to minimize the gap between children's ability to testify and the demands of the legal system. Specifically, this chapter concerns preparation (i.e. training) programs to equip children for the task of testifying. Before addressing such programs, we discuss the legal context in which children testify, and we analyze its task demands; this analysis identifies areas in which children may be ill-equipped to meet the challenges posed by the legal system. Then, sample studies are described that explore the efficacy of preparation programs that we developed. Finally, guidelines for futher research are suggested.

THE LEGAL CONTEXT

When the victim-witness is a child, the judicial process has a dual responsibility—to discover the truth and safeguard the child's emotional well-being (Federal Rules of Evidence 611(a)(3); *Maryland v. Craig*, 1990; Myers, 1987). But current sociolegal practices were designed neither to maximize the accuracy of children's reports nor to minimize their stress. Take, for example, the practice of generously granting delays and continuances. The resulting retention intervals, extended by months and sometimes years, may differentially erode younger children's memories (Brainerd, Reyna, Howe, & Kingma, 1990). Further, recent studies suggest that duration of legal involvement is negatively related to resuming healthy emotional functioning (Runyan, Everson, Edelsohn, Hunter, & Coulter, 1988; Whitcomb, Shapiro, & Stellwageon, 1985). Thus, recovery from the often traumatic events that bring children to the attention of the court could be thwarted inadvertently by such delays (Weiss & Berg, 1982).

Although some states have been progressive in their efforts to accommodate to child witnesses, several reforms have been criticized as knee jerk reactions that violate defendants' rights. For example, placing a screen in front of the child witness in a jury trial has been determined to possess the potential for prejudicial bias against the accused (*Coy v. Idaho*, 1988). Notwithstanding the need for system-wide reform, advance preparation of child witnesses could prove to be a partial solution that does not raise legal, ethical, or constitutional dilemmas.

Preparation alone will not eliminate the mismatch between the requirements of the system and the capabilities, limitations, and needs of young children. Preparation is one of many factors that mediate children's testimonial performance and their subjective experience of the process (see Spencer & Flin, 1990, for a review). However, preparation may diminish the gap. Preparation of children for painful medical procedures has proven successful in lowering children's perceptions of pain and raising their level of cooperation (Jay, 1984). Children facing similarly stressful forensic procedures deserve no less. Moreover, carefully tested preparation methods may advance the course of justice by improving the quality of evidence children provide to fact finders.

The Task of Testifying

The legal system demands a prompt, clear and consistent report of a recognizable crime. A witness must be able to communicate effectively and demonstrate an understanding of the difference between truth and falsehood. The witness must be able to perform under stress and face the accused in open court. These demands are often taxing even for adult witnesses, not to mention children. We next discuss these demands in relation to children's abilities.

Language Skills

The system expects that witnesses possess sufficient language skills to translate their memories into words and convey what happened in a question–answer format. As reviews of courtroom transcripts and the example at the beginning of this chapter highlight, child witnesses are often asked questions that are semantically and syntactically too complex for them to comprehend about concepts too abstract for them to understand (Brennan & Brennan, 1988; Goodman et al, 1989; Saywitz, Jaenicke, & Comparo, 1990; Shuy, 1986). Yet, young children have a limited ability to monitor comprehension of incoming questions or to cope with instances of noncomprehension (Dickson, 1981; Flavell, Speer, Green, & August, 1981; Markman, 1977, 1979). They often fail to evaluate their own utterances or those of others for possible errors, inconsistencies, or contradictions (Flavell, 1981; Singer & Flavell, 1981). In short, they may not recognize when they do not understand the question and may fail to request clarification. They may not recognize when they have been misunderstood by others and may take no steps to correct the misunderstanding. These circumstances can obscure the fact-finding process.

Memory Skills

The system also requires that witnesses possess sufficient memory skills to provide complete, accurate, and organized reports. Even 3-year-olds can provide accurate information about personally experienced, real-life events that would be meaningful in a criminal investigation (Fivush, Gray, & Fromhoff, 1987; Miller & Sperry, 1988). Although young children's free recall (e.g., responses to the question "what happened?") is found to be quite accurate, it is also incomplete in comparison to older children's and adults' free recall. We are all familiar with the skeletal nature of young children's narrative reports: "What did you do after school?" "I played." More information is forthcoming when adults ask specific questions. "Where did you play?" "In the backyard." "Who was there?" "Joan and Mary," and so forth. Children's brevity results, at least in part, from the need for cues to stimulate reporting of additional information (see Pipe, Gee, & Wilson, Chapter 2, this volume). However, specific questions may generate not only cues to accurate information but also unintended increases in errors, especially errors concerning details of an event (Ceci, Ross, & Toglia, 1987a; Goodman & Reed, 1986). Recall of details is often important in order to file charges, identify suspects, and locate events in time and place.

Resistance to Suggestion

The system also expects child witnesses to possess the cognitive and social–emotional skills necessary to resist potentially misleading questions from authority figures. Although studies do not find children over 10 to 11 years of age to be more susceptible to suggestion than adults, 3-year-olds have been reported to have more difficulty resisting misleading questions than do older children or adults (Ceci et al., 1987a; Zaragoza, 1987). Although studies suggest that 4- to 9-year-olds can be highly resistant to leading questions about central aspects of events and abuse-related experiences (Rudy & Goodman, 1991; Saywitz, Goodman, Nicholas, & Moan, 1991), their susceptibility to some types of misleading information may compromise a subset of their responses, especially those about peripheral details (Goodman & Reed, 1986; Saywitz et al., 1991).

Knowledge of the Legal System

The system also expects that witnesses have some knowledge of the judicial process in order to participate with competence and credibility.

An understanding of the system provides a frame of reference from which to make sense of the experience and the expectations of adults. Victims often cope with the stress of testifying by using their knowledge of the system and the purpose of adjudication to put fears in perspective, perhaps minimizing negative effects on performance. Studies of age-related trends suggest that children under 10 years of age may have limited knowledge of the legal system with misconceptions that lead to false expectations or unrealistic fears (Flin, Stevenson, & Davies, 1989; Sas, 1991; Saywitz, 1989; Saywitz, Jaenicke, & Camparo, 1990; Spencer & Flin, 1990; Warren-Leubecker, Tate, Hinton, & Ozbek, 1989). For example, in several studies, researchers have found that children feared that they would be sent to jail if they made even a minor mistake on the stand (Flin et al., 1989; Saywitz, 1989). A lack of knowledge of the legal system may hinder children's abilities to testify by fostering unrealistic expectations and misguided beliefs, lack of metacognitive awareness of task demands, and anxiety related to the unknown and unfamiliar. Social-motivational theories of memory suggest that beliefs, attitudes, and expectations can interfere with memory performance (Paris, 1988). For example, if children believe that the consequences for memory failure are minimal, they may behave in such a way as to end the situation as soon as possible, putting little effort into generating and implementing retrieval strategies.

Emotional Factors

Moreover, the system requires child witnesses to perform to the best of their ability despite emotional factors that may interfere with optimal performance in the forensic context. Witnesses must have emotional maturity sufficient to cope with the anxiety of an unfamiliar situation. They must be able to overcome several possible fears, including fear of public speaking and scrutiny, losing control, embarrassment, and rejection by peers. Child witnesses have expressed such fears (Sas, 1991; Saywitz & Nathanson, in press; Spencer & Flin, 1990). Other prominent fears noted by child witnesses are of testifying on the stand, being screamed at in court, not being believed, facing the accused who might lie in court, and, especially in cases of intrafamilial abuse, angering family members (Sas, 1991). Studies show certain aspects of participation are also experienced as stressful by child witnesses, such as number of interviews, unfamiliarity of interviewers, duration of the case, and, of course, removal from home (Goodman, et al., 1989; Runyan et al., 1988; Spencer & Flin, 1990; Tedesco & Schnell, 1987).

The link between emotional factors and performance in the forensic context is not fully understood. Recently, proponents of motivated-remembering theories have hypothesized that the discrepancy between children's memory capability and memory performance may be mediated by emotions (Paris, 1988; Saywitz, Goodman, Nicholas, & Moan, 1991; Verdonik, 1988). Emotions may affect testimony in at least four ways. First, memory for emotionally laden material, like traumatic events, may be heightened or impaired in comparison to memory for innocuous stimuli. Studies tend to show few effects of stress on memory or slightly positive effects (Goodman, Hirschman, Hepps, & Rudy, 1991; Oschner & Zaragoza, 1988; Warren-Leubecker & Springfield, 1987) but one researcher has consistently shown negative effects (Peters, 1991).

A second way in which emotions may affect testimony concerns affective states at the time of retrieval (e.g., anxiety related to the courtroom atmosphere). There is evidence to suggest that children's reports are less complete in the courtroom context or in front of the accused than are those of agemates in other settings (Dent, 1977; Hill & Hill, 1987; Peters, 1991; Saywitz & Nathanson, in press). Emotions present at the time of retrieval could render memories temporarily inaccessible, lead to inefficient memory searches, or result in an inability to generate needed retrieval strategies. Such emotions might also lead to inconsistencies between courtroom testimony and out-of-court statements made under less stressful conditions.

Third, strategies for coping with emotions may interfere with memory performance (Paris, 1988). For example, the coping pattern of "defensive avoidance," employed when aversive consequences are anticipated, could lead to insufficient levels of energy and motivation applied to a memory task (Mann & Janis, 1982). "Hypervigilance," a coping pattern in which people panic and seize impulsively on solutions to achieve immediate relief, could result in an illogical search for retrieval methods. It is possible that childern, due to normal limits on their emtional maturity, resort to the use of such strategies, which could impair their ability to give reliable and complete testimony (Cramer, 1991).

Fourth, children's testimony may be further compromised by preexisting emotional disorders that affect concentration, motivation, self-esteem, and mood, like clinical depression or negative psychological effects from abuse. Although children's responses to abuse vary widely (Beitchman, Zucker, Hood, Da Costa, & Akman, 1991; Browne & Finkelhor, 1986), some children experience sequelae that could influence their testimony, such as flashbacks of the trauma that accompany Posttraumatic Stress Disorder and result in children's reliving, not merely retelling, what happened. In sum, emotions may influence testimony through a variety of mechanisms that are only beginning to be explored experimentally and theoretically.

Summary

A task analysis of testifying suggests that children's communication, memory, social, cognitive, and emotional abilities all influence children's testimony. A child's ability to meet the impinging demands of the legal system varies depending on developmental factors (e.g., stage of language and memory development), individual differences (e.g., premorbid emotional functioning, family functioning), and situational factors (e.g., whether the child was a victim or bystander, exposure to force or threats, the availability of protective measures in court).

RESEARCH ON PREPARATION

When attorneys prepare children for court, they typically provide a tour of the courtroom and perhaps a cursory review of the facts of the case. Despite the lack of empirical evidence, these steps are assumed to decrease anxiety and improve performance on the stand. Attorneys usually feel they have done their job after escorting a young witness through the courtroom and saying, for example, "There's the jury box. That's where the judge sits." This is only the beginning. Such an introduction addresses neither an explanation of the investigative or judicial process nor the challenges child witnesses face within the legal system.

There are few programs designed to prepare children for the investigative or judicial process, and those that do exist are rarely empirically based. Few techniques have been tested; hence, their efficacy is unknown. Further, it is difficult to determine which, if any, of the components of these programs actually improve children's performance and reduce stress. The published literature on preparing child witnesses is mainly limited to anecdotal accounts and clinical suggestions (Bauer, 1983; Wolfe, Sas, & Wilson, 1987).

One important exception is a recently completed clinical study suggesting that preparation may increase conviction rates and lower child witnesses' fears (Sas, 1991). In this study, preparation of child abuse victims focused on demystifying the process with education about the legal system and reducing children's anxiety with techniques such as relaxation training. Although promising, this study could not test the effects of preparation on memory performance; we can safely assume that, in most cases, there was no objective record of the crime under investigation against which to compare children's testimony.

On the one hand, clinical studies with actual witnesses must comprise a substantial part of any program of research designed to make recommendations to the judicial system. On the other hand, methods must also be tested in a rigorous manner to examine their effects on the accuracy of children's reports, both intended positive effects and unintended negative effects. To whatever extent possible, research and development of preparation methods should take into consideration (1) the ecological validity of stimuli, retention tests, and retention intervals; (2) theories of memory and development; (3) the emotional needs of child victim/witnesses; (4) the constraints of the legal process (e.g., rules of evidence); and (5) the rights of the accused.

In an ideal world, not only would preparation improve children's performance and reduce their stress, it would be neither time-consuming nor costly. It could be implemented by professionals and lay advocates alike. Techniques would be tested to ensure that they are devoid of unintended side effects before generalization to the legal setting. Despite our best intentions, a long process of revision and refinement would likely be needed to ensure that preparation does no harm.

At every turn, preparation would be distinguished from coaching. Care would be taken to protect the rights of the accused and to avoid the possibility or appearance of contamination. Although in many cases, preparation may require some prudent discussion of the facts of the case, much could be accomplished with minimal discussion of the case by preparing children for the task demands of the forensic context itself. Such an approach may be limited, especially with witnesses who are highly vulnerable due to psychiatric disturbance from severe abuse, but it is still extremely useful in numerous cases.

There are many places to turn for both theoretical and empirical guidance to begin a program of research in this area. A cognitive–behavioral perspective might predict success with stress inoculation training, desensitization, and guided imagery (Meichenbaum, 1985). Educational efforts to guide children's expectations and beliefs about what will happen and why may also improve children's memory performance. From a family-systems perspective, efforts to reduce the anxiety of parents and siblings who would otherwise continue to stimulate the child witness' anxiety would be most worthwhile. A psychodynamic approach might recommend doll play with a model of a courtroom to identify a child's fears, wishes, and conflicts about testifying. Regardless of the approach chosen, the methods should be well grounded in theory and empirically tested with regard to their effect on memory performance. The remainder of this chapter focuses on three sample studies that turn to the literature in developmental psychology for direction in developing and testing methods for preparing child witnesses.

RESEARCH ON IMPROVING THE
COMPLETENESS OF CHILDREN'S REPORTS

Children bring both strengths and weaknesses to the stand. Their reports are often quite accurate but also quite incomplete. Given this situation, how can adults help children report events more fully without influencing what is reported? Previous attempts to improve children's memory performance have been successful in constrained laboratory settings on tasks such as paired associate learning (see Schneider & Pressley, 1989, for a comprehensive review). Unfortunately, in memory-training studies, the to-be-remembered stimuli are typically innocuous pictures, word lists, or stories, not personally salient, real-life events in which children are participants. In these studies, retention intervals are very short, unlike the weeks or months child witnesses often wait before being interviewed. Further, children in memory-training studies usually know ahead of time that their memory will be tested, unlike child witnesses who are unaware at the time of the event that they will need to retrieve the information at a later date. The children are representative of the norm, not children who might be suffering the psychological effects of abuse. Thus, for the most part, these studies fail to address the discrepancy noted earlier between memory ability and memory performance mediated by motivational, social, and communicative factors salient in the forensic context (Garbarino et al., 1989; Paris, 1988; Saywitz, Goodman, Nicholas, & Moan, 1991).

Having called the reader's attention to these limitations on generalization, it is important to note that the memory-training studies do provide a wealth of information through the rigor and control found only in the laboratory. These studies suggest that external cues, categorization, and metamemory strategies, when accompanied by a rationale for their use, aid children's recall (e.g., Bartlett, 1932; Fivush, Hudson, & Nelson, 1984; Kobasigawa, 1974, 1977; Kurtz & Borkowski, 1984; Lodico, Ghatala, Levin, Pressley, & Bell, 1983; Pressley, Forrest-Pressley, & Elliot-Faust, 1988; Pressley, Ross, Levin, & Ghatala, 1984; Ryan, Hegion, & Flavell, 1970).

Effect of Preparation on Completeness of Free Recall

In a recent study, Saywitz, Snyder, and Lamphear (1990) used these methods to prepare children to report a past event. Attention was paid to ecological validity for generalization to the forensic context. In a previous study, interviews with child witnesses, ages 4 to 14 years, led to speculation that younger children have poorly elaborated schemata for the forensic task before them (Saywitz, 1989). It was hypothesized that young children are unaware of the types of information or the level of detail required of them in forensic questioning. In the present study, children were trained to use external visual cues to remind them to report a specified level of detail from categories of information that would be useful in a criminal investigation. The categories represented a schema for organizing recall and are a version of the Stein and Glenn (1978) story grammar. The categories included setting, participants, conversations, affective states, actions, and consequences (Nelson, Fivush, Hudson, & Lucariello, 1983; Stein & Glenn, 1978).

One hundred and thirty-two children (sixty-five 7- to 8-year-olds; sixty-seven 10- to 11-year-olds) were randomly assigned to one of three treatment groups: (1) narrative elaboration intervention; (2) instruction-based intervention; or (3) control group. Children in the narrative elaboration group were given training (described below) to increase the completeness of their reports. Children in the instruction-based intervention group were told to be as complete and accurate as possible, to report incidences of novelty, and to report the beginning, middle, and end of the event. This group was included because researchers have found that instructing adults (Geiselman, Fisher, MacKinnon, & Holland, 1985; Fisher, Geiselman, & Amador, 1989) and even children (Geiselman, Saywitz, & Bornstein, Chapter 4, this volume; Saywitz, Geiselman, & Bornstein, 1992; Wellman, Fabricus, & Wan, 1987; Wellman, Ritter, & Flavell, 1975; Yussen, 1974) to be more detailed during interviews increases completeness of reports. Children in the control group did not receive any training or special instructions. Children in all three groups were later questioned and the accuracy of their testimony compared.

At the start of the study, all children participated in a videotaped classroom event designed to be rich in detail and action as well as emotionally involving. Professional actors were hired to depict student teachers who came into the classroom for 30 minutes to teach a history lesson. Midway through, a confederate teacher entered, accusing one teacher of taking his materials without asking. She had already distributed the materials to the class who then became involved in the problem and its resolution, the latter accomplished through appropriate social problem-solving skills. The event was fairly salient and compelling. In some classes children clapped when the disagreement was resolved.

Two weeks later, half-hour training or placebo sessions took place at the schools. A brief description of the narrative elaboration training follows: Children were taught that there are better and worse ways to do things by having them compare a tiger they drew freehand and one drawn with a stencil. This was done to provide a rationale for strategy usage. Then children were told that similarly, there are better and worse ways to recount a past event. It was explained that a good way to tell everything remembered is to tell about the parts of what happened. Then children were taught the five parts (categories) mentioned previously from the story-recall literature. Each category corresponded to a schematic drawing on a card (see Figure 6.1). After learning the name

"Who was there?"
Participants

"Where did it happen?"
Setting

"What happened?"
Actions

"What were they saying and feeling?"
Conversation/Affective State

FIGURE 6.1. Sample of reminder cards used to prepare for questioning.

and purpose of each "reminder" card, children viewed and then recalled videotaped vignettes, using the cards to remind them to describe each category in a specified level of detail. They also practiced with autobiographical memories.

For example, the setting card was referred to as the "where" card. It depicted a sketch of a generic house beside a tree. Children practiced using the card to remind themselves to include details about characteristics of the setting in their free recall of the vignette (indoors–outdoors, time of day, weather, etc.), with the examiner providing feedback on accuracy and modeling level of detail expected in the forensic context. To discourage task-inefficient responses, children were cautioned not to guess or push themselves too hard for details that might be inaccurate. The same was repeated for the "who" card (participants), the "feelings/saying" card (affective states and conversations), and the others. After mastering each card individually, children practiced using the entire set by retelling a recent school event and a final videotaped vignette.

One day later, there was a brief booster session for all groups after which all children were interviewed about the classroom event with (1) a free-recall task, (2) a cued-recall task during which they were allowed to use the reminder cards if they liked, and (3) open-ended questions. A checklist for coding children's free-recall data was developed by applying Turner and Greene's (1977) propositional analytic system to the script of the staged classroom event. Although the psychological reality of the levels of representation generated by this system have been well documented in the literature (Kintsch & Van Dijk, 1978; Van Dijk & Kintsch, 1983), the psychological reality of this particular checklist was subjected to a verification study based on Snyder and Downy's (1991) research.

Transcripts of children's responses were coded and compared to videotapes of the classroom event. The results revealed that the group that received the narrative elaboration training package reported significantly more correct units of information in free-recall and cued-recall tasks than did children in the other two groups, who did not differ from each other. This increased free recall was accomplished without significant increases in error rates (see Table 6.1). However, merely instructing 7- to 11-year-olds to be more complete was not effective.

The results of this study demonstrate that the completeness of 7- to 11-year-olds' eyewitness memory can be increased by relatively brief preparation that does not generate an increased rate of error and would not infringe on the rights of the accused if implemented in the forensic context. More complete recall could produce the added benefit of reducing the need for leading questions and consequently the risk of contaminating testimony with preconceived notions.

TABLE 6.1. Mean Number Correct and Incorrect Responses on Free and Cued Recall Tasks by Training Condition

Test	Treatment condition		
	Training[a]	Instructions[b]	Control[c]
Free recall			
Number correct	16.23	10.96	12.29
Number incorrect	0.98	0.45	0.53
Cued recall			
Number correct	5.33	1.45	1.77
Number incorrect	0.27	0.03	0.11

Note. Cued recall scores were comprised only of nonredundant information elicited with reminder cards in addition to initial free recall.
[a]n = 45; [b]n = 40; [c]n = 47.

Although the intervention was successful in the context of this experiment, young children have a limited ability to transfer new skills to unfamiliar situations, such as the courtroom, unless given reminders or cues (Borkowski & Cavanaugh, 1979; Schneider & Pressley, 1989). Thus, we anticipate that child witnesses would need to be reminded to use the strategies immediately before they begin an investigative interview or courtroom examination. Although this is not a feasible approach to initial emergency interviews, comprehensive interviews are typically conducted at later dates and often there is time for preparation by the professional who conducts the interview. In addition, advance preparation and reminders are feasible when attorneys or advocates prepare children for depositions or courtroom examinations.

Although it may seem unusual for children to use visual cues to aid retrieval in front of a jury, this should be no more problematic than the use of other demonstrative tools such as drawings that are frequently used to supplement children's limited language skills. Moreover, the majority of interviews and examinations children undergo are not in front of juries in criminal cases. Use of visual cues in the present study represents one example of a technique that could be pursued to improve children's reports through preparation.

RESEARCH ON IMPROVING RESISTANCE TO MISLEADING QUESTIONS

Two previous laboratory studies have shown reductions in children's suggestibility. In one study, researchers reduced the status differential between questioner and witness when 7-year-olds presented misleading questions to preschoolers. Suggestibility was decreased although not eliminated (Ceci, Ross, & Toglia, 1987b). In another study, children were warned that questions might be tricky and instructed to tell only what they really remembered. A small increase in resistance to misleading questions was induced (Warren, Hulse-Trotter, & Tubbs, 1991). Although encouraging, both of these studies involved story recall, not memory for real-world events in which children participate. Children's perceptions of the interviewer's knowledge of the story were not controlled. In the latter study, children were aware that their memory would later be tested. As practical methods of reducing suggestibility, these procedures would be problematic to implement without potentially violating the rights of the accused or rules of evidence and procedure.

As these and other studies have indicated, suggestibility appears to be multiply determined by the interaction among mnemonic, social, and emotional factors (Goodman, Rudy, Bottoms, & Aman, 1990; Zaragoza, 1987). Some determinants of suggestibility, such as the strength of the initial memory trace, may be difficult, if not impossible, to modify. Others may be more amenable to intervention. Saywitz, Moan, and Lamphear (1991) postulated that one potential contributor to children's suggestibility might not be difficult to modify. This was children's expectations and beliefs about the rules for sociolinguistic interaction in the forensic context.

Because children have limited knowledge of the legal system and they rely on everyday rules of communication even in the forensic context, they may fail to appreciate that adults are operating under quite a different set of sociolinguistic principles. The result may be a gap between the child's view and the adult's view of the task before them, a gap that could contribute to children's increased suggestibility.

Children develop an understanding of the functions of language and the rules for conversation gradually with age (Irwin, 1982). For example, listeners assume speakers are sincere unless presented with information to the contrary (Grice, 1975). Children under 9 to 13 years of age tend to interpret all remarks as sincere (Demorest, Meyer, Phelps, Gardner, & Winner, 1984). Due to the adversarial nature of the judicial process, unexpected violations of the "sincerity postulate" are likely to be frequent. Failure to understand the speaker's intent due to limited role-taking skills and limited knowledge of the legal system could influence how readily children acquiesce to misleading questions.

Children may expect that adults ask questions to which they already know the answer. This is common with teachers and parents. In fact, with leading questions, by definition, the answer is implied in the question. Children may come to trust the adult's knowledge base more than their own, undermining their confidence in their own view of the event in question.

Effect of Preparation on Resistance to Misleading Questions

In a study by Saywitz, Moan, and Lamphear (1991), fifty-five 7-year-olds (34 males, 21 females) from public schools were assigned randomly to one of two treatment conditions: (1) training group—training to resist misleading questions (n = 28) or (2) control group—motivating instructions for children to do their best (n = 27). Children participated in a staged event described previously in Saywitz, Snyder, and Lamphear, 1990. Two weeks later, they individually participated in training or placebo sessions and were then interviewed about the classroom event with a standardized questionnaire composed of misleading, nonleading, and correctly leading questions.

The training was designed to expose children to an alternate set of expectations and beliefs about answering questions. First, children read a story about a child who goes along with others' questions for a variety of social and emotional reasons (e.g., doesn't want to hurt their feelings, is intimidated). Each time there are negative consequences. Finally, the character learns that it is best to tell the truth. Children discuss having had similar feelings and experiences. Next, in response to vignettes, children practice answering leading questions posed in the vignettes by police officers. The children receive explicit feedback and modeling. For example, "What would you say if you were the boy in the story and the policeman asked you this question . . . ?" Researchers reinforced resistance to suggestive questions that referred to the story: "Good, you said you didn't know instead of guessing or going along with his question." Acquiescence to a suggestion was responded to with comments like, "Sometimes kids feel like they should go along with an adult's question. They might feel scared to say something different. Like when Mary had to tell the principal he made a mistake."

Last, children watched a videotape and their memory was tested with leading and nonleading questions about what happened in the tape. To counter the belief that they must answer each question or else adopt the adult's version when they were unsure, children were told that they might not know all the answers and warned that some questions would be hard and to be on guard against being fooled by questions. We have come to believe that it is best to define a leading question to children as one in which the speaker puts a guess or hope into the question, explaining the speaker's intent in terms of his or her job in the legal setting (e.g., to bring out all the facts so that the wrong person won't be punished). To change beliefs about consequences for error and to increase children's confidence in their own knowledge, unintended consequences of acquiesence were highlighted, for example, that the wrong person might get punished if witnesses acquiesce to suggestions by questioners who were not present at the event under investigation. Children were told the goal was to tell the truth, not to please the adult.

Suggestibility was measured by the proportion of incorrect responses to misleading questions. Correctly leading and nonleading questions were included to measure unintended effects on such questions. The training group made significantly fewer errors than did the control group on misleading questions, indicating that they "resisted" the suggestions more often and that the training was successful in reducing false responses (see Table 6.2).

Surprisingly, the control group responded correctly more frequently than did the training group to nonleading and correctly leading questions, suggesting that the training had the unintended effect of lowering correct responses on these questions. Instead, the training group responded more frequently with "I don't know" than did the control group. This is not surprising because they were trained to say "I don't know" when they did not know the answer, instead of

TABLE 6.2. Mean Proportion Correct, Incorrect, and "Don't Know/Remember" Responses by Treatment Condition

Responses	Treatment condition	
	Training	Control
Misleading		
Correct	0.45	0.42
Incorrect	0.39	0.53**
Don't know/remember	0.15	0.05*
Correctly leading		
Correct	0.73	0.82**
Incorrect	0.18	0.15
Don't know/remember	0.09	0.03*
Nonleading		
Correct	0.56	0.62*
Incorrect	0.31	0.34
Don't know/remember	0.13	0.03*

$*p < 0.05$. $**p < 0.01$.

guessing or going along with the suggestion. However, the training may have created a response set and children may have been more cautious in responding than necessary. This cautioussness may reflect overgeneralization of the "I don't know/remember" strategy to leading questions even when the suggestion was in the correct direction. Such cautiousness may also result in reduced correct guesses on nonleading questions. Still, it could be argued that admitting "I don't know/ remember" is a better method of coping with an uncomfortable situation than acquiescence.

In sum, results indicated that the training group showed a 26% decline in percentage of error in response to misleading questions relative to the control group, without generating an increase in acquiescence errors to other types of questions. Overgeneralization of the "I don't know" strategy demonstrates the need for rigorous testing of interventions used with child witnesses. Unintended side effects must be identified and eliminated through revision, refinement, and retesting.

A replication study by Moan (1991) modifying the training package to focus on when and how to apply resistance strategies suggested that the decline in correct responses can be eliminated. For example, in her study, an attempt was made to focus children's attention on the content and truth value of each question. Children were encouraged to trust their memories and were instructed that when they knew the answer they were to tell it. They were vigorously reinforced for correct responses to nontarget questions with comments like "Good, you knew the answer and you told it." The training group showed reduced error to nonleading as well as misleading questions, without reductions in correct responses on any question type.

Neither of these studies tested whether children's expectations changed. Future studies need to focus on developing measures to identify changes in children's beliefs and expectations about the rules of sociolinguistic interaction in the forensic context as well as the relationship between such expectations and memory performance.

In the present study, error on misleading questions was reduced but not eliminated. The effect size was modest. This is not surprising if, as mentioned previously, suggestibility is multiply determined. Of course, many determinants are difficult to modify in real cases. However, if preparation can prevent instances of children agreeing to untrue statements in the forensic context, it merits serious consideration. Thus, despite the difficulty inherent in addressing such a multifaceted phenomenon, further research into efforts to reduce children's suggestibility is warranted.

RESEARCH ON IMPROVING CHILDREN'S COMPREHENSION SKILLS

The ability to monitor whether you fully understand what others are communicating to you is often referred to as comprehension monitoring. It is a skill that develops gradually with age. Preschoolers may recognize when they are having difficulty understanding the utterances of others; they may be able to implement strategies for resolving such difficulties. However, they are primarily able to do so in naturalistic settings when tasks and stimuli are simple and familiar and require nonverbal responses to physically present referents (Gallagher, 1981; Garvey, 1977; Revelle, Wellman, & Karabenick, 1985). In contrast, in experimental studies, where settings, tasks, and stimuli tend to be complex, verbal, and unfamiliar, young children have difficulty detecting the adequacy of questions, may not know when they have failed to understand a question, and rarely recognize ambiguous messages or request clarification from adults (Asher, 1976; Cosgrove & Patterson, 1978; Ironsmith & Whitehurst, 1978; Markman, 1977; Patterson, Massad, & Cosgrove, 1978). Children may demonstrate similar difficulties in the forensic context because the task taxes not only comprehension but also memory: The setting is unfamiliar, lacks physically present referents, and relies on questions that are not well matched to the child's level of language development.

Efforts to improve comprehension monitoring in the laboratory have not been conducted in the context of an interview about a past real-life event. Previous studies to enhance comprehension monitoring have come from disparate fields, focusing on reading comprehension (Capelli & Markman, 1982; Harris, Kruithof, Terwogt, & Visser, 1981), referential communication games (Cosgrove & Patterson, 1978), and language-impaired children (Dollaghan & Kaston, 1986). Therefore, the relation between improved comprehension monitoring skills and memory performance remains unknown.

Based on current theories of cognition (Dickson, 1981), the developmental literature suggests several factors that influence comprehension monitoring. Children's comprehension monitoring may be improved by manipulating the following listener variables: (1) metacognitive knowledge of task demands (Borkowski, Carr, & Pressley, 1987; Flavell, 1981; Harris et al., 1981; Schneider & Pressley, 1989) and response consequences (Deshler, Alley, Warner, & Schumaker, 1981; Paris, 1988); (2) motivation (Borkowski, Millstead, & Hale, 1988; Markman, 1977; Paris, 1988); (3) rationale for strategy usage (Pressley et al., 1984; Reid & Borkowski, 1985), and (4) perception of the speaker's intent (Ackerman, 1986a, 1986b). Message variables, such as message complexity, also have been identified and can be manipulated to increase the frequency with which children detect and react to noncomprehension (Flavell et al., 1981; Patterson, O'Brien, Kister, Carter, & Kotsonis, 1981).

Effect of Preparation on Comprehension Monitoring

Preliminary results from a recent study address the question of how to improve children's comprehension monitoring. Saywitz and Snyder (1991) examined how children cope when they do not understand a question about a past event and whether their performance can be improved by preparation. The authors speculated on the basis of pilot data that whether or not children are aware that they do not comprehend a question, they are likely to try to answer the question anyway. Their response may be an association to a part of the question that was understood, but not necessarily the answer to the intended question.

One hundred and eighty-six children, half 6- and half 8-year-olds, were randomly assigned within age group to one of three treatment conditions (training, instructions, control) and one of two interviewer conditions (trainer, unfamiliar authority). Children participated in the same classroom event as described previously (Saywitz, Snyder, & Lamphear, 1990). Two weeks later, children participated in treatment or placebo sessions. Then memory was tested with a set of questions that varied in comprehension difficulty. When children indicated that they did not understand a question, it was rephrased using a simpler grammatical construction.

Training focused on several listener variables: (1) expanding metacognitive knowledge of a witness's role (e.g., helper) and the task demands of a question–answer session (e.g., children were warned that they might not understand all the questions); (2) increasing awareness of the unintended consequences of answering questions one does not fully understand; (3) expanding awareness of the speaker's intentions; (4) increasing awareness of the consequences of strategy usage; and (5) providing rationales for putting forth the energy to employ the strategies.

First, children viewed videotaped vignettes that demonstrated a mind-set about the interview context focusing on the role of the witness, speaker's intent, and cost of error. For example, the first vignette was about a child who witnessed a friend's bicycle being stolen and who is now being interviewed by a policeman. The tape was stopped several times and the researcher discussed with the child that some of the questions were easy and some were hard, some were well understood and some misunderstood. It was explained that some adults are not used to talking to children; they are used to talking to other adults. Other vignettes followed, with examples and discussion focused on the cost of trying to answer a question one does not understand (e.g., missing out on a desired field trip, getting the wrong meal at a restaurant, making mistakes).

The next section of training focused on detecting incomprehensible questions. This approach was modeled after Dollaghan and Kaston's (1986) method for improving comprehension monitoring in language-impaired children. Initially, the examiner mumbled or coughed her way through questions. Once children demonstrated an ability to detect such obvious obstacles to comprehension, the examiner introduced intelligible sentences that contained increasingly more complex syntactic structures.

In the last section, children were taught a strategy for coping with noncomprehension once detected. Children were taught that they could elicit a rephrased question by telling the adult that they did not understand and by putting out their hand in the same manner a policeman does to stop traffic and saying, "I don't get it. What do you mean?" They practiced applying this response to questions that varied in comprehensibility, regarding memory for a previously viewed video. Explicit feedback was provided. Inhibition of task-inappropriate or task-inefficient responses (e.g., guessing) was encouraged.

Motivating instructions were used with the control group to provide them with an experience comparable to that of the training group (i.e., insuring similar tasks and effort) but not specific to comprehension monitoring. Also, children in both groups were reinstructed to use what they learned (i.e., trying their hardest or using the strategy). This was done because studies of memory training suggest that generalization is promoted by such prompts (see Schneider & Pressley, 1989, for a review).

The role of interviewer was varied because it was expected that children might apply what they learned to please only the person who taught them, but fail to use the new behavior in interviews with other adults. Thus, in order to test both near and far transfer of newly acquired skills, half the children were interviewed by the person who conducted the training (near). The other half were interviewed by an unfamiliar person who posed as the college professor of the student teachers (far). To heighten meaningfulness and perceived consequences of error, she said she needed to use the children's reports to grade her students.

To create the questionnaire, a preliminary study had been conducted with an additional 66 children to ensure that the information tested was relatively easy to recall when questions were phrased simply (Saywitz & Snyder, 1991). Then half the questions were rephrased in difficult-to-comprehend form. For example, "What were the markers in?" became "What were the markers that were given to the class to use to decorate the scarves for your dance costume in?" Question forms were modeled after transcripts of child witness direct- and cross-examinations in actual cases.

Preliminary results on data from 126 children indicated that when children in the control group were confronted with difficult-to-comprehend questions about easily recalled information, they tried to answer anyway, even when they were unlikely to have understood the question. Despite their effort, they were as likely to respond incorrectly as correctly (see Table 6.3). Children in the training group tended to tell the examiner when they did not understand a question and requested that it be rephrased. When these and other less frequently used strategies were combined, training group children responded correctly significantly more often (M = 12.38) and made significantly fewer errors (M = 1.94) than did children in the control group (M = 6.51 and M = 6.05, respectively).

On the easy-to-comprehend questions, the groups performed comparably, suggesting that the training itself had no adverse effects on nontarget questions. Future analyses of the "instructions" group should illuminate to what degree results are a function of changing

TABLE 6.3. Mean Number of Correct and Incorrect Responses to Difficult to Comprehend Questions by Common Response Strategies

Response strategy	Treatment condition[a]	
	Training	Control
Try to answer		
Correct	1.97	4.55
Incorrect	1.17	5.32
Ask for rephrase		
Correct	9.73	0.62
Incorrect	0.60	0.02
Ask for repetition		
Correct	0.03	0.22
Incorrect	0.01	0.19

Note. Total number of difficult to comprehend questions was 15.
[a]Each treatment condition comprised of 63 subjects.

children's perceptions of task demands with instructions alone and to what degree results are a function of training in detection and coping with noncomprehension.

These results highlight the potential for communication breakdown when children are asked, and try to answer, questions they do not fully understand. The data imply that adults should not rely on children to monitor their own comprehension to inform adults of a misunderstanding. Although children's limited communication skills present a barrier to reliable testimony, perhaps it is one that can be minimized by advance preparation.

FUTURE RESEARCH

In all three of the the studies reported here, there are noteworthy limits on generalization to the courtroom setting. For example, in the latter study, the interview may have been more heavily loaded with difficult-to-comprehend questions than is the average forensic interview. Also, the courtroom context involves additional demands on children's processing skills that may make it more difficult to apply newly learned skills in that setting. Clearly a great deal more research is necessary before these methods can be adapted for forensic application. Further research is also necessary to fully understand the precise mechanisms by which preparation affects testimony. These studies demonstrate the value of preparation methods that are based on developmental theory, using ecologically valid methodologies subjected to empirical testing. The results suggest the potential for children to be prepared for questioning in such a way that it is likely to enhance their competence as participants in the judicial process without infringing on the rights of the accused.

Future researchers will need to attend not only to the development of more ecologically valid paradigms, the constraints of the legal system, the rights of the accused, and the emotional reactions of victim/witnesses, but also to an expansion of current theories of children's memory. The theories that guide preparation efforts must encompass the social, emotional, and motivational factors salient in the forensic context. For example, we should strive to develop theories that can explain the effects of ambivalence on children's testimony (e.g., on the testimony of children who are asked to testify against a parent on whom they depend for emotional and physical survival). Theories need to address moments of inadequate information processing and skewed coping patterns. These may arise when children with immature or disturbed psychological functioning try to recall emotionally laden information in stressful social situations. For example, Paris (1988) has postulated that if a memory task is perceived as a threat to self-esteem, the effort to remember may be reduced. What are the implications of this hypothesis for the effects on testimony of a cross-examiner's attempts at impeachment and character defamation? Preparation may need to focus on children's self-image, their perceptions of recall- strategy utility, perceptions of the effort required, analysis of whether successful recall is worth the effort, and beliefs about the consequences (rewards or punishments) of reporting. Such an approach would need to be based on a model of everyday remembering that views memory performance as embedded within a complex network of expectations, goals, and motivations.

CREATING A CLOSER MATCH

The ability of a child to provide competent testimony is determined not only by the child's strengths and weaknesses but also by the formal and informal procedures of the system, and the training and sensitivity of the professionals involved. How can a better match between task requirements and children's abilities be achieved? Our research has led us to postulate two paths for closing this gap: modifications from the "top down" (adult to child) and from the "bottom up" (child to adult).

Top down solutions involve additional training for legal professionals regarding the norms of child development—perhaps a specialization of pediatric law for attorneys who represent minors and also for judicial officers who pursue a career in courts that frequently hear cases involving children. For example, judges who monitor children's direct and cross-examinations should be able to require rephrasing questions into grammatical constructions that children can understand. Similarly, juvenile detectives or attorneys who routinely question child witnesses should be trained in relevant aspects of cognitive development so as to be aware of the ages at which children typically learn to count, tell time, and so forth. These skills are often required to respond to questions intended to determine charges, jurisdictions, identifications, and alibis. These types of accommodations do not raise ethical or constitutional dilemmas regarding defendant's rights, yet they would help children provide more credible and reliable testimony. Still, these efforts alone would not be sufficient. For most attorneys and judges, child witness cases comprise only a small fraction of their case load. It may not be cost- effective for them to devote too much energy to learning about child development. Moreover, some attorneys may be less than enthusiastic about clarifying children's confusions and simplifying their speech, especially if it is not in the best interest of their client to do so. Thus, in addition to statutory reforms and education of legal professionals at the top of the system, preparing and fortifying children, to whatever degree possible, is probably also necessary.

Bottom-up solutions involve preparing children for the cognitive, communicative, emotional, and social challenges they face as witnesses. A good deal of further investigation, both theoretical and experimental, is needed to identify characteristics and conditions necessary to enhance eyewitness performance and reduce distress. This task requires attention not only to developmental factors but also to individual differences and situational factors that vary across cases. These variables have only begun to be incorporated into our models of the strengths and weaknesses of child witnesses. Closing the gap between system requirements and children's capabilities and needs will require innovative thinking from both researchers and theoreticians in law, public policy, mental health, and psychology. It will be well worth the effort if we can improve the fact-finding process and establish a just and safe environment for both children and adults.

ACKNOWLEDGMENTS

The studies described in this chapter were funded by a grant to Karen J. Saywitz from the National Center on Child Abuse and Neglect, Department of Health and Human Services. We would like to thank Vivian Lamphear, Brenda Burke, Rebecca Nathanson, Michael Espinoza, Richard Romanoff, and Patricia Savich for their contributions. Appreciation is also extended to all the students and research assistants who worked on these projects: Susan Moan, Lorinda Comparo, Sharon Ezop, Maria Bucmaniuk, Kathy Lawrence, Raven Sosnowski, Valerie Ishida, Ephi Betan, Todd Westra, Marjorie Graham-Howard, Mary Hamrick, Saghi Samadani, Andrea Aguiar, Monica Morlan-Magallanes, Eric Hoe, Steve Benson, Kimberly Noyes, Christine Droege, James Nagasaki, and Ricci Ryall. We also thank the faculty, parents, and children of the Redondo Beach and Torrance Unified School Districts, and Coast Christian Schools.

REFERENCES

Ackerman, B. P. (1986a). Interpreting children's responses to ambiguous messages: A reply to Robinson and Whittaker (1985). *Developmental Psychology, 22*, 701–703.

Ackerman, B. P. (1986b). Children's sensitivity to comprehension failure in interpreting a nonliteral use of an utterance. *Child Development, 57*, 485–497.

Asher, S. R. (1976). Children's ability to appraise their own and other person's communication performance. *Developmental Psychology, 12,* 24–32.

Bartlett, F. C. (1932). *Remembering.* Cambridge, England: Cambridge University Press.

Bauer, H. (1983). Preparation of the sexually abused child for court testimony. *Bulletin of the American Academy of Psychiatry and Law, 11*(3), 287–289.

Beitchman, J. H., Zucker, K. J., Hood, J. E., Da Costa, G. A., & Akman, D. (1991). A review of the short-term effects of child abuse. *Child Abuse and Neglect, 15,* 537–556.

Borkowski, J. G., Carr, M., & Pressley, M. (1987). "Spontaneous" strategy use: Perspectives from metacognitive theory. *Intelligence, 11,* 61–75.

Borkowski, J. G., & Cavanaugh, J. C. (1979). Maintenance and generalization of skills and strategies by the retarded. In N. R. Ellis (Ed.), *Handbook of mental deficiency: Psychological theory and research* (pp. 569–617). Hillsdale, NJ: Erlbaum.

Borkowski, J. G., Millstead, M., & Hale, C. (1988). Components of children's metamemory: Implications for strategy generalization. In F. E. Weinert & M. Perlmutter (Eds.), *Memory development: Universal changes and individual differences* (pp. 73–100). Hillsdale, NJ: Erlbaum.

Brainerd, C.J., Reyna, V.F., Howe, M.L., & Kingma, J. (1990). The development of forgetting and reminiscence. *Monographs of the Society for Research in Child Development, 55* (3–4, Serial No. 222).

Brennan, M., & Brennan, R. (1988). *Strange language: Child victims under cross examination.* Riverina, Australia: Charles Stuart University.

Browne, A., & Finkelhor, D. (1986). Impact of child sexual abuse: A review of the research. *Psychological Bulletin, 99,* 66–77.

Capelli, C. A., & Markman, E. M. (1982). Suggestions for training comprehension monitoring. *Topics in learning & learning disabilities, 2*(1), 87–96.

Ceci, S., Ross, D., & Toglia, M. (1987a). Suggestibility of children's memory: Psycholegal implications. *Journal of Experimental Psychology: General, 116* (1), 38–49.

Ceci, S., Ross, D., & Toglia, M. (1987b). Age differences in suggestibility: Narrowing the uncertainties. In S. Ceci, M. Toglia, & D. Ross (Eds.), *Children's eyewitness memory* (pp. 79–91). New York: Springer-Verlag.

Cosgrove, J., & Patterson, C. (1978). Generalization of training for children's listener skills. *Child Development, 49,* 513–516.

Coy v. Idaho, 487 U.S. 1012 (1988).

Cramer, P. (1991). *The development of defense mechanisms.* New York: Springer-Verlag.

Demorest, A., Meyer, C., Phelps, E., Gardner, H., & Winner, E. (1984). Words speak louder than actions: Understanding deliberately false remarks. *Child Development, 55,* 1527–1534.

Dent, H. R. (1977). Stress as a factor influencing person recognition in identification parades. *Bulletin of the British Psychological Society, 30,* 339–340.

Deshler, D. D., Alley, G. R., Warner, M. M., & Schumaker, J. B. (1981). Instructional practices for promoting skill acquisition and generalization in severely learning disabled adolescents. *Learning Disability Quarterly, 4,* 415-421.

Dickson, W.P. (1981). *Children's oral communication skills.* New York: Academic Press.

Dollaghan, C., & Kaston, N. (1986). A comprehension monitoring program for language impaired children. *Journal of Speech and Hearing Disorders, 51,* 264–271.

Federal Rules of Evidence, 611(a)(3)(1975).

Fisher, R. P., Geiselman, R. E., & Amador, M. (1989). Field test of the cognitive interview: Enhancing the recollection of actual victims and witnesses of crime. *Journal of Applied Psychology, 74*(5), 722–727.

Fivush, R., Gray, J., & Fromhoff, F.A. (1987). Two-year-olds talk about the past. *Cognitive Development, 2,* 393–409.

Fivush, R., Hudson, J., & Nelson, K. (1984). Children's long term memory for a novel event: An exploratory study. *Merrill-Palmer Quarterly, 30,* 303-316.

Flavell, J.H. (1981). Cognitive monitoring. In W.P. Dickson (Ed.), *Children's oral communication skills* (pp. 35–60). New York: Academic Press.

Flavell, J. H., Speer, J. R., Green, F. L., & August, D. L. (1981). The development of comprehension monitoring and knowledge about communication. *Monographs of the Society for Research in Child Development, 46* (5, Serial No. 192).

Flin, R., Stevenson, Y., & Davies, G. M. (1989). Children's knowledge of court proceedings. *British Journal of Psychology, 80,* 285–297.

Gallagher, T. (1981). Contingent query sequences within adult–child discourse. *Journal of Child Language, 8,* 51–62.

Garbarino, J., Stott, F.M., & Faculty of the Erikson Institute. (1989). *What children can tell us.* San Francisco: Jossey-Bass.

Garvey, C. (1977). The contingent query: A dependent act in conversation. In M. Lewis & L. Rosenblum (Eds.), *Interaction, conversation and the development of language* (pp. 63-93). New York: Wiley.

Geiselman, R.E., Fisher, R.P., MacKinnon, D.P., & Holland, H.L. (1985). Eyewitness memory enhancement in the police interview: Cognitive retrieval mnemonics versus hypnosis. *Journal of Applied Psychology, 70*(2), 401–412.

Goodman, G. S., Hirschman, J., Hepps, D., & Rudy, L. (1991). Children's memory for stressful events. *Merrill-Palmer Quarterly, 37,* 109–158.

Goodman, G., Pyle, E., Jones, D., England, P., Port, L., Rudy, L., & Prado, L. (1989). *Emotional effects of criminal court testimony on child sexual assault victims* (final report). Washington, DC: National Institute of Justice.

Goodman, G., & Reed, R. (1986). Age differences in eyewitness testimony. *Law and Human Behavior, 10,* 317-332.

Goodman, G., Rudy, L., Bottoms, B., & Aman, C. (1990). Children's concerns and memory: Issues of ecological validity in the study of children's eyewitness testimony. In R. Fivush & J. Hudson (Eds.), *Knowing and remembering in young children* (pp. 249–284). New York: Cambridge University Press.

Grice, P. (1975). Logic and conversation. In R. Cole & J. Morgan (Eds.), *Syntax* and semantics: *Speech acts* (pp. 41–58). New York: Academic Press.

Harris, P. A., Kruithof, A., Terwogt, M. M., & Visser, T. (1981). Children's detection and awareness of textual anomaly. *Journal of Experimental Child Psychology, 31,* 212–230.

Hill, P. E., & Hill, S. M. (1987). Videotaping children's testimony: An empirical view. *Michigan Law Review, 85,* 809–833.

Ironsmith, M., & Whitehurst, G.J. (1978). The development of listener abilities in communication: How children deal with ambiguous information. *Child Development, 49,* 348–352.

Irwin, J. (1982). *Pragmatics: The role in language development.* La Verne, CA: Fox.

Jay, S. M. (1984). Pain in children: An overview of psychological assessment and intervention. In A. Zener, D. Bendell, & C. E. Walker (Eds.), *Health psychology treatment and research issues* (pp. 167–196). New York: Plenum Press.

Kintsch, W., & Van Dijk, T. A. (1978). Toward a model of text comprehension and production. *Psychological Review, 85,* 363–394.

Kobasigawa, A. (1974). Utilization of retrieval cues by children in recall. *Child Development, 45,* 127–134.

Kobasigawa, A. (1977). Retrieval strategies in the development of memory. In R. V. Kail & J. W. Hagen (Eds.), *Perspectives on the development of memory and cognition* (pp. 177–201). Hillsdale, NJ: Erlbaum.

Kurtz, B. E., & Borkowski, J. G. (1984). Children's metacognition: Exploring relations among knowledge, process, and motivational variables. *Journal of Experimental Child Psychology, 43,* 129–148.

Lodico, M. G., Ghatala, E. S., Levin, J. R., Pressley, M., & Bell, J. A. (1983). The effects of strategy-monitoring on children's selection of effective memory strategies. *Journal of Experimental Psychology, 35,* 263–277.

Mann, L., & Janis, I. (1982). Conflict theory of decision making and the expectancy value approach. In N. Feather (Ed.), *Expectations and actions: Expectancy value models in psychology* (pp. 342–364). Hillsdale, NJ: Erlbaum.

Markman, E. M. (1977). Realizing that you don't understand: A preliminary investigation. *Child Development, 48,* 986–992.

Markman, E. M. (1979). Realizing that you don't understand: Elementary school children's awareness of inconsistencies. *Child Development, 50,* 643–655.

Maryland v. Craig, 110 S. Ct. 3157 (1990).

Meichenbaum, D. (1985). *Stress inoculation training.* New York: Pergamon Press.

Miller, P. J., & Sperry, L. L. (1988). Early talk about the past: The origins of conversational stories of personal experience. *Journal of Child Language, 15,* 293–315.

Moan, S. (1991). *Reducing suggestibility in children's eyewitness testimony: A training program to improve children's competence to resist misleading questions and aid retrieval.* Unpublished doctoral dissertation, University of California, Los Angeles.

Myers, J. (1987). *Child witness law and practice.* New York: Wiley.

Nelson, K., Fivush, R., Hudson, J., & Lucariello, J. (1983). Scripts and the development of memory. In M. Chi (Ed.), *Current trends in memory development research* (pp. 52–69). New York: Karger.

Oschner, J. C., & Zaragoza, M. (1988, March). *Children's eyewitness testimony: Accuracy and suggestibility of a memory for a real event.* Paper presented at the Biennial Meeting of the American Psychology-Law Society, Miami, FL.

Paris, S. G. (1988). Motivated remembering. In F. E. Weinert & M. Perlmutter (Eds.), *Memory development: Universal changes and individual differences* (pp. 221–242). Hillsdale, NJ: Erlbaum.

Patterson, C. J., Massad, C. M., & Cosgrove, J. M. (1978). Children's referential communication: Components of plans for effective listening. *Developmental Psychology, 14,* 401–406.

Patterson, C., O'Brien, C., Kister, M., Carter, D., & Kotsonis, M. (1981). Development of comprehension monitoring as a function of context. *Developmental Psychology, 17,* 379–389.

Peters, D. (1991). Confrontational stress and children's testimony. In M. DeSimone & M. Toglia (Chairs), *Living and truthfulness among young children.* Symposium presented at the Society for Research in Child Development Meetings, Seattle, WA.

Pressley, M., Forrest-Pressley, D. J., & Elliot-Faust, D. J. (1988). What is strategy instructional enrichment and how to study it: Illustrations from research on children's prose memory and comprehension. In F.E. Weinert & M. Perlmutter (Eds.), *Memory development: Universal changes and individual differences* (pp. 101–130). Hillsdale, NJ: Erlbaum.

Pressley, M., Ross, K. A., Levin, J. R., & Ghatala, E. S. (1984). The role of strategy utility knowledge in children's strategy decision making. *Journal of Experimental Child Psychology, 38,* 491–504.

Reid, M. K., & Borkowski, J. G. (1985). *The influence of attribution training on strategic behaviors, self management, and beliefs about control in hyperactive children.* Paper presented at the biennial meeting of the Society for Research in Child Development, Toronto, Canada.

Revelle, G. L., Wellman, H. M., & Karabenick, J. D. (1985). Comprehension monitoring in preschool children. *Child Development, 56,* 654–663.

Rudy, L., & Goodman, G. S. (1991). Effects of participation on children's reports: Implications for children's testimony. *Developmental Psychology, 27,* 527–538.

Runyan, D., Everson, M., Edelsohn, G., Hunter, W., & Coulter, M. (1988). Impact of legal intervention on sexually abused children. *Journal of Pediatrics, 113,* 647–653.

Ryan, S. M., Hegion, A. G., & Flavell, J. H. (1970). Nonverbal mnemonic mediation in preschool children. *Child Development, 41,* 539–550.

Sas, L. (1991). *Reducing the system-induced trauma for child sexual abuse victims through court preparation, assessment and follow-up* (Project #4555-1-125). Final Report for the National Welfare Grants Division, Health and Welfare, Canada.

Saywitz, K. J. (1989). Children's conceptions of the legal system: Court is a place to play basketball. In S. J. Ceci, D. F. Ross, & M. P. Toglia (Eds.),

Perspectives on children's testimony (pp. 131–157). New York: Springer-Verlag.

Saywitz, K. J., Geiselman, R. E., & Bornstein, G. (1992). Effects of cognitive interviewing and practice of children's recall. *Journal of Applied Psychology, 77*(5), 744–756.

Saywitz, K. J., Goodman, G. S., Nicholas, E. & Moan, S. (1991). Children's memories of physical examinations involving genital touch: Implications for reports of child sexual abuse. *Journal of Consulting and Clinical Psychology, 59,* 682–691.

Saywitz, K. J., Jaenicke, C., & Camparo, L. (1990). Children's knowledge of legal terminology. *Law and Human Behavior, 14,* 523–535.

Saywitz, K. J., Moan, S., & Lamphear, V. (1991, August). *The effect of preparation on children's resistance to misleading questions.* Paper presented at the annual meeting of the American Psychological Association, San Francisco, CA.

Saywitz, K. J., & Nathanson, R. (in press). Effects of environment on children's testimony and perceived stress. *International Journal of Child Abuse and Neglect.*

Saywitz, K. J., & Snyder, L. (1991, April). *Preparing child witnesses: The efficacy of comprehension monitoring training.* Paper presented at the biennial convention of the Society for Research on Child Development, Seattle, WA.

Saywitz, K. J., Snyder, L., & Lamphear, V. (1990, August). *Preparing child witnesses: The efficacy of memory strategy training.* Paper presented at the annual convention of the American Psychological Association, Boston, MA.

Schneider, W., & Pressley, M. (1989). *Memory development between 2 and 20.* New York: Springer-Verlag.

Shuy, R. W. (1986, August). *Linguistic perspectives on the child sexual abuse interview.* Paper presented at the meeting of the American Psychological Association, Washington, DC.

Singer, J., & Flavell, J. (1981). Development of knowledge about communication: Children's evaluations of explicitly ambiguous messages. *Child Development, 52,* 1211–1215.

Snyder, L., & Downy, D. M. (1991). The language–reading relationship in normal and severely disabled children. *Journal of Speech and Hearing Research, 34,* 129–140.

Spencer, J. R., & Flin, R. (1990). *The evidence of children.* London: Blackstone Press.

Stein, N., & Glenn, C. (1978). *The role of temporal organization in story comprehension* (Tech. Rep. No. 71). Urbana: University of Illinois, Center for Study of Reading.

Tedesco, J. F., & Schnell, S. V. (1987). Children's reactions to sex abuse investigation and litigation. *Child Abuse and Neglect, 11,* 267–272.

Turner, S., & Greene, E. (1977). *The construction and use of a propositional text base.* Boulder, CO: Institute for the Study of Intelligent Behavior.

Van Dijk, T. A., & Kintsch, W. (1983). *Strategies of discourse comprehension.* New

York: Academic Press.

Verdonik, F. (1988). Reconsidering the context of remembering: The need for a social description of memory processes and their development. In F. Weinert & M. Perlmutter (Eds.), *Memory development: Universal changes and individual differences* (pp. 257–274). Hillsdale, NJ: Erlbaum

Warren, A., Hulse-Trotter, K., & Tubbs, E. (1991). Inducing resistance to suggestibility in children. *Law and Human Behavior, 15,* 273–286.

Warren-Leubecker, A., & Springfield, M. (1987, April). *Flashbulb memory revisited: Children recall the space shuttle accident.* Paper presented at the Society for Research on Child Development Meetings, Baltimore, MD.

Warren-Leubecker, A., Tate, C., Hinton, I., & Ozbek, N. (1989). What do children know about the legal system and when do they know it? In S. Ceci, D. Ross, & M. Toglia (Eds.), *Perspectives on children's testimony* (pp. 158–183). New York: Springer-Verlag.

Weiss, E., & Berg, R. (1982). Child victims of sexual assault: Impact of court procedures. *Journal of the American Academy of Child Psychiatry, 21,* 513–518.

Wellman, H. M., Fabricus, W. V., & Wan, C. (1987). Considering every available instance: The early development of a fundamental problem-solving skill. *International Journal of Behavioral Development, 10,* 485–500.

Wellman, H. M., Ritter, K., & Flavell, J. H. (1975). Deliberate memory behavior in the delayed reactions of very young children. *Developmental Psychology, 11,* 780–787.

Whitcomb, D., Shapiro, E. R., & Stellwagen, L. D. (1985). *When the victim is a child: Issues for judges and prosecutors* (Contract # J-LEAA-011-81). Washington, DC: National Institute of Justice.

Wolfe, V. V., Sas, L., & Wilson, S. K. (1987). Some issues in preparing sexually abused children for courtroom testimony. *Behavior Therapist, 10,* 107–113.

Yussen, S. R. (1974). Determinants of visual attention and recall in observational learning by preschoolers and second graders. *Developmental Psychology, 10,* 93–100.

Zaragoza, M. (1987). Memory, suggestibility, and eyewitness testimony in children and adults. In S. Ceci, M. Toglia, & D. Ross (Eds.), *Children's eyewitness memory* (pp. 52–78). New York: Springer-Verlag.

7

Lies and Secrets: Implications for Children's Reporting of Sexual Abuse

Kay Bussey and Kerry Lee
Macquarie University

Elizabeth J. Grimbeek
University of New South Wales

Although there has been a dramatic increase in the number of children who have had contact with the legal system over the past decade, there is still a great deal of controversy associated with child witnesses (Haugaard & Reppucci, 1988). Sensationalized media reports of multiple abuse allegations such as the McMartin case in the United States and the Mr. Bubbles case in Australia have fueled this controversy in the public arena. Despite the accompanying upsurge of research to clarify issues surrounding child witnesses, many questions still remain unanswered.

The body of research to date has primarily been concerned with whether young children are capable of reporting witnessed events (Melton, 1987). That is, *can* children provide reliable testimony? This focus has largely resulted from the questioning by the courts of young children's competence to accurately report witnessed events. Research on children's memory-related abilities has yielded invaluable data relevant to this issue. Not surprisingly, particularly for events in which children have been active participants, it is difficult to discount children's memory simply on the basis of age. While 3- and 4-year-old children do not spontaneously report as much information as accurately as their older counterparts, overall, their reports are usually quite accurate (Goodman, Aman, & Hirschman, 1987; Goodman, Bottoms, Schwartz-Kenny, & Rudy, 1991; Goodman, Hirschman, & Rudy, 1987; Goodman & Reed, 1986). Further, and most important, for children appearing as witnesses in the legal context, younger children's reporting accuracy can be enhanced by multiple interviews about a witnessed event and by conducting the interviews in a supportive manner (Goodman et al., 1991). The facilitatory role of a supportive interviewing style highlights aspects other than cognitive memorial processes that may contribute to accurate reporting.

To date, however, scant attention has been paid to the impact of sociocognitive factors on children's eyewitness reporting. Specifically, the influence of motivational factors on the accuracy of reporting witnessed events has received little attention by most cognitive theorists (see Neisser, 1982). Social cognitive theory (Bandura, 1986, 1989), however, provides a perspective in which the accuracy of reporting is construed as multidetermined in that not only cognitive but also affective and motivational factors contribute to accurate reporting. Thus, from this view, apart from memory for the event, a major determinant of the veracity of a witness's reporting is the anticipated outcome of reporting that event (Bandura, 1986, 1991). For example, if children expect punishment, or if they believe that their life will be jeopardized by reporting an event, there is little likelihood that they will actively seek to disclose information. Rather, they may withhold the information. By intentionally concealing the occurrence of an event, it remains a secret. This may in part account for the underreporting of sexual abuse (Burgess & Holmstrom, 1978; Rush, 1980). Hence, the aim of many school-based child abuse prevention programs is not only to prevent abuses occurring but also to encourage the disclosure of present and past abusive events. Alternatively, the anticipated reward for pleasing an adult, for example, an interviewer or parent involved in a custody dispute, may lead children to falsely allege abuse.

In this chapter, rather than focusing on memory-related issues, we concentrate on the veracity of children's reporting of witnessed events and cognitive motivational factors that may influence their veracity. Before addressing whether children might be more or less motivated to lie or tell the truth in certain situations, we review the research on children's knowledge of lying and truthfulness. We examine whether young children can differentiate a lie from a truthful statement and whether they understand the importance of telling the truth. We review this research because it is often asserted, particularly in courts of law, that without consciously lying, young children sometimes make false statements. Also, it is often claimed that either coaching or suggestive interviewing by adults renders children incapable of accurately reporting their experiences. The premise underlying such assertions is that children cannot be relied on to distinguish accurately between what really happened and what others want them to believe really happened. By casting doubt on children's ability to wittingly lie, doubt is also cast on their ability to wittingly tell the truth. Therefore, in the first section of this chapter, three questions are addressed in relation to children's lying and truthfulness: Do children know what constitutes a false statement; that is, do they know the difference between a lie and a truthful statement? Do they make intentional false statements; that is, do they lie? If they are capable of making intentional false statements, what might motivate them to do so? These issues are then examined within the context of children reporting on sexual abuse. In particular, two major types of false statements that children may make in the sexual abuse context are discussed: (1) reporting an event as if it had occurred (false allegation), and (2) denying information about an event that has occurred (false denial). This latter type of falsehood is discussed within the broader context of children's nondisclosure of information about an event. Although nondisclosure can take many forms, we focus on the child's lack of disclosure of information once suspicions of abuse exist. More specifically, we examine instances in which the child actively tries to keep secret an event that he or she does not want to disclose by denying it. Although only such false denials qualify as lies, many forms of nondisclosure involve wittingly keeping secrets. Hence, we examine children's use of secrets to prevent disclosure of information. A range of strategies, varying in the extent to which they involve deception, can be used by children to maintain secrets.

We also briefly discuss false allegations. These lies are of primary concern in courts of law since false allegations can lead to the conviction of innocent persons. However, greater attention is devoted in this chapter to the discussion of false denial, not only because of its previous omission from the literature, but also because of its importance in understanding the difficulty that children experience in disclosing sexual abuse. False denials also have a bearing on the anecdotal reports of children's recantations of sexual abuse. Helping victims disclose rather than withhold information may further the protection of victims of sexual abuse. Researchers, practitioners, and members of the legal profession need to concern themselves not only with possible false allegations but also with possible false denials if justice is to prevail for both the accused and the victim.

CHILDREN'S UNDERSTANDING OF
LYING AND TRUTHFULNESS

As a legacy from Piaget's (1965) research reported in *The Moral Judgement of the Child*, it is often held that young children do not know the difference between lying and truthfulness. Piaget wrote:

> Without actually for the sake of lying, i.e. without attempting to deceive anyone, and without even being definitely conscious of what he is doing, he distorts reality in accordance with his desires and his romancing. To him a proposition has value less as a statement than as a wish, and the stories, testimony and explanations given by a child should be regarded as the expression of his feelings rather than of beliefs that may be true or false. (p. 157)

Conjectures of this nature both inform and reinforce jurors' and judges' skepticism about the testimony of young children.

Piaget (1965) wrote that children under age 6 subscribed to overinclusive definitions of lies that encompassed swearing and every kind of false statement including mistaken guesses. Between the ages of 6 and 10, children defined a lie as something that was not true, but they were unable to differentiate between intentional and unintentional statements: "a lie is what does not agree with the truth independently of the subject's intention" (p. 141). By 10 or 11 years old, intentionality was accommodated and only false statements intended to be false were defined as lies. Apart from investigating age differences in children's definitions of lies, Piaget (1965) also researched children's evaluations of lies. As with definitions, he reported that objective responsibility was replaced by subjective responsibility with increasing age; the older the child, the more likely intentionality was taken into account in evaluating lies. For children under age 6, the more a lie departed from reality the worse it was judged. Exaggerations such as saying that a dog was as big as a cow were judged more harshly by younger than older children. One exception to this general rule was for acts of clumsiness, where even older children judged the seriousness of the lie in terms of its material consequences, not its degree of falsity or intentionality.

Contemporary researchers have demonstrated that several aspects of Piaget's methods have worked against younger children and seriously underestimated their capabilities (Peterson, Peterson, & Seeto, 1983; Wimmer, Gruber, & Perner, 1984, 1985). Most notably, Peterson et al. (1983) have shown that children as young as 5 years can correctly identify lies, particularly lies involving misdeeds. For statements involving exaggeration and mistaken guesses, used extensively in Piaget's research, Peterson et al. found that, "95% of 11-year-olds called the exaggerations a lie, while some 30% of the 33-year-old adults defined the guess . . . as such" (Peterson et al., 1983, p. 1534). The data from that study do not support Piaget's assertion that all factually untrue statements are treated as lies, independent of intentions, only by young children. Older children and adults took little account of intentions in correctly identifying these statements. Yet both adults and children, from as young as 5 years, had no difficulty in correctly defining a false statement about a misdeed as a lie. This is perhaps not surprising in view of Stouthamer-Loeber's (1987) findings that mothers reported the most frequent reason their 4-year-olds lied was to conceal a misdeed. Lies about misdeeds were also the most frequent that children themselves, across the age range of 4 to 12 years, reported telling (Bussey, 1990b). Thus, these lie types might provide a more valid assessment of children's understanding of lying and truthfulness than those used in Piaget's studies. Further, apart from lies about misdeeds being more relevant to children, these lie types are the most pertinent in the court context as children's testimony often hinges on their being able to truthfully report on another's or their own misdeed. Indeed, it has been demonstrated in a recent study (Bussey, 1989a), using lies and truthful statements about misdeeds, that 7- and 10-year-olds were completely accurate in their identification of lies and truthful statements and that 4-year-olds obtained an 88% accuracy score.

Haugaard and Crosby (1989) also showed that children as young as 4 years of age could differentiate a lie from a truthful statement not only when the character in a vignette lied, but also when the character was coached by her mother to lie about a man touching her when he had not done so. These findings are particularly important for the courts, where, as a legacy from Piaget, it is often suggested that children are unable to make this differentiation until many years later, and that coaching from parents renders children incapable of distinguishing a lie from a truthful statement about an event.

Thus, contrary to Piaget's findings, it has been demonstrated that even young children are able to differentiate a lie from a truthful statement, particularly when the statement has a specific behavioral referent. The falsity of a statement determines a child's judgment of it as a lie, irrespective of an adult's having coached the child to make the statement or not (Haugaard & Crosby, 1989). Further, Piaget's findings on children's evaluations of lies have also been challenged in recent research. Even 4-year-olds understand that it is "good" to tell the truth and that it is "bad" to lie (Bussey, 1992). If children as young as 4 years of age can differentiate lies from truthful statements and evaluate false statements more negatively than truthful statements, do they lie intentionally and why?

Do Children Lie and Why?

It would appear that children's first lies are told to avoid getting into trouble, particularly when they have committed a misdeed (Stouthamer-Loeber, 1987). In Stouthamer-Loeber's study, mothers reported that the majority of the lies they detected their 4-year-olds telling were in reaction to something the child had done wrong, a misdeed, such as having broken a rule, having taken something they were not supposed to take, damaging something, or hurting someone. Mothers further reported that their perceived motivation for their children's telling these lies was fear of punishment for the misdeed. In this context, children's lies were more likely to follow the form of simple denial such as "no" and to a lesser extent blame of others, for example, "The cat knocked it over."

The finding that children do lie in reaction to their own misdeeds was supported by Lewis, Stanger, and Sullivan (1989), who observed children's misdeeds (looking at a prohibited toy) and their subsequent lies. Of the 88% of 3-year-old children who looked at the toy, approximately one third lied about looking. In an extension of Lewis et al.'s study, 5-year-olds were included (Bussey, 1990a), and it was found that they were less likely to commit this misdeed (69%) than the 3-year-olds (96%). However, the 5-year-olds who looked at the prohibited toys were more likely to lie about looking (95%) than were the 3-year-olds (40%) who looked (Bussey, 1990a). It was also found that when children anticipated punishment for the misdeed, they were more likely to lie; the 5-year-olds were more likely to anticipate punishment than were the 3-year-olds. These studies support the hypothesis that an important factor governing children's lying and truth telling is the anticipated outcome of disclosure. The more children anticipated getting into trouble for being honest, the less likely they were to be truthful. Simply knowing the difference between a lie and a truthful statement, and knowing that it is wrong to lie and important to tell the truth, may therefore not be sufficient to guarantee honesty. Anticipated punishment for truthfulness can induce children to lie.

These findings are consistent with the principles of social cognitive theory (Bandura, 1986, 1989) which are clearly demonstrated in a classic study of children's aggression (Bandura, 1965). Children who had witnessed a model behaving aggressively were more likely to perform the aggressive behaviors spontaneously when the behavior met with no consequences, or was praised, than when the behavior was punished. Subsequently, the children who had witnessed the model being punished and who had not spontaneously performed the aggressive behaviors were explicitly asked what they had seen and were offered a reward for reproducing or reporting the modeled aggression. It was found that these children could reproduce as many responses as the children who had spontaneously performed the aggressive behaviors after having witnessed models who were not punished for their aggressive behavior. From this study we infer that if children anticipate censure for doing or reporting something, they will be reluctant to enact or report it even though they are quite capable of doing so. Thus, an important determinant of the course of action an individual chooses to take, such as lying or telling the truth, will depend on what they think will happen to them as a result of choosing that particular course of action.

IMPLICATIONS FOR CHILDREN'S REPORTING OF CHILD SEXUAL ABUSE

What are the implications of these findings for children's false statements about sexual abuse? The research reviewed in the preceding sections showed that children as young as 4 years of age are capable of differentiating a lie from a truthful statement, and that they are capable of wittingly lying or telling the truth. A major factor influencing their lying or truthfulness was the anticipated outcome associated with each type of statement, lie or truth. Therefore, children could conceivably be coerced into falsely alleging abuse when it has not occurred (false allegation) and could be persuaded by threats of punishment, for example, to deny occurrences of abuse (false denial). However, in the preceding section it has been shown that young children's lies were mostly in response to a misdeed, that is, they were reactive to an event that had occurred (Bussey, 1990b; Stouthamer-Loeber, 1987), rather than a fabrication of an event that did not occur. Hence, we can speculate that if young children were to lie about sexual abuse, it is more likely that they would deny that such abuse occurred than fabricate a false allegation about its occurrence. Yet, the issue that has received the most attention is children's false allegations of sexual abuse against innocent persons (Faller, 1984; Jones & McGraw, 1987; Mantell, 1988). We next discuss these two types of false statements that children may make in relation to sexual abuse.

False Allegations

The debate about false allegations has at times been characterized by the adoption of rather extreme positions. Some professionals working with abused children have argued that children never make false allegations (see Mantell, 1988), while others have argued that such allegations are reasonably prevalent (Gardner, 1991; Wakefield & Underwager, 1989). Given the frequent attacks on the veracity of young children's testimony in the legal context, and the disbelief that many children encounter when they first disclose their abuse (Bussey & Boerma, 1990), it is understandable why many clinicians, in particular, have taken the view that children's allegations of sexual abuse should be believed. Such a viewpoint has intuitive appeal for those who have to do battle with the legal system to get the child's view heard. Indeed, there may be good reason to believe children who make such allegations, because "the general veracity of children's reports is supported by relatively high rates of admission by the offenders" (Berliner & Barbieri, 1984, p. 127). However, statements made by both adults and children are sometimes dishonest and more so in some situations than in others; statements of both adults and children need to be evaluated on their own merits. To always believe or indeed disbelieve young children seems just as questionable as always believing or disbelieving adults. Although we might like to believe that children never lie about abuse, it does sometimes occur. However, this clearly does not mean that children should never be believed when they disclose sexual abuse.

Those professionals who insist that children have a propensity for false allegations argue that children usually resort to such allegations to please a third party, either a sexual abuse investigator who wants to believe that the child has been abused or a parent who coaches their child to allege abuse (Wakefield & Underwager, 1989). There has, however, been little empirical evidence to support these claims.

In a recent analogue study, Tate and Warren-Leubecker (1989) addressed the possibility of coaching children to make false statements. Children either played or did not play with a magnetic building toy. Children who did not play with the toy were encouraged by the experimenter to trick another adult by telling the adult that they had played with the toy. Children were coached in detail about what to tell the other adult. Results revealed that children across the 3–7 years age range were equally likely to comply with the experimenter's request to lie. Eleven out of the 20 children who had not played with the magnetic building toy indicated to the second adult, the interviewer, that they had played with it. However, by the end of the interview, only 3 of the 20 children still maintained that they had played with the toy. Children who had actually played with the toy provided more detailed elaborations (free report = 6.7 words; answers to specific questions = 17.7 words) about their play than did the children who had not played with the toy (free report = 3.0 words; answers to specific questions = 8.1 words). Further, older children who had not played with the toy provided more detailed elaborations than did the younger children. Although the authors demonstrated that children could be coached into making false statements, they reported that it was difficult to encourage such false statements, and that the statements, particularly of the younger children, were not very credible. Does this mean that there should be more concern about the false allegations of older rather than younger children? If no other mitigating factors were present, the answer would be in the affirmative. However, from the sociocognitive perspective (Bandura, 1986, 1991), increasing cognitive competence is often accompanied by internalization of societal norms, so that increasingly lying and truthfulness become subject to self-regulatory control. From about 7 years of age, perhaps even earlier, children adopt standards of valuing truthfulness and deprecating lying such that they anticipate feelings of pride for truthfulness and feelings of remorse and guilt for lying (Bussey, 1992).

To the extent that individuals actively engage their anticipated self-evaluative reactions, they are more likely to act in accord with these standards. Sometimes, of course, external factors, such as severe threats for truth telling, or rewards for lying, may override an individual's reliance on internal standards. Certainly such external pressures will have a powerful impact on a young child. Therefore, false allegations are possible for younger and older children but the allegations of younger children would be less likely to stand up to scrutiny than those of older children and adults. However, for some children who have been abused, threats, sometimes life threatening, will be major factors influencing their lack of reporting abuse (Blume, 1991; Rush, 1980; Summit, 1983). Hence, it is possible that children will deny or recant their alleged abuse.

Nondisclosure

Why would children deny or retract information about abuse? Why would children try to keep secret the fact that they have been abused? A number of reasons have been proposed in the literature: fear of getting into trouble from the accused (Bussey & Cashmore, 1990), anticipating blame for the abuse (Goodman et al., 1989), not wanting the perpetrator to get into trouble (Bottoms, Goodman, Schwartz-Kenney, Sachsenmaier, & Thomas, 1990) and/or embarrassment

(Saywitz, Goodman, Nicholas, & Moan, 1989). Which of these reasons prevents a child from disclosing abuse will partly depend on the strategy used by the abuser to silence the child.

Although there are many strategies that can be used to prevent children from disclosing abuse, threat is the most widely mentioned in the literature. Children are often sworn to secrecy to prevent them from disclosing the abuse. Summit (1983), in the following excerpt, provides some lucid examples of how children are sworn to secrecy:

> Virtually no child is prepared for the possibility of molestation by a trusted adult; that possibility is a well- kept secret even among adults. The child is, therefore, entirely dependent on the intruder for whatever reality is assigned to the experience. Of all the inadequate, illogical, self-serving, or self-protective explanations provided by the adult, the only consistent and meaningful impression gained by the child is one of danger and fearful outcome based on secrecy. . . . "This is our secret; nobody else will understand." "Don't tell anybody." "Nobody will believe you." "Don't tell your mother; (a) she will hate you, (b) she will hate me, (c) she will kill you, (d) she will kill me, (e) it will kill her, (f) she will send you away, (g) she will send me away, or (h) it will break up the family and you'll end up in an orphanage." "If you tell anyone (a) I won't love you anymore, (b) I'll spank you, (c) I'll kill your dog, or (d) I'll kill you." However gentle or menacing the intimidation may be, the secrecy makes it clear to the child that this is something bad and dangerous. The secrecy is both the source of fear and the promise of safety: "Everything will be all right if you just don't tell." (p. 181)

Whatever the reason for nondisclosure, children who do not disclose abuse must maintain their secret. However, Piaget would have us believe that children cannot keep secrets. According to Piaget (1959), young children are "unable to keep a single thought secret." In his view:

> Apart from thinking by images or autistic symbols which cannot be directly communicated, the child, up to an age, as yet undetermined but probably somewhere about seven, is incapable of keeping to himself the thoughts which enter his head. He says everything. He has no verbal continence. (p. 38)

However, this assertion is at variance with adult survivors' recollections of their abuse and accounts of how they maintained the secret (Blume, 1991).

Secrets

Secrecy requires intentional concealment.

> To keep a secret from someone, then, is to block information about it or evidence of it from reaching that person, and to do so intentionally: to prevent him from learning it, and thus from possessing it, making use of it, or revealing it. The word "secrecy" refers to the resulting concealment. (Bok, 1983, pp. 5–6)

In Piaget's view, young children cannot keep secrets because their thinking is egocentric. Piaget concluded that children are egocentric from his classic three-mountains task (Piaget & Inhelder, 1956), where children younger than 7 or 8 years of age attributed their own view of the mountain to a doll that was facing another part of the papier-mache mountain. However, recent studies employing tasks simpler than those administered by Piaget, have not found such pervasive egocentric thought among young children. Of course, young children may not have a fully developed capacity for overcoming egocentricism, just as on occasions adults' thinking is egocentric, but they do have a greater capacity for taking into account others' perspectives than was shown in Piaget's studies. For example, even 18-month-old children attempt to solicit the attention of others by gesturing and pointing (Rheingold, Hay, & West, 1976), and 4-year-olds have been observed modifying their speech when talking to younger children (Shatz & Gelman, 1973). So it might not be surprising if young children, contrary to Piaget's assertions, can keep secrets. Unfortunately, apart from anecdotal evidence, there is little contemporary research addressing this issue. The research that can inform us at this stage comes from studies that have investigated children's concealment of information about their own or others' misdeeds.

It was shown earlier in this chapter that children sometimes lie when they commit a misdeed and anticipate punishment for owning up to the misdeed (Bussey, 1990a; Lewis et al., 1989; Stouthamer-Loeber, 1987). But what about the situation where children witness a misdeed committed by another, particularly an adult? Do they also lie in this situation, a situation more analogous to a sexually abusive episode, in which the adult rather than the child commits the misdeed and asks the child to conceal the event? Will children withhold reporting such information or will they freely disclose it? Obviously, it is impossible to investigate these issues in actual sexual abuse encounters. Hence, we conducted an analogue study in which we attempted to capture certain dynamics often involved in sexually abusive situations. To this end, we investigated children's propensity to report on the transgression of an adult who had instructed them not to report it (Bussey, 1990a). The transgressor was an adult male, since in most court cases involving sexual abuse, the child witness testifies against an adult male (Goodman et al., 1989; Harshbarger, 1987; Sas, 1990). As noted earlier, in many cases of child sexual abuse the child has been instructed by the accused not to disclose the incident. This instruction may undermine the child's propensity to report the truth. Thus, we investigated the likelihood of 3- and 5-year-old children reporting on a witnessed transgression committed by an adult male who broke a "prized" glass and then hid the broken pieces to conceal his misdeed. The adult male asked the child not to tell the female interviewer about what had happened. The results revealed that when children 3 and 5 years of age were simply asked not to tell on the adult, more of the 3-year-olds (86%) than the 5-year-olds (57%) disclosed the transgression. It is instructive to note that some of the 3-year-olds (14%) and quite a large percentage of the 5-year-olds (43%) were capable of keeping a secret. In this study, children were simply requested not to tell about the adult's transgression. But what about other appeals such as bribes, threats, trickery, and concern that adults use to inhibit disclosure?

A further study was undertaken to assess the differential impact of these various appeals on children's disclosure of an adult male's transgression (Bussey, Lee, & Rickard, 1990). Again, across all types of appeal children were more likely to disclose (70%) than not to disclose (30%) the transgression. As in the previous study, it was the 3-year-olds rather than the 5-year-olds who showed the greatest propensity for disclosure; 79% of the 3-year-olds disclosed the transgression compared to 61% of the 5-year-olds. Disclosure rates were lowest for both the 3-year-olds (64%) and 5-year-olds (50%) in the threat condition. Not surprisingly, the sterner the request by the adult not to disclose his transgression, the more likely children from both age groups were to comply.

It is important to note in these studies that overall disclosure rates were quite high. Although it could be argued that the task was not sufficiently serious or important to warrant withholding information, comments made by the children confirmed that they had regarded the transgression as serious. For example, the following excerpt starts after a 5-year-old child had answered a number of questions asked by the female interviewer about the game that the adult male (who was also the transgressor) taught the child.

INTERVIEWER: Did anything else happen while I was gone?
CHILD: Yes. It's sad.

INTERVIEWER: Would you like to tell me what happened?
CHILD: Don't get angry. Your special glass broke.
INTERVIEWER: Oh, what happened?
CHILD: Mr. X was going to get a cup of water and it was kinda slippery. Don't tell him that you heard, 'cause he'll get angry.

At this stage it is important to clarify the relationship between children's lack of disclosure and their lying. Although Bok (1983) states that "lies are part of the arsenal used to guard and to invade secrecy; and secrecy allows lies to go undiscovered and to build up" (p. xv), we suggest that maintaining a secret often results in lying, although this is not necessarily always the case. Confusion currently exists in the literature regarding the classification of nondisclosure of information as lying. This has effectively meant that little research has focused on the nondisclosure of information. Whether or not the nondisclosure of information should be regarded as lying has been the subject of much debate by moral philosophers (Bok, 1978). This debate is clearly beyond the scope of this chapter. We consider, however, that lack of disclosure can take three forms, of which only the last form listed here can readily be classified as a lie. First, something untoward occurs (e.g., abuse), but it is not suspected and the child does not disclose it (disclosure omission). Second, something untoward occurs (e.g., abuse), and it is suspected, but the child refuses to disclose the relevant information (disclosure refusal); he or she does not lie, however, by denying that something has happened. He or she simply refuses to disclose the information. Third, something untoward occurs (e.g., abuse), and it is suspected, but the child denies that anything has happened or retracts information previously disclosed (false denial). We believe that our use of the term "false denial" qualifies as a lie in terms of Bok's (1978) definition of a lie as "an intentionally deceptive message in the form of a statement" (p. 15). In the studies reported above, lack of disclosure could take the form of either disclosure refusal or false denial. Since the last question in the interview specifically asked children if they knew what had happened to the glass, it was not possible for children to evade disclosure through omission. Both disclosure refusal and false denial involve keeping a secret, but only false denial involves lying to protect the secret. Although the majority of children who did not disclose the adult's transgression in these studies (Bussey, 1990a; Bussey et al., 1990) lied about the transgression by denying that they knew what had happened to the glass (false denial), about 20% of the children across the various conditions and age groups maintained their secret by refusing to disclose it, but without lying about the transgression. An example of a 5-year-old's refusal to reveal the transgression is provided below:

INTERVIEWER: Did anything else happen while I was gone?
CHILD: I don't know.

[The interviewer and child proceed with the balance scale task and then the interviewer announces that she is quite thirsty and is going to have a drink of water. The child declines the offer of a drink of water. The interviewer looks for her glass but can't find it. She expresses surprise about not being able to find her special glass where she had left it.]

INTERVIEWER: Have you seen my special glass?
CHILD: I'm not going to tell you about it. I don't want to tell you 'cause Mr. X says if I tell you he'll get angry at me. I don't want to tell you.

The studies discussed above reveal that an adult's instruction about reporting an event observed by a child can influence the child's subsequent reporting of it—even 3-year-olds can be coerced into keeping secrets. Bottoms et al. (1990) also found that disclosure of information by 5- and 6-year-olds varied as a function of instruction by their mothers. Specifically, when mothers engaged their children in play with a prohibited set of toys and asked their children to keep this a secret, fewer children reported the activities than did children who were permitted to play with the toys and whose mothers did not ask their children to keep this a secret. Younger children, 3- and 4-year-olds, in that study were unaffected by the request to keep the information secret. However, for a very salient event, such as the mother's accidentally breaking and hiding a Barbie doll, only 1 out of the 49 children in the study spontaneously reported what had happened. Apparently, little pressure is needed to silence children when adults attempt to cover up their mistakes or transgressions. In this case, hiding the broken Barbie doll may have signaled to the children that the breakage needed to be kept secret. Therefore, for children who are sexually abused, it is possible that the more concern they feel for the alleged transgressor, the more serious the transgression, and the greater the threat for reporting the abuse, the more likely they would be to comply with the transgressor's request or demand not to report the witnessed event. Further, on the basis of these studies it would seem that for children who have been persuaded to secrecy by an abuser, the conditions under which they are questioned might affect their propensity to report it. Specifically, the courtroom situation may undermine their ability to disclose an abusive episode. We examine this issue next.

Reporting Abuse in the Courtroom

On the basis of the findings from the studies reported above, it would not be surprising if children were reluctant to report their abuse, or recant earlier disclosures, when required to report it in front of the perpetrator in a courtroom. There is, however, little research to substantiate this hypothesis. Many believe that facing the accused is a source of major distress to child witnesses (Burgess & Holmstrom, 1978; Libai, 1969; Parker, 1982; Whitcomb, Shapiro, & Stellwagen, 1985), and children themselves have anticipated strong negative affect about having to testify in front of the accused in a courtroom (Goodman et al., 1989). In Goodman et al.'s (1989) study, children's evaluations of various aspects of the court procedure were more positive after their court appearance than before it; however, their feelings about testifying in front of the accused remained highly negative (Goodman et al., 1989; Sas, 1990). A direct result of these concerns has been a barrage of legislation in many countries to allow children to present their testimony other than in face-to-face confrontation with the accused. These include shielding the child from the defendant with a screen and various procedures associated with closed-circuit television. Although such procedures have been applauded by attorneys for the prosecution, they have met with criticism from the defense.

In law it has been assumed that it is necessary for the accuser to face the accused to ensure the veracity of the testimony. In the United States, the rights of the accused to face his or her accuser is enshrined in the Constitution, specifically the Sixth Amendment. This has been reiterated in a recent Supreme Court case where it was stated that, "The premise of the Confrontation Clause is that it is more difficult for a witness to lie, and more likely that the trier of fact will be able to detect lying from the witness' demeanor, if the witness must accuse the defendant to his face" (*Coy*, 108 S. Ct. at 2800-2802). However, in its submission to the U.S. Supreme Court in *Maryland v. Craig*, the American Psychological Association (APA) (Goodman, Levine, Melton, & Ogden, 1991) argued that such a premise may have limits when applied to young children. Children may be afraid to disclose the abusive event and therefore may give less than complete accounts when testifying before the accused. Consequently, the APA advocated the use of protective measures to eliminate the child's confrontation with the defendant. These procedures would serve two aims: (1) protect child witnesses from severe emotional distress and (2) obtain the most complete and truthful possible testimony from child witnesses in sexual abuse cases. Researchers have found support for the first aim (Goodman et al., 1989), and the lack of completeness in children's responses when they face the accused (Hill & Hill, 1987) provides partial support for the second aim. In a recent study, we focused on that aspect of the second aim, which deals with the veracity of children's reports when they face the accused.

In that study we investigated the influence of the presence or absence of a transgressor on children's reporting of a transgression committed by an adult (Bussey, Ross, & Lee, 1991). To reiterate, the general wisdom is that children will be more likely to disclose an adult's transgression when the adult is not present during disclosure, although there is little data to support this position. Obviously, it is impossible to investigate this issue in the actual courtroom, hence this study relied on an analogue investigation. As in the studies reported earlier in this chapter, an adult male transgressed by breaking a "prized" glass and then hiding the broken pieces. Children 3, 5, and 9 years of age witnessed the transgression and were subsequently questioned by a second interviewer either in the presence or absence of the transgressor. Results revealed that 3- and 5-year-old children were less likely to disclose the adult's transgression in his presence (31% and 25% disclosed the transgression, respectively), than in his absence (63% and 69% disclosed the transgression, respectively). However, the transgressor's presence or absence did not impact on the disclosure of the 9-year-olds, since 88% of the children disclosed the transgression in both the present and absent conditions. All of the 5- and 9-year-olds and the majority of the 3-year-olds (62%) who did not disclose the adult's transgression, actively denied (false denial) that they knew anything about the broken glass. In this study, only 3-year-olds refused to disclose the adults' transgression without denying that they knew what had happened to the glass (disclosure refusal). Thirty-eight percent of the children who did not disclose the transgression, distributed equally across the transgressor present and absent conditions, did not attempt to lie about the transgression by denying any knowledge of it. They simply said, "I can't tell."

These results suggest that the presence of the perpetrator is likely to reduce disclosure of the perpetrator's transgression by young witnesses. Not surprisingly, it is difficult for anybody to "tell" on someone else, but apparently this is extremely difficult for young children. Although future research must clarify the reason for children's nondisclosure when they face the perpetrator, it would seem that fear of punishment is a major factor silencing them. Younger children therefore particularly need encouragement for disclosure and a supportive environment in which to disclose sensitive information. Although the older children were more likely to disclose in the presence of the perpetrator in this study, this does not mean that this was an easy task for these children. The following responses of two 9-year-olds in answer to a question about how they felt about disclosing the transgression illustrate this: "Awful, 'cause I promised not to tell you," and "Felt a bit funny telling you a lie, but I felt bad after I told the truth" (this child initially denied the transgression but later disclosed it). Had the consequences for disclosure been more severe, perhaps even these children's truthfulness would have been compromised. Although lacking conclusive evidence, we can speculate that children who have been sexually abused, threatened with dire consequences for disclosure, and who have to report on embarrassing material would be even more reticent to report the event in the presence of the perpetrator than has been shown in this study.

These findings provide empirical support for the U.S. Supreme Court's decision to uphold *Maryland v. Craig*, alluded to earlier, that permitted a 6-year-old child to testify by closed-circuit television. It should be noted, however, that the Supreme Court ruled that it is only possible for children to provide their testimony via this medium once it has been established that they would suffer severe emotional trauma such that they could not communicate adequately if they had to testify in front of the accused. The court held that the essence of the confrontation clause was not face-to-face confrontation between witnesses and criminal defendants:

> The Clause's central purpose, to ensure the reliability of the evidence against a defendant by subjecting it to rigorous testing in an adversary proceeding before the trier of fact, is served by the combined effects of the elements of confrontation: physical presence, oath, cross-examination, and observation of demeanor by the trier of fact. Although face-to-face confrontation forms the core of the Clause's values, it is not an indispensable element of the confrontation right. (*Maryland v. Craig*, Syllabus, p. II)

Hence, provided the child submits to cross-examination via closed-circuit television, the child's evidence does not, in the opinion of the Supreme Court, usurp the constitutional rights of the accused. In other countries, however, where it is not possible for children to testify without face-to-face confrontation with the accused, it would seem essential that children be adequately prepared for providing their testimony. Desensitization and confidence-building programs for testifying before the accused would seem crucial components of any child witness preparation program.

It must be remembered that even though it has been shown that younger children's propensity to tell the truth in the presence of the accused may be compromised, the use of closed-circuit television to overcome this may not be the best or the only way of dealing with this difficulty. If subsequent studies demonstrate that closed-circuit television procedures compromise the credibility of children giving testimony, then obviously little has been gained. Future research needs to address optimal procedures that enable young children, in particular, to be heard in courts of law without accompanying undue emotional distress that may render them incapable of disclosing the event about which they are to testify, and without compromising their credibility.

CONCLUSION

The conditions surrounding children's reports of witnessed events are crucial, since certain factors facilitate while others inhibit truthfulness. Even if younger children do make false allegations, these allegations appear less credible than those made by older children, and could be expected not to survive the scrutiny of prudent questioning. Older children who have the ability to make more plausible false statements are also more likely to exercise self-regulatory control of their own lying and truthfulness and act in accord with their internal standards for lying and truthfulness (Bandura, 1986, 1991). That is, individuals who have learned to value truthfulness, and feel pride for truthfulness and deprecate lying, and feel remorse and guilt for lying are more likely to be truthful through the active engagement of self-evaluative reactions. So, are adults and older children more honest than their younger counterparts because of their internalization of standards for truthfulness? The answer is clearly, "no." First, not all adults and older children develop standards that value truthfulness and deprecate lying. Second, even if such standards were developed they could be readily disengaged through justification. Adults have a greater capacity than do children for being deceitful and getting away with it, justifying their deceit, and concealing it through masking their feelings (Bandura, 1986, 1990).

As well as examining research findings on false allegations, this chapter has drawn attention to an equally important issue, children's nondisclosure of events, specifically highlighting false denials. This chapter has focused on those situations in which children have been told not to tell about a witnessed event. Here, in the presence of a transgressor, young children were especially reluctant to disclose information. The presence of the transgressor compromises the truthfulness of children possibly by reminding them of their agreement not to tell about the event. Not all young children who did not report the truth about an event lied about it. Some children simply refused to disclose the information. They kept the truth secret but did not lie. These findings have implications for programs that aim to facilitate children's disclosure of abuse. In addition, the findings suggest that young children may be likely to report their alleged abuse in courtrooms if they give their testimony in the absence of the accused. Although the presence or absence of the transgressor did not affect the veracity of older children's testimony, if the threat had been more extreme or life threatening, their disclosure might also have been affected. Obviously, threats are usually more severe in cases of sexual abuse than those that are reproduced in analogue studies.

On the basis of the studies reviewed in this chapter, some speculations about the truthfulness of certain age groups with respect to reporting sexual abuse are offered. It would be expected that young children 3 to 5 years of age, for example, would have more difficulty telling the truth about sexual abuse if they had been threatened for disclosing it and/or have to face the perpetrator than would older children, 9- and 10-year-olds, whose truthfulness is less reliant on external factors and whose positive internal standards for truthfulness are more firmly established. In fact, these older children may be even more truthful in such situations than adolescents are and adults since they may have less ready access to justifications for disengaging their internal standards. These speculations warrant further investigation. However, because an individual's truthfulness is multidetermined, ultimately there is no way to predict whether an individual of any age will be truthful or not in a specific situation.

In sum, on the basis of the studies reviewed here it is proposed that the less censure children anticipate for truthfulness, the more likely they are to be truthful. Hence, professionals and parents who provide situations that facilitate truthfulness, say by appropriately reassuring children about the positive outcomes of disclosure, will be more likely to obtain truthful and complete testimony from children.

ACKNOWLEDGMENTS

The research reported in this chapter was supported by an Australian Research Council Grant (8615687) to Kay Bussey. We wish to acknowledge Albert Bandura for his helpful comments on an earlier version of this chapter.

REFERENCES

Bandura, A. (1965). Influence of models' reinforcement contingencies on the acquisition of imitative responses. *Journal of Personality and Social Psychology, 1,* 589–595.

Bandura, A. (1986). *Social foundations of thought and action: A social cognitive theory.* Englewood Cliffs, NJ: Prentice-Hall.

Bandura, A. (1989). Social cognitive theory. In R. Vasta(Ed.), *Annals of child development. Six theories of child development* (Vol. 6, pp. 1–60). Greenwich, CT : JAI Press.

Bandura, A. (1990). Selective activation and disengagement of moral control. *Journal of Social Issues, 46,* 27–46.

Bandura, A. (1991). Social cognitive theory of moral thought and action. In W. M. Kurtines & J. L. Gewirtz (Ed.), *Handbook of moral behavior and development* (Vol. 1, pp. 45–103). Hillsdale, NJ: Erlbaum.

Berliner, L., & Barbieri, M. K. (1984). The testimony of the child victim of sexual assault. *Journal of Social Issues, 40,* 125–137.

Blume, E.S. (1991). *Secret survivors: Uncovering incest and its aftereffects in women.* New York: Ballantine Books.

Bok, S. (1978). *Lying: Moral choices in public and private life.* New York: Pantheon.

Bok, S. (1983). *Secrets: On the ethics of concealment and revelation.* New York: Vintage Books.

Bottoms, B., Goodman, G. S., Schwartz-Kenney, B., Sachsenmaier, T., & Thomas, S. (1990, March). *Keeping secrets: Implications for children's testimony.* Paper presented at the biennial meeting of the American Psychology and Law Society, Williamsburg, VA.

Burgess, A. W., & Holmstrom, L. L. (1978). Accessory-to-sex: Pressure, sex, and secrecy. In A. W. Burgess, A. N. Groth, L. L. Holmstrom, & S. M. Sgroi (Eds.), *Sexual assault of children and adolescents* (pp. 85–98). Lexington, MA: D. C. Heath.

Bussey, K., (1989a, April). *Children's definitions and evaluations of lies and truths involving a misdeed.* Paper presented at the Meeting of the Society for Research in Child Development, Kansas City, MO.

Bussey, K. (1990a, August). Adult influence on children's eyewitness reporting. In S. Ceci (Chair), *Do children lie? Narrowing the uncertainties.* Symposium conducted at the American Psychology and Law Society Biennial Meeting, Williamsburg, VA.

Bussey, K. (1990b). *The content and purpose of children's lies.* Manuscript submitted for publication.

Bussey, K. (1992). Lying and truthfulness: Children's definitions, standards and evaluative reactions. *Child Development, 63,* 129–137.

Bussey, K., & Boerma, E. M. (1990). *Sexually abused and non-abused girls' conceptions of sexual abuse.* Manuscript submitted for publication.

Bussey, K., & Cashmore, J. (1990). *Children's conceptions of the witness role.* Manuscript in preparation.

Bussey, K., Lee, K., & Rickard, K. (1990). *Children's reports of an adult's transgression.* Manuscript in preparation.

Bussey, K., Ross, C., Lee, K. (1991). The effect of the transgressor's presence on children's truthfulness. Manuscript in preparation.

Coy v. Iowa, 487 U.S. 1012 (1988).

Faller, K. C. (1984). Is the child victim of sexual abuse telling the truth? *Child Abuse and Neglect, 8*, 473–481.

Gardner, R. A. (1991). *Sex abuse hysteria: Salem witch trials revisited*. Cresskill, NJ: Creative Therapeutics.

Goodman, G. S., Aman, C. J., & Hirschman, J. (1987). Child sexual and physical abuse: Children's testimony. In S. J. Ceci, M. P. Toglia, & D. F. Ross (Eds.), *Children's eyewitness memory* (pp. 1–23). New York: Springer-Verlag.

Goodman, G. S., Bottoms, B. L., Schwartz-Kenney, B. M., & Rudy, L. (1991). Children's testimony about a stressful event: Improving children's reports. *Journal of Narrative and Life History, 1*, 69–99.

Goodman, G. S., Hirschman, J., & Rudy, L. (1987, April). Children's testimony: Research and policy implications. In S. Ceci (Chair), *Children as witnesses: Research and social policy implications*. Symposium presented at the Society for Research in Child Development, Baltimore, MD.

Goodman, G. S., Jones, D. P. H., Pyle-Taub, E., England, P., Port, L., Rudy, L., & Prado-Estrada, L. (1989, August). *Children in court: The emotional effects of criminal court involvement*. Paper presented at the American Psychological Association Convention, New Orleans, LA.

Goodman, G. S., Levine, M., Melton, G. B., & Ogden, D. W. (1991). Child witnesses and the confrontation clause: The American Psychological Association brief in *Maryland v. Craig*. *Law and Human Behavior, 15*, 13–29.

Goodman, G. S., & Reed, R. S. (1986). Age differences in eyewitness testimony. *Law and Human Behavior, 10*, 317–332.

Harshbarger, S. (1987). Prosecution is an appropriate response in child sexual abuse cases. *Journal of Interpersonal Violence, 2*, 108–112.

Haugaard, J. J., & Crosby, C. (1989). *Children's definitions of the truth and their competency as witnesses in legal proceedings*. Paper presented at the Southeastern Psychological Association Conference, Washington, DC.

Haugaard, J. J., & Reppucci, N. D. (1988). *The sexual abuse of children: A comprehensive guide to current knowledge and intervention strategies*. San Francisco: Jossey-Bass.

Hill, P. E. & Hill, S. M. (1987). Videotaping children's testimony: An empirical view. *Michigan Law Review, 85*, 809–833.

Jones, D. P. H., & McGraw, J. M. (1987). Reliable and fictitious accounts of sexual abuse to children. *Journal of Interpersonal Violence, 2*, 27–45.

Lewis, M., Stanger, C., & Sullivan, M.W. (1989). Deception in 3-year-olds. *Developmental Psychology, 25*, 439–443.

Libai, D. (1969). The protection of the child victim of a sexual offense in the criminal justice system. *Wayne Law Review, 15*, 977–1032.

Mantell, D. M. (1988). Clarifying erroneous child sexual abuse allegations. *American Journal of Orthopsychiatry, 58*, 618–621.

Maryland v. Craig, 110 S. Ct. 3157 (1990).

Melton, G. B. (1987). Children's testimony in cases of alleged sexual abuse. In M. Wolraich, & D. K. Routh (Eds.), *Advances in developmental and behavioral pediatrics* (Vol. 8, pp. 179–203). Greenwich, CT: Jai Press.

Neisser, U. (Ed.). (1982). *Memory observed: Remembering in natural contexts.* San Francisco: W.H. Freeman.

Parker, J. (1982). The rights of child witnesses: Is the court a protector or perpetrator? *New England Law Review, 17,* 643–717.

Peterson, C. C., Peterson, J. L., & Seeto, D. (1983). Developmental changes in ideas about lying. *Child Development, 54,* 1529–1535.

Piaget, J. (1959). *The language and thought of the child.* London: Routledge & Kegan Paul. (Original work published 1929)

Piaget, J. (1965). *The moral judgment of the child.* Harmondsworth, England: Penguin Books. (Original work published 1932)

Piaget, J., & Inhelder, B. (1956). *The child's conception of space.* London: Routledge & Kegan Paul.

Rheingold, H. L., Hay, D. F., & West, M. J. (1976). Sharing in the second year of life. *Child Development, 47,* 1148–1158.

Rush, F. (1980). *The best kept secret: Sexual abuse of children.* New York: McGraw-Hill.

Sas, L. (1990). *Reducing the system-induced trauma for child sexual abuse victims through court preparation, assessment and follow-up.* London, Ontario: London Family Court Clinic.

Saywitz, K., Goodman, G.S., Nicholas, E., & Moan, S. (1989, April). Children's memories of genital examinations: Implications for cases of child sexual assault. In G. S. Goodman (Chair), *Can children provide accurate eyewitness testimony?* Symposium presented at the biennial meetings of the Society for Research in Child Development, Kansas City, MO.

Shatz, M., & Gelman, R. (1973). The development of communication skills: Modifications in the speech of young children as a function of listener. *Monographs of the Society for Research in Child Development, 38* (5, No. 152).

Stouthamer-Loeber, M. (1987, April). *Mothers' perceptions of children's lying and its relationship to behavior problems.* Presented at the annual meeting of the Society for Research on Child Development, Baltimore, MD.

Summit, R. C. (1983). The child sexual abuse accommodation syndrome. *Child Abuse and Neglect, 7,* 177–193.

Tate, C. S., & Warren-Leubecker, A. (1989, April). *The effects of adult coaching on children's willingness to provide false reports.* Paper presented at Meeting of Society for Research in Child Development, Kansas City, MO.

Wakefield, H., & Underwager, R. (1989). Evaluating the child witness in sexual abuse cases: Interview or inquisition. *American Journal of Forensic Psychology, 7,* 43–69.

Whitcomb, D., Shapiro, E. R., & Stellwagen, L. D. (1985). *When the victim is a child.* Washington, DC: U.S. Department of Justice.

Wimmer, H., Gruber, S., & Perner, J. (1984). Young children's conception of lying: Lexical realism—moral subjectivism. *Journal of Experimental Child Psychology, 37,* 1–30.

Wimmer, H., Gruber, S., & Perner, J. (1985). Young children's conception of lying: Moral intuition and the denotation and connotation of "to lie." *Developmental Psychology, 21,* 993–995.

8

Discernibility or Discrimination?: Understanding Jurors' Reactions to Accurate and Inaccurate Child and Adult Eyewitnesses

Michael R. Leippe
Adelphi University

Andrew P. Manion
St. Mary's College of Minnesota

Ann Romanczyk
Slippery Rock University

"Can you really believe everything that these children . . . were saying?" (*Nightline*, 1990 p. 2).

That is how one juror summed up the well-publicized McMartin Preschool trial. The jury returned a decision of "not guilty" on 52 counts of lewd and lascivious acts against 11 children, which had been filed against defendants Ray Buckey and his mother, Peggy McMartin Buckey. During the course of this extraordinarily long (2½ years) trial, 11 children, all alleged victims of sexual abuse, testified and underwent cross-examination. Although all told similar stories, the jury failed to convict the defendants on any count. Thirteen other counts against Ray Buckey resulted initially in a mistrial, but later he was acquitted of these as well. Jurors reported that they felt the methods used to obtain the evidence were questionable. A major concern was that the questioning of the children had been too leading. Among other things, the children who admitted to abuse were rewarded, while those who did not were verbally ridiculed and nonverbally rejected. Ultimately, although seven of the jurors believed that some abuse had taken place, they could not determine what portion of the children's testimony had been fact and what portion fancy. This case dramatically illustrates a problem of children's testimony in the courtroom. How do jurors and other fact finders react to the eyewitness testimony of children?

One encouraging aspect of the McMartin trial is that the attention it received reflects an increasing social awareness of and concern about the existence and impact of child abuse. Reports of sexual abuse against children increased more than 300% between 1980 and 1986 (National Center on Child Abuse and Neglect, 1988). A result of this increase is a corresponding increase in the frequency with which young children are called on to testify in court or in pretrial interviews (Goodman, 1984). With larger numbers of children taking the stand a growing need has emerged for legal reform to accommodate these young witnesses.

Historically, minors (as old as 14 years) have had to undergo a competency hearing before their testimony was considered admissible as evidence (Goodman, 1984). Additionally, the testimony of children was not afforded full weight unless corroborated by an adult (Bulkley, 1982). Judges also often gave explicit warnings to jurors about children's susceptibility to suggestion, memory failure, and confusion of fact with fantasy (Bulkley, 1982; Graham, 1983).

In recent years many of these legal restrictions to children's testimony have been lifted. For example, rules of corroboration are fast becoming obsolete (Whitcomb, Shapiro, & Stellwagen, 1985), particularly in cases involving alleged abuse (Myers, 1987). Similarly, the federal court and many states no longer require competency hearings for all child witnesses (Melton, 1984). Rather, it is now left up to the trial judge to make case-by-case determinations of whether a child's competency to testify needs to be demonstrated by a hearing. In fact the states of Colorado, Connecticut, Missouri, and Utah have established rules of evidence specifying that children who are alleged victims of sexual abuse are *automatically* competent to testify. Apparently, in these states even young children are no longer assumed to be incapable of testifying about crimes allegedly perpetrated against them. Some progressive courts have even introduced methods to facilitate child eyewitness testimony, such as the use of anatomically correct dolls and videotaped rather than live testimony (Altman & Lennon, 1986, Nance, 1989).

Despite these advances many prosecutors (and lawyers in general) remain wary of using the testimony of children in a trial (Leippe, Brigham, Cousins, & Romanczyk, 1989; *Harvard Law Review*, 1985).

Their fears seem somewhat justified in light of highly publicized unsuccessful trials (from the perspective of the prosecution) like the McMartin Preschool case. Psychological theory and research also do little to bolster a would-be prosecutor's determination to bring to trial a case relying heavily on the testimony of a child. Those diligent attorneys who consult the psychological literature of the '80s will find considerable disagreement about whether young children are sufficiently reliable eyewitnesses. They will also find similar uncertainty about the level of credibility ascribed to young witnesses by fact finders such as police officers, social workers, judges, and jurors (e.g., Leippe et al., 1989; Leippe & Romanczyk, 1987; Yarmey & Jones, 1983). Are young children underbelieved or overbelieved? Can fact finders discriminate between accurate and inaccurate child witnessess? This chapter describes a program of research designed to address these questions.

CHILDREN'S MEMORY VERSUS ADULTS': A BRIEF LOOK AT THE LITERATURE AND SOME NEW DATA

Traditionally, child eyewitness research has placed the child in the role of a passive bystander observing a staged crime (either live or videotaped) or a crime-like event (e.g., heated arguments). These episodes are typically quite brief (less than 30 seconds in most cases). A major criticism of this research is that the simulated crime events do not closely approximate those about which children typically testify (e.g., Raskin & Yuille, 1989). Children appear in court more often as alleged victims of sexual abuse or as victim-bystanders of some other form of protracted domestic violence (Goodman, 1984; Leippe et al., 1989). Therefore, extrapolating from bystander experiments to the courtroom is problematic. More recently, researchers have begun testing children's memory for events in which they were active participants.

Research relevant to the accuracy of children's memory has yielded inconsistent results. On the negative side of the ledger, some studies of children's memory and communication have shown that, compared to adults, children are poorer at recalling events and faces (Brigham, Van Verst, & Bothwell, 1986; Chance & Goldstein, 1984; Yarmey, 1984). Children also have been shown to be more susceptible to suggestive questioning (Ceci, Ross, & Toglia, 1987; Cohen & Harnick, 1980), more likely to misremember statements of actions as actual actions (Lindsay, 1990; Lindsay & Johnson, 1987), and more error prone when communicating a remembered event (Pratt &

MacKenzie-Keating, 1985) than adults. Children's free recall descriptions of remembered events also tend to be shorter and less complete than those of adults (Cohen & Harnick, 1980; Marin, Holmes, Guth, & Kovac, 1979). Further, Chance, Turner, and Goldstein (1982) and King and Yuille (1987) reported that children are more likely to make false identifications than adults on a face recognition task, suggesting a greater willingness to guess when unsure of the correct response. In a study reported by Davies, Tarrant, and Flin (1989), nearly one child in five made a false identification when attempting to identify a man with whom they had interacted for 5 minutes. This study also showed differences in recall accuracy among children of different ages. One week after participating in a medical exam, 9–10-year-olds demonstrated superior recall for the event than did 6–7-year-olds.

On the other hand, evidence indicates that developmental differences are smaller if the situations in which the events occur are equally familiar across age groups (Chi & Ceci, 1987). Studies employing more forensically relevant events as well as simple, direct questioning also have found small or nil differences between adults and children in recall accuracy (Goodman & Reed, 1986; Goodman, Rudy, Bottoms, & Aman, 1990). This is especially true for activities and events that are attention getting and highly involving—as the critical events of sexual abuse would be. Marin et al. (1979) found that although children gave less complete free-recall reports about a staged argument between two adults, they seldom volunteered false information and were as accurate as adults in answering objective questions about the event. Children were also as capable as adults at later identifying one of the adults in a six-person photo lineup.

Experiment 1: A Study of Memory for a "Touching Experience"

If any conclusion can be reached from studies of children's testimony, it is that children may approach adults in memory skills as conditions of witnessing and questioning improve—but they may very well fall short of adults in reporting unfamiliar and fast-moving events. In the initial experiment reported here, we sought further insights about children's memory by comparing adults' and children's memory reports regarding an experience that included a leisurely yet brief encounter with a stranger who wins the witness's trust and initiates a sequence of interpersonal touching—an experience, in other words, that innocently mimicked some features of molestation cases. The memory reports from this experiment served a second purpose; they were the stimulus materials presented to subject-jurors for their judgments of credibility in the remaining experiments reported in this chapter.

Method

The witnesses in this experiment (Leippe, Romanczyk, & Manion, 1991) were white, mostly middle-class males and females who represented three age groups: 5–6-year-olds (*n* = 26), 9–10-year-olds (*n* = 31), and adults (college students with an average age of 19) (*n* = 27). Each witness participated individually in two successive sessions. In the first session, the witness spent 5–7 minutes alone with a male experimenter who administered a bogus test of skin sensitivity. The session began with "small talk" and the experimenter removing his lab and his suit coat. The experimenter (henceforth the "toucher") then repeatedly touched the witness's hands, arms, and face both with his hands and with a Von Frey aesthesiometer (a small, hand-held instrument with plastic filaments of varying diameters with which the subject is touched), each time asking the witness whether or not he or she felt the touch. At one point, the witness was also invited to touch the toucher with the instrument. At another point a female adult (the "intruder") entered the room for 8 seconds to ask the toucher a question. After the last of nine sets of predesignated touch trials the toucher collected his coats and left the room.

After a brief pause, a second experimenter (the "interviewer") arrived and escorted the witness to a second room where the second session took place. After spending 5 minutes on an irrelevant task, the witness was asked to describe everything that had happened "while you were in the room with the man." The interviewer followed up this free narrative report with five open-ended questions like, "Can you tell me anything else about what the man looked like?" The interviewer then asked approximately 30 specific questions about the physical features of the toucher and intruder, the toucher's and witness's actions, the physical surroundings of the testing room, and the places the witness was touched. Finally, witnesses attempted to identify the toucher and the intruder from separate six-person photospread lineups. For half of the subjects a photo of the toucher was actually among the six photos (target-present), whereas for the other half his picture was not included in the lineup (target-absent). The intruder was always present in her lineup. The entire memory report session was videotaped.

Results

A transcript was made from the videotaped memory report of each witness and scored on a number of dimensions. The major results are presented in Table 8.1. Not surprisingly, 5–6- year-olds gave significantly briefer free-recall reports than did either the 9–10-year-olds or the adults, using only an average of 125 words to answer the "Tell me everything" question and the five follow-up questions, in contrast to 260 and 329 words for the successively older witness groups. The shorter narratives of the young children were also less complete, containing fewer accurate statements than the free-recall reports of either the older children or the college students. However, as can be seen in Table 8.1, children and adults, in their free-recall, did not differ in number of commission errors (assertions that something happened that did not or incorrect attributes of persons or objects). Consistent with past research, the little that children said in free recall tended to be quite accurate.

Five- to six-year-olds correctly answered significantly fewer objective items about the toucher, the intruder, the places they had been touched, and the events that had occurred during the session. Moreover, unlike in free recall, the younger children made more commission errors in answering the objective questions. However, it is encouraging to note that neither group of children made more commission errors about where they had been touched.

Whereas only the youngest children performed more poorly than did the adults on the free-recall and objective questions tasks, both 5–6-year-olds and 9–10-year-olds performed significantly more poorly than did adults on the recognition tasks (lineup identifications), particularly on the intruder lineup. As can be seen in Table 8.1, adults were able to correctly identify the toucher from the target-present lineup or to correctly reject the target-absent lineup 92% of the time, whereas children of both age groups were accurate about 74% of the time. Yet children were not significantly more likely than adults to make a false identification of the toucher from either a target-present or target-absent lineup. In contrast, only half as many children (39% of 5–6-year-olds, 45% of 9–10-year-olds) as adults (81%) correctly identified the intruder, and significantly more children identified the wrong person (about 23% in both age groups) than did college students (0%).

Discussion

Young children didn't fare as well as older children and college students in this study. Consistent with earlier findings, they said less

TABLE 8.1. Witness Memory Results of Experiment 1

Measure	Witness age		
	5–6 yrs.	9–10 yrs.	Adult
Free recall			
Number of items recalled	12.46[a]	28.77[b]	33.69[b]
Number of commission errors	2.08	2.31	2.23
Objective questions			
Proportion of correct answers			
Overall	.60[a]	.71[b]	.75[b]
Toucher	.73[a]	.84[b]	.86[b]
Intruder	.67[a]	.78[b]	.88[c]
Events/actions	.51[a]	.65[b]	.67[b]
Places touched	.44[a]	.59[b]	.63[b]
Surroundings	.60	.66	.65
Number of commission errors			
Overall	8.88[a]	5.90[b]	4.22[c]
Places touched	0.46	0.39	0.59
Photospread recognition			
Proportion of correct identification			
Of toucher	.73[a]	.74[a]	.92[b]
Of intruder	.39[a]	.45[a]	.82[b]

Note. Within a row, means with different superscripts differ significantly at $p < .05$.

and reported fewer facts about the touching experience than did the older children or the adults. On the other hand, again consistent with past inquiries, the information that children did provide during free recall was fairly accurate. It does not appear that children fabricate information during free recall.

Unlike some past research on children's eyewitness memory (Goodman & Reed, 1986; Marin et al., 1979) the young children in our study also performed worse than did older children and adults in answering objective questions. Younger children answered fewer questions correctly than did older children and adults. Our impression is that these differences reflect primarily a deficit in memory among the younger children rather than communication or comprehension deficits. The objective questions were posed in simple, straightforward language and the interviewer encouraged all witnesses to verbalize any confusion about any question they might have. Moreover, one-word answers and even appropriate gestures were sufficient as correct responses to some questions.

One positive aspect of the children's testimony is that they made very few commission errors about the places they had been touched—a central aspect of the situation that would be particularly important in cases of alleged sexual abuse. It is also noteworthy that no children implied during testimony that any inappropriate behavior had taken place.

However, also consistent with previous findings, children of both age groups performed with less accuracy than did the adults when attempting to identify the experimenter and the intruder in lineups. Children were fairly poor at identifying the briefly seen intruder, but they were much more "adult-like" when it came to the toucher lineup. It is encouraging that children's performance approaches that of adults as witnessing conditions improve. Remember that the intruder was present only for a few seconds and her appearance was (intentionally) a peripheral aspect of the event. The toucher, on the other hand, was the initiator of the central aspect of the session (the touching). Contact with him was slow paced and lasted about six minutes (several minutes of which were spent engaged in direct eye contact). Although not on par with the adults, children did reasonably well at the task of identifying the toucher.

One disturbing finding is the rate of false identifications made by children on the intruder lineup. Considered with the greater number of commission errors during objective questioning a pattern emerges that reflects a greater willingness on the part of children to guess when they are unsure of the correct response (cf. Chance et al., 1982; King & Yuille, 1987; Parker & Carranza, 1989). In their defense, it should be noted that the children in this study knew there were no dire consequences of "fingering" the wrong person in the intruder lineup or providing inaccurate information during questioning. Many of the children seemed to enjoy themselves during the experiment. It is quite possible that under more serious circumstances children would monitor their decisions with greater care.

All in all, this study suggests that 5–6-year-old children will provide less complete and accurate memory reports than will older children and adults about both the people and some aspects of the actions in a participatory experience. But their memory errors are not likely to involve the most critical or central aspects of their experience, and commission errors are not likely by these youngsters unless questioning gets specific and very structured. In short, young children's memory for a touching experience was subadult but, in our opinion, not so bad.

Some children's memory reports were, in fact, quite accurate. Yet, from a legal standpoint, any witness's memory is only as good as the jury's evaluation of it. More realistically, it is only as good as the credibility judgments it receives from the fact finders (e.g., police officers, social workers) who are instrumental in deciding if a case should go to trial (indeed, whether there is a case at all). The remaining studies reported in this chapter examined children's credibility as compared to adults', and whether fact finders know an accurate child (or adult) when they see one.

REACTIONS TO CHILDREN'S (VERSUS ADULTS') TESTIMONY: JUDGMENTS OF BELIEVABILITY AND THEIR VALIDITY

The Believability Issue

Questionnaire studies that have sampled parents, lawyers, psychologists, and college students have found that, in general, people believe children under 10 years of age have somewhat poorer recall skills and are more suggestible than adults (Leippe et al., 1989; Leippe & Romanczyk, 1987; Yarmey & Jones, 1983).[1] Consistent with those impressions, which amount to a negative stereotype of children-as-memory-sources (Leippe & Romanczyk, 1989; Ross, Dunning, Toglia, & Ceci, 1990), a number of trial simulation studies have found that a prosecution case that relies heavily on a child's eyewitness testimony is less effective than one that relies on the same testimony by an adult. For example, Leippe and Romanczyk (1989) presented written descriptions of a criminal trial (of a robbery or mugging resulting in a homicide) in which the sole eyewitness was either 6 or 30 years old. Even though the eyewitness provided the same information in both age conditions, the 6-year-old eyewitness, in contrast to the 30-year-old, was rated as less credible and the case he supported garnered fewer guilty verdicts. Similar mock-trial studies by Goodman, Golding, Helgeson, Haith, and Michelli (1987) found that even a 10-year-old eyewitness received a lower credibility rating than did an adult eyewitness who provided the same account.

Interestingly, and of considerable importance, this skepticism toward children's testimony has its counterpoint in several recent studies that found just the opposite—that child witnesses are more readily believed than adults. This typically happens in studies in which testimony is presented in the witness's *own words*—via videotape, audiotape, or verbatim printed transcript (Leippe & Romanczyk, 1989; Ross et al., 1990)—or when child witnesses are considered less likely than adults to be able or willing to fabricate the allegations they are making (e.g., sexual abuse) (see Goodman, Bottoms, Herscovici, & Shaver, 1989). Relevant to the former potential condition of greater belief in children, Leippe and Romanczyk (1989) found that the testimony of a 6-year-old was associated with more guilty verdicts and was generally seen as more credible than that of a 30-year-old when mock jurors read verbatim testimony, whereas the reverse was true when mock jurors read a description of testimony containing the same information. Ross et al. (1990) presented a videotaped trial to subjects in which the key eyewitness was 8 or 21 years old. The witnesses were judged equally credible, but the 8-year-old was seen as more accurate, consistent, intelligent, and truthful.

Why are young children sometimes less and sometimes more believed than adults are? Leippe and Romanczyk (1989) attribute both effects to the negative stereotype of "children as memory sources." When testimony is simply described by a third party and attributed to a child, the stereotype has full play in the minds of the fact finders. They *assume* the child is not credible. But when they can see the child or read exactly what the child said, fact finders may be surprised. The real thing may be better than the stereotype suggests, possibly because the stereotype is based on only limited experience with children's testimony or on extrapolation from known developmental differences in more general cognitive and communicative skills. If the negative expectations are disconfirmed in this way, the child may be seen as especially believable. The contrast with expectations will stand out and belief in the child may be augmented by reasoning that the report seems compelling and thorough *in spite* of the age of the witness (cf. Kelley, 1972).

Overbelief in child witnesses could be as much a problem as underbelief. Commentators and researchers have already begun worrying that overbelief in children's memory reports may contribute to the growing number of sexual allegations that turn out to be unsubstantiated (Raskin & Yuille, 1989). Of course, it may be that mock-jury studies that found greater belief in children than in adults did so only because they employed exceptional child actors as eyewitnesses or wrote impressive (for a child) eyewitness transcripts. Indeed, in a recent study by Romanczyk (1990) that presented extensive (but fabricated) written transcripts of testimony to mock jurors, a 6-year-old was seen as more credible than an adult only when he or she admitted to no memory failures during cross-examination, giving flawless testimony. On the other hand, in a study in which actual testimony of numerous children and adults about a staged crime was presented to college students, 8-year-old children subjected to cross-examination were rated just as believable as adults—despite the fact that their reports were less accurate (apparently due to the confusion and pressure of the cross-examination) (Wells, Turtle, & Luus, 1989). In effect, these children were overbelieved.

Although the roles of prior expectations and stereotypes help explain the possibility of both over- and underbelief of child witnesses, the existing "juror reaction" studies have shortcomings that leave important questions unanswered. First, the question about over- or underbelief cannot be definitively answered without knowledge of the *actual* accuracy of actual witnesses—information provided in only one past study that compared child and adult witnesses (Wells, Turtle, & Luus, 1989). Second, because they used fabricated or acted out testimony, these studies tell us little about what communicative styles (if any) of child witnesses contribute to their credibility or lack thereof.

The Discernibility Issue

Questions of underbelief and overbelief of children, and of prior expectations and communicative styles as determinants of reactions to children, beg an even more basic question: Can fact finders discriminate between accurate and inaccurate child witnesses (or, for that matter, adult witnesses)? If so, what behavioral cues from the child do they use? One of the jurors in the McMartin Preschool trial described her experience this way:

> [I]t was hard for many of the jurors . . . [to determine] if we were knowing their personal experience or if we were just hearing about what their parents had talked to them about. . . . It was very difficult to tell the difference. (*Nightline*, 1990, p. 6)

Apparently, it was difficult for the jurors to tell whether the children were reporting memories for real or suggested (imagined) events. Determining the accuracy and credibility of a child (or any) eyewitness is the critical task of jurors and other fact finders such as police and social workers. The task is difficult enough when the eyewitness is an adult. The ability of mock jurors to validly judge the accuracy of an adult eyewitness has been shown to be slim at best (Wells & Leippe, 1981; Wells, Lindsay, & Ferguson, 1989; Wells, 1984). One aspect of testimony that jurors seem to use to determine accuracy is the confidence with which it is delivered (Deffenbacher, 1980; Leippe, 1980; Wells, Lindsey, & Ferguson, 1979). For example, Wells, Lindsey, and Ferguson (1979) showed that when subjects evaluated a witness they had seen answer direct and cross-examination questions, the witness's actual accuracy failed to influence these evaluations. Rather, the confidence with which the memory report was delivered had the most influence on subjects' evaluations. However, Wells and Murray

(1984), in a review of relevant literature, concluded that confidence generally is a weak predictor of accuracy.

More recent evidence that is somewhat more encouraging (about the possibility of discerning eyewitness accuracy) was provided by Schooler, Gerhard, and Loftus (1986), who showed that descriptions of real and imagined events differ in identifiable ways. In this study, some subjects actually saw a traffic sign during a slide presentation while others merely had its presence implied later during questioning. Compared to the reports of subjects who had the sign suggested to them, descriptions of the object were briefer, contained fewer hedges and references to cognitive operations, and were delivered more confidently when subjects had actually seen the stimuli. Schooler et al. (1986) also demonstrated that when told of these differences, subjects made modestly successful use of them as cues to discriminate between memory reports of real and suggested stimuli.

While these results give us confidence that fact finders will have at least modest skill at telling a good memory from a bad one, the situation may be quite different when the witnesses are children. A good part of any success at discerning the accuracy of others' memories probably comes from looking for the same cues in others' reports that we use to "reality monitor" our own memory. However, as Lindsay and Johnson (1987) suggested, children may monitor their memories— decide whether they are strong and real—differently than adults do. As a result, children may also emit fewer valid cues for the juror to interpret. It is also possible that evaluating children's testimony is more difficult than evaluating that of adults because jurors (who are adults) are less able to self-reference (e.g., "Would I have remembered that?") when evaluating the testimony of a child.

Experiment 2: A Study of Reactions to Real Memory Reports (about the Touching Experience)

In our next study (Leippe, Manion, & Romanczyk, 1992, Experiment 1), we began to address the believability and discernibility questions. We presented college students with the videotaped memory reports of the very best and very worst child and adult participant/witnesses in the "touching experience" memory experiment. Our student fact finders were asked to judge the memory accuracy and believability of the witnesses, thereby telling us if children giving real memory reports come across as more or less credible than adults reporting the same experience, and also whether accurate witnesses garner higher marks on accuracy than do their more forgetful counterparts. We also asked the participants to rate the witnesses on various communication dimensions, to determine if they see differences in *how* children (vs. adults) deliver their testimony.

Method

Using a composite memory score that took into account performance on objective questions and identification tasks, we identified the three most (*high-accurate*) and three least (*low-accurate*) accurate males and females in each age group from the touching experience study.[2] Videotapes of the recall and objective questions portions of these witnesses served as stimulus materials.[3] Each of 288 college students watched two videotaped memory reports, one of a high-accurate witness and the other of a randomly paired low-accurate witness of the same age and sex. All subjects saw witnesses respond to objective questions. Half of the subjects first saw the witnesses provide an unstructured narrative description of the event (*free recall*), whereas the other half did not (*no free recall*). This variable was included on the hunch that any tendency to perceive children as less believable would be especially likely when subjects hear their narrative free recall, which tends to be short and inarticulate (see, e.g., Leippe, Romanczyk, & Manion, 1991; Yarmey, 1984).

Order of presentation (high-accurate first or second) was counter-balanced, yielding a 3 (witness age: 5–6 years, 9–10 years, or adult) x 2 (witness sex) x 2 (free recall or no free recall) x 2 (order) x 2 (witness accuracy) mixed factorial design, with specific witness-pair-watched nested within the age and sex variables. After watching each tape, subjects (1) rated the witness on 7-point scales covering a number of dimensions, including believability, confidence, consistency, etc.(see Table 8.2), (2) estimated the percentage of objective questions the witness answered correctly, and (3) gave "lineup predictions" of whether or not the witness correctly identified the toucher and the intruder from target-present lineups, and correctly rejected a target-absent lineup regarding the toucher. The three lineup predictions included a dichotomous (yes or no) guess of whether the witness made an accurate decision and a rating on a 7-point scale (7 = most confident) of the subject's confidence in that prediction. In turn, a confidence-in-accuracy score was created for the subject in which the confidence rating was multiplied by -1 if the subject predicted the witness would be inaccurate or by a +1 if the subject predicted the witness would be accurate. The result was a 14-point scale with −7 being maximally confident that the witness would be inaccurate on a lineup decision and +7 being maximally confident that the witness would be accurate.

Results

Table 8.2 presents mean ratings and estimates of witnesses' memory performances as a function of witness age and accuracy level. Whereas witness sex, presentation order, and (contrary to our hunch) presence versus absence of the free-recall portion of the memory report had few effects, witness age and witness accuracy were significantly related to judgments on most memory and communication variables. In addition, the age and accuracy effects tended to be consistently present—albeit to different degrees—across the numerous stimulus witnesses used in the experiment.

As can be seen, the nature of most of these effects is that 5–6-year-old witnesses receive lower, more skeptical, ratings than the adult witnesses, with 9–10-year-olds falling in between but generally

TABLE 8.2. Mean Memory Estimates and Communication Attribute Ratings in Experiment 2

Witness age:	5–6 yrs.		9–10 yrs.		Adult	
Witness accuracy:	Low	High	Low	High	Low	High
Objective questions[a]**	.62	.62	.64	.74	.71	.74
Toucher ID (present)[b]**++	.66	.87	.51	3.25	1.67	4.15
Toucher ID (absent)[b]**++	.58	−.32	−.80	2.23	1.29	3.01
Intruder ID[b]*+	−.80	−.73	−1.09	1.17	−.20	1.29
Rating of:[c]						
Believability***+	4.19	4.54	4.57	5.23	4.98	5.18
Confidence	4.30	4.11	3.71	4.23	4.11	4.54
Consistency**	4.21	4.33	4.60	4.94	4.88	4.94
Nervousness	3.93	3.41	4.23	3.99	3.39	3.52
Likability**	5.55	5.52	5.31	5.06	5.04	4.77
Narrativeness*	3.05	2.58	3.14	3.82	3.21	3.78
Speech strength*	3.39	3.26	2.89	3.14	3.41	3.54

Note. Narrativeness refers to the extent to which speech is characterized by long utterances and verbal elaboration. Speech strength refers to the extent to which language contains few verbal hedges, qualified statements, or intensifiers.

[a] Mean proportion of objective memory questions answered correctly.

[b] Mean confidence-in-accuracy ratings (−7 = most confident that witness made an inaccurate lineup decision, 7 = most confident that witness made an accurate lineup decision).

[c] Ratings made on 7-point scales in which higher numbers indicate more of the attribute as listed.

* = near-significant ($.05 < p < .10$) main effect of witness age

** = significant ($p < .05$) main effect of witness age

+ = near-significant main effect of witness accuracy

++ = significant main effect of witness accuracy

closer to the adults. On average, subjects gave 5–6-year-olds a believability rating of 4.36, in contrast to ratings of 4.90 and 5.08 given to older children and adults, respectively. Whereas subjects estimated that older children and adults answered 68.7% and 72.4% of the objective questions accurately, they estimated only 62.2% for the 5–6-year-olds. In addition, less optimistic predictions were made about the children's lineup identifications. With increasing age of the witness, subjects expressed significantly increasing confidence that the witness accurately identified the toucher (Ms = 0.77, 1.88, and 2.91) and the intruder (Ms = -0.77, 0.04, and 0.55) from target- present lineups and correctly asserted, "He's not there" when confronted with a lineup from which the toucher was absent (Ms = 0.13, 0.72, and 2.15). We can see these same trends by examining the percentage of subjects predicting correct lineup decisions. For example, most subjects (76%) who watched an adult give a memory report predicted an accurate identification of the toucher by that witness, but only 58% of those who watched a 5- or 6-year-old predicted accuracy. The figure was 67% for those who watched a 9- or 10-year-old.

On the communication side, subjects judged young children's memory reports as the most inconsistent and fragmented (least narrative) giving 5–6-year-olds mean ratings of 4.27 and 2.82 on these dimensions in contrast to ratings of 4.77 and 3.48 for 9–10-year-olds and 4.91 and 3.50 for adults.

In a fashion that bodes well for the possibility that accuracy can be discerned, significant or near-significant effects of witness accuracy were obtained on believability and all three confidence-in-accuracy measures. As the mean differences in Table 8.2 convey, although the differences were not dramatic, high-accurate witnesses generally were judged more believable and more accurate than their low-accurate counterparts. A close look at Table 8.2 would seem to indicate as well that this accuracy discernment was less for younger children than for adult witnesses. However, none of the Accuracy x Age interactions on the memory credibility measures were statistically significant. Still, the numerical trends suggest that the matter of differential discernibility might be pursued in future research designed to be more statistically sensitive to these interactions.

Recall that subjects saw two witnesses in succession. When we tallied believability and memory judgments of first- and second-seen witnesses separately, the data presented in Table 8.3 emerged. It can be seen that the main effect of witness age is present to about the same extent in both cases. The effect of witness accuracy, however, is decidedly larger for second-seen witnesses, especially the 5–6-year-olds.[4] This suggests that, with practice, the ability to discern the accuracy of a witness may improve.

Discussion

When they gave testimony about a novel, participatory event that they actually experienced, child witnesses—especially younger ones—were less believed on average than adult witnesses to the same event. This was true even when their testimony was quite accurate. Figure 8.1 shows actual and estimated accuracy in responding to objective memory questions for all three age groups of witnesses. It can be seen that high-accurate 5–6 year-olds answered more objective questions accuractely than did low-accurate adults—yet subject fact finders estimated they answered *fewer* such questions accurately. Thus, it does not seem to be the case that the negative stereotype of children's memory is readily disconfirmed by "live memory performances," as Leippe and Romanczyk (1989) have speculated. It would appear that the findings from some mock-juror studies that children are more credible than adults is at least partly a result of presenting exceptionally impressive children's testimony. Most children, judging from our results, do not look *that* exceptional. As a matter of fact, the younger

TABLE 8.3. Mean Believability and Memory Estimates for First-Seen and Second-Seen Witnesses in Experiment 2

Witness age:	5–6 yrs.		9–10 yrs.		Adult	
Witness accuracy:	Low	High	Low	High	Low	High
First-seen witness						
Believability rating[a]	4.33	4.69	4.73	5.35	5.02	4.75
Questions estimate[b]	.64	.60	.62	.73	.72	.69
Toucher ID (present)[c]	1.46	.10	.13	2.90	1.98	3.50
Toucher ID (absent)[c]	.15	-.79	-.40	1.19	.65	2.77
Intruder ID (present)[c]	-.56	-2.33	-.23	.44	-.19	.06
Second-seen witness						
Believability rating	4.04	4.40	4.47	5.10	4.94	5.60
Questions estimate	.61	.65	.66	.74	.70	.79
Toucher ID (present)	-.15	1.63	.90	3.60	1.35	4.79
Toucher ID (absent)	1.02	.15	-1.21	3.27	1.94	3.25
Intruder ID (present)	-1.04	.88	-1.98	1.90	-.21	2.52

[a] Ratings were made on a 7-point scale in which higher numbers indicate more of the attribute as listed.
[b] Mean proportion of objective-questions subjects estimated were answered correctly.
[c] Mean "confidence-in-accuracy" rating (-7 = most confident that witness made an inaccurate lineup decision, 7 = most confident that witness made an accurate lineup decision).

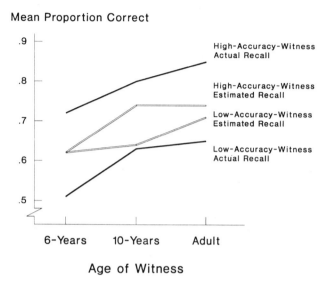

Mean Proportion Correct

FIGURE 8.1. Proportions of objective cued-recall items anwsered correctly by subject-witensses in Experiment 1 and proportions estimated by subject-jurors in Experiment 2.

ones in our study appeared to subjects to be more inconsistent and to speak less narratively, in a more fragmented, choppy style than did adults. If children look this way, it is perhaps not surprising that they routinely draw less positive credibility ratings.

The accuracy discernment findings are encouraging as evidence that fact finders, to an extent, can tell an accurate adult's or child's memory report when they see one. The fact that this discernibility was greater for second-seen witnesses than for first-seen witnesses raises the possiblity that discriminating accurate from inaccurate child witnesses can be improved with experience or practice. Our next experiment explored this possibility further.

Before moving to the next experiment, we should note that the lesser belief in the testimony of 5–6-year-olds is, in one sense, justified. The memory reports of the younger children were, in fact, poorer than those of the older children and adults in Experiment 1, and some of this difference necessarily characterized the subsets of reports evaluated in Experiment 2. While encouraging from this point of view, a less optimistic conclusion emerges from a close look at Figure 8.1. It can be seen that high-accurate 5–6-year-olds' objective-questions performance was underestimated to about the same degree as that of high-accurate older witnesses. Inaccurate 5–6-year-olds, however, were more *overbelieved* than their older counterparts, a finding also observed by Wells, Turtle, and Luus (1989). Factfinders' difficulty in discerning the accuracy of young children creates judgment errors in both directions.

Experiment 3: Does "Practice Make Perfect" in Judging Child and Adult Testimony?

To test for a "practice effect," we varied whether or not college students saw a moderately accurate memory report before evaluating a high- or low-accurate report by a witness of the same age (Leippe, Manion, & Romanczyk, 1992, Experiment 2). If practice in the form of prior exposure to a different witness helps, there should be a greater difference in the believability and accuracy ratings of accurate and inaccurate witnesses when fact finders have prior exposure than when they do not.

Method

A different sample of memory reports of the touching experience was used. In this sample, about half the reports used in Experiment 2 were replaced with different reports, with the new selections being based on maintaining a large separation between high-accurate and low-accurate reports. Overall, 36 target witness reports were used, including six high-accurate and six low-accurate witnesses in each of the three age groups. Each of 216 college students watched and rated one of these reports, which included both free recall and responses to objective questions. Half the students saw their target report immediately following introductory instructions (*no-practice* condition). The other half first watched and rated a practice memory report given by a witness of the same age whose composite accuracy was near the median among witnesses in that age group (*practice* condition). In essence, subjects saw a high-accurate or low-accurate memory report by either a 5–6-year-old, 9–10-year-old, or adult witness after either having or not having first seen another witness report the same event. Six different stimulus witnesses, each seen by six subjects, were nested in each of the 3 (Witness Age) x 2 (Witness Accuracy) x 2 (Practice or No-Practice) conditions. The dependent measures were the same as in Experiment 2.

Results

The results of Experiment 3 turned out to be complex and only partially consistent with the results of Experiment 2. On the consistent side of the ledger, a modest accuracy discernment effect was evident. Overall, high-accurate witnesses received significantly higher ratings of believability (M = 5.13) and estimates of objective-questions accuracy (M = 72.69) than did low-accurate witnesses (Ms = 4.63 and 66.24), as well as near significantly (ps < .10) higher confidence-in-accuracy regarding their correct identifications of the toucher (Ms = 2.94 vs. 1.73 for high- and low-accurate witnesses, respectively) and rejection of the toucher target-absent lineup (Ms = 1.93 vs. 0.49). The practice effect did not emerge, as there were no significant Accuracy x Practice interactions. Nor were there any Accuracy x Age interactions. Hence, with or without prior exposure to another witness, subjects judged more accurate witnesses as more credible whether they were adults or children.

Whereas reactions to witness accuracy were the same in Experiment 3 as they were in Experiment 2, reactions to witness age were not. Age did not have an overall significant effect on any of the judgments of witness believability and accuracy. Instead, there were significant Age x Practice interactions on believability ratings and the three confidence-in-accuracy scores. The relevant means are shown in Table 8.4, where it can be seen that, in the practice condition, there were small, nonsignificant age differences favoring 9–10-year-olds followed by adults and 5–6-year-olds. In the practice condition, by contrast, significant age differences emerged in which 9-10 year-olds fared the worst, receiving lower ratings than did either their older or younger counterparts.

Both witness age and witness accuracy had significant effects on ratings of communications dimensions. Noteworthy are the effects that replicate those of Experiment 2. Adults again were perceived as most consistent (Ms = 4.46, 4.50, 5.07, for 5–6-year-olds, 9–10 year-olds, and adults, respectively) and children as more likable (Ms = 5.70, 5.30, 4.85). High-accurate witnesses (M = 4.49) were seen as near-signficantly (p = .07) more confident than low-accurate witnesses, M = 3.97, a relationship that concurs with noticeable but nonsignificant trends among the 9–10-year-old and adult witnesses in Experiment 2 (see Table 8.2).

Discussion

We learned from Experiment 3 that the accuracy discernment effect is robust—at least for the "touching experience" memory report. And it is there even for our youngest child witnesses. On the other hand, the age-credibility effect of Experiment 2, in which young children come across as less believable and accurate, failed to emerge in Experiment 3.

TABLE 8.4. Mean Believability and Memory Estimates Ratings in Experiment 3

	Witness age		
	5–6 yrs.	9–10 yrs.	Adult
No practice condition			
Believability	4.78	5.06	4.86
Questions estimate[a]	.69	.70	.70
Confidence-in-accuracy[b]			
Toucher ID	1.64	2.86	2.00
Toucher rejection	−0.33	1.58	0.31
Intruder ID	1.14	−1.50	−0.75
Practice condition			
Believability*	4.81	4.44	5.36
Questions estimate	.68	.65	.75
Confidence-in-accuracy			
Toucher ID**	3.61	−0.25	4.17
Toucher rejection**	2.50	−0.28	3.47
Intruder ID**	0.17	−2.94	2.61

[a]Mean proportion of objective-questions subjects estimated were answered correctly.
[b]Means based on 14-point scale in which −7 corresponds to maximum confidence that lineup ID was inaccurate and +7 corresponds to maximum confidence that lineup ID was accurate.
*near significant ($.05 < p < .10$) main effect of witness age.
**significant ($p < .05$) main effect of witness age

Instead, 5–6-year-old witnesses received similar ratings to adults, and 9–10-year-olds received either similar ratings to adults (if subjects did not first see another witness) or the very lowest ratings (if a practice witness was seen first).

One explanation of the dramatic turn of fortune in the impact of the very same 9–10-year-old witnesses could be a contrast effect. Perhaps the focal witnesses of that age looked less believable than did the practice witness. The practice witness in each age group (always a male) was chosen for his average accuracy and without regard to communicative qualities. Judging from the ratings he received, the 9–10-year-old practice witness made a better impression than did a number of the 9–10-year-old focal witnesses. The latters' ratings, as a result, may have suffered in contrast, thereby accounting for the exceedingly low ratings they received in the practice condition.

This contrast explanation, of course, cannot at all explain the relative absence of age effects on credibility judgments in the no-practice condition. It would seem that when witnesses give memory reports in their own words, the age-credibility relationship is not particularly robust. Although adults may come across as more credible than young children on average, some not insignificant number of children may appear just as credible, or more credible, than some number of adults. Experiment 3 may have included, by the luck of the draw, a good number of such cases. This suggestion concurs with both the inconsistencies in the results of previous research on witness age and credibility that we discussed at the beginning of this chapter and with social–psychological knowledge that idiosyncratic communicative qualities play a large role in persuasion and communication (see, e.g., Zimbardo & Leippe, 1991).

Still, the failure to obtain a significant overall age effect in Experiment 3 is frustrating in that it blocks our goal of discerning a reliable overall pattern amidst the "noise" of individual differences among witnesses. Faced with the null finding of Experiment 3, must we conclude that the results of Experiment 2 were merely a chance fluke? Or was the reliable age difference of Experiment 2 a valid indicator that age effects, when they do show up, favor adult witnesses. To increase our confidence either way, we decided to conduct one more experiment.

Recall that the primary goal of Experiment 3 was to test whether practice increases fact finders' ability to discern eyewitness accuracy. We obtained no evidence to support this. Subjects discriminated between high-accurate and low-accurate witnesses to the same modest but significant degree whether or not they had already evaluated another witness. In retrospect, however, it is questionable whether we actually varied practice. Typically, practice involves feedback from one trial to the next. Our subjects were given no such feedback. Experiment 4 was designed in part to give the practice hypothesis, like the age-credibility relationship, one more chance.

Experiment 4: Judging Child Witnesses When You Are Married with (or without) Children

We examined a group of subjects whom we felt likely had practice in evaluating the truthfulness and accuracy of children—parents (Leippe, Manion, & Romanczyk, 1992, Experiment 3). We showed the memory reports of high- and low-accurate 5–6-year-olds and college students to parents and nonparents of elementary school children. If prior exposure to children facilitates ability to discern the accuracy of their memory reports, parents should be able to discriminate between high- and low-accurate children to a greater extent than nonparents.

Method

Forty-eight people who had been married between 5 and 18 years and were mostly middle-class suburbanites served as subjects. Half the subjects (the married-with group) had at least one child who was currently between the ages of 5 and 7, whereas the other half had no children over the age of 2 years (the married-without group). Each subject watched videotapes of *four* memory reports from Experiment 1. Two were reports of adult witnesses, and two of 5–6-year-old witnesses. Within witness age, one witness was a high-accurate and the other a low-accurate witness. The order of presentation was systematically varied across subjects. In addition, the 2 (Age) x 2 (Accuracy) design was repeated 3 times with different foursomes of witnesses. After watching each memory report, subjects rated the witness on believability, confidence, and consistency, gave a recall estimate, and predicted lineup recognition. Finally, after they went through all four reports, subjects were asked to indicate which of the two adults and which of the two children they had evaluated seemed more accurate.

Results

Accuracy effects emerged once again. As can be seen in Table 8.5, compared to low-accurate witnesses, high-accurate witnesses were rated as significantly more believable, confident, and consistent; were estimated to have answered significantly more questions correctly; and were more often predicted to have made accurate lineup choices. Importantly, rather strong age effects reemerged in this experiment. As in Experiment 2, 5–6-year-olds received significantly lower ratings of believability and estimates of objective-questions and lineup accuracy. The children also were rated less confident and consistent than were the adults. Age and accuracy, as a rule, did not interact. These results restore our confidence that the negative age-credibility relationship in eyewitness testimony is reliable, if not inevitable. The results also inform us that the accuracy discernment and lesser-credibility-given-to-children effects occur when fact finders are jury-eligible, noncollege, older adults and when the fact finders see both adult and child witnesses.

The effects of age and accuracy also occur whether or not fact finders have extensive experience with (their own) children. For the most part, the results were the same for the married-with and married-without samples. On one measure only did we get evidence that "unpracticed" married-withouts can less readily discern the accuracy of 5–6-year-olds than that of adults. When asked to choose which adult was more accurate, both married-withs (67%) and married-withouts (83%) chose the high-accurate witness the majority of the time. In contrast, when asked to choose the more accurate child, married-withs made the right choice most of the time (71%), whereas

TABLE 8.5. Mean Ratings and Predictions of High-Accurate and Low-Accurate Adult and Child Witnesses in Experiment 4

Witness age:	5–6 yrs.		Adult	
Witness accuracy:	Low	High	Low	High
Questions estimate[a]	.59	.63	.72	.84
Lineup predictions[b]				
Toucher	.63	.69	.71	.88
Intruder	.33	.31	.54	.75
Ratings of:[c]				
Believability	4.56	4.92	5.21	6.10
Confidence	4.23	4.41	4.29	5.40
Consistency	4.21	4.71	5.19	5.92

[a]Mean estimated proportion of objective questions answered correctly (out of 45).
[b]Proportion of subjects who predicted that the witness would make a correct identification.
[c]Ratings were made on a 7-point scale in which higher numbers indicate more of the attribute as listed.

married-withouts guessed with only chance accuracy (46%). The witness Age x Parental Status interaction on this measure proved significant.

Determinants of Believability and Cues to Accuracy

By measuring a number of subjective and objective witness variables in Experiments 2 and 3, we hoped to gain some insight into the witness behaviors or styles that lead fact finders to believe or not believe them, as well as to discriminate between those witnesses who are more accurate and those who are less accurate. In pursuit of this insight, we conducted a series of multiple regression analyses on six subsets of data. These subsets were comprised of the coded behaviors and subjects' ratings of the 5–6-year-olds, 9–10-year-olds, and adults in Experiment 2 (first-seen witness condition only) and Experiment 3. The analyses included the following variables.

To-Be-Predicted Criteria

Within each of the six data subsets, three multiple regressions were conducted in which the criterion, to-be-predicted variable was either (1) *believability ratings*, (2) *objective-questions estimate* (the percentage of objective questions subjects estimated a witness answered correctly), or

(3) *actual accuracy* of the witness (a "composite accuracy score" consisting of performance on objective questions and lineup tasks—see note 2). Note that the first two criteria are *perceptions* of memory, whereas the third criterion is the real thing.

"Communication Style" Predictors

In each regression, we examined the extent to which several aspects of how the witnesses communicated related to, or predicted, either perceptions of memory or the real thing. The predictors included subjects' ratings of the witnesses on *confidence, consistency, narrativeness, likability, and the other ratings dimensions* of Experiments 2 and 3. To these subjective predictors, we added three qualities of the witnesses' communication styles, which we measured off transcripts of the memory reports. One was *report length*, the number of words comprising the witness's free-recall narrative. A second was *don't-knows*, the number of times the witness responded "I don't know" to an objective memory question. And the third was speech *powerfulness*. Following the work of O'Barr (1982; Erickson, Lind, Johnson, & O'Barr, 1978), we counted the number of "powerless verbalizations" in the free recall of the witness, including verbal hedges (e.g., "sort of"), hesitations (e.g., "uh, um"), intensifiers (e.g., "very definitely"), and gestures as substitutes for words (e.g., pointing while saying "he touched me here and here"). In turn, the ratio of report length to number of powerless verbalizations was used as our measure of speech powerfulness—the larger this value was, the less often the witness used powerless speech forms.

Results

So what did these analyses reveal? Let us look first at predictors of perceptions of memory. The strongest and most consistently significant predictors of both believability and objective questions estimate were rated confidence and rated consistency (standardized regression coefficients [betas] ranged from 0.20 to 0.69 for these predictors). In both Experiment 2 and Experiment 3, witnesses in all three age groups received higher believability ratings and higher objective-questions estimates the more they were seen to be *confident* and *consistent*. In addition, in Experiment 2, 9–10-year-olds who spoke more powerfully were seen as more believable and accurate (betas = 0.22 and 0.22). Interestingly, in both experiments, both 5–6- and 9–10-year-olds received higher believability ratings (but not objective-questions estimates) the more often they admitted they "don't know" (betas range = 0.16–0.22).

A sharp contrast presents itself when we move to an examination of the communication variables associated with actual accuracy. How witnesses of any age actually performed on the memory tasks was unrelated to how consistent subjects judged those witnesses. And judgments of confidence were positively related only to actual accuracy only among adult witnesses in Experiment 3 (beta = 0.48). Instead of rated confidence and consistency, it was the objectively measured communication variables that were associated with actual memory accuracy. For adults and older children, longer memory reports (betas = 0.51 and 0.48 in Experiment 2), fewer don't-knows (betas = -0.31 and -0.43 in Experiment 2, and -0.31 for adults in Experiment 3), and more powerful speech (betas = 0.42 and 0.24 in Experiment 2, and 0.75 for 9–10-year-olds in Experiment 3) were associated with higher accuracy. For the younger—5–6-year-old—children, *just the reverse* of these relationships prevail (betas = -0.39 [report length, Experiment 2], 0.26 [don't-knows, Experiment 2], -0.41 [powerfulness, Experiment 3]). We will have more to say about these intriguing relationships presently.

CONCLUSIONS

Believability and Age

We began this chapter with a memory experiment in which children between the ages of 5 and 6 years, compared to adults, gave less complete free-recall reports, made more commission errors in responding to objective memory questions, and (along with even older children, ages 9 and 10 years) were less able to accurately identify both a momentarily seen stranger and one with whom they interacted closely for about 6 minutes. This research, like other studies before it, suggests that young children cannot match adults in remembering unusual events and unfamiliar people whom they encounter for a rather brief time. On the other hand, the research also found that our young witnesses almost never offered incorrect information when giving uninterrupted or cued free recall. Moreover, in our opinion as objective observers who knew "what happened," practically all the children reported the main activities and "spirit" of their "touching experience" in an accurate and appropriate manner.

Our major questions, though, concerned how naive (regarding the reported incident) fact finders would react to the children's reports. Two of three experiments found that college students, as well as parents with and without elementary school children, judged 5–6-year-old witness-participants in the touch experiment as less believable and less accurate than their adult counterparts. A third experiment failed to find this age pattern to a statistically reliable degree but did suggest that 5–6-year-olds scored at least slightly lower than adults on all memory credibility dimensions. Children ages 9–10, overall, did not receive believability and accuracy ratings that were terribly lower than those given adult witnesses (except in a condition of Experiment 3 in which a contrast effect may have worked against them). All in all, then, it seems that younger children—the 5–6-year-olds—are judged as less credible memory sources than are adults when they give testimony in their own words. Indeed, no matter how accurate a 5–6-year-old witness was, he or she seldom fared better on memory credibility ratings than did a *less* accurate adult.

Why is this? Part of it would seem to involve the way in which young children communicate memories. Young children were consistently (in all three "reactions" experiments) rated less consistent than adults. In one experiment, they also were judged to give more fragmented, less smooth reports, and in another experiment they looked less confident. All three of these qualities have been found in past research to decrease the credibility of witnesses (Leippe & Romanczyk, 1989; O'Barr, 1982; Wells & Murray, 1984; Whitley & Greenberg, 1986). And the regression analyses of fact finder judgments in Experiments 2 and 3 revealed that, for child and adult witnesses alike, impressions of confidence and consistency were the strongest predictors of believability and accuracy. Ratings of confidence, moreover, were themselves moderately to highly correlated in each age group with rated narrativeness, $rs(70) > 0.39$, and rated speech strength, $rs(70) > 0.70$. The "look of confidence" seems to involve subjective impressions of speaking in longer, more elaborate sentences with few hesitations—a look that naturally may be seen less in children.

The lower consistency ratings received by children are particularly important. They concur with empirical research showing that young children may appear inconsistent because certain of their communication-relevant skills are not fully developed (see Goodman, Golding, & Haith, 1984; Melton, 1981). Young children's sense of time may not have reached adult levels. Their reports of lengthy events may be less likely to be temporally sequential or may exclude connecting events they consider unimportant. Observers quite readily may infer poor memory from such qualities of inconsistency. Judging from our data, however, this is a shaky inference. Rated consistency did not predict the accuracy of children's memory reports.

The strong roles of rated consistency and confidence indicate that a negative stereotype is not the only cause of the negative age-believability relationship. *How* young children communicate also seems important. But the stereotype probably contributes to the relationship even when fact finders watch actual testimony. As we have seen, even highly accurate and reasonably articulate children received somewhat lower accuracy and believability ratings than did comparably accurate adults. Moreover, objectively, children's reports were delivered just as "powerfully" as were adults'. The average speech powerfulness scores in Experiments 2 and 3 were 12.73 and 12.10 for 5–6-year-olds, 14.54 and 14.82 for 9–10-year-olds, and 11.25 and 12.68 for adults.

It would seem that people increase their a priori skepticism at least a little when an eyewitness is a child. This may be appropriate because, on average, young children *are* less accurate. But, on the downside, the heightened skepticism may become a hurdle that even very good testimony may not fully overcome. Accordingly, the courts should consider using pretrial instructions to juries that—to the contrary of what traditional instructions have stressed—urge jurors to guard against using any preconceptions to judge any witness, including a child.

Discernibility and Age

What about accuracy discernibility? The evidence that subjects, at least to a moderate extent, more readily believed high-accurate witnesses than low-accurate witnesses is good news for the criminal justice system, which relies on the assumption that police officers and jurors can make valid decisions about eyewitness memory. Previous research (e.g., Lindsay, Wells, & Rumpel, 1981; Wells, Lindsay, & Ferguson, 1979) has questioned this assumption, but this work may have methodological limitations (see Leippe et al., 1992). Our studies suggest that at least modest discernment occurs, in part because fact finders rely on apparent witness confidence, which weakly, but significantly, discriminates between accurate and less accurate witnesses in our research (i.e., the witness accuracy effect on rated confidence observed in Experiments 3 and 4 and as a trend in Experiment 2) and other eyewitness studies (see Bothwell, Deffenbacher, & Brigham, 1987). Our findings (from the multiple regressions) also suggest, however, that memory judges could do a lot better if they used powerful speech, long free-recall narratives, and relative lack of memory failure admissions as positive cues to high accuracy among adults and older children. Should these relationships be replicated in studies involving eyewitness reports of different events in different contexts, it might be possible to train interviewers and jurors to use them in assessing credibility (cf. Schooler et al., 1986).

Children, like adults, were discernible—an encouraging finding, to be sure. But, in our first reactions study (Experiment 2), we encountered signs that the younger children were nonsignificantly less discernible than the adults. Future research should examine whether, in fact, adults may have a somewhat harder time self-referencing when it comes to children—putting themselves "in their shoes" as it were. The present studies do not reveal much about that possibility, but an examination of the behavioral correlates of witness accuracy revealed by the multiple regressions does suggest that some cues to accuracy are different, indeed, *opposite* for 5–6-year-old witnesses than they are for 9–10-year-old and adult witnesses. More accurate younger children gave *shorter* narrative reports, spoke with *more* hesitations, hedges, and intensifiers, and admitted memory failures *more* often than did less accurate younger children.

These findings make sense in light of memory studies (including Experiment 1) that show that young children are prone to commission errors when specific or forced-choice memory items are posed that tacitly invite guessing (King & Yuille, 1987; Parker & Carranza, 1989). This may be because young children have an overly optimistic sense of their own memory skills (Flavell, 1979). It stands to reason that the children most prone to these errors—and thus those with the least accurate memory reports—would be those who gave rambling, indiscriminate narratives, always guessed, never said, "I don't know," and did all this without much hesitation. More accurate children, by contrast, would give concise reports, admit memory failures, and perhaps "hem and haw" a bit—all reflective of greater self-scrutiny.

If this sounds intuitive and reasonable, remember that it is also after the fact. Subjects in our research did not grasp these relationships before the fact, since there is no evidence that they used the cues sufficiently to guide their judgments. If they had, they would have done a better job at discerning accuracy. Of course, there is a clear need for future studies to find out whether the communicative correlates of children's accuracy in the present studies are *generally* valid cues to accuracy in forensically relevant memory situations. In the event that they are, or that other valid cues are discovered, we may eventually have the knowledge to train fact finders and triers-of-fact to be better judges of children's memory. One of the trial lawyers in the McMartin case said, "I think we are on the brink . . . of an American child movement. We are now paying attention to the children. Perhaps . . . the 90's will be the decade of the child" (*Nightline*, 1990, p. 14).

He may be right. However, we not only need to pay attention to the children; we also need to learn *how* to pay attention to them.

ACKNOWLEDGMENTS

The research reported in this chapter was supported by a grant from the National Science Foundation (No. SES - 8711659) awarded to Michael R. Leippe. The authors would like to thank Joyce Bloom, Lenore Heller, Alexandra Jacoby, Laura Livingston, Amy Manion, Tim Miller, Seth Oberstein, and Roz Sackoff for assistance at various stages of the research.

NOTES

1. Interestingly, although the majority of respondents in Leippe and Romanczyk (1987) believed that children were less capable rememberers than adults, a notable minority reported that they believed children to be superior to adults in memory skills.
2. A composite accuracy score was computed for each memory report within age group. Two points were given for a correct decision on the toucher lineup while 1 point was given for accurately identifying the intruder. The same number of points was subtracted for incorrect decisions. Within age group, memory scores (i.e., the proportion of objective questions answered correctly) regarding the toucher, the intruder, the surroundings, and actions/touches were ordered from best to worst and quartiles were assigned appropriately. Witnesses were given an additional point for being in the top quartile on a memory measure while a point was subtracted for being in the bottom quartile. Composite accuracy was the sum of these scores and ranged from -7 to +7 (i.e., $2 + 1 + 1 + 1 + 1 + 1$).
3. Photospread IDs were excluded from the memory reports. Jurors in real trials do not see the initial witness ID of the alleged perpetrator. Instead, they hear testimony and are informed that an ID was made.
4. A statistical test of this apparent interaction was not possible. To achieve a manageable design, the order of report presentation (high- or low-accurate first) was confounded with prior-report-seen (high- or low-accurate). This pattern, therefore, is only suggestive.

REFERENCES

Altman, M. J., & Lennon, D. (1986, March). Child witnesses in felony trials—competency and protection. *New York Law Journal*, pp. 1–3.

Bothwell, R. K., Deffenbacher, K. A., & Brigham, J. C. (1987). Correlation of eyewitness confidence and accuracy: The optimality hypothesis revisited. *Journal of Applied Psychology, 72,* 691–695.

Brigham, J. C., Van Verst, M., & Bothwell, R. K. (1986). Accuracy of children's eyewitness identifications in a field setting. *Basic and Applied Social Psychology, 7,* 295–306.

Bulkley, J. A. (1982). *Recommendations for improving legal interventions in intrafamilial child sexual abuse cases.* Washington, DC: American Bar Association.

Ceci, S. J., Ross, D. F., & Toglia, M. P. (1987). Suggestibility of children's memory: Psycholegal implications. *Journal of Experimental Psychology: General, 116,* 38–49.

Chance, J. E., & Goldstein, A. G. (1984). Face recognition memory: Implications for children's eyewitness testimony. *Journal of Social Issues, 40,* 69–86.

Chance, J. E., Turner, A. L., & Goldstein, A. G. (1982). Development of differential recognition for own- and other-race faces. *Journal of Psychology, 112,* 29–37.

Chi, M. T. H., & Ceci, S. J. (1987). Content knowledge: Its role, representation, and restructuring in memory development and reorganization of memory. In W. H. Reese (Ed.), *Advances in child development and behavior* (Vol. 20, pp. 91–142). Orlando, FL: Academic Press.

Cohen, R. L., & Harnick, M. A. (1980). The susceptibility of child witnesses to suggestion: An empirical study. *Law and Human Behavior, 4,* 201–210.

Davies, G., Tarrant, A., & Flin, R. (1989). Close encounters of the witness kind: Children's memory for a simulated health inspection. *British Journal of Psychology, 80,* 415–429.

Deffenbacher, K. A. (1980). Eyewitness accuracy and confidence: Can we infer anything about their relationship? *Law and Human Behavior, 4,* 243–260.

Erikson, B., Lind, E. A., Johnson, B. C., & O'Barr, W. B. (1978). Speech style and impression formation in a court setting: The effects of "powerful" and "powerless" speech. *Journal of Experimental Social Psychology, 14,* 266–279.

Flavell, J. H. (1979). Metacognition and cognitive monitoring: A new era of cognitive developmental inquiry. *American Psychologist, 34,* 906–911.

Goodman, G. S. (1984). Children's testimony in historical perspective. *Journal of Social Issues, 40,* 9–32.

Goodman, G. S., Bottoms, B. L., Herscovici, B. B., & Shaver, P. (1989). Determinants of the child victim's perceived credibility. In S. J. Ceci, D. F. Ross, & M. P. Toglia (Eds.), *Perspectives on children's testimony* (pp. 1–22). New York: Springer-Verlag.

Goodman, G. S., Golding, J. M., & Haith, M. M. (1984). Jurors' reactions to child witnesses. *Journal of Social Issues, 40,* 139–156.

Goodman, G. S., Golding, J. M., Helgeson, V. S., Haith, M. M., & Michelli, J. (1987). When a child takes the stand: Jurors' perceptions of children's eyewitness testimony. *Law and Human Behavior, 11,* 27–40.

Goodman, G. S., & Reed, R. S. (1986). Age differences in eyewitness testimony. *Law and Human Behavior, 10,* 317–332.

Goodman, G. S., Rudy, L., Bottoms, B. L., & Aman, C. (1990). Children's memory and concerns: Ecological issues in the study of children's testimony. In R. Fivush & J. Hudson (Eds.), *What young children remember and why.* New York: Cambridge University Press.

Graham, M. H. (1983). *Evidence.* St. Paul, MN: National Institute for Trial Advocacy.

Harvard Law Review. (1985). The testimony of child victims in sex abuse prosecutions: Two legislative innovations. *98*, 806–827.

Kelley, H. H. (1972). Attribution in social interaction. In E. E. Jones, D. E. Kanouse, H. H. Kelley, R. E. Nisbett, S. Valins, & B. Weiner (Eds.), *Attribution: Perceiving the causes of behavior* (pp. 1–26). Morristown, NJ: General Learning Press.

King, M. A., & Yuille, J. C. (1987). Suggestibility and the child witness. In S. J. Ceci, M. P. Toglia, & D. F. Ross (Eds.), *Children's eyewitness memory* (pp. 24–35). New York: Springer-Verlag.

Leippe, M. R. (1980). Effects of integrative memorial and cognitive processes on the correspondence of eyewitness accuracy and confidence. *Law and Human Behavior, 4*, 261–274.

Leippe, M. R., Brigham, J. C., Cousins, C., & Romanczyk, A. (1989). The opinions and practices of criminal attorneys regarding child eyewitnesses: A survey. In S. J. Ceci, D. F. Ross, & M. P. Toglia (Eds.), *Perspectives on children's testimony* (pp. 100–130). New York: Springer-Verlag.

Leippe, M. R., Manion, A. P., & Romanczyk, A. (1992). Eyewitness persuasion: How and how well do fact finders judge the accuracy of adults' and children's memory reports. *Journal of Personality and Social Psychology, 63*, 181–197.

Leippe, M. R., & Romanczyk, A. (1987). Children on the witness stand: A communication/persuasion analysis of jurors' reactions to child witnesses. In S. J. Ceci, M. P. Toglia, & D. F. Ross (Eds.), *Children's eyewitness memory* (pp. 155–177). New York: Springer-Verlag.

Leippe, M. R., & Romanczyk, A. (1989). Reactions to child (versus adult) eyewitnesses: The influence of jurors' preconceptions and witness behavior. *Law and Human Behavior, 13*, 103–132.

Leippe, M. R., Romanczyk, A., & Manion, A. P. (1991). Eyewitness memory for a touching experience: Accuracy differences between child and adult witnesses. *Journal of Applied Psychology, 76*, 367–379.

Lindsay, D. S. (1990). *Brief summary of children's study.* Unpublished data and analysis, Williams College, Williamstown, MA.

Lindsay, D. S., & Johnson, M. K. (1987). Reality monitoring and suggestibility: Children's ability to discriminate among memories from different sources. In S. J. Ceci, M. P. Toglia, & D. F. Ross (Eds.), *Children's eyewitness memory* (pp. 92–121). New York: Springer-Verlag.

Lindsay, R. C. L., Wells, G. L., & Rumpel, C. (1981). Can people detect eyewitness identification accuracy within and across situations? *Journal of Applied Psychology, 66*, 79–89.

Marin, B. V., Holmes, D. L, Guth, M., & Kovac, P. (1979). The potential of children as eyewitnesses: A comparison of children and adults on eyewitness tasks. *Law and Human Behavior, 3*, 295–306.

Melton, G. B. (1981). Children's competency to testify. *Law and Human Behavior, 5*, 73–85.

Melton, G. B. (1984). Child witnesses and the first amendment: A psychological dilemma. *Journal of Social Issues, 40*, 109–125.

Myers, J. E. B. (1987). The child witness: Techniques for direct examination, cross-examination, and impeachment. *Pacific Law Journal, 18,* 801–942.

Nance, S. (1989, September 5). Child witnesses in court raise problems. *New York Law Journal.*

National Center on Child Abuse and Neglect. (1988). *Study of national incidence and prevalence of child abuse and neglect: 1988.* Washington, DC: U.S. Government Printing Office.

Nightline. (1990, January 18). D.C. Mayor Arrested/McMartin Trial Verdict [transcript]. New York: Journal Graphics.

O'Barr, W. M. (1982). *Linguistic evidence: Language, power, and strategy in the courtroom.* New York: Academic Press.

Parker, J. F., & Carranza, L. E. (1989). Eyewitness testimony of children in target-present and target-absent lineups. *Law and Human Behavior, 13,* 133–149.

Pratt, M. W., & MacKenzie-Keating, S. (1985). Organizing stories: Effects of development and task difficulty on referential cohesion in narrative. *Developmental Psychology, 21,* 350–356.

Raskin, D. C., & Yuille, J. C. (1989). Problems in evaluating interviews of children in sexual abuse cases. In S. J. Ceci, D. F. Ross, & M. P. Toglia (Eds.), *Perspectives on children's testimony* (pp. 184–207). New York: Springer-Verlag.

Romanczyk, A. (1990). *Attributions of witness credibility: The effects of response bias information and stereotype-based expectancies.* Unpublished doctoral dissertation, Adelphi University, Garden City, NY.

Ross, D. F., Dunning, D., Toglia, M. P., & Ceci, S. J. (1990). The child in the eyes of the jury: Assessing mock jurors' perceptions of the child witness. *Law and Human Behavior, 14,* 5–24.

Schooler, J. W., Gerhard, D., & Loftus, E. F. (1986). Qualities of the unreal. *Journal of Experimental Psychology: Learning, Memory and Cognition, 12,* 141–181.

Wells, G. L. (1984). How adequate is human intuition for judging eyewitness testimony? In G. L. Wells & E. F. Loftus (Eds.), *Eyewitness testimony: Psychological perspectives* (pp. 256–272). New York: Cambridge University Press.

Wells, G. L., & Leippe, M. R. (1981). How do triers of fact infer the accuracy of eyewitness identification? Using memory for detail can be misleading. *Journal of Applied Psychology, 66,* 682–687.

Wells, G. L., Lindsay, R. C., & Ferguson, T. J. (1979). Accuracy, confidence, and juror perceptions in eyewitness identifications. *Journal of Applied Psychology, 64,* 440–448.

Wells, G. L., & Murray, D. M. (1984). Eyewitness confidence. In G. L. Wells & E. F. Loftus (Eds.), *Eyewitness testimony: Psychological perspectives* (pp. 155–170). New York: Cambridge University Press.

Wells, G. L., Turtle, J. W., & Luus, C. A. E. (1989). The perceived credibility of child eyewitnesses: What happens when they use their own words? In S. J. Ceci, D. F. Ross, & M. P. Toglia (Eds.), *Perspectives on children's testimony* (pp. 23–46). New York: Springer-Verlag.

Whitcomb, D., Shapiro, E. P., & Stellwagen, C. D. (1985). *When the victim is a child: Issues for judges and prosecutors.* Washington, DC: National Institute of Justice.

Whitley, B. E., Jr., & Greenberg, M. S. (1986). The role of eyewitness confidence in juror perceptions of credibility. *Journal of Applied Social Psychology, 16,* 387–409.

Yarmey, A. D. (1984). Age as a factor in eyewitness memory. In G. L. Wells & E. F. Loftus (Eds.), *Eyewitness testimony: Psychological perspectives* (pp. 142–154). New York: Cambridge University Press.

Yarmey, A. D., & Jones, H. P. T. (1983). Is the psychology of eyewitness identification a matter of common sense? In S. M. A. Lloyd-Bostock & B. R. Clifford (Eds.), *Evaluating eyewitness evidence* (pp. 13-40). Chichester, England: Wiley.

Zimbardo, P. G., & Leippe, M. R. (1991). *The psychology of attitude change and social influence.* Philadelphia: Temple University Press.

9

Blaming the Child: Attribution of Responsibility to Victims of Child Sexual Abuse

Peter K. Isquith and
Murray Levine
State University of New York at Buffalo

Janine Scheiner
*Child and Family Services of Sullivan County
for West Central Services, New Hampshire*

Until the 1980s, reports of child sexual abuse were rare and were handled primarily by the family or juvenile court systems. As public awareness and concern over this issue and reported cases of child sex abuse have increased, the courts have responded with changes designed to facilitate the criminal prosecution of such cases (Bulkley, 1989). Each modification in procedure designed to facilitate prosecution poses a set of empirical questions as to its efficacy and subsequent ramifications (see *Maryland v. Craig*, 1990; American Psychological Association, 1990).

Given the increased emphasis on criminal prosecution and changes in state laws allowing children to give uncorroborated testimony in criminal court, the likelihood that children will testify in court is increased. These factors have stimulated a great deal of research on the capability of children as witnesses and their credibility to jurors. There are disparate results in the literature on jurors' reactions to children's testimony, partly because studies deal with children as bystander/witnesses, and as victim/witnesses (Goodman,

Golding, Helgeson, Haith, & Michelli, 1987; Leippe & Romanczyk, 1989; Nigro, Buckley, Hill, & Nelson, 1989; Ross, Dunning, Toglia, & Ceci, 1990; Ross, Miller, & Moran, 1987). Efforts to reconcile disparate results have begun to shed some theoretical light on how jurors might perceive children's testimony under different circumstances (see Goodman, Bottoms, Herscovici, & Shaver, 1989; Leippe & Romanczyk, 1987; Ross, Dunning, Toglia, & Ceci, 1989, 1990).

The credibility of child witnesses, particularly in child sexual abuse trials, may be a function of attributions jurors make about children's cognitive capacities and their motivations (Goodman, Golding, & Haith, 1984; Pynoos & Eth, 1984; Goodman et al., 1989). Two studies suggest that child complaining witnesses in sex abuse trials may be perceived as more credible than adult witnesses, but this advantage appears to diminish as the child's age increases to 11 or 12 years (Duggan et al., 1989; Goodman et al., 1989).

Goodman et al. (1989) theorize that in trial scenarios where the witness's accuracy is more salient than honesty in determining credibility, such as when the child is a bystander/witness, children may be judged to be less credible than adults. In contrast, if the trial is one that rests more on the witness's honesty than on accuracy, such as in a sexual abuse trial, a child witness may be judged to be as credible or even more credible than an adult. Perhaps jurors in the Goodman et al. (1989) study believed that the 6-year-old child was more honest, and thus more credible, than either the 14- or the 22-year-old.

Dugan (1987; Dugan et al., 1989) found similar results using a videotaped trial, subject/jurors from the community, and deliberations. They presented subject/jurors with a simulated sex abuse trial in which the alleged victim was either a 5-, 9-, or 13-year-old female and the defendant was a 38-year-old male known to the child. The principal results indicated that the 9-year-old alleged victim was rated the most credible and drew the most votes to convict the defendant, while the 13-year-old child was rated the least credible and drew the fewest votes to convict. Juror votes and credibility ratings in the case of the 5-year-old fell in between. Jurors may have perceived the 9-year-old as more cognitively capable than the younger child, yet more honest than the older child.

But what might account for the perception that the 13-year-old was less honest? Duggan et al. (1989) suggest that jurors may have attributed some measure of responsibility for the sexual abuse to this witness, thereby reducing her perceived honesty and credibility. Indeed, the authors report that jurors attributed more responsibility for the abuse to the 13-year-old than to either the 5- or the 9-year-olds. Aubrey (1989) also examined the jury deliberations from the Duggan et al. (1989) study and found that jurors discussed the child's responsibility for the abuse in the case of the 13-year-old complaining witness only and not when the younger witnesses testified. Similarly, Goodman et al. (1989) note that no statements attributing responsibility to the alleged victim were made when the child was a 6-year-old, but some statements to this effect were made when the alleged victim was either a 14- or a 22-year-old.

Perhaps jurors' attribution of responsibility to an older child witness in a sexual abuse trial factors into their credibility judgments by compromising their perceptions of the child's motivation. Little is known about the kinds of attributional biases that may influence jurors in cases of child sexual abuse. In the case of adult sexual assault, evidence indicates that the probability of convicting the defendant of rape decreases as a function of jurors' tendencies to perceive the victim as somehow having provoked the rape (Edwards, 1981). Jurors are more likely to attribute responsibility to the rape victim when she is attractive (Berscheid & Walster, 1974; Deitz & Byrnes, 1981), provocatively clothed (e.g., Kanekar and Kolsawalla, 1980), or when the victim's lifestyle implies an active sexual history (e.g, Smith, Keating, Hester, & Mitchell, 1976). The tendency of jurors to "blame the victim" of rape who possesses such characteristics makes obtaining convictions difficult.

Does a similar attribution bias exist for jurors in cases of child sexual abuse? If so, will the attributional bias vary as a function of the age of the child? Finally, does this bias obtain for both male and female victims of sexual abuse?

This chapter reports the results of two sets of studies. The first, a series of three experiments, examines the extent to which children of different ages who testify as complaining witnesses in a sexual abuse trial may be held responsible for the abuse and how this attribution of responsibility might affect perceptions of the child's credibility. The second series of two experiments explores whether jurors' tendency to attribute responsibility to the child can be controlled by judicial instructions.

ATTRIBUTION OF RESPONSIBILITY TO CHILD SEX ABUSE VICTIMS

Given that a simulated trial has already demonstrated that subject-jurors attributed responsibility to an older child (age 13) testifying as a complaining witness and were less likely to believe her (Duggan et al., 1989), we designed a study to assess the external validity of the simulation results, that is, to determine whether the tendency to attribute responsibility to the 13-year-old child for the sexual abuse was an artifact of the particular actress chosen to portray the 13-year-old victim. We used the "minimalist vignette" method (Scheiner, 1988), or brief written vignettes providing subjects with a minimum amount of information on which to base their judgments, to explore this issue further. This method provides a means of tapping into subjects' stereotypes about children at different ages by not providing them with visual or auditory information about the particular child. By concentrating the mock jurors' attention on the concept, generalizability may be enhanced.

In the first experiment, 76 undergraduate psychology students enrolled in psychology courses were told that a recent study had been conducted in which either a 5-, 9-, or 13-year-old female testified in court that she was sexually abused by an adult male familiar to her. We then asked the participants to place themselves in the role of juror, and indicate their agreement with the statement, "As a juror, I would hesitate to vote guilty if I perceived that the 5-year-old alleged victim encouraged the abuse." Subjects were then asked to respond for a 9-year-old and a 13-year-old witness. We asked the question tapping the attribution of responsibility indirectly because some evidence suggests that college students may be cautious in answering a more direct question regarding this issue (Isquith, 1988).

A large within-subject repeated-measures main effect for child age, $F (1, 142) = 17.81$, $p < .0001$, $f = .61$, was obtained.[1] Pairwise comparisons indicated significant differences between all three age cells, with the hesitation to convict appearing greatest if the subject perceived that the 13-year-old encouraged the sexual abuse.

We repeated this study with another group of subjects using a between-groups design to ensure that the repeated-measures design itself did not create an inadvertent demand on Ss to report a differentiated hesitation to convict based on the age of the child victim. In the second experiment, 41 college students in psychology courses were told that, in a trial, either a 5-, 9-, or 13-year-old child alleged that she was inappropriately touched by an adult male defendant. As in the first experiment, participants were asked to indicate on a 4-point scale the extent to which they would hesitate to vote guilty if they perceived that the child encouraged the sexual abuse.

Again the results indicated that participants would be more likely to consider an older child's responsibility for the abuse than they would a younger child's. A significant main effect for child age was obtained, ($F(1, 39) = 11.44$, $p < .001$, $f = .67$) with posthoc probing using

Scheffe' procedure (p = .01), confirming that hesitation to convict was greatest for the 13-year-old victim.

These two experiments are consistent with the Duggan et al. (1989) finding that victim responsibility may be considered in some way by jurors, particularly when the female is as young as 13 years old, and even when consent is not a legal issue. A third study was designed to answer three questions: (1) for what age child do jurors begin to attribute responsibility to the child victim for the occurrence of the abuse, (2) will jurors attribute responsibility to male as well as female victims of sexual abuse, and (3) is the tendency to attribute responsibility to child victims of sexual abuse related to the age at which jurors believe children become interested in sexual contact?

We used the same scenario and between-subjects design as before. Subjects were undergraduate psychology, and sociology students (N = 342). They were administered a brief questionnaire describing an allegation by a child that an adult male had touched him or her on the genitals. The age of the child (5, 7, 9, 11, 13, or 15 years), and sex of the child (male, female) were varied between questionnaires. Subjects completed 7-point Likert scales on the believability of the child's allegation and on their hesitation to vote guilty if they perceived that the child encouraged the abuse. Further, subjects were asked at what age they believe children develop a desire for sexual contact.

As expected, the believability and hesitation-to-convict variables were inversely correlated (r = −.22, p < .0001). An analysis of variance (ANOVA) computed on the hesitation-to-convict variable showed a main effect for child age, $F(5, 310)$ = 6.22, p <.001), f = .30, with hesitation increasing systematically with the age of the child. Scheffe's probes showed that the 13-year-old and the 15-year-old alleged victims were significantly different from the younger age victims on the variable of hesitation to convict. A main effect was also obtained for the sex of subject, $F(1, 310)$ = 11.79, p <.001, f = .34, with men showing greater hesitation to convict defendants if they perceived that the child was responsible for the abuse. Women were more likely to believe the child, $F(1, 310)$ = 22.39, p <.001, f = .60. There were no differences depending on whether the child was portrayed as a male or female, $F(1, 442)$ = .473, p = .47, and there were no significant higher-order interactions. Figure 9.1 shows the relation between the child's age and the jurors' hesitation to convict the defendant.

Figure 9.1 shows a similar pattern for the age by which subjects feel children develop an interest in sexual contact. The curve represents the cumulative number of subjects who indicated that children desire sexual contact by each age. The overall mean age of 12.4 years for

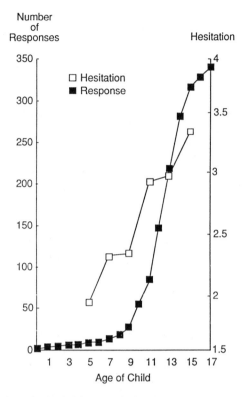

FIGURE 9.1. Age by which children are believed to develop an interest in sexual contact and jurors' hesitancy to convict if alleged victim encouraged abuse. The left ordinal and line on the figure designated "response" show the cumulative number of mock jurors who believed children developed interest in sexual contact at each age shown on the abscissa; the right ordinal and the line of the figure "hesitation" show the mean rating by mock jurors of hesitancy to convict at each age shown on the abscissa.

development of desire for sexual contact roughly coincided with the age at which the substantial increase in hesitation to convict occurred. Perceptions of the age at which sexual desire develops varied as a function of the alleged victim's gender. Boys were perceived as developing an interest in sexuality at a slightly younger age ($M = 11.7$) than girls ($M = 13.0$), $F(1, 310) = 16.99$, $p < .001$, $f = .45$. Both men and women judged the age at which children develop an interest in sexual contact similarly, $F(1, 310) = .02$, $p = .878$, $f = .09$.

   These three studies identify a constellation of beliefs that generate insight into jurors' perceptions of the credibility of child witnesses in cases of alleged sexual abuse. It is not just the cognitive capacities of children that may be questioned by jurors. Children, like adult rape victims, may be vulnerable to the perception that they may have provoked the abuse. The tendency for mock jurors to hold a child perhaps as young as 11 or 12 responsible for his or her own victimization is a robust finding that transcends method and population. In each study, whether using written vignettes or a videotaped trial simulation, participants indicated that they would be more likely to hesitate to convict the defendant if they thought the child was responsible when the child was 11 years old; the hesitancy to convict increases directly as the age of the child increases. This hesitation to convict coincides with the age at which subjects believe children develop an interest in sexual contact. This is also about the same age that children are perceived to have cognitive abilities approximating an adult's (Leippe & Romanczyk, 1989). The attribution of responsibility to the child is also associated with a decrease in the perceived credibility of a child sexual abuse victim.

This tendency for subject jurors to hold a child responsible for sexual abuse is troublesome. Many states have changed their laws in order to increase the number of child sexual abuse cases brought to trial (Bulkley, 1989). However, older children may not be perceived as credible if jurors hold them responsible for the sexual abuse. The successful prosecution of many child sexual abuse cases may depend on the development of techniques to counteract jurors' tendencies to disbelieve a child's testimony once they have "blamed the victim" for encouraging the abuse. Can jurors be persuaded to remove consideration of the child's responsibility from their decision making?

CONTROLLING JUROR BIAS

A similar phenomenon of attributing responsibility to the victim has been well documented in the rape literature (Aubrey, 1986; Calhoun, Selby, & Warring, 1976; Deitz & Byrnes, 1981; Fulero & Delara, 1976; Pugh, 1983). Holding a rape victim responsible bears a prima facie resemblance to holding an older child sex abuse victim responsible. Indeed, surveys of court records indicate that cases of sexual abuse involving victims between the ages of 12 and 40 are significantly less likely to result in convictions than are those involving victims under age 12 and over age 40 (Williams, 1981). In other words, jurors may view a child over the age of 12 as more like an adult than a younger child. Thus, it may be possible to draw inferences from the relative wealth of rape trial studies about ways in which jurors' attributional bias can be controlled.

Three issues must be decided by a jury in a rape trial: First, can the alleged victim accurately identify the rapist? Second, did the crime actually take place? And third, did the alleged victim consent to the sexual act? When a consent defense is used, the victim's character and credibility may be assailed and her sexual history reviewed to support the defendant's allegation that she consented. Borgida and White (1978) found that the amount of testimony regarding the victim's sexual history affects jury verdicts: An increase in testimony results in a decrease in convictions (see also Aubrey, 1986; LaFree, Reskin, & Visher, 1985).

Although blaming child sex abuse victims and blaming rape victims may be similar behaviorally, they are different legally. While jurors in a rape case may be asked to determine whether the alleged victim consented to the sexual act, this is not an appropriate consideration in a child sexual abuse case. In child sexual abuse cases only two issues, identification of the defendant and whether or not the abuse occurred, need to be decided. Consent is predetermined by the law: Children under an age specified by statute are not considered capable of consent. A consent defense is inapplicable in child sex abuse cases. A child's sexual history and provocativeness would probably be barred from admission because to include them would be both irrelevant and prejudicial. Jurors are also not routinely given a "cautionary charge" in child sexual abuse trials, although jury instructions might warn jurors to use caution in accepting a child's testimony (see Goodman et al., 1984).

How, then, might jurors' attributional bias toward child sex abuse victims be limited? One possibility would be to instruct jurors that they are not to consider the child's consent or responsibility in reaching a verdict. The New York Pattern Jury Instructions (Pattern Instructions) used in Duggan et al. (1989) did not explicitly instruct jurors that the child, by virtue of her age, is not capable of consent and that the responsibility for the sexual act rests solely on the defendant.

Would jurors react differently to older child witnesses in sexual abuse trials if they were reminded by the judge of the responsibility and consent issue? That is, if jurors were admonished to remove any consideration of the child's responsibility for the sexual abuse from their decision, would they be able to do so, and would this lead to higher credibility judgments of the child witness and/or a greater likelihood of convicting the defendant? We conducted a second series of two experiments designed to examine the effect of such an instruction in a child sex abuse case.

RESPONSE TO JUDICIAL INSTRUCTIONS

Before turning to these experiments, let us examine the effects of altering the judge's instructions. Devlin (1966) cautioned against tampering with jury rules: "Since no one really knows how a jury works or indeed can satisfactorily explain to a theorist why it works at all, it is not wise to tamper with it until the need for alteration is shown to be overwhelming." Devlin is cautioning that we cannot always predict the outcome of a change in jury procedure. In this instance, how might jurors react to a specific instruction regarding children's responsibility in a sexual abuse trial?

Since the judge is the most powerful authority in the courtroom and has the last word before the jury begins deliberating, the judge's instructions to the jury may have far-reaching implications for the jury's decision. The most influential statements from judge to jury are included in the "charge," the set of instructions outlining the jurors' task, the relevant law or laws to apply, the presumption of innocence, the burden of proof, and the standard of proof. These instructions are intended to form the "communicative link between the citizen-juror and the presiding judicial authority" (Buchanan, Pryor, Taylor, & Strawn, 1978, p. 31). In other words, the jury charge represents the judge's attempt to provide the jury with an understanding of the relevant law and legal concepts to apply, and to provide the jury with a framework within which they are to decide the particular case.

Despite the importance attached to the judge's instructions to the jury, it is unclear whether elements of the charge have the desired effect and under what conditions the effect is felt. Can jurors understand and apply the judge's instructions (Buchanon et al., 1978; Elwork, Sales, & Alfini, 1977, 1982; O'Mara, 1972; Severence, Green, & Loftus, 1984; Strawn & Buchanan, 1976; Sue, Smith, & Pedroza, 1975)? Are they willing to follow the instructions (see Gordon & Temerlin, 1971; Thompson, Fong, & Rosenhan, 1981)?

When extralegal or biasing evidence is introduced during the course of a trial, the judge may instruct the jury to disregard the evidence. Some studies investigating jurors' ability to disregard inadmissible evidence have found that jurors appear to be able to do so (L.S.E. Jury Project, 1973; Kassin & Wrightsman, 1985; Miller, 1975). For example, the L.S.E. Jury Project (1973) presented either an audiotaped theft trial or rape trial to potential jurors and allowed some subject jurors to hear evidence indicating that the defendant had prior convictions. In each case, when jurors were instructed to ignore the evidence, they returned significantly fewer convictions than did jurors who had not heard the same inadmissible evidence or jurors who had heard the same evidence that the judge had ruled admissible.

In contrast, a number of studies suggest that jurors find it difficult to ignore evidence when instructed to do so (Doob & Kirschenbaum, 1972; Hoiberg & Stires, 1973; Kassin & Wrightsman, 1980, 1981; Padawer-Singer & Barton, 1975; Sue, Smith, & Caldwell, 1973; Sue, Smith, & Gilbert, 1974; Thompson et al., 1981; Werner, Kagehiro, & Strube, 1982), or may even be led to pay greater attention to the inadmissible evidence (Broeder, 1959; Oros & Elman, 1979; Wolf & Montgomery, 1977). This latter phenomenon has been referred to as the "boomerang effect" (Oros & Elman, 1979).

Two studies of the effect of judicial instructions to cautiously examine the testimony of a rape victim bear directly on the present study. Oros and Elman (1979) compared the cautionary charge with a similar charge designed to neutralize bias against the defendant whose race was varied. While neither instruction affected juror votes for conviction, jurors given the cautionary charge to be skeptical of the alleged rape victim's testimony were indeed more lenient toward the defendant. The instruction to ignore personal biases against the defendant, however, produced an effect that was opposite from the anticipated direction. Oros and Elman (1979) suggest that jurors develop a skeptical cognitive set while hearing testimony, and that drawing attention to one particular witness or portion of testimony may lead jurors to attach a greater weight to it, thereby producing the "boomerang effect."

The L.S.E. Jury Project (1973) also found a "boomerang effect" when using the cautionary charge in a rape trial study. Jurors were able to follow the judge's instructions to disregard inadmissible evidence. However, the study found the opposite reaction to a second instruction by the judge to consider the uncorroborated testimony of the alleged rape victim with caution. Jurors who were instructed that such testimony is not likely to be credible returned a greater proportion of guilty verdicts than did jurors who were not given the cautionary charge.

It is not clear, however, under what conditions instructions to ignore biasing information will have an impact, and if they have an impact, if the impact will be the expected one. The lack of findings may reflect the weight of the evidence which may be strongly in favor of the defendant or the plaintiff. Judicial instructions may be more influential when the evidence is less clearly weighted one way or the other. In addition, the effects of jury instructions may be enhanced as a function of engaging in a deliberation (Kassin & Wrightsman, 1985; Wolf & Montgomery, 1977), a feature lacking in many mock jury studies.

In the case of a child sex abuse trial, if jurors are instructed not to consider the child's responsibility and to place all responsibility on the defendant, will jurors do so, or will they demonstrate the "boomerang effect?"

EXPERIMENT 1: JURY INSTRUCTIONS TO CONTROL JUROR BIAS

In order to explore the potential for revised jury instructions to limit jurors' attributions of responsibility to older child sex abuse victims, we asked 124 men and 113 women in psychology courses to read a one-page summary of the videotaped sex abuse trial used by Duggan et al. (1989) and used by us in Experiment 2. Our subject jurors read that a 13-year-old female had alleged that the male defendant, a 38-year-old neighbor, took her into the woods, sat her on his lap, placed his hand inside her pants, and rubbed her vaginal area. The defendant testified that the alleged victim was "running around" in the woods, and that he attempted to calm her down by sitting her on his lap and telling her a story.

The vignette was followed by either a summary of the Pattern Instructions or a summary of the Revised Instructions. Both sets of instructions included identical statements as to the presumption of innocence, the standard of proof, and the relevant law to apply in reaching a verdict. The Pattern Instructions, the same instructions used by Aubrey (1989), Duggan et al. (1989), and reported in Experiment 2 here, include explanations of the presumption of innocence, the burden of proof, the reasonable-doubt standard of proof, and the relevant law the jurors are to apply. With regard to the issue of the child complaining witness's consent or responsibility, the Pattern Instructions state:

> A person is guilty of sexual abuse in the second degree when he subjects another person to sexual contact and when such person is less than 14 years old. Usually, a number of points must be proven in a case of this kind. However, here, due to the age of the child not being in question, only one issue needs to be proven in order for you to find the defendant guilty of this crime.

With the aid of prosecuting and defense attorneys, this section of the jury instructions was revised to read:

> A person is guilty of sexual abuse in the second degree when he subjects another person to sexual contact and when such person is less

than 14 years old. Usually, a number of points must be proven in a case of this kind. In cases where the victim is under 14 years of age, as is the case here, consent is not an issue.

The revision also included the following:

The decision you are to reach in no way depends upon any consideration that the child was somehow responsible for the sexual contact. The law says the adult is responsible for refraining from sexual contact with a child under 14 years of age. Whether or not the child was a willing participant has no bearing on your decision. The state of her appearance or maturity does not matter.[2]

After reading the vignette and instructions, participants were asked to indicate their vote preference (guilty vs. not guilty) and respond to seventeen 7-point scale items measuring their perceptions of the credibility, motivations, and responsibility of each actor.

The Revised Instructions led to a significant increase in jurors' votes for conviction. A 2 (Pattern, Revised Instructions) x 2 (subject gender) analysis of variance on juror votes revealed a main effect of the instructions, $F(1, 236) = 14.52$, $p < .001$, $f = .25$. Overall, 65% of the subject jurors who read the revised instruction summary voted to convict, compared with 40% of those who heard the Pattern Instructions summary.

Figure 9.2 shows the effect of the instructions as well as a main effect of subject juror gender. Women were more likely to convict in this case than men, $F(1, 236) = 19.89$, $p < .001$, $f = .28$. Sixty-seven percent of women voted to convict, compared with only 40% of the men, regardless of the instructions. How men and women voted was not differently affected by which instruction they heard, $F(2, 236) = .003$, $p = .96$.

Juror perceptions of the actors were similarly examined in a 2 (instructions) x 2 (subject gender) ANOVA. To reduce the number of dependent measures, the 17 scales were first entered into a principal-components factor analysis with a varimax rotation. A sampling adequacy measure indicated that a good factor solution was possible (Kaiser, 1974; KMO = .91); three factors emerged from the raw data, accounting for 60% the variance. Subsequently, one score for each of the three factors was computed for each juror by multiplying the juror's standardized ratings on each scale by the factor loading and summing across all items comprising the factor.

The Credibility and Guilt factor accounts for 41% of the variance. Jurors who scored high on this factor felt that the child was fabricating the incident, her testimony was inaccurate and unbelievable, and the

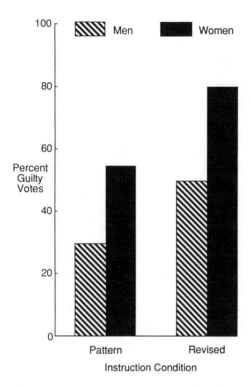

FIGURE 9.2. Juror gender and vote to convict with Pattern and Revised Instructions.

defendant was believable Moreover, these jurors doubted that the defendant committed the act.

The second factor, Responsibility, accounts for 12% of the variance and includes five scales that reflect how jurors felt about the child's responsibility for the abuse. A juror who scored high on this factor believed that the alleged victim encouraged, provoked, and should have foreseen the abuse and was responsible for it.

The Cognitive-Emotional factor, which suggests a cognitive and emotional set of responses, accounts for an additional 7% of the variance. A person scoring high felt that the defendant was responsible, that the child did not misunderstand his intentions, that the abuse was harmful to the victim, and that she was aware of the seriousness of her accusation.

When subjects' scores on each factor were entered into the 2 (instructions) x 2 (male, female jurors) analysis of variance design, only main effects for gender were found. The instructions did not seem to affect subjects' perceptions of the actors in the trial as measured by the factors. However, jurors seemed to understand the instruction that they were not to consider the child's responsibility in reaching a decision, and further were able to act on that understanding as exemplified by their votes of guilty or not guilty.

Men and women differed on each of the three factors. Women were more likely to believe the child, to perceive her as more aware of the seriousness of the accusation and of the defendant's intentions, and as harmed more by the abuse. Men were more likely to believe the defendant and to attribute greater responsibility to the alleged victim.

This study suggests jurors may be able to separate their attitudinal biases from their verdict decisions. Although there was no observable effect of the instructions on jurors' perceptions and attributions of responsibility, the Revised Instructions did result in an increase in guilty votes for both men and women. These results must be considered with caution, however. Although the vignette method is an efficient means of exploring trends, it would be more convincing if the same effect were demonstrated with a more ecologically valid study using subject jurors more like actual jurors, a trial simulation, and jury deliberations.

EXPERIMENT 2: VIDEOTAPED SIMULATION[3]

Based on the vignette study, we undertook a videotaped simulation. Forty 6-member juries, balanced for gender and comprised of participants recruited from the voter registration roles and from undergraduate psychology courses,[4] viewed a videotaped trial. A 13-year-old child testified that she was sexually abused by an adult male. A slightly modified version of Duggan et al.'s (1989) videotaped trial was used for this study. The videotape of a trial with a 13-year-old alleged victim but no corroborating testimony was chosen for this study because it had produced an approximately equal number of votes to convict and to acquit. Moreover, jurors' attribution of responsibility to the 13-year-old alleged victim was significantly higher than for any other age child (Duggan et al., 1989).

The script was a composite of the common elements found in this type of trial and was created in cooperation with the district attorney's sex crimes unit. The trial included the judge's introduction, opening and closing arguments by prosecuting and defense attorneys, and direct and cross-examination of a 38-year-old male defendant described as the stepfather and a 13-year-old female complaining witness.

The details of the testimony were the same as in Duggan et al. (1989). The testimony is summarized in Experiment 1, discussed above. Following the closing arguments, the judge concluded with either Pattern Instructions or Revised Instructions, as described in Experiment 1.

After viewing the trial, but before deliberating, participants indicated their inclination to vote guilty or not guilty on a continuous scale. Each six-person jury then deliberated for between 15 and 45 minutes and attempted to reach a unanimous verdict. Following deliberations, jurors again voted and completed a questionnaire assessing their perceptions of the alleged victim's and the defendant's credibility, and responsibility for the sexual act, the child's cognitive abilities, and their own ability to empathize with each actor.

The unit of analysis for all postdeliberation measures is the jury rather than the juror. To control for the interdependence of jurors' ratings, all dependent variables were transformed into means for each jury. Male and female responses were considered separately within each jury to allow analyses for gender differences. As a result, each jury has a mean score for males and a separate mean score for females for each observation made.

Did the Revised Instructions affect the rate of conviction? Of the 20 juries who heard the Pattern Instructions, 30% voted unanimously to convict, 35% voted unanimously to acquit, and 35% remained hung at the end of deliberations. Of the 20 juries who heard the Revised Instructions, 25% voted unanimously to convict, 55% voted unanimously to acquit, and 20% remained hung. This difference between juries in the two instruction conditions was not significant, $\chi^2(2, N = 40) = 1.79, p = .407$. Thus, the Revised Instructions apparently did not have the hypothesized effect of increasing the number of convictions when compared with Pattern Instructions. If anything, juries who heard the Revised Instruction appeared to be more inclined to acquit than juries who heard the Pattern Instructions.

Despite the lack of significant findings in jury verdicts between the two instruction conditions, we decided to examine whether the effectiveness of the Revised Instructions was altered as a result of deliberating and whether it was altered differently for men and women jurors.

To address these issues, men and women jurors' votes were entered as within-juries dependent variables in a 2 (Pattern, Revised Instructions) x 2 (male, female jurors) x 2 (predeliberation, postdeliberation votes) analysis of variance with instructions as a between-groups factor and juror gender and pre- versus postdeliberation vote as within-groups factors. Figure 9.3 shows the effect of the Revised

Instructions on men and women jurors' votes both prior to and following deliberations. There was no statistically significant main effect of jury instructions $F(1, 36) = 1.87$, $p = .19$, $f = .20$. Women tended to vote to convict ($M = .49$) more than men ($M = .43$), $F(1, 36) = 8.01$, $p = .007$, $f = .12$. However, the gender effects were subsumed under an interaction between juror gender and the instruction factor, $F(1, 36) = 5.69$, $p = .022$, and a second interaction between juror gender and pre- versus postdeliberation vote, $F(1, 36) = 18.20$, $p < .001$. Men and women responded differently to the two instructions. Both before and after deliberating, males were more likely to acquit the defendant in response to the Revised Instructions ($M = .34$) than in response to the Pattern Instructions ($M = .51$), $F(1, 39) = 3.96$, $p = .05$, $f = .28$. In contrast, women were not affected by the instructions, $F(1, 39) = .370$, $p = .548$, $f = .09$, voting equally often to convict with the Pattern ($M = .52$) and the Revised ($M = .48$) Instructions. Thus, while the instructions had no observable effect on women jurors, men appear to have responded to the Revised Instructions in the opposite of the expected direction. That is, when instructed by the judge not to consider the child's responsibility and to place all responsibility on the defendant, males were actually more likely to find the defendant not guilty, a "boomerang effect."

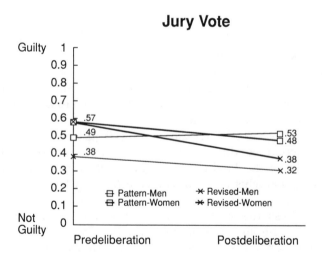

FIGURE 9.3. Juror gender and vote to convict with Pattern and Revised Instructions before and after deliberation.

Women and men responded differently as a result of deliberating. Women in both instruction conditions changed their vote as a result of deliberations, $F(1, 39) = -4.71, p < .001, f = .21$, while men did not, $F(1, 39) = .036, p = .847, f = .01$. Prior to deliberating, women ($M = .57$) were significantly more likely to convict than men ($M = .44$). After deliberating, however, women voted similarly to men ($M = .43$ and .43, respectively). It would appear that men in this study did not change their vote during the course of deliberations, but that women changed their vote as a function of deliberations toward not guilty.

There was no interaction between the instruction factor and pre- versus postdeliberation votes, $F(1, 36) = .56, p = .460$.

Given the pattern of gender differences in jury votes in response to the judge's instructions, do men and women differ in their ratings of the actors and their testimony? Men and women jurors' responses to 33 rating scales were factor analyzed using a principal components extraction technique and submitting the factors to a varimax rotation. Four factors emerged that account for 62% of the variance in the 25 variables. (Eight items were eliminated on the basis of statistical criteria.) Factor scores for men and women jurors within each jury were compared between the instruction conditions.

The Victim Credibility factor accounts for 41% of the variance and is made up of nine items. High scores suggest that the jurors felt that the child was believable; her testimony was accurate, consistent, honest, and factual; her recall for the event was accurate; she appeared confident, and that it was unlikely she gave false testimony.

The Responsibility factor, composed of seven questions, accounts for 9% of the variance. High scores suggest that the jurors perceived the child as responsible for the sex abuse and believed she provoked, encouraged, and wanted the sexual contact. They also believed that the defendant was not responsible.

The third factor, Defendant Credibility, captures an additional 7% of the variance and focuses on belief of the defendant. Jurors with high scores on this factor found the defendant likable, believed him, doubted he planned the sexual contact, and doubted his guilt. In conjunction with this set of beliefs, they did not like the alleged victim and perceived her as motivated by revenge.

Finally, the fourth factor, Suggestibility, accounts for 5% of the variance. Jurors who scored high believed that the child was susceptible to the influence and suggestion of her mother and the attorneys, and that she was generally suggestible.

The four factor scores for male and female jurors were submitted to a 2 (Pattern, Revised Instructions) x 2 (male, female jurors) multivariate analysis of variance with juror gender as a within groups variable. There were no interactions or main effects involving instruction condition: Jurors' perceptions of the evidence did not vary as a result of having heard different sets of instructions.

The multivariate test for the gender within-groups factor revealed a significant main effect, $F(4, 33) = 3.30$, $p = .022$. Males and females differed significantly on the Responsibility factor, $F(1, 36) = 4.40$, $p = .043$, $f = .20$, and the Suggestibility factor, $F(1, 36) = 5.56$, $p = .024$, $f = .25$. Males were significantly more likely to attribute responsibility to the alleged victim ($M = .089$) than were females ($M = -.162$). Males also saw the child witness as more susceptible to influence ($M = .152$) than did females ($M = -.161$). Both males and females similarly evaluated the victim's credibility, $F(1, 36) = .046$, $p = .833$, $f = .02$, and the defendant's credibility, $F(1, 36) = 2.13$, $p = .153$, $f = .13$.

To summarize, men and women jurors responded differently to some portions of the evidence in this trial, but their perceptions were independent of the instructions. Although they perceived the alleged victim's and defendant's credibility and the likelihood of guilt similarly, differences are apparent in more subtle measures of their evaluation of the evidence. Men, who were more likely to vote not guilty, attributed more responsibility to the child and saw her as more suggestible than did women.

To probe the nature of the relationships between juror perceptions and decisions further, jury guilt votes were correlated with each of the factor scores. The pattern of relationships suggests first that votes are most strongly related to perceptions of the child's and the defendant's credibility. Jurors in both instruction conditions who viewed the child as more credible were more likely to vote to convict ($r = .72$ and $r = .70$, $N = 40$, $p < .01$), as were those who viewed the defendant as not credible ($r = -.62$ and $r = -.42$, $N = 40$, $p < .01$). Second, jurors' perception of the child's responsibility was important in their decisions only in the Pattern Instructions condition and not in the Revised Instructions condition. In the Pattern Instructions condition, jurors who thought the child was responsible were more likely to vote to acquit, $r = -.45$, $N = 40$, $p < .01$. However, in response to the Revised Instructions, juror votes were unrelated to their perceptions of the child's responsibility, $r = .16$, $N = 40$, n.s. The Revised Instructions seemed to have some effect on jurors' consideration of the child's responsibility in relation to their votes.

If jurors who were instructed not to consider the child's responsibility in reaching a verdict indeed did not do so as the correlations suggest, what can account for the "boomerang effect?" Returning to the correlations, we noted that, at the same time the relation between responsibility and vote diminishes, the relationship between suggestibility and vote increases from −.03, n.s., in the Pattern Instructions condition to −.42, $p < .05$, in the Revised Instructions condition. Perhaps jurors who felt that their freedom to consider the child's responsibility was limited by the judge's instructions instead chose to express their doubt of her credibility in terms of her susceptibility to influence.

Two theories have been proffered to account for the "boomerang effect." One explanation, based on information processing theory, suggests that reminding jurors of a piece of evidence just prior to their deliberations simply serves to focus their attention on the evidence they are supposed to ignore (Broeder, 1959; Oros & Elman, 1979). Thus, jurors may attach more weight to the particular piece of evidence. In this case, the theory would predict that all jurors who were instructed not to consider the child's responsibility for the sexual abuse would actually consider it more in their decision. The data from this study do not support this explanation. It was only men who reacted in this way to the instruction, in spite of the fact that both men and women heard the instruction and would have been expected to respond similarly.

The second explanation, offered by Wolf and Montgomery (1977), is based on reactance theory (Brehm, 1966). Jurors who are admonished to ignore evidence may feel that their freedom to consider any evidence they choose is threatened and they are aroused to restore that freedom. Reactance theory would predict, in this case, that jurors who felt threatened by not being allowed to consider all the evidence would respond by weighing the forbidden evidence more heavily in their decision.

The data from the present study appear to support an explanation based on reactance theory. First, men are more likely than women to empathize with the defendant and more likely to attribute responsibility to the child. Admonishing the male jurors might have been threatening to them if they experienced a limitation of their freedom to consider the child's responsibility. In contrast, women, who did not appear to have empathized with the defendant and were unlikely to have held the child responsible, may not have felt a similar threat or limitation in response to the judge's instruction. We can reach a tentative conclusion that, in sex abuse cases, reactance in men may be aroused by an instruction limiting their freedom to find fault with the child, resulting in the "boomerang effect." Women, who may not perceive a limitation on their freedom by the judge's instruction, would not be expected to react in the same manner as men.

Wolf and Montgomery (1977) suggest also that engaging in deliberations might have an impact on jurors' reactance to a judge's instructions. Although these authors did not include deliberations in their study, they predicted that if jurors discussed the sanctioned information during deliberations, their sense of freedom would be restored and the reactance would be reduced. However, they also claim that if jurors were prevented from discussing the salient issue during deliberations, their reactance would be maintained and would be manifested in the final verdict.

Some anecdotal evidence from the deliberations in the present study suggests that jurors did indeed discuss the issue of responsibility. In all but a few of the community-participant juries, the child's responsibility for the abuse was raised for discussion at least once. The juries who had heard the Pattern Instructions typically mentioned her responsibility briefly before moving onto another topic. In a number of instances, however, when the issue of the child's responsibility was raised in a jury that had been given the Revised Instructions, the juror who raised it was reminded of the judge's instructions by another juror. The following excerpt from the jury deliberations in the Revised Instructions condition is illustrative of jurors' use of the instructions:

JUROR 1: Why didn't she refuse him?
JUROR 2: The judge said you can't consider that.
JUROR 3: She's gone back to the woods with a lot of men.
JUROR 2: You're saying that she's responsible. It doesn't matter whether she liked it or not.
JUROR 1: A 13-year-old girl could be in love with him.
JUROR 2: Again, the judge said that doesn't matter.

These examples further support Wolf and Montgomery's (1977) application of reactance theory to the "boomerang effect." When the judge's instructions were raised during deliberations, they appear to have been used to limit the discussion of responsibility. However, by limiting jurors' freedom to consider all the issues they deemed important, their reactance was maintained and manifested in the final verdicts.

CONCLUSION

The first series of experiments demonstrated a robust and replicable finding that children over the age of 12 may be held partially responsible for their own sexual victimization by jurors and, as a result, may be perceived as less credible witnesses. This finding is consistent in part with the theory developed by Goodman et al. (1989) to account for jurors' perceptions. This theory predicts that children may be less credible than adult witnesses in cases where memory or accuracy are more salient, such as when the child is a bystander-witness to a homicide or auto theft. However, in cases where honesty is more salient such as in sex abuse cases, children may be perceived as more honest than adults and therefore may be more credible witnesses. The perceived honesty, however, may be mediated by a third factor—that of responsibility. Goodman et al.'s (1989) theory may need to be modified to take into account that when children reach the age of 12 they may be perceived as honest, but jurors may attribute responsibility to the child and be less likely to convict the defendant. The responsibility attribution is apparently less important with prepubertal children.

The law, however, is clear on the issue of responsibility in child sex abuse cases. When the alleged victim is under an age specified by statute, the child is legally incapable of consent. Therefore, the defendant should be found guilty if the jurors are confident that the sexual abuse occurred, regardless of the jurors' perceptions of the child's responsibility. Nonetheless, subject jurors do appear to consider this issue in reaching their decision.

The second series of experiments explored whether jurors could be induced to remove consideration of the child's responsibility from their decision-making process. We did this by simply instructing jurors that the law places sole responsibility on the defendant when the child is under 14 years of age. The first of these experiments suggested that, while jurors' perceptions of responsibility and credibility remained unchanged by the modified set of instructions, jurors were more likely to convict the defendant. The second experiment, however, yielded a "boomerang effect," particularly for male jurors. That is, men who were instructed to disregard any perceptions that the child was in some way responsible for the abuse were actually less likely to convict. Women jurors, who were less likely to perceive the child as responsible, were unaffected by the instructions, but by the end of deliberations their votes were swayed toward not guilty.

The issue of holding a child responsible for her own victimization is an important one and deserves further attention. The failure of the Revised Instructions to increase the chances of a conviction in the final experiment does not imply that these instructions would have the same effect in all cases. Perhaps, as Wolf and Montgomery (1977) suggest, the particular instructions used here were too strong, giving rise to reactance in jurors. Issuing somewhat milder instructions, while still raising the issue of responsibility, might lead jurors to be more aware of their biases but not cause the reactance we found here.

This series of studies also underlines the importance of examining the robustness of findings across methods. In the first set of studies examining attributions of responsibility to different age victims, we obtained consistent results with several different methods. However in the second set of studies examining jury instructions to control juror bias, we obtained different results using written vignettes compared to a videotaped, simulated trial.

In addition to exploring the possibility that instructions of different strength might have different effects, we need to know more about the conditions under which jurors do and do not attribute responsibility to child sex abuse victims. Perhaps there are victim characteristics in addition to age or specific juror characteristics and attitudes that lead some jurors to hold children more responsible. Juror gender may offer a clue, but juror gender doesn't explain much in and of itself. Juror gender is a proxy for other attitudes and processes associated with gender. That area may be profitably explored in the future.

NOTES

1. Effect sizes are reported here as f, the proportion of between groups standard deviation to within groups standard deviation. Cohen (1977) differentiates among "small" effects (i.e., $f = .10$), "medium" effects (i.e., $f = .30$) and "large" effects (i.e., $f = .50$).
2. This Revised Instruction makes the issue clear, and may appear strong. When included in the full set of instructions, however, it is less forceful. The attorneys who reviewed this instruction felt it was clear, but would still be acceptable in court.
3. This study is abstracted from Isquith's doctoral dissertation (Isquith, 1990).
4. The design included a comparison of college students and community participants as subject-jurors. There were, however, no significant differences between college student and community participant juries on any dependent measure in this study. Therefore, the two groups are combined in this presentation.

REFERENCES

American Psychological Association. (1990) *Motion for leave to file brief amicus curiae and brief for amicus curiae American Psychological Association in support of neither party. Maryland v. Craig,* (U.S., October Term, 1989) (No. 89–478).

Aubrey, M. R. (1986). *Factors associated with victim credibility in rape cases.* Unpublished master's thesis, State University of New York at Buffalo, Buffalo, NY.

Aubrey, M. R. (1989). *A content analysis of jurors' deliberations in response to a simulated child sexual abuse trial.* Unpublished doctoral dissertation, State University of New York at Buffalo, Buffalo, NY.

Berscheid, E., & Walster, E. (1974). Physical attractiveness. In L. Berkowitz (Ed.), *Advances in experimental social psychology.* (Vol. 7). New York: Academic Press.

Borgida, E., & White, P. (1978). Social perception of rape victims. *Law and Human Behavior, 2,* 339–351

Brehm, J. W. (1966). *A theory of psychological reactance.* New York: Academic Press.

Broeder, D. (1959). The University of Chicago jury project. *Nebraska Law Review, 38,* 744–760.

Buchanan, R. W., Pryor, B., Taylor, K. P., & Strawn, D. U. (1978). Legal communication: An investigation of juror comprehension of pattern instructions. *Communications Quarterly, 26,* 31–35.

Bulkley, J. A. (1989). The impact of new child witness research on sexual abuse prosecutions. In S. J. Ceci, D. F. Ross, & M. P. Toglia (Eds.), *Perspectives on children's testimony* (pp. 208–229). New York: Springer-Verlag.

Calhoun, L. G., Selby, J. W., & Warring, L. J. (1976). Social perception of the victim's causal role in rape: An exploratory examination of four factors. *Human Relations, 29,* 517–526.

Cohen, J. (1977). *Statistical power analyses for the behavioral science (2nd ed.).* New York: Academic Press.

Deitz, S. R., & Byrnes, L. E. (1981). Attribution of responsibility for sexual assault: The influence of observer empathy and defendant occupation and attractiveness. *The Journal of Psychology, 108,* 17–29

Devlin, P. (1966). *Trial by jury.* London: Stevens and Son.

Doob, A. N., & Kirschenbaum, H. M. (1972). Some empirical evidence of the effect of s.12 of the Canada Evidence Act upon an accused. *Criminal Law Quarterly, 15,* 88–96.

Duggan, L. M. (1987). *The credibility of child witnesses in a simulated child sex abuse trial.* Unpublished doctoral dissertation, State University of New York at Buffalo, Buffalo, NY.

Duggan, L. M., Aubrey, M., Doherty, E., Isquith, P., Levine, M., & Scheiner, J. (1989). The credibility of children as witnesses in a simulated child sex abuse trial. In S. Ceci, D. Ross, & M. P. Toglia (Eds.), *Perspectives on children's testimony* (pp. 71–99). New York: Springer-Verlag.

Edwards, S. (1981). *Female sexuality and the law.* Oxford: Martin Robertson

Elwork, A., Sales, B. D., & Alfini, J. J. (1977). Juridic decisions: In ignorance of the law or in light of it? *Law and Human Behavior, 1,* 163–189.

Elwork, A., Sales, B. D., & Alfini, J. J. (1982). *Making jury instructions understandable.* Charlottesville, VA: Michie.

Fulero, S. M., & Delara, C. (1976). Rape victims and attributed responsibility: A defensive attribution approach. *Victimology: An International Journal, 1,* 551–563.

Goodman, G. S., Bottoms, B. L., Herscovici, B. B., & Shaver, P. R. (1989).

Determinants of the child victim's perceived credibility. In S. J. Ceci, D. F. Ross, & M. P. Toglia (Eds.), *Perspectives on children's testimony* (pp. 1–22). New York: Springer-Verlag.

Goodman, G. S., Golding, J. M., & Haith, M. M. (1984). Jurors' reactions to child witnesses. *Journal of Social Issues, 40,* 139–156.

Goodman, G., Golding, J. M., Hegelson, V. S., Haith, M. M., & Michelli, J. (1987). When a child takes the stand: Jurors' perceptions of children's eyewitness testimony. *Law and Human Behavior, 11,* 27–40.

Gordon, R., & Temerlin, M. (1971). Forensic psychology: The judge and the jury. In G. Winters (Ed.), *The jury-selected readings.* Chicago: American Judicial Society.

Hoiberg, B., & Stires, L. (1973). The effect of several types of pre-trial publicity on the guilt attributions of simulated jurors. *Journal of Applied Social Psychology, 3,* 267–275.

Isquith, P. K. (1988, April). A comparison of students and community subjects as jurors. In M. Levine (Chair), *Simulated jury research on the child as a witness.* Symposium conducted at the meeting of the Eastern Psychological Association, Buffalo, NY.

Kaiser, H. F. (1974). An index of factorial simplicity. *Psychometrika, 39,* 31–36.

Kanekar, S., & Kolsawalla, M. (1980). Responsibility of a rape victim in relation to her respectability, attractiveness, and provocativeness. *Journal of Social Psychology, 40,* 153–154.

Kassin, S. M., & Wrightsman, L. S. (1980). Prior confessions and mock juror verdicts. *Journal of Applied Social Psychology, 10,* 133–146.

Kassin, S. M., & Wrightsman, L. S. (1981). Coerced confessions, judicial instruction, and mock juror verdicts. *Journal of Applied Social Psychology, 11,* 489–506.

Kassin, S. M., & Wrightsman, L. S. (1985). Confession evidence. In S. M. Kassin & L. S. Wrightsman (Eds.), *The psychology of evidence and trial procedure* (pp. 67 94). Beverly Hills, CA: Sage.

L.S.E. Jury Project. (1973, April). *Criminal Law Review,* 208–223.

LaFree, G., Reskin, B., & Visher, C. (1985). Jurors' responses to victims' behavior and legal issues in sexual assault trials. *Social Problems, 32,* 389–407.

Leippe, M. R., &,Romanczyk, A. (1987). Children on the witness stand: A communication/persuasion analysis of jurors' reactions to child witnesses. In S. J. Ceci, M. P. Toglia, & D. F. Ross (Eds.), *Children's eyewitness memory* (pp. 155-177). New York: Springer-Verlag.

Leippe, M. R., & Romanczyk, A. (1989). Reactions to child (versus adult) eyewitnesses: The influence of jurors' preconceptions and witness behavior. *Law and Human Behavior, 13,* 103-132.

Maryland v. Craig, 110 s. Ct. 3157 (1990).

Miller, G. R. (1975). Jurors' responses to videotaped trial materials: Some recent findings. *Personality and Social Psychology Bulletin, 1,* 561-569.

Nigro, G. N., Buckley, M. A., Hill, D. E., & Nelson, J. (1989). When juries "hear" children testify: The effects of eyewitness age and speech style on jurors' perceptions of testimony. In S. J. Ceci, D. F. Ross, & M. P. Toglia (Eds.),

Perspectives on children's testimony (pp. 57–70. New York: Springer-Verlag.

O'Mara, J. J. (1972). Standard jury charges—Findings of pilot project. *Pennsylvania Bar Association Quarterly, 43,* 166–175.

Oros, C. J., & Elman, D. (1979). Impact of judge's instructions upon jurors' decisions: The "cautionary charge" in rape trials. *Representative Research in Social Psychology, 10,* 28-36.

Padawer-Singer, A. M., & Barton, A. H. (1975). The impact of pretrial publicity on jurors' verdicts. In R. J. Simon (Ed.), *The jury system in America: A critical overview* (pp. 123–139). Beverly Hills, CA: Sage.

Pugh, M. D. (1983). Contributory fault and rape convictions: Loglinear models for blaming the victim. *Social Psychology Quarterly, 46,* 233–242.

Pynoos, R. S., & Eth, S. (1984) The child as witness to homicide. *Journal of Social Issues, 40,* 87–108.

Ross, D. F., Dunning, D., Toglia, M. P., & Ceci, S. J. (1990). The child in the eyes of the jury: Assessing mock jurors' perceptions of the child witness. *Law and Human Behavior, 14,* 5–23.

Ross, D. F., Miller, B. S., & Moran, P. B. (1987). The child in the eyes of the jury: Assessing mock jurors' perceptions of the child witness. In S. J. Ceci, M. P. Toglia, & D. F. Ross (Eds.), *Children's eyewitness memory* (pp. 142–154). New York: Springer-Verlag.

Scheiner, J. (1988, April). The use of the minimalist vignette as a method for assessing the generalizability of videotape trial simulation results. In M. Levine (Chair), *Simulated jury research on the child as a witness.* Symposium conducted at the meeting of the Eastern Psychological Association, Buffalo, NY.

Severence, L. J., Green, E., & Loftus, E. F. (1984). Toward criminal jury instructions that jurors can understand. *Criminology, 75,* 198-233.

Smith, R., Keating, J., Hester, R., & Mitchell, H. (1976) Role of justice considerations in the attribution of responsibility to a rape victim. *Journal of Research in Personality, 10,* 346–357.

Strawn, D. U., & Buchanan, R. W. (1976). Jury confusion: A threat to justice. *Judicature, 59,* 478–483.

Sue, S., Smith, R. E., & Caldwell, C. (1973). Effects of inadmissible evidence on the decisions of simulated jurors: A moral dilemma. *Journal of Applied Social Psychology, 3,* 345–353.

Sue, S., Smith, R. E., & Gilbert, R. (1974). Biasing effects of pretrial publicity on judicial decisions. *Journal of Criminal Justice, 2,* 163–171.

Sue, S., Smith, R. E., & Pedroza, G. (1975). Authoritarianism, pretrial publicity, and awareness of bias in simulated jurors. *Psychological Reports, 37,* 1299–1302.

Thompson, W. C., Fong, G. T., & Rosenhan, D. L. (1981). Inadmissible evidence and juror verdicts. *Journal of Personality & Social Psychology, 40,* 453–463.

Werner, C. M., Kagehiro, D. K., & Strube, M. J. (1982). Conviction proneness and the authoritarian juror: Inability to disregard information or attitudinal bias? *Journal of Applied Psychology, 67,* 629–636.

Williams, K. (1981). Few convictions in rape cases: Empirical evidence concerning some alternative explanations. *Journal of Criminal Justice, 9,* 29–39.

Wolf, S., & Montgomery, D. A. (1977). Effects of inadmissible evidence and level of judicial admonishment to disregard on the judgements of mock jurors. *Journal of Applied Social Psychology, 7,* 205–219.

10

Individual Differences in Perceptions of Child Sexual Assault Victims

Bette L. Bottoms
University of Illinois at Chicago

Ours is a legal system designed for adults. When children enter that system, problems are inevitable. Nevertheless, more and more children are being called to testify in courts, especially in child sexual assault trials. Given the inherently private nature of child sexual abuse, one special difficulty encountered in these trials is that jurors must often struggle to make decisions based on little evidence other than the word of a child witness.

Although children may be more reliable witnesses than once thought (e.g., Goodman & Reed, 1986; Goodman, Rudy, Bottoms, & Aman, 1990), recent research unfortunately suggests that jurors' decisions may not be based on the actual accuracy of child witnesses (Goodman, Bottoms, Herscovici, & Shaver, 1989; Leippe, Manion, & Romanczyk, Chapter 8, this volume; Leippe & Romanczyk, 1989). Rather, there may be a number of case, victim, and juror factors that in part determine judgments in cases involving child witnesses (Bottoms, 1989; Bottoms & Goodman, 1992). This chapter focuses on one factor in particular: individual differences among jurors in their reactions to child sexual assault victims. One important individual difference factor that has emerged in research is juror gender: Women and men often make different evaluations and judgments in child sexual abuse cases. Why? Do men and women carry different pretrial biases with them into the courtroom? Do they differ in what they think and feel about

229

issues relevant to decision making in cases of child sexual abuse? How do these differences influence their judgments about child victim credibility and defendant guilt in child sexual assault cases?

In the course of discussing possible answers to these questions, I review relevant literature and formulate specific hypotheses concerning pretrial biases and their relation to decisions in child sexual assault cases. Although theoretically framed research on the determinants of social perceptions of child sexual assault victims is quite limited, a larger body of conceptually driven research has explored the perceived credibility of adult rape victims. Because many of the findings from that research parallel findings from studies of perceptions of child victims, particularly with regard to gender differences, I rely on research on the perceived credibility of adult rape victims to direct much of my discussion. Specifically, I begin with a review of research on jurors' perceptions of child sexual abuse victims and then illustrate parallel findings from literature on perceptions of adult rape victims. Using the adult rape victim credibility literature as a guide, I then hypothesize specific determinants of individual differences, particularly gender differences, in reactions to child sexual abuse victims. I argue that individual differences in evaluations of child sexual abuse victims are influenced by jurors' empathy for child victims and attitudes toward issues relevant to child sexual abuse cases. Finally, I present preliminary data supporting my hypotheses and discuss theoretical and practical implications of my work.

THE PERCEIVED CREDIBILITY OF CHILD SEXUAL ASSAULT VICTIMS

To date, much of the research on mock jurors' reactions to children's testimony has focused on children as bystander witnesses to crimes such as theft or vehicular homicide (e.g., Goodman, Golding, Helgeson, Haith, & Michelli, 1987; Leippe & Romanczyk, 1987, 1989). Such studies typically find that children are perceived to be less credible witnesses than adults. However, children's testimony is actually most likely to be heard by a jury in trials in which children are the alleged victims of sexual assault (Bulkley, 1989; see also Leippe et al., Chapter 8, this volume). This is true because, in contrast to cases involving crimes such as theft, in sexual abuse cases it is usually not feasible to pursue a trial without the child victim's testimony, given the paucity of other evidence to corroborate the complaint.

Research concerning jurors' reactions to child victims of sexual assault is limited, but indicates that jurors may be predisposed to find young child victims of this crime particularly credible. For example, Duggan et al. (1989; see also Isquith, Levine, & Scheiner, Chapter 9, this volume) found that mock jurors considered a 5- and a 9-year-old female molestation victim more credible than a 13-year-old victim. Deliberation comments indicated that the younger victims' heightened credibility may have been due to perceived naivete and inability to fabricate sexual abuse claims, and that the older child's lack of credibility may have stemmed from jurors' attributions of dishonesty and responsibility for the crime to her. The latter explanation was confirmed in a replication study by Scheiner (1988), and is supported by results from a study by Waterman and Foss-Goodman (1984) in which more blame was attributed to a 15-year-old sexual assault victim than to a 7- or 11-year-old victim. Other research similarly finds younger child victims of sexual assault to be considered by mock jurors as more credible than older victims (Bottoms & Goodman, 1992; Gabora, Spanos, & Joab, 1991). For example, Bottoms and Goodman (1992) found that more pro-defense evaluations were made in cases with a 14-year-old as compared to those with a 6- or 11-year-old victim–witness (see also Goodman et al., 1989).

Survey studies on perceptions of child sexual abuse victims' ability to give testimony also indicate that young child witnesses may often be perceived as particularly credible. Laypersons surveyed by Limber and Castrianno (1990) had expectations that, for example, younger incest victims (4-year-olds) would be more "confused" than older child victims (13-year-olds), but respondents generally endorsed sympathetic views of victims and thought it probable that children would tell the truth in reporting sexual assault. Social workers surveyed by Everson and Boat (1989) estimated that older children, especially adolescents over the age of 12, would be more likely than younger children to give false reports of sexual abuse. Community jurors (Corder & Whiteside, 1988), judges (Saunders, 1986), and police officers (Saunders, 1987) were also found to believe that young children could be credible witnesses in sexual assault cases.

Thus, when other considerations are held constant in child sexual abuse cases, younger victim–witnesses may often be perceived to be quite credible, while older witnesses may not be perceived to be as credible because they may be assigned blame for sexual encounters with adults. But will all jurors be predisposed to perceive even young children as credible victim–witnesses in sexual assault cases? Survey and experimental research suggests not. There may be important individual differences among jurors in the way child sexual assault victims are perceived. For example, in Duggan et al.'s (1989) study, mock jurors who considered themselves more experienced with children were less likely to attribute responsibility to the child witness, were less influenced by the child's age, and were more confident of the defendant's guilt than were jurors who considered themselves less experienced.

One individual difference factor that seems to be particularly important in determining the perceived credibility of child sexual abuse victims is perceiver gender. In the Duggan et al. (1989) study, compared to men, women on average believed child witnesses more and expressed more confidence that the defendant was guilty. Women also considered child witnesses to be more aware of the seriousness of the crime and more harmed by the act and by testifying. In a follow-up study, Scheiner (1988) found that men were more likely than women to consider victim responsibility in evaluating the victim's credibility. In predeliberation judgments given by mock jurors in the study by Gabora et al. (1991), women were more likely than men to convict the defendant and to consider the victim more credible. Similarly, in studies by Bottoms and Goodman (1992), Goodman et al. (1989), and Limber and Castrianno (1990), women considered child witnesses more favorably than did men.

In sum, research investigating decision making in child sexual abuse cases has revealed important information about the age at which child victims are perceived as credible witnesses, and also about individual differences in the way child victims are perceived. In general, women are more pro-victim in their judgments and evaluations in cases of child sexual assault than are men. Although many men are as pro-victim as women and many women are as pro-defense as men, gender differences emerge with surprising consistency when group means are considered.

Although this is an interesting finding, left open is the important question of what might account for gender differences. As noted previously, research on the perceived credibility of adult rape victims may serve as a guide for investigating factors that underlie individual differences in perceptions of child sex abuse victims. One might well expect commonalities in empirical findings in the child sexual assault and adult rape literatures since both deal with sex crimes. Thus, findings from the adult rape literature pertinent to the exploration of children's perceived credibility are reviewed below.

THE PERCEIVED CREDIBILITY OF ADULT RAPE VICTIMS

An increase in societal awareness of women's issues over the past two decades has been accompanied by attention to rape and investigation of jurors' biases as they affect the perceived credibility of rape victims (for a review, see Borgida & Brekke, 1985). In general, research indicates that mock jurors often regard the credibility of an adult rape victim with skepticism because they assign responsibility for the rape to her (e.g., Deitz & Byrnes, 1981; Luginbuhl & Mullin, 1981). This may be especially true of men, who are more likely than women to blame and attribute responsibility to a rape victim (Calhoun, Selby, & Warring, 1976; Deitz & Byrnes, 1981; Feild, 1978b; Luginbuhl & Mullin, 1981; Rumsey & Rumsey, 1977; Smith, Keating, Hester, & Mitchell, 1976), and less likely than women to identify and empathize with the victim (Deitz, Blackwell, Daley, & Bentley, 1982; Kahn et al., 1977; Krulewitz & Nash, 1979). Compared to women, males may also appear to be less conviction prone when deciding cases of rape (Davis, Kerr, Atkin, Holt, & Meek, 1975; Kerr et al., 1976; Nagao & Davis, 1980). It is important to note, however, that some studies have not replicated gender differences in guilt judgments or sentencing in rape cases (e.g., Kaplan & Miller, 1978; Jones & Aronson, 1973; Villemur & Hyde, 1983; see Borgida & Brekke, 1985, for a review).

A large body of research has sought to understand evaluations and judgments made in rape cases and to understand the gender differences in these judgments. A focus of much of this research has been on perceiver variables such as attitudes and empathy, briefly reviewed below (for detail, see Borgida & Brekke, 1985).

For example, attitudes toward women have been found to be significantly related to attributions of rape victim responsibility (Thorton, Ryckman, & Robbins, 1982) and predictive of judgments in rape cases (Spanos, DuBreuil, & Gwynn, in press; Thorton et al., 1982). Attitudes toward feminism and sex roles have also been linked to perceptions in rape cases (Burt, 1980; Krulewitz & Paine, 1978). Further, women are more likely than men to endorse pro-women, feminist attitudes (Spence, Helmreich, & Stapp, 1973; Thorton et al., 1982); thus, gender differences in these attitudes may partially account for the differences observed between men's and women's judgments in rape cases.

Attitudes toward rape itself have also been linked to evaluations in rape cases. For example, acceptance of rape myths is negatively correlated with the likelihood of labeling forced sexual contact as rape (Burt, 1980; Burt & Albin, 1981) and positively correlated with the degree of responsibility attributed to rape victims (Krahe, 1988). Feild (1978b) has also reported significant correlations between perceivers' rape beliefs and decision making in rape cases (Barnett & Feild, 1977; Feild, 1978a). Finally, research reveals that, compared to men, women hold more negative attitudes and fewer misconceptions about rape itself (Barnett & Feild, 1977; Larsen & Long, 1988), suggesting that gender differences in attitudes and knowledge about rape may also contribute to gender differences in judgments.

In addition, it has been suggested that attitudes toward sexuality, or sexual conservatism, may be linked to perceptions of rape victims. On the one hand, persons who have very conservative attitudes toward sexuality might react quite strongly against rape, which might lead to greater outrage against a defendant and less blame toward a victim. In fact, research suggests that women are more sexually conservative than men (Small, Teagno, & Selz, 1980); thus, sexual conservatism may in part underlie gender differences in perceptions of rape victims.

On the other hand, however, Burt (1980) suggests that sexual conservatism is actually associated with assignment of blame to adult rape victims. She theorized that very sexually conservative persons would be so disturbed by the sexuality involved in the act of rape that they might make a "just word" attribution; that is, wanting to believe that the world is a just place where misfortune befalls only the deserving (Lerner, 1970; Lerner & Miller, 1978), they might be driven to attribute responsibility to an adult rape victim.

Although many (but not all) studies find that women on average are more pro-victim than men, there are certainly many women who do blame victims, just as there are many men who do not. Strictly conservative attitudes toward sexuality may characterize that subset of women who do blame victims.

Finally, researchers have also proposed that jurors' empathy for defendants and victims in rape cases may be important in determining decision making in rape cases (Barnett, Tetreault, Esper, & Bristow, 1986; Deitz et al., 1982; Deitz & Byrnes, 1981; Weir & Wrightsman, 1990). For example, in her consideration of empathy and its relation to judgments in rape cases, Deitz noted the role of empathy in mediating attributions of blame to victims. She reasoned that jurors' "rape empathy" ("the relative tendency for subjects to assume the psychological perspective of the rape victim or the rapist in viewing a rape incident," Deitz et al., 1982, p. 374) would influence their attributions of responsibility to a rape victim and, in turn, influence their judgments of defendant and victim credibility in rape cases. Thus, persons able to empathize with a rape victim would consider her more credible than would persons unable to empathize with a rape victim. Deitz et al. (1982) constructed the Rape Empathy Scale (RES) to measure rape empathy. In a mock-jury study, RES scores were predictive of jurors' ratings of defendant guilt, sentencing, and attributions of responsibility for a rape. Similarly, Weir and Wrightsman (1990) found that rape empathy predicted verdicts in a mock rape trial (but see Coller & Resick, 1987).

There also appear to be individual differences in rape empathy. For example, research indicates that people who know a rape victim may be more empathic toward victims, including rape victims (Barnett et al., 1992). There is also mounting evidence for gender differences in rape empathy: Research has revealed that men are less empathic toward rape victims than are women (Barnett et al., 1992; Deitz et al., 1982). Weir and Wrightsman (1990) also found gender differences in rape empathy, noting interestingly that low-empathy females were the most pro-defense of all perceivers. Further, research indicates that women who have experienced a rape situation personally are more victim empathic than women who have not been in such a situation (Barnett et al., 1986; Barnett, Tetreault, & Masbad, 1987; Deitz et al., 1982; but see Coller & Resick, 1987). These findings follow from research indicating that people are most empathic toward victims when they consider it likely that they themselves could be in a smilar situation (Aderman, Archer, & Harris, 1975; Aderman, Brehm, & Katz, 1974; Lerner & Miller, 1978), or when they consider the victim to be like themselves (Krebs, 1970). Women are much more likely than men to be raped (Finkelhor, 1984) and are probably well aware of it. Thus, more so than men, women should be expected to consider rape a threatening possibility for themselves and, in turn, identify and empathize more easily with a rape victim and assign less blame to her than would men. This formulation would be especially true for women who have previously been victimized, who would probably be even more acutely aware of their vulnerability and their similarities to the victim.

In sum, just as in research considering perceptions of the credibility of child sexual assault victims (Bottoms & Goodman, 1992; Duggan et al., 1989; Gabora et al. 1991; Scheiner, 1988), gender differences have been found in investigations of adult rape victim credibility (e.g., Calhoun, Selby, & Warring, 1976; Deitz & Byrnes, 1981; Luginbuhl & Mullin, 1981). In general, compared to men, women are more pro-victim. Further, researchers have identified several likely determinants of these gender differences, including individual differences in attitudes toward women, rape, and sexuality, as well as individual differences in empathy for victims.

Much can be gained by considering individual differences in reactions to child sexual assault victims in relation to these findings. For example, just as researchers have revealed links between certain pretrial attitudes and perceptions of rape victims (e.g., Krahe, 1988), I propose that child sexual assault victims' credibility is related to perceivers' attitudes toward various issues such as child sexual abuse.

Further, just as Deitz et al. (1982) found rape victim empathy to be an important factor in rape case judgments, empathy for child victims may underlie gender differences in perceptions of child victims. The remainder of this chapter, then, focuses specifically on pretrial attitudes and victim empathy as they relate to juror decision making in cases of child sexual abuse.

DETERMINANTS OF INDIVIDUAL DIFFERENCES IN THE PERCEIVED CREDIBILITY OF CHILD SEXUAL ASSAULT VICTIMS

Attitudes

In general, attitudes have been a widely researched topic in psychology, and it is generally accepted, although conditionally, that they influence our perceptions, intentions, and behaviors (e.g., Ajzen, 1985, 1988; Johnson, 1991). It is important, then, to identify possible attitudinal determinants of jurors' perceptions and behavior (judgments) in the context of child sexual assault cases, just as they have been researched in the context of adult rape cases.

Research specifically about attitudes toward child sexual assault victims is limited, but extrapolation from the literature on adult rape victim credibility (as reveiwed above), and literature on attitudes toward child witnesses of various crimes and toward the act of child sexual assault (as mentioned above and developed below), suggests several attitudinal constructs that might influence decision making in child sexual assault cases. These, considered in detail below, include attitudes toward (1) children's general believability, (2) women and feminism, (3) adult/child sexual relations (child sexual abuse), and (4) sexuality in general (sexual conservatism).

Attitudes Toward Children's General Believability

Attitudes toward children's cognitive abilities and general believability are likely to be related to judgments in cases involving child witnesses. For example, people may believe that children are generally not as cognitively sophisticated as adults and thus lack the ability to provide as accurate testimony about past events. Research on adults' perceptions of children's cognitive abilities is largely limited to studies of parental beliefs about their own children's abilities and the relation of those beliefs to child rearing (see Sigel, 1985, for review). Such research has illustrated (perhaps not surprisingly) the tendency for parents to overestimate their own young children's developmental level and abilities (e.g., Hunt & Paraskevopoulos, 1980; Miller, White, & Delgado, 1980).

In contrast, research aimed at understanding perceptions of the cognitive abilities of child witnesses has found that people generally consider young children to be more suggestible and to have worse recall than adults (Leippe & Romanczyk, 1987; Leippe, Brigham, Cousins, & Romanczyk, 1989; Yarmey & Jones, 1983), especially until about age 12. This belief appears to lead to decreased perceived credibility for child bystander–witnesses of crimes in which recall of details is important, such as traffic accidents (Goodman, Golding, & Haith, 1984; Goodman et al., 1987; Leippe & Romanczyk, 1987, 1989). However, perceived cognitive deficits may not necessarily lead to decreased credibility for children in all types of cases (e.g., Leippe & Romanczyk, 1987; Nigro, Buckley, Hill, & Nelson, 1989; Ross, Miller, & Moran, 1987), especially cases like sexual victimization in which a child's sincerity and trustworthiness rather than cognitive abilities are often highlighted (Goodman et al., 1984; Goodman et al., 1989). Specifically, although children may be perceived as fairly cognitively astute at around age 12 to 13 or older (thus better able to give accurate testimony), Scheiner (1988) and Bottoms (1989) found that children of that age may also be considered capable of fabricating false allegations of sexual abuse (thus less likely to be accurate witnesses). Therefore, Bottoms and Goodman (1992) and Goodman et al. (1989) have suggested that in cases of child sexual assault, jurors may rely heavily on judgments of a child's honesty and trustworthiness in deciding credibility, and further, that a perceived lack of cognitive sophistication may actually increase a child's perceived credibility. That is, a young child who is perceived as cognitively deficient will be thought to be incapable of fabricating stories of sexual abuse, not deserving of blame for sexual contact (as might be deemed the case for older victims, see Duggan et al., 1989), and, in turn, a trustworthy and credible witness (unless a cognitively related factor, such as increased suggestibility, is a significant issue in the case). This theory accounts for the finding that mock jurors sometimes perceive younger child sexual assault victims to be more credible than older victims (e.g., Bottoms & Goodman, 1992; Duggan et al., 1989; Gabora et al., 1991). It also predicts important differences in the way young child witnesses versus adolescent and teen witnesses will be perceived.

There is evidence of gender differences in perceptions of children's general believability. For example, Bull, Borgida, Gresham, Swim, and Gray (in press) found that, compared to men, women were more likely to think that: (1) children's witness abilities are not necessarily poor, (2) children are able to accurately identify their assailants, (3) children have memory abilities equal to that of adults for trauma, and (4) children are not prone to sexual fantasy. Also, in a mock jury study by Bottoms and Goodman (1992), compared to men, women considered alleged child sexual assault victims to be less suggestible. However, men rated the victims as more intelligent than women did.

In sum, attitudes toward child sexual assault victims' believability may be based in part on beliefs about children's cognitive abilities and about children's ability to fabricate sexual abuse allegations. Further, these attitudes toward children's general believability may be an important determinant of judgments made in child sexual assault cases. In support, recent research by Gabora et al. (1991) revealed a weak but significant correlation between attitudes toward children's ability to fabricate false allegations of sexual assault and mock jurors' ratings of defendant guilt and child victim credibility. Finally, there may be gender differences in beliefs about children's believability that lead to gender differences in credibility and guilt judgments made by men and women in child sexual assault cases.

Attitudes Toward Women and Feminism

Child physical and sexual abuse, like adult rape, have been embraced as issues of concern by the feminist movement. Feminist writings on the topic lead to the prediction of gender differences in reactions to child and adult rape victims (Brownmiller, 1975; Herman, 1981; Herman & Hirschman, 1977; Rush, 1980). In this literature, the sexual abuse of women and children is conceptualized as an outgrowth of dominant, possessive positions held by men in relation to women and children throughout history: For example, men may consider it their right to treat women and children as they see fit. In fact, research has shown that, compared to women, men are less likely to endorse certain types of legal rights for children (Morton & Dubanoski, 1982; Rogers & Wrightsman, 1978), and less likely to endorse pro-women attitudes in general (Spence et al., 1973; Thorton et al., 1982).

As previously noted, research has found that antifeminist, sex-stereotyped attitudes are related to pro-defense evaluations in adult rape cases (e.g., Spanos et al., in press). It appears that this may be true for judgments and perceptions in child sexual abuse cases as well. In a mock-jury study focusing on a case of child sexual abuse, Gabora et al. (1991) found that pro-women attitudes were correlated positively with jurors' ratings of victim credibility and negatively with defendant credibility. Thus, compared to persons with pro-female or pro-feminist views, persons with antifeminist views may not react as negatively to child sexual abuse or judge child sexual assault victims to be as credible.

Attitudes Toward Adult / Child Sexuality

Just as attitudes toward rape are related to evaluations made in adult rape cases (Burt & Albin, 1981; Feild, 1978b), jurors' attitudes toward child sexual abuse itself may predict their reactions to alleged victims of this crime. Discussions of attitudes toward adult/child sexuality can be found in clinical and research literatures dealing with child sexual abuse.

Historically, attitudes toward child maltreatment have been equivocal (Levine & Levine, 1992). As late as 1970, a researcher of attitudes toward physical abuse of children concluded that physical injury was still an "almost normal occurrence in the course of caring for a child" (Gil, p. 55). Interestingly, Gil also noted that compared to females, males were more tolerant of parents who abused their children and considered it more likely that they themselves could injure a child. Although physical battering of children was recognized as a serious social problem by the 1960s (Kempe, Silverman, Steele, Droegenmueller, & Silver, 1962), child sexual abuse has been considered a child welfare concern of considerable magnitude only within the last 2 decades (Finkelhor, 1984, 1986).

In fact, within some clinical writings there are still widely varying attitudes toward adult/child sexual relations (Goldstein, 1987). Most respected child abuse researchers condemn sexuality between adults and children, asserting that children are incapable of sexual consent and that sexual abuse is harmful to children (Constantine & Martinson, 1981; Faller, 1988; Finkelhor, 1984, 1986; Summit, 1988). Literature assessing the long-term effects of childhood sexual abuse indicates that sexual abuse may be associated with loss of self-esteem, self-destructive behavior, depression, suicidal ideations, character disorder, and psychosis (Beitchman et al., 1992; Browne & Finkelhor, 1986; Constantine & Martinson, 1981; deYoung, 1982; MacFarlane et al., 1986; Mrazek & Mrazek, 1981; Wolfe, 1987; Wyatt & Powell, 1988a).

Others, however, suggest that sexual contact between children and adults may be a normal act with few ill effects (Bender & Grugett, 1952; Bender & Blau, 1937; Brongersma, 1984; Lukianowicz, 1972; Schultz, 1982; see DeMott, 1980; deYoung, 1982, for discussion), that adults who engage in sex with children are not necessarily deviant (DeLora & Warren, 1977), and that children may be naive or even willing seducers who are responsible for sexual abuse (Bender & Blau, 1937; Bender & Grugett, 1952; Lukianowicz, 1972; Moll, 1929; see Katz & Mazur, 1979, for review). It is not hard to imagine that jurors holding such attitudes may be more pro-defense than persons who do not condone adult/child sexual relations, believing them to be harmful and unnatural. In fact, not surprisingly, research finds that known child molesters endorse such condoning attitudes. For example, abusers often believe that (1) the prohibition of adult/child sex is a meaningless cultural taboo (Abel, Becker, & Cunningham-Rathner, 1984; Finkelhor, 1984); (2) children are capable of consenting to and enjoying sexual activities with adults; (3) children are responsible for their abuse; and (4) adult/child sexual contact is beneficial for children (Stermac & Segal, 1989).

Persons who hold such attitudes may find child victims not credible by assigning responsibility to them for reported abuses. It is an interesting twist, however, that clinical literature also suggests that although some adults find the idea of sex with children abhorrent, they may still be unlikely to consider a particular child victim credible because they do not want to and cannot believe that sex between adults and children actually occurs (Faller, 1988; Waterman & Lusk, 1986). Some trace the origins of such denial to Freud's retraction of his seduction theory (Freud, 1962; Masson, 1984; Wyatt & Powell, 1988b). Thus, a juror who holds negative attitudes toward sexual contact between adults and children may not necessarily consider child sexual assault victims to be credible witnesses.

Survey research on lay and professional attitudes toward adult/ child sexual relations has revealed interesting individual differences that may partially explain the discrepancy between men's and women's perceptions of child sexual assault victims (e.g., Bottoms & Goodman, 1992; Duggan et al., 1989). For example, Bull et al. (1991) found gender differences in attitudes toward child sexual assault and its victims among members of the Society for Traumatic Stress Studies. Compared to male members, female members were more likely to believe that (1) recantations do not necessarily indicate initial false reports; (2) it would not be wrong to convict on the testimony of a child; (3) children are not prone to sexual fantasy; (4) prevention programs do not make children more likely to misinterpret innocent behaviors as sexual ones; and (5) the rate of convictions for child sexual abuse should increase. In a survey of practitioners including psychologists, psychiatrists, pediatricians, and family counselors, Attias and Goodwin (1985) found that, compared to women practitioners, male practitioners gave lower estimates of the incidence of incest, gave higher estimates of the prevalence of false accusations of incest, and were less likely to indicate that they would report incest. Finlayson and Koocher (1991) found the same gender bias with regard to the reporting of child sexual abuse generally within a group of doctoral-level child clinical practitioners. Similarly, in a survey of English health professionals, Eisenberg, Owens, and Dewey (1987) found that women considered child sexual abuse more serious than did males, and in a survey of teachers and social workers, Johnson, Owens, Dewey, and Eisenberg (1990) found that women considered incest more harmful to children than did men. Finally, although gender differences were not pervasive among community jurors surveyed about child sexual abuse by Corder and Whiteside (1988), there was a greater tendency for men than for women to consider incest with an older female as "understandable."

Finally, experimental research also reveals gender differences in attitudes toward sexual activity between children and adults. Kelly (1984; Kelly & Tarran, 1983, 1984) found that, in general, women react more negatively than men do to child sexual abuse. Finkelhor (1984) found similar gender differences in observers' perceptions of the abusiveness of fabricated sexual abuse vignettes. Women consistently rated acts depicted in vignettes as more abusive than did men. Finally, Broussard and Wagner (1988) found that males, but not females, considered a 15-year-old's encouragement or lack thereof in assigning responsibility to the perpetrator in a sex abuse vignette.

In sum, attitudes toward adult/child sexual contact may be influential in decision making in child sexual abuse cases. Further, just as women seem to hold more negative attitudes toward rape than men do (Barnett & Feild, 1977; Larsen & Long, 1988), they may also hold more negative attitudes toward child sexual abuse (e.g., Bull et al., 1991; Finkelhor, 1984; Kelly, 1984), and these gender differences in attitudes may in part underlie differences in reactions to child sexual assault victims and judgments in child sexual assault cases.

Attitudes Toward Sexuality (Sexual Conservatism)

Personal beliefs about sexuality may also influence reactions to child sexual assault victims and decisions made in cases involving them. Just as Burt (1980) theorized that persons high in sexual conservatism might blame rape victims because of a "just world" attribution, one might expect the same for child victims. However, based on examinations of jurors' perceptions of child sexual assault victims in previous studies, it appears that jurors generally begin considering responsibility in their judgments when sex abuse cases involve victim–witnesses of about 13 years of age or older (Duggan et al., 1989; Goodman et al., 1989). Thus, on the one hand, an attribution process similar to that hypothesized by Burt may be used by sexually conservative jurors deciding a sexual assault case in which the victim is over the age of 13 (unless, as suggested by Deitz, empathy mediates this attribution—see below). On the other hand, in cases with younger children, responsibility is less likely to be an issue; therefore, it seems reasonable to expect that sexually conservative persons might react more negatively toward adult/child sexuality than those with liberal attitudes, and, in turn, be more positive in their evaluations of child victims and more prosecution oriented in their case judgments. However, one could also argue the opposite: Although sexual conservatives might react more negatively to confirmed child sexual abuse, they might be less willing to believe allegations without irrefutable evidence, thus reacting negatively to children who make abuse allegations.

In what appears to be the only research testing the relation of sexual conservatism to blame attributed to child victims of sexual assault, Waterman and Foss-Goodman (1984) found that sexually conservative jurors assigned more fault to victims than did liberal jurors. However, the variance in blame accounted for by this construct was small, and, unfortunately, although the study included cases with child victims of different ages (7, 11, and 15 years), the authors did not report analyses exploring a possible relation between sexual conservatism and blame to victims as a function of age.

Further, as noted earlier, evidence suggests that women on average have more sexually conservative attitudes than men (Small, Teagno, & Selz, 1980); thus, attitudes toward sexuality may be another construct underlying gender differences in child sexual abuse cases.

Summary

To summarize, jurors' attitudes toward (1) children's general believability, (2) women and feminism, (3) adult/child sexuality, and (4) sexuality in general may determine their perceptions, evaluations, and judgments in cases of child sexual assault. Further, given research indicating that there are gender differences in these attitudes, it is plausible that these differences may contribute to gender differences revealed in studies investigating the credibility of child sexual abuse victims.

Empathy

Finally, as in adult rape cases (Deitz et al., 1982), juror empathy may influence reactions to child witnesses and decisions made in child sexual assault cases. Taking into consideration definitions of empathy and sympathy proposed by theorists such as Batson, Fultz, and Schoenrade (1987) (the two constructs are presumed to be highly related for purposes of the present discussion),[1] I define child victim empathy as "the tendency for subjects to identify cognitively and emotionally with child victims of sexual assault, having feelings of concern, compassion, and understanding for their experience." Simply put, a person with a high level of child victim empathy would be expected to make favorable evaluations of child witnesses and pro-prosecution case decisions.[2]

Interestingly, judging from the literature on jurors' reactions to child and adult sexual assault victims, one might expect the mechanism by which empathy affects evaluations and judgments to differ for cases involving younger versus older children. Specifically, just as in adult rape cases (e.g., Burt, 1980; Coller & Resick, 1987), in cases involving children about age 12 or older, jurors may consider responsibility an issue, regardless of laws mandating that the issue of consent must be ignored in child sexual abuse cases because children are not deemed capable of consenting to sexual relations with an adult. Thus, jurors may make attributions of responsibility to older children for their victimization, resulting in attenuated perceptions of the their credibility as witnesses (Duggan et al., 1989; Waterman & Foss-Goodman, 1984). But, as Deitz et al. (1982) proposed in the context of rape cases, empathy may mediate these attributions of responsibility and result in the victim's being judged credible. That is, a juror who might otherwise be driven to blame a child for participation in a sexual abuse situation might be hindered from making such an attribution by feelings of compassion for and identification with the child victim.

Although Johnson et al. (1990) suggest that there is a "popular belief" that young children are blamed for sexual encounters with adults, there is little evidence in the scientific literature that jurors assign responsibility to younger child victims for child sexual abuse, as noted in the literature review above (e.g., Duggan et al., 1989; Isquith et al., Chapter 9, this volume).[3] Thus, in cases involving very young witnesses, empathy may be less likely to mediate attributions of blame than in cases involving adult or older child victims. Instead, the effect of empathy on evaluations and judgments may be more direct: Emotional and cognitive identification with child victims may simply predispose observers to consider child witnesses favorably (perhaps protectively) and to make pro-victim judgments.

Finally, gender differences in empathy may underlie gender differences in response to child victims. Compared to men, women are sometimes found to be more empathic in general (Barnett et al., 1992; Batson et al., 1988; Davis, 1983; Hoffman, 1977; but see Eisenberg, Fabes, Schaller, & Miller, 1989; Eisenberg & Lennon, 1983). Perhaps the only mention of gender differences in empathy toward child sexual assault victims is in a report of a study by Leippe et al. (1989) exploring attorneys' attitudes toward child sexual abuse victims. Female attorneys differed from male attorneys in reasons given for why they thought children might retract allegations of sexual assault. Compared to men, women thought it more likely that children make retractions because of embarrassment or fear of retaliation for the accusations. The authors suggested that this difference might reflect women's more empathic approach to children, which might elicit more self-disclosure from children about their reasons for recantation, or allow women to be more responsive than men to cues from children's behavior indicative of fear and embarrassment. This empathic stance might lead women to more pro-prosecution judgments.

In summary, although untested in the empirical literature, there is good reason to suspect that jurors' empathy for child sexual assault victims may be significantly related to judgments in cases of child sexual abuse, that men and women may differ on average in their levels of empathy for child victims, and that these differences may contribute to gender differences in child sexual abuse case judgments.

EMPIRICAL VALIDATION OF PROPOSED IDEAS

In this chapter, I have reviewed various literatures to support several hypotheses regarding jurors' perceptions and judgments in child sexual abuse cases; specifically, that men and women differ in their level of empathy for child victims and in attitudes relevant to child abuse (e.g., attitudes toward children's believability in general, adult/child sex, feminism, and sexuality), and that these differences explain to some extent gender differences in judgments made in child sexual assault cases. Preliminary research has been conducted as a first step in a series of studies testing those hypotheses.

Method and Predictions

In a laboratory experiment, over 300 student participants indicated their level of agreement with items designed to tap child victim empathy and the proposed attitudinal constructs. From these data, meaningful scales were statistically determined: (1) the Children's General Believability Scale, which measures attitudes toward the honesty or trustworthiness of children, especially with regard to reporting of sexual abuse; (2) the Child Victim Empathy Scale, which includes items reflecting the ability of respondents to empathize with the experiences of a child sexual abuse victim both during an assault and during a trial for this crime; and (3) the Adult/Child Sexuality Attitudes Scale, which focuses on the seriousness of sexual contact between children and adults as well as on the idea that children are sexual beings. Participants also completed measures that assessed degree of sexual conservatism (Simpson & Gangestad, 1991) and feminism. To test the predictive validity of the scales, subjects were presented with scenarios of child sexual assault cases and were asked to make individual judgments about victim believability and defendant guilt. The relation between subjects' scale scores and case judgments was then determined.

It was expected that there would be significant gender differences in victim credibility and defendant guilt judgments, with women making more pro-victim evaluations than men. But, it was also expected that persons who had empathy for children, who considered children to be generally believable, who reacted negatively to adult/child sexuality, who held pro-feminist views, and who held conservative attitudes toward sex would be most likely to make pro-child victim and anti-defendant judgments in child sexual assault cases, regardless of gender. Overall, however, it was expected that more women would fit that profile than men, and thus, that gender differences would be accounted for by individual differences in scale measures of attitudes and empathy.

In addition, it was expected that juror experiential factors, such as a personal history of abuse, would also be related to judgments. It was reasoned that people who had been victimized themselves as adults or children would hold stronger pro-victim attitudes than nonvictimized persons, and that these attitudes would influence their evaluative behavior as jurors.

Results and Discussion

Preliminary examination of the data from this initial study revealed support for major predictions. Specifically, there were pervasive gender differences in scale scores and in victim credibility and defendant guilt judgments: Across the four hypothetical case scenarios, females were significantly more pro-victim than males (see Table 10.1). Also, each of the proposed multi-item scales was found to be internally reliable (coefficient alphas ranged from .70 to .88), and multiple regression analyses revealed that scale scores were predictive of case judgments. Most important, however, when both gender and scale scores were included in stepwise regression analyses as predictors of victim credibility and defendant guilt judgments, gender did not enter into the equations (see Table 10.2 for significant scale-score predictors). Differences in mock jurors' empathy and attitudes were more informative in "explaining" their case judgments than was their gender alone. Thus, as hypothesized, differences in empathy and attitudes appear to underlie in part gender differences in case judgments: Although there were gender differences in judgments, men who were more empathic toward child victims and who held attitudes relevant to child abuse cases similar to those more often held by women tended to be more pro-victim; women who were less empathic toward child victims and who held relevant attitudes more like men were generally less pro-victim.

The constructs of child victim empathy and the various attitudes were, however, predictive of case judgments to different degrees. As can be seen from Table 10.2, although scores on multi-item measures of attitudes toward women, sexuality, and adult/child sexuality were generally related to judgments as hypothesized (especially evaluations of child witness credibility), scores on scales concerning children's general believability and child victim empathy were the most successful predictors of judgments. Although attitudes toward feminism were significantly correlated with judgments in several of the cases, with less feminist views being associated more with pro-defense judgments, the other constructs were more highly related to judgments.

TABLE 10.1. Mean Credibility and Guilt Ratings as a Function of Participant Gender

| | Participant gender | | |
	Male	Female	Significance
Case 1: Father/Daughter Incest Case			
Victim credibility	3.88	4.43	$F(1, 322) = 17.71, p < .001$
Defendant guilt	0.56	0.76	$F(1, 322) = 12.64, p < .001$
Degree of guilt	3.73	4.44	$F(1, 322) = 18.26, p < .001$
Case 2: Teacher/Student Case			
Victim credibility	4.08	4.65	$F(1, 323) = 19.96, p < .001$
Defendant guilt	0.67	0.84	$F(1, 322) = 8.98, p < .01$
Degree of guilt	4.20	4.77	$F(1, 322) = 12.32, p < .001$
Case 3: Day-Care Case			
Victim credibility	4.19	4.69	$F(1, 322) = 14.29, p < .001$
Defendant guilt	0.72	0.82	$F(1, 318) = 3.88, p < .05$
Degree of guilt	4.43	4.86	$F(1, 318) = 6.83, p < .01$
Case 4: Stranger Abduction Case			
Victim credibility	3.72	4.18	$F(1, 228) = 6.93, p < .01$
Defendant guilt	0.26	0.20	NS
Degree of guilt	2.51	2.72	NS

Note. Credibility ratings range from 1 "not at all believable" to 6 "extremely believable"; guilt ratings range from 0 "not guilty" to 1 "guilty"; degree of guilt ratings range from 1 "not guilty/very confident" to 6 "guilty/very confident."

TABLE 10.2. Multivariate Prediction of Case Judgments: Results of Separate Multiple Regression Analyses with Scale Scores Entered Stepwise

	Scales entering equations, in order	Beta	t
Case 1: Father/Daughter Incest Case			
Victim credibility	Children's believability	.36	6.75****
	Child victim empathy	.14	6.75**
	Sexual conservatism	.11	2.03*
Degree of guilt	Children's believability	.28	5.18****
	Sexual conservatism	.16	3.08**
	Child victim empathy	.17	2.99**
Case 2: Teacher/Student Case			
Victim credibility	Children's believability	.35	6.33****
	Child victim empathy	.16	2.98**
Degree of guilt	Children's believability	.23	4.05****
	Child victim empathy	.21	3.77***
Case 3: Day-Care Case			
Victim credibility	Children's believability	.33	5.96****
	Child victim empathy	.13	2.24*
Degree of guilt	Children's believability	.22	3.90****
Case 4: Stranger Abduction Case			
Victim credibility	Children's believability	.29	3.84***
	Adult/child sexuality	−.19	−2.62**
	Child victim empathy	.17	2.34*
Degree of guilt	N/S	—	—

Note. Credibility ratings range from 1 "not at all believable" to 6 "extremely believable." Degree of guilt ratings range from 1 "not guilty/very confident" to 6 "guilty/very confident."
* $p < .05$, ** $p < .01$, *** $p < .001$, **** $p < .0001$.

Finally, as predicted, persons with a history of abuse were significantly more pro-victim with regard to judgments and scale scores than were those who had not been abused.

Thus, results of the study supported hypotheses outlined in this chapter: There seems to be a disparity in the decisions made by men and women in some cases involving alleged child sexual assault victims, but this may be explained by individual differences in empathy for and attitudes relevant to child victims.

Data from two follow-up studies are now being collected to test and improve the reliability and validity of the proposed scale measures of empathy and attitudes. The generalizability of findings across cases with varying characteristics (such as cases with younger vs. older child victims) and the relative importance of such case factors on juror decision making is also being explored.

Preliminary Model for Understanding
Judgments in Child Sexual Abuse Cases

Although the preliminary results presented herein must be interpreted with caution until ongoing experiments have provided additional support for the reliability and predictive validity of the proposed scales, the data and literature review support a tentative model for understanding mock jurors' reactions to child sexual assault cases (see Figure 10.1). According to this model, juror factors such as gender and personal abuse history will be associated with specific attitudes and the level of empathy one has for child victims. These attitudes and empathic tendencies will in turn be predictive of evaluations of the credibility of child witnesses and guilt judgments rendered in child sexual assault cases. Also important, perhaps in influencing the relation between empathy and attitudes and judgments, will be case characteristics (e.g., case strength, victim age). According to this model, a case verdict will be determined, in the end, primarily by the perceived credibility of the victim (see Borgida & Brekke, 1985).

As now conceptualized, the model reflects the possibility of a relationship between attitudes and empathy. Although the literature on both attitudes and empathy in any context is largely silent on the possibility of a causal relation between empathy and attitudes, it seems plausible that attitudes contribute to the ability to empathize with child sexual assault victims. One of the few empirical or theoretical considerations of this issue appears to be in the context of reactions to AIDS sufferers: Persons with homophobic attitudes are less empathic toward AIDS victims (Dhooper, Royse, & Tran, 1988; Connors & Heaven, 1990; Royse, & Birge, 1987). Similarly, it may be that persons who are most empathic with child sexual assault victims will be those who hold, for example, strong favorable attitudes toward children's believability and feminism and negative attitudes toward child sexual abuse. Intuitively, it seems unlikely that a person could have empathy for child sexual assault victims without first having such an attitudinal basis for feeling positively toward child victims. In fact, Karniol (1982) suggests that empathic tendencies are a product of information retrieved from memory that guide responses to a target. It seems reasonable to consider attitudes as a type of "information retrieved from memory," and, thus, as possible determinants of empathic responses. Nonetheless, the direction of causality between attitudes and empathy, if it exists at all, may be reversed (see Shelton & Rogers, 1981).

In summary, although this model is tentative and may change with data from ongoing studies, it is useful as an initial framework for

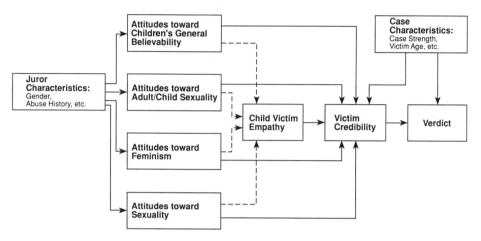

FIGURE 10.1. Tentative model of factors influencing decision making in child sexual assault cases.

considering the mechanisms responsible for juror decision making in child sexual assault cases.

INDICATIONS FOR FUTURE RESEARCH

Obviously, this review cannot be exhaustive of all possible attitudinal determinants or correlates of perceptions of child sexual assault victims. For example, Barnett and Sinisi (1990) have recently developed a measurement that assesses general "liking of children," which has shown females to be more pro-children than men. Thus, future research needs to validate ideas proposed herein as well as to extend the line of inquiry by exploring other constructs that might be significantly related to evaluations of child sexual assault victims. I am currently seeking to do this in follow-up studies by exploring, for example, individual differences such as experience with children and general pro-prosecution/pro-defense juror biases.

Even as attitudinal bases for gender differences are empirically established, another important question will remain for future research: Why do men and women differ in those underlying attitudes or empathic tendencies? One answer may be related to the fact that, as previously mentioned, prior abuse experience may have an impact on attitudes, child victim empathy, and, consequently, perceptions of child victims and judgments in child sexual assault cases. Specifically, concerning gender differences in attitudes, basic attitude research has revealed that attitudes are more likely to be related to behaviors if the attitudes are the product of personal, firsthand experience (Fazio, Zanna, & Cooper, 1978) or are of particular self-importance (Young, Borgida, Sullivan, & Aldrich, 1987). Because females, as adults or children, are more likely to be sexually victimized than males (Finkelhor, 1984) and are likely to be aware of this threat due to societal attention to the issue (e.g., Brownmiller, 1975), even nonvictimized women may feel threatened. Thus, potential sexual victimization may be a much more personally important issue for women than for men, and this may be responsible for women's stronger negative attitudes toward sexual abuse and positive attitudes toward child victims.

Similarly, concerning gender differences in empathy, just as research reveals that we are most empathic toward people who are like ourselves (Krebs, 1970), previously victimized persons have been found to be more empathic toward other victims than are persons who have not been abused (Barnett et al., 1986; Barnett et al., 1987; Deitz et al., 1982). Similarly, survivors of sexual abuse, especially child sexual abuse, may be more likely than nonsurvivors to identify and empathize with a child victim because they have suffered a similar negative event. In support, Waterman and Foss-Goodman (1984) found that previously victimized subjects attributed less fault to child victims than nonvictimized subjects. Because, as noted above, women are more likely than men to be sexually victimized, even nonvictimized women may identify more with child victims than men and thus have more empathy for them.

Finally, it will be important to consider basic research on the determinants of gender differences in interpreting gender differences in empathic and attitudinal constructs related to child sexual abuse. Important gender differences are being noted in psychological research, and theory and experimentation have emerged in an attempt to identify the causes of these differences. For example, Eagly and colleagues (Eagly, 1987; Eagly & Wood, 1991) advocate a social role, or "gender role," explanation for gender differences. In general, Eagly suggests that the behaviors and personalities of members of our society are shaped by internalization of their respective gender roles: Women, who are identified with childrearing and a generally submissive societal role (Chodorow, 1978), are more "communal" than men: Having been socialized from childhood for their roles, they are more empathic (Hoffman, 1977), caring, concerned, helpful, and expressive (Gilligan, 1982), and have more favorable attitudes toward children and child raising (Barnett & Sinisi, 1990). In contrast, Eagly suggests that men are more "agentic": more assertive, dominant, forceful, and less concerned with the needs of others. Thus, it follows that compared to men, women would be more concerned about child welfare, and that this might manifest itself in more negative attitudes toward child sexual abuse, more positive attitudes toward children's ability to testify about victimization, and more empathic reactions to child victims. Empirical validation of these ideas is needed.

PRACTICAL AND THEORETICAL IMPLICATIONS OF THE RESEARCH

At present, there has been very little theoretically sound research on factors that influence jurors' perceptions of child witnesses and the role of these factors in case decisions. The proposed line of research is a significant step toward expanding and fostering such research by developing scales measuring specific biases related to perceptions and judgments in child sexual assault cases and by proposing an empirically testable theoretical model for conceptualizing the influence of those biases on juror decisions. The research is also of interest with regard to understanding basic gender differences and clarifying issues regarding attitudes, empathic tendencies, and their effects on perceptions and behaviors.

In addition to the theoretical importance of the proposed ideas, there is also potential for practical applications of this research. For example, understanding general reactions to child sexual abuse and its victims may facilitate therapeutic preparation of child victims for reactions that they may encounter inside or outside a courtroom setting should their victimization be made public (Kelly, 1984). Also, the identification of specific biases that influence decisions might also make it possible to design jury instructions to educate jurors about their own biases and to caution them against approaching trial evidence from a biased perspective. Further, some have advocated screening jurors in rape cases based on pretrial biases such as an inability to empathize with victims (see Deitz et al., 1982); similarly, information from this line of research might be useful in identifying individual prospective jurors holding biases that might jeopardize impartial jury composition in child sexual assault cases. Importantly, I refer here to jurors who might be particularly biased against believing defendants as well as those who might be biased against believing child witnesses. Benefits of assuring fairer juries by the exclusion of or education of biased jurors include the protection of children from revictimization by unconvicted perpetrators, as well as the protection of innocent defendants from unjust conviction.

CONCLUSION

In sum, jurors' pretrial biases may overshadow what little hard evidence is presented in child sexual abuse cases and threaten the integrity of the judicial system by hindering fair, impartial trials for defendants and victims. As a framework for understanding biases in decision making in child sexual abuse cases, particularly gender differences in reactions to child victims, the present discussion has considered empathy and attitudinal constructs as determinants of perceptions, evaluations, and case judgments.

Research on the issues raised herein promises to advance psychological theory regarding attitudes, empathy, and juror decision making, and to provide practical benefits for children's involvement in the legal system. Given the rising incidence of child sexual assault cases, the special problems that arise when jurors hear such cases, and our societal obligation to assure fair trials, we cannot afford to neglect inquiry into determinants of children's perceived credibility.

ACKNOWLEDGMENTS

This research was supported by grants from the American Psychology/Law Society, Sigma Xi, and the Department of Health and Human Services (90CA1473). Sincerest thanks are extended to Gail S. Goodman, Phillip R. Shaver, and Murray Levine for insightful comments on earlier drafts, and to Tracey Schneider and Cathleen Carter for invaluable research assistance.

NOTES

1. A review of the literature concerning empathy reveals a debate over the distinction between empathy and sympathy, a closely related concept (e.g., Wispé, 1986). Eisenberg and Miller (1987) suggest that sympathy is "an emotional response stemming from another's emotional state or condition that is not identical to the other's emotion, but consists of feelings of sorrow or concern for another" (p. 292). This is in contrast to empathy defined by Eisenberg (1989) as "the sharing of the perceived emotion of another . . . an affective state that stems from the apprehension of another's emotional state or condition and that is congruent and quite similar to the perceived state of the other" (p. 1). Many researchers, however, have not considered it necessary to distinguish between the two; for example, Batson et al. (1987) point out that both are "other-oriented feelings of concern, compassion, and tenderness experienced as a result of witnessing another person's suffering" (p. 174).

2. The present discussion focuses on a hypothesized enduring construct of empathy for child victims; however, temporarily induced empathy may also be at issue in trial settings: Consider the jury that is exposed to prosecution lawyers adept at creating a very compelling empathic atmosphere toward a child, or a defense attorney who asks the jurors to place themselves in the shoes of the defendant, as trial lawyers have instinctively done for years (Archer, Fouchee, Davis, & Aderman, 1979; Belli, 1956). For discussion of temporarily induced empathy as a mediator of dispositional attributions of fault, see Aderman et al. (1975), Archer et al. (1979), and Regan and Totten (1975).
3. Although research suggests that very young child sexual assault victims are not blamed, there are vivid anecdotal examples to the contrary. For example, a judge, who sentenced a man found guilty of sexually abusing a 5-year-old girl to a minimum 90-day work-release program, commented on the logic of his decision: "I am satisfied we have an unusually sexually promiscuous young lady. And [the defendant] did not know enough to refuse. No way do I believe he initiated sexual contact" (Finkelhor, 1984, p. 108).

REFERENCES

Abel, G. G., Becker, J. V., & Cunningham-Rathner, J. (1984). Complications, consent and cognitions in sex between children and adults. *International Journal of Law and Psychiatry, 7*, 89–103.

Aderman, D., Archer, R. L., & Harris, J. L. (1975). Effects of emotional empathy on attribution of responsibility. *Journal of Personality, 43*, 156–167.

Aderman, D., Brehm, S. S., & Katz, L. B. (1974). Empathic observation of an innocent victim: The just world revisited. *Journal of Personality and Social Psychology, 29*, 342–347.

Ajzen, I. (1985). From intentions to actions: A theory of planned behavior. In J. Kuhl & J. Beckmann (Eds.), *Action control: From cognition to behavior* (pp. 11–39). New York: Springer-Verlag.

Ajzen, I. (1988). *Attitudes, personality and behavior.* Chicago: Dorsey Press.

Archer, R. L., Fouchee, H. C., Davis, M. H., & Aderman, D. (1979). Emotional empathy in a courtroom simulation: A person–situation interaction. *Journal of Applied Social Psychology, 9*, 275–291.

Attias, R., & Goodwin, J. (1985). Knowledge and management strategies in incest cases: A survey of physicians, psychologists and family counselors. *Child Abuse and Neglect, 9*, 527–533.

Barnett, M. A., Feierstein, M. D., Jaet, B. P., Saunders, L. C., Quakenbush, S. W., & Sinisi, C. S. (1992). The effect of knowing a rape victim on reactions to other victims. *Journal of Interpersonal Violence, 7*, 44–56.

Barnett, N. J., & Feild, H. S. (1977). Sex differences in university students' attitudes toward rape. *Journal of College Student Personnel, 18*, 93–96.

Barnett, M. A., & Sinisi, C. S. (1990). The initial validation of a liking of children scale. *Journal of Personality Assessment, 55*, 161–167.

Barnett, M. A., Tetreault, P. A., Esper, J. A., & Bristow, A. R. (1986). Similarity and empathy: The experience of rape. *Journal of Social Psychology, 126,* 47–49.

Barnett, M. A., Tetreault, P. A., & Masbad, I. (1987). Empathy with a rape victim: The role of similarity of experience. *Violence and Victims, 2,* 255–262.

Batson, C. D., Dyck, J. L., Brandt, J. R., Batson, J. G., Powell, A. L., McMaster, M.R., Griffitt, C. (1988). Five studies testing two new egoistic alternatives to the empathy-altruism hypothesis. *Journal of Personality and Social Psychology, 55,* 52–77.

Batson, C. D., Fultz, J., & Schoenrade, P. A. (1987). Adults' emotional reactions to the distress of others. In N. Eisenberg & J. Strayer (Eds.), *Empathy and its development* (pp. 163–184). New York: Cambridge University Press.

Beitchman, J. H., Zucker, K. J., Hood, J. E., DaCosta, G. A., Akman, D., & Cassavia, E. (1992). A review of the long-term effects of child sexual abuse. *Child Abuse and Neglect, 16,* 101–118.

Belli, M. M. (1956). *Blood money: Ready for the plaintiff.* New York: Grosset & Dunlap.

Bender, L., & Blau, A. (1937). The reaction of children to sexual relations with adults. *American Journal of Orthopsychiatry, 7,* 500–518.

Bender, L., & Grugett, A. E. (1952). A follow-up on children who had atypical sexual experiences. *American Journal of Orthopsychiatry, 22,* 825–837.

Borgida, E., & Brekke, N. (1985). Psychological research on rape trials. In A. W. Burgess (Ed.), *Research handbook on rape and sexual assault.* New York: Garland.

Bottoms, B. L. (1989). *Courtroom evaluation of children's testimony: Factors influencing the jury.* Unpublished master's thesis, University of Denver, Denver.

Bottoms, B. L., & Goodman, G. S. (1992). *Perceptions of children's credibility in sexual abuse cases.* Manuscript submitted for publication.

Brongersma, E. (1984). Aggression against pedophiles. *International Journal of Law and Psychiatry, 7,* 79–87.

Broussard, S. D., & Wagner, W. G. (1988). Child sexual abuse: Who is to blame? *Child Abuse and Neglect, 12,* 563–569.

Browne, A., & Finkelhor, D. (1986). Impact of child sexual abuse: A review of the research. *Psychological Bulletin, 99,* 66–77.

Brownmiller, S. (1975). *Against our will: Men women and rape.* New York: Simon & Schuster.

Bulkley, J. A. (1989). The impact of new child witness research on sexual abuse prosecutions. In S. Ceci, D. Ross, & M. Toglia (Eds.), *Perspectives on children's testimony* (pp. 208–229). NY: Springer-Verlag.

Bull, M. A., Borgida, E., Gresham, A. W., Swim, J., & Gray, E. (in press). Do child sexual abuse experts hold pro-child beliefs? A survey of the International Society for Traumatic Stress Studies. *Journal of Traumatic Stress.*

Burt, M. R. (1980). Cultural myths and support for rape. *Journal of Personality and Social Psychology, 38,* 217–230.

Burt, M. R., & Albin, R. S. (1981). Rape myths, rape definitions, and probability of conviction. *Journal of Applied Social Psychology, 11,* 212–230.

Calhoun, L. G., Selby, J. W., & Warring, L. J. (1976). Social perception of the victim's causal role in rape: An explanatory examination for four factors. *Human Relations, 29,* 517–526.

Chodorow, N. (1978). *The reproduction of mothering: Psychoanalysis and the sociology of gender.* Berkeley: University of California Press.

Coller, S. A., & Resick, P. A. (1987). Women's attributions of responsibility for date rape: The influence of empathy and sex-role stereotyping. *Violence and Victims, 2,* 115–125.

Connors, J., & Heaven, P. C. L. (1990). Belief in a just world and attitudes toward AIDS sufferers. *Journal of Social Psychology, 130,* 559–560.

Constantine, L., & Martinson, F. M. (Eds.) (1981). *Children and sex: New findings, new perspectives.* Boston: Little, Brown.

Corder, B. F., & Whiteside, R. (1988). A survey of jurors' perception of issues related to child sexual abuse. *American Journal of Forensic Psychology, 6*(3), 37–43.

Davis, M. H. (1983). Measuring individual differences in empathy: Evidence for a multidimensional approach. *Journal of Personality and Social Psychology, 44,* 113–126.

Davis, J. H., Kerr, N. L., Atkin, R. S., Holt, R. W., & Meek, D. (1975). The decision processes of 6- and 12-person juries assigned unanimous and two thirds majority rules. *Journal of Personality and Social Psychology, 32,* 1–14.

Deitz, S. R., Blackwell, K. T., Daley, P. C., & Bentley, B. J. (1982). Measurement of empathy toward rape victims and rapists. *Journal of Personality and Social Psychology, 43,* 372–384.

Deitz, S. R., & Byrnes, L. E. (1981). Attribution of responsibility for sexual assault: The influence of observer empathy and defendant occupation and attractiveness. *Journal of Psychology, 108,* 17–29.

Delora, J., & Warren, C. (1977). *Understanding sexual interactions.* Boston: Houghton Mifflin.

DeMott, B. (1980). The pro-incest lobby. *Psychology Today, 13*(10), 11.

deYoung, M. (1982). *The sexual victimization of children.* Jefferson, NC: McFarland.

Dhooper, S. S., Royse, D. R., & Tran, T. V. (1988). Social work practitioners' attitudes towards AIDS victims. *Journal of Applied Social Sciences, 12,* 108–123.

Duggan, L. M., III, Aubrey, M., Doherty, E., Isquith, P., Levine, M., & Scheiner, J. (1989). The credibility of children as witnesses in a simulated child sex abuse trial. In S. J. Ceci, D. F. Ross, & M. P. Toglia (Eds.), *Perspectives on children's testimony* (pp. 71–99). New York: Springer-Verlag.

Eagly, A. H. (1987). *Sex differences in social behavior: A social role interpretation.* Hillsdale, NJ: Erlbaum.

Eagly, A. H., & Wood, W. (1991). Explaining sex differences in social behavior: A meta-analytic perspective. *Personality and Social Psychology Bulletin, 17,* 306–315.

Eisenberg, N. (Ed.). (1989). *Empathy and related emotional responses.* San Francisco: Jossey-Bass.

Eisenberg, N., Fabes, R. A., Schaller, M., & Miller, P. A. (1989). Sympathy and personal distress: Development, gender differences, and interrelations of indexes. In N. Eisenberg (Ed.), *Empathy and related emotional responses* (pp. 107–127). San Francisco: Jossey-Bass.

Eisenberg, N., & Lennon, R. (1983). Sex differences in empathy and related capacities. *Psychological Bulletin, 94,* 100-131.

Eisenberg, N., & Miller, P. A. (1987). Empathy, sympathy, and altruism: Empirical and conceptual links. In N. Eisenberg & J. Strayer (Eds.), *Empathy and its development* (pp. 292–316). New York: Cambridge University Press.

Eisenberg, N., Owens, R. G., & Dewey, M. E. (1987). Attitudes of health professionals to child sexual abuse and neglect. *Child Abuse and Neglect, 11,* 109–116.

Everson, M. D., & Boat, B. W. (1989). False allegations of sexual abuse by children and adolescents. *Journal of the American Academy of Child and Adolescent Psychiatry, 28*(2), 230–235.

Faller, K. C. (1988). *Child sexual abuse.* New York: Columbia University Press.

Fazio, R. H., Zanna, M. P., & Cooper, J. (1978). Direct experience and attitude–behavior consistency: An information processing analysis. *Personality and Social Psychology Bulletin, 4,* 48–51.

Feild, H. S. (1978a). Attitudes toward rape: A comparative analysis of police, rapists, crisis counselors, and citizens. *Journal of Personality and Social Psychology, 36,* 156–179.

Feild, H. S. (1978b). Juror background characteristics and attitudes toward rape: Correlates of jurors' decisions in rape trials. *Law and Human Behavior, 2,* 73–93.

Finkelhor, D. (1984). *Child sexual abuse: New theory and research.* New York: Free Press.

Finkelhor, D. (1986). *A sourcebook on child sexual abuse.* Beverly Hills, CA: Sage.

Finlayson, L. M., & Koocher, G. P. (1991). Professional judgment and child abuse reporting in sexual abuse cases. *Professional Psychology: Research and Practice, 22,* 464–472.

Freud, S. (1962). The etiology of hysteria. In J. Strachley (Ed. and Trans.), *The complete psychological works of Sigmund Freud.* London: Hogarth Press. (Original work published 1933)

Gabora, N. J., Spanos, N. P., & Joab, A. (1991). *The Effects of complainant age and expert psychological testimony in a simulated child sexual abuse trial.* Unpublished manuscript, Carleton University, Millbrook Correctional Centre, Ottawa, Ontario, Canada.

Gil, D. G. (1970). *Violence against children.* Cambridge, MA: Harvard University Press.

Gilligan, C. (1982). *In a different voice: Psychological theory and women's development.* Cambridge, MA: Harvard University Press.

Goldstein, S. (1987). *The sexual exploitation of children.* New York: Elsevier.

Goodman, G. S., Bottoms, B. L., Herscovici, B. B., & Shaver, P. R. (1989). Determinants of the child victim's perceived credibility. In S. J. Ceci, D. F.

Ross, & M. P. Toglia (Eds.), *Perspectives on children's testimony* (pp. 1–22). New York: Springer-Verlag.

Goodman, G. S., Golding, J. M., & Haith, M. M. (1984). Jurors' reactions to child witnesses. *Journal of Social Issues, 40*(2), 139–156.

Goodman, G. S., Golding, J. M., Helgeson, V. S., Haith, M. M., & Michelli, J. (1987). When a child takes the stand: Jurors' perceptions of children's eyewitness testimony. *Law and Human Behavior, 11*, 27–40.

Goodman, G. S., & Reed, R. S. (1986). Age differences in eyewitness testimony. *Law and Human Behavior, 10*, 317–332.

Goodman, G. S., Rudy, L., Bottoms, B. L., & Aman, C. (1990). Children's memory and concerns: Ecological issues in the study of children's eyewitness testimony. In R. Fivush & J. Hudson (Eds.), *Knowing and remembering in young children.* (pp. 249– 284). New York: Cambridge University Press.

Herman, J. (1981). *Father–daughter incest.* Cambridge, MA: Harvard University Press.

Herman, J., & Hirschman, L. (1977). Father-daughter incest. *Signs, 2*, 1–22.

Hoffman, M. L. (1977). Sex differences in empathy and related behaviors. *Psychological Bulletin, 84*(4), 712–722.

Hunt, J. McV., & Paraskevopoulos, J. (1980). Children's psychological development as a function of the inaccuracy of their mother's knowledge of their abilities. *Journal of Genetic Psychology, 136*, 285–298.

Johnson, B. T. (1991). Insights about attitudes: Meta-analytic perspectives. *Personality and Social Psychology Bulletin, 17*, 289–299.

Johnson, P. A., Owens, R. G., Dewey, M. E., & Eisenberg, N. E. (1990). Professionals' attributions of censure in father–daughter incest. *Child Abuse and Neglect, 14*, 419–428.

Jones, C., & Aronson, E. (1973). Attribution of fault to a rape victim as a function of the respectability of the victim. *Journal of Personality and Social Psychology, 26*, 415–419.

Kahn, A., Gilbert, I. A., Latta, R. M., Deutsch, C., Hagen, R., Hill, M., McGaughey, T., Ryan, A. N., & Wilson, D. W. (1977). Attribution of fault to a rape victim as a function of respectability of the victim: A failure to replicate or extend. *Representative Research in Social Psychology, 8*, 98–107.

Kaplan, M. F., & Miller, L. E. (1978). Effects of jurors' identification with the victim depend on likelihood of victimization. *Law and Human Behavior, 2*, 353–361.

Karniol, R. (1982). Settings, scripts, and self-schemata: A cognitive analysis of the development of pro-social behavior. In N. Eisenberg (Ed.), *The development of pro-social behavior* (pp. 251–278). New York: Academic Press.

Katz, S., & Mazur, M. A. (1979). *Understanding the rape victim: A synthesis of research findings.* New York: Wiley.

Kelly, R. J. (1984). *Gender and incest factors in reactions to adult–child sex.* Unpublished dissertation, State University of New York at Buffalo, Buffalo.

Kelly, R. J., & Tarran, M. J. (1983, April). *Gender differences in childhood sexual experiences and subsequent attitudes toward child sexual abuse.* Paper presented at the meeting of the Eastern Psychological Association, Philadelphia, PA.

Kelly, R. J., & Tarran, M. J. (1984, April). Negative homosexuality bias in reactions to adult-child sex. Paper presented at the meeting of the Western Psychological Association, Los Angeles, CA.

Kempe, C. H., Silverman, F. N., Steele, B. F., Droegenmueller, W., & Silver, H. K. (1962). The battered child syndrome. *Journal of the American Medical Association, 181*, 17–24.

Kerr, N. L., Atkin, R., Stasser, G., Meek, D., Holt, R., & Davis, J. (1976). Guilt beyond a reasonable doubt: Effects of concept definition and assigned rule on the judgments of mock jurors. *Journal of Personality and Social Psychology, 34*, 282–294.

Krahe, B. (1988). Victim and observer characteristics as determinants of responsibility attributions to victims of rape. *Journal of Applied Social Psychology, 18*, 50–58.

Krebs, D. L. (1970). Altruism: An examination of the concept and a review of the literature. *Psychological Bulletin, 73*, 258–303.

Krulewitz, J. E., & Nash, E. J. (1979). Effects of rape victim resistance, assault outcome, and sex of observer on attributions about rape. *Journal of Personality, 47*, 557–574.

Krulewitz, J. E., & Paine, E. J. (1978). Attributions about rape: Effects of rapist force, observer sex and sex role attitudes. *Journal of Applied Social Psychology, 8*, 291–305.

Larsen, K. S., & Long, E. (1988). Attitudes toward rape. *Journal of Sex Research, 24*, 299–304.

Leippe, M. R., Brigham, J. C., Cousins, C., & Romanczyk, A. (1989). The opinions and practices of criminal attorneys regarding child eyewitnesses: A survey. In S. J. Ceci, D. F. Ross, & M. R. Toglia (Eds.), *Perspectives on children's testimony* (pp. 100–130). New York: Springer-Verlag.

Leippe, M. R., & Romanczyk, A. (1987). Children on the witness stand: A communication/persuasion analysis of jurors' reactions to child witnesses. In S. J. Ceci, M. P. Toglia, & D. F. Ross (Eds.), *Children's eyewitness memory* (pp. 155–177). New York: Springer-Verlag.

Leippe, M. R., & Romanczyk, A. (1989). Reactions to child (versus adult) eyewitnesses: The influence of jurors' preconceptions and witness behavior. *Law and Human Behavior, 13*(2), 103–132.

Lerner, M. (1970). The desire for justice and reactions to victims. In J. Macaulay & L. Berkowitz (Eds.), *Altruism and helping behavior.* New York: Academic Press.

Lerner, M., & Miller, D. T. (1978). Just world research and the attribution process: Looking back and ahead. *Psychological Bulletin, 85*, 1030–1051.

Levine, M., & Levine, A. (1992). *Helping children: A social history.* New York: Oxford University Press.

Limber, S. P., & Castrianno, L. M. (1990, August). *Laypersons' perceptions of sexually abused children.* Paper presented at the meeting of the American Psychological Association, Boston, MA.

Luginbuhl, J., & Mullin, C. (1981). Rape and responsibility: How and how much is the victim blamed? *Sex Roles, 7,* 547–559.

Lukianowicz, N. (1972). Incest I: Paternal incest; Incest II: Other types of incest. *British Journal of Psychiatry, 120,* 301–313.

MacFarlane, K., Waterman, J., Conerly, S., Damon, L., Durfee, M. & Long, S. (Eds.) (1986). *Sexual abuse of young children.* New York: Guilford Press.

Masson, J. M. (1984). *The assault on truth: Freud's suppression of the seduction theory.* New York: Farrar, Straus, & Giroux.

Miller, S. A., White, N., & Delgado, M. (1980). Adults' conceptions of children's cognitive abilities. *Merrill-Palmer Quarterly, 26,* 135-151.

Moll, A. (1929). *The sexual life of the child.* New York: MacMillan.

Morton, T. L., & Dubanoski, R. A. (1982). Children's rights: Attitudes and perceptions. *Educational Perspectives, 19*(4), 24–27.

Mrazek, P., & Mrazek, D. (1981). The effects of child abuse: Methodological considerations. In P. Mrazek & C. H. Kempe (Eds.), *Sexually abused children and their families* (pp. 2354–256). New York: Pergamon Press.

Nagao, D. H., & Davis, J. H. (1980). Some implications of temporal drift in social parameters. *Journal of Experimental Social Psychology, 16,* 479–496.

Nigro, G., Buckley, M., Hill, D., & Nelson, J. (1989). When juries "hear" children testify: The effects of eyewitness age and speech style on jurors' perceptions of testimony. In S. Ceci, D. Ross, & M. Toglia (Eds.), *Perspectives on children's testimony* (pp. 57–70). New York: Springer-Verlag.

Regan, D. T., & Totten, J. (1975). Empathy and attribution: Turning observers into actors. *Journal of Personality and Social Psychology, 32,* 850–856.

Rogers, C. M., & Wrightsman, L. S. (1978). Attitudes towards children's rights: Nurturance or self-determination? *Journal of Social Issues, 34,* 59–68.

Ross, D. F., Miller, B. S., & Moran, P. B. (1987). The child in the eyes of the jury: Assessing mock jurors' perceptions of the child witness. In S. J. Ceci, M. P. Toglia, & D. F. Ross (Eds.), *Children's eyewitness memory* (pp. 142–154). New York: Springer-Verlag.

Royse, D., & Birge, B. (1987). Homophobia and attitudes towards AIDS patients among medical, nursing, and paramedical students. *Psychological Reports, 61,* 867–870.

Rumsey, M. G., & Rumsey, J. M. (1977). A case of rape: Sentencing judgments of males and females. *Psychological Reports, 41,* 459–465.

Rush, F. (1980). *The best kept secret: Sexual abuse of children.* New York: McGraw-Hill.

Saunders, E. J. (1986). Judicial attitudes toward child sexual abuse: A preliminary examination. *Judicature, 70*(2), 95–98.

Saunders, E. J. (1987). Police officers' attitudes toward child sexual abuse: An exploratory study. *Journal of Police Science and Administration, 15*(3), 186–191.

Scheiner, J. L. (1988, April). The use of the minimalist vignette as a method for assessing the generalizability of videotape trial simulation results. In M. Levine (Chair), *Simulated jury research on a child as a witness*. Symposium conducted at the meeting of the Eastern Psychological Association, Buffalo, NY.

Schultz, L. G. (1982). Child sexual abuse in historical perspective. *Journal of Social Work and Human Sexuality, 1,* 21–36.

Shelton, M. L., & Rogers, R. W. (1981). Fear-arousing and empathy-arousing appeals to help: The pathos of persuasion. *Journal of Applied Social Psychology, 11,* 366–378.

Sigel, I. E. (1985). *Parental belief systems.* Hillsdale, NJ: Erlbaum.

Simpson, J. A., & Gangestad, S. W. (1991). Individual differences in sociosexuality: Evidence for convergent and discriminant validity. *Journal of Personality and Social Psychology, 60,* 870–883.

Small, A., Teagno, L., & Selz, K. (1980). The relationship of sex role to physical and psychological health. *Journal of Youth and Adolescence, 9,* 305–314.

Smith, R. E., Keating, J. P., Hester, R. K., & Mitchell, H. E. (1976). Role and justice considerations in the attribution of responsibility to a rape victim. *Journal of Research in Personality, 10,* 246–257.

Spanos, N. P., DuBreuil, S. C., & Gwynn, M. I. (in press). The effects of expert testimony concerning rape on the verdicts and beliefs of mock jurors. *Imagination, Cognition, and Personality.*

Spence, J. T., Helmreich, R., & Stapp, J. (1973). A short version of the Attitudes Toward Women Scale. *Bulletin of the Psychonomic Society, 2,* 219–220.

Stermac, L. E., & Segal, Z. V. (1989). Adult sexual contact with children: An examination of cognitive factors. *Behavior Therapy, 20,* 573–584.

Summit, R. C. (1988). Hidden victims, hidden pain: Societal avoidance of child sexual abuse. In G. E. Wyatt & G. J. Powell (Eds.), *Lasting effects of child sexual abuse* (pp. 39–60). Newbury Park, CA: Sage.

Thorton, B., Ryckman, R. M., & Robbins, M. A. (1982). The relationship of observer characteristics to beliefs in the causal responsibility of sexual assault. *Human Relations, 35,* 321–330.

Villemur, N. K., & Hyde, J. S. (1983). Effects of sex of defense attorney, sex of juror, and age and attractiveness of the victim on mock juror decision making in a rape case. *Sex Roles, 9,* 879–889.

Waterman, C. K., & Foss-Goodman, D. (1984). Child molesting: Variables relating to attribution of fault to victims, offenders, and nonparticipating parents. *Journal of Sex Research, 20,* 329–349.

Waterman, J., & Lusk, R. (1986). Scope of the problem. In K. MacFarlane, J. Waterman, S. Conerly, L. Damon, M. Durfee, & S. Long (Eds.), *Sexual abuse of young children* (pp. 3–12). New York: Guilford Press.

Weir, J. A., & Wrightsman, L. S. (1990). The determinants of mock jurors' verdicts in a rape case. *Journal of Applied Social Psychology, 20,* 901–919.

Wispé, L. (1986). The distinction between sympathy and empathy: To call forth a concept, a word is needed. *Journal of Personality and Social Psychology, 50,* 314–321.

Wolfe, D. A. (1987). *Child abuse*. Newbury Park, CA: Sage.

Wyatt, G. E., & Powell, G. J. (Eds.). (1988a). *Lasting effects of child sexual abuse*. Newbury Park, CA: Sage.

Wyatt, G. E., & Powell, G. J. (1988b). Identifying the lasting effects of child sexual abuse. In G. E. Wyatt & G. J. Powell (Eds.), *Lasting effects of child sexual abuse* (pp. 11–17). Newbury Park, CA: Sage.

Yarmey, A. D., & Jones, H. P. T. (1983). Is the psychology of eyewitnesses identification a matter of common sense? In S. M. A. Lloyd-Bostock & B. R. Clifford (Eds.), *Evaluating witness evidence: Recent psychological research and new perspectives* (pp. 13–40). Chichester, England: Wiley.

Young, J., Borgida, E., Sullivan, J., & Aldrich, J. (1987). Personal agendas and the relationship between self-interest and voting behavior. *Social Psychology Quarterly, 50,* 64–71.

11

The Emotional Impact of Societal Intervention into Child Abuse

Desmond K. Runyan
University of North Carolina School of Medicine at Chapel Hill

*P**rimum non nocere* (First of all, do no harm). This ancient aphorism embodies the dilemmas inherent in child protection involvement by physicians and other mandated reporters. Those required to report suspected child maltreatment often find themselves troubled by the apparent risk–benefit ratio of involving protective services, foster and shelter care, and both civil and criminal courts in the effort (Newberger, 1987). Only a brief exposure to the child protective service system is necessary to realize that social workers are overloaded, the mental health treatment of child victims is haphazard or unavailable, foster care may be overused or even hazardous to children's health, and crowded court dockets and procedural rules minimize the likelihood that a timely and just determination of the truth will occur. Against this background a reasonable person might well wonder whether involving the child in the "system" is in the child's best interests.

This chapter details a series of investigations undertaken to understand the impact of intervention. Beginning with an examination of the determinants of foster care for child maltreatment, these studies include examinations of both foster care and the court process as part of an attempt to assess whether intervention might be, in itself, contributory to the adverse outcomes noted among victims.

DETERMINANTS OF SOCIETAL INTERVENTION

As a medical student, I observed among physicians a reluctance to become involved in reporting child maltreatment because of expressed concern that the protective service system could not be trusted to intervene appropriately. Some saw social service agencies as too aggressive, disrupting families and placing many children in foster care "needlessly," while others perceived that protective service workers never did "anything." "Anything" was operationally defined as not removing the children from the offending home. My colleagues and I undertook a study to determine which children receive in-home services and which are removed and placed into custody (Runyan, Gould, Trost, & Loda, 1981). Through a careful study of the use of foster care, the most controversial of interventions, I expected to inform health care professionals about the nature of the child abuse intervention process and increase communication between social workers and physicians concerned about child welfare.

Using the data from the 4,611 children reported to protective service agencies in North Carolina for the year 1979, stratified analyses and mathematical modeling procedures were conducted to ascertain which children were at risk for foster care placement on the basis of abuse and child, family, environmental, or agency characteristics. The North Carolina Central Child Abuse Registry database held data on over 250 variables pertinent to these areas. The nature of the abuse itself, along with the child, family, and environmental conditions surrounding the abuse, were poorly predictive of the decisions about the use of foster care. Only 17% of the decisions about foster care could be explained by information contained in the central registry record. No clear patterns emerged related to any specific type of injury or even to the social worker's perception of the maltreatment severity. Suprisingly, no patterns emerged relating placement to either race or family income.

After controlling for variables such as type of abuse and age of the child, it was clear that referrals to social service from police and the courts were somewhat more likely to result in out-of-home placement than referrals from medical or school officials. The single most important determinant of the use of foster care was the identity and/or location of the investigating agency. Although one urban county social service department placed nearly one of every two children substantiated as victims in foster care, 10 North Carolina county agencies placed no children in foster care during the year. It was not possible to determine whether social service agencies were more or less influential than the district courts; in several cases neighboring counties with common court districts appeared to share a common propensity to either favor or avoid foster care.

The wide variation in the application of foster care was troubling and our study seemed unlikely to produce the increased understanding of the system by mandated reporters and the trust between professions that had been the hope. It was apparent that there was no widespread agreement between social work agencies, or even within agencies, on the goals of foster care. Was foster care meant to be protective or therapeutic? Clearly more data about the impact of foster care were needed if a consensus about the proper use of foster care was to be developed.

THE IMPACT OF FOSTER CARE

Although the apparent haphazard use of foster care is troubling from a service delivery standpoint, it permitted a natural experiment in which children in foster care could be compared to children left in their own homes to examine the psychological impact of intervention. Gould and I undertook a retrospective or historical cohort study of maltreated children in foster care and in their own homes to examine the relative impact of this form of intervention (Runyan & Gould, 1985a, 1985b). Time and money limitations prompted us to undertake this work with existing records. We chose involvement in juvenile delinquency subsequent to reported abuse and school function as the outcomes of interest. Delinquency and crime have been thought to be the results of abuse from at least the latter half of the 1800s during what has been termed "the House of Refuge movement" (Pfoul, 1977). Evidence of antisocial and criminal behavior is readily available in records maintained by society for other purposes. We theorized that antisocial and criminal behavior, if causally related to prior abuse, could serve as markers of successful therapeutic intervention. The other major area of childhood function, school, also produced existing records and had standardized ways of assessing child progress; it seemed another natural area to explore for evidence of successful therapeutic intervention.

We identified children in foster care for abuse reported at some time in the past and followed the children until the present. A cohort of abused children who were left in the home, matched for date of report, gender, age, and race, was followed in an identical fashion. Children originally left in the home but subsequently moved to foster care were excluded. After identifying the cohorts of children at risk; social service, school, and court records were reviewed from the time of entry into care and thereafter. The "incidence" of criminal charges and convictions and the incidence of school failure were directly compared between the foster children and the "home care" children to assess the impact of foster care. We used "odds ratios" (ORs) to estimate the increased incidence for adverse outcomes related to "exposure" of the children to foster care. ORs estimate how much more likely an outcome is to develop among persons exposed to an experience compared to persons without the exposure and are easily interpreted in clinical decision making. As such, they translate readily into data that can be used for policy formation or clinical interpretation (Fletcher, Fletcher, & Wagner, 1988).

We found 114 children in six urban North Carolina counties who had been in foster care for at least 3 years because of abuse or neglect. A control group of 106 children maltreated during the same year but left in their home after the report was also identified through social service records. To control for the severity of abuse or neglect, the children in the control group had to have received at least three visits by social workers after abuse or neglect was substantiated. The average time of follow-up after the original report was about 8 years. The rate of delinquency for the children during their adolescent years was the same for the children in home care and those in foster care; the rate was 0.05 crimes per child per year after the age of 11 years, for a total risk of 0.367 crimes per child for the 7 years of adolescence between 11 and 18 years of age.

Within the foster care group there was a strong relationship between number of placements and the risk of subsequent delinquency. Children who had been in four or more homes were 3.77 times more likely to be charged with a crime than children in home care ($p < .05$). Whereas children who experienced just one foster home over the intervening years had a lower rate of delinquency than children in home care, a "dose-response" effect appeared; after more than two home placements, the risk increased with the number of placements. A review of the reasons for multiple placements indicated that child behavior causing difficulties for the foster parent was the most common reason given for change of placement. We concluded that children failing even two homes were at much higher risk of subsequent delinquency and that special efforts should be directed at children failing first and second placements.

Permission from either the parents or the protective service agencies with custody was required to review school records of the children. Permission was granted and school records found for 96 of the children in foster care and 69 of the children in home care. The records revealed significant educational problems for most of the children; nearly two thirds of both groups were either failing the current grade in school or had been retained in a school grade in a previous year. There were no systematic differences in school performance between foster and home-care children with the single exception that the children in foster care had better attendance for the most recent year of school.

Neither the school data nor the delinquency data supported the theory that foster care has an important adverse effect on children. Significantly, no therapeutic effect was noted either. Although our analysis was limited to retrospective data and the measures were very crude approximations of mental health status, we concluded that the use of foster care is not, in itself, an adequate therapeutic plan. The "parentectomy" of foster care does not appear to do more than assure physical protection. Even physical protection was not assured by foster care as further reports of child abuse were received for 25% of the home care group and 12% of the foster-care group. Among the foster children who were reported for subsequent abuse, half were reported to have been abused by foster parents and half were reported to have been abused by the natural parents during parental visits.

In our study of foster care, we chose to include children who were victims of all forms of maltreatment. Our rationale for combining victims of all forms of abuse was that we were interested in the response to the interventions, not the abuse, and we needed a large sample for sufficient statistical power to conduct the analysis. However, because of the limitations inherent in archival data and our concern that delinquency and school performance were not complete measures of child mental health, we were not convinced that the impact of foster care had been definitively examined. We were concerned that the impact of intervention might be modified by the type of maltreatment the children had suffered. In further pursuit of foster care impact, we undertook a prospective study of the impact of foster care and added an examination of court intervention (Runyan, Everson, Edelsohn, Hunter, & Coulter, 1988). We intended to characterize the impact of foster care by following through the intervention process a group of children who were victims of the same form of child maltreatment. However, because of the short period available for follow-up for each child imposed by funding restrictions, our initial efforts addressed the impact of court involvement on the children. We hoped that subsequent funding would then permit us to revisit the foster-care issue.

THE IMPACT OF LEGAL INTERVENTION

Justice is thought to be best served when persons disputing the truth each present their side to an audience of judge and jury (Whitcomb, Shapiro, & Stellwagen, 1985). The adversarial nature of the court process is supposed to facilitate the discovery of truth. Indeed, the right to confront one's accuser is grounded in the U.S. Constitution. This process may not work so well when the disputants are as clearly unevenly matched as child and adult. Whether or not the process of discovering the truth is enhanced in adversarial procedures, many are concerned that the process confers additional harm on child victims. Because the nature of the societal response and its impact on the victims is so salient to mandated reporters of abuse, we continued our examination of the response process by examining the impact of the courts.

We again chose a cohort study design. We prospectively assessed the degree of improvement in mental health over time in sexually abused children to discern whether there were patterns of improvement that could be related to the patterns of intervention each child experienced. The study sample was composed of children, between 6 and 18 years of age, reported to social services as victims of sexual abuse in 11 North Carolina counties over a 22-month recruitment period. An important design consideration was the use of standard mental health measures to assess the functioning of the children. Too few studies of abused children have used standard assessment tools that permit comparisons across samples and sites. All children received a structured psychiatric interview, the Child Assessment Schedule (CAS) (Hodges, 1985), while their caretaker completed a Child Behavior Checklist—Parent (CBCL) form (Achenbach & Edelbrock, 1983). The Child Assessment Schedule is a child-friendly structured interview with established reliability and validity. Other instruments included a measure of cognitive function, the Peabody Picture Vocabulary Test, and an interview about court experiences. We recruited nearly 75% of the eligible children from 10 of the counties and about 20% of the eligible children from the remaining county. A disproportionately large number of families in this latter county appeared for the initial protective service interview with an attorney who suggested that the family not participate while others apparently refused because our study was the second of two research projects in which they were asked to participate. Data about the events leading to a maltreatment report and subsequent intervention efforts were collected from the child's social worker in order to spare the child from having to repeat these details. Where possible, observers attended court proceedings in which the child might have been expected to participate.

One hundred children were recruited from the social service department case load in the North Carolina counties; 75 children returned for a follow-up interview 5 months later. The sample was 82% female and 66% white. The mean age was 11.9 years. The perpetrator was the biological father in 31% of the cases, a stepfather for 43%, and the mother's boyfriend for 15%. The remaining 11% of the cases included adult siblings, grandparents, and two mothers. Penetration or oral–genital sex had occurred to 73% of the children; 53% had been victims of abuse lasting more than one year. The estimated verbal IQ of the sample was 87.

The data indicate that the degree of distress reported by sexually abused children is significant. The mean score at referral on the CAS was 44, which was similar to the average score observed for psychiatric inpatients at the University of Missouri (Hodges, 1985). The mean behavior problem T-score on the parent form of the CBCL was 66.6, which is approximately at the cut point for the clinical range on this instrument (Achenbach & Edelbrock, 1983). In our study the CAS distinguished between subgroups of subjects in expected directions and appeared sensitive to changes in living circumstances. The CAS appeared to be more sensitive to change than parent report and appeared to be more sensitive to capturing "affective" issues than the other instrumentation used with the children.

By the time of the 5-month follow-up, 63% of the children had been removed from the abusing home and 10 children had returned to the home. The rate of foster care and other out of home placement was higher than previously reported in other studies and likely reflected both a more complete recruitment of foster children into the study and the increased use of foster care in the current social service environment. Nearly 45% of the children had juvenile court hearings by the time of the follow-up. Just 12 children (15%) were asked to testify in juvenile court. Of the 44 children involved in the criminal courts at follow-up, half were through the process and half were still pending. Among the completed cases there had been 4 trials, 17 plea bargains, and 1 acquittal.

To create a risk or benefit estimate for the testimony experience, we developed a series of logistic models in which a categorical outcome related to improvement in mental health status was associated with specific experiences. Modeling was necessary because of the need to control potential confounding by such factors as the age of the child and the relationship between the perpetrator and the child. Logistic models predict the probability of dichotomous outcomes (e.g., improvement vs. lack of improvement) and can estimate the relative risk or OR for the independent variables (e.g., legal involvement) while controlling for the influence of multiple potential confounders (Kleinbaum, Kupper, & Morgenstern, 1991). We used a maximum likelihood model with multiple iterations to produce a "best fit" for the complete model. We categorized the children into two groups, improved and not improved, based on whether they had lowered their scores on the CAS and CBCL by the equivalent of one standard deviation from the first to the second administrations. This arbitrary standard, 18 points on the CAS total score and 10.5 points on the CBCL total score, was considered clinically significant. Categorical improvement was also noted for the CAS subscales of anxiety, depression, and conduct disorder using one standard deviation as the standard for the subscale scores.

Based on a logistic model that controlled for age of the child, verbal IQ score, provision of therapy, identity of the perpetrator, percentage of life abused, and whether penetration occurred, we found that children left in limbo by the criminal court system were only 8 percent as likely to evidence improvement in depression as were their peers who were not in the court system or who had resolved all court issues (see Table 11.1). Testimony in juvenile court appeared to be beneficial as indexed by improvement on the anxiety subscale. The other outcome measures showed similar trends but did not reach statistical significance. The estimates of risk that were developed had large confidence intervals but were statistically significant. Other potential confounders were not controlled for in the model because of the limited sample size.

We were surprised by the apparent salutary effect of juvenile court testimony. We had hypothesized, using the theoretical formulation by Finkelhor and Browne (1985), that testimony would be traumatic because it would increase the child's sense of stigma and cause the child to feel more responsible for the events that followed disclosure. However, several other effects may have occurred. Testimony may improve the child's sense of control and treat the sense of powerlessness induced by the abuse. We did not have sufficient data to analyze the impact of criminal court testimony. In North Carolina the juvenile court has less onerous operating procedures, standards of evidence, and jurisdiction than those of the criminal court. Juvenile courts are conducted without juries and the standard of proof is "the preponderance of the evidence" instead of "beyond a reasonable doubt" as used in criminal courts. Further, while the juvenile court has jurisdiction over where the child lives and can send children into detention or foster-care living arrangements, it has no power to send an adult to

TABLE 11.1. Adjusted Odds Ratios for improving CAS and CBCL Scores by Specific Court Experiences

Outcomes	Odds of improving (95% confidence interval)
Waiting for court vs. no prosecution groups	
CAS General Pathology Score	0.23 (0.03–1.6)
CAS Depression Score	0.08 (0.006–0.9)
CAS Anxiety Score	0.14 (0.009–2.1)
CBCL report	0.11 (0.006–1.7)
Testimony in juvenile court vs. all other children	
CAS General Pathology Score	3.94 (0.5–29.7)
CAS Depression Score	6.38 (0.8–48.7)
CAS Anxiety Score	20.1 (1.6–249)
CBCL-P Score	18.0 (0.7–499)

Note. The OR is determined by categorizing children as having improved if their CAS or CBCL score at follow-up was lower than the equivalent of one standard deviation of the baseline scores for the group and using logistic regression to control for potential confounders. The variables controlled for these estimates were verbal IQ, provision of therapy, relationship to the perpetrator, and whether the abuse involved penetration. ORs greater than 1 reflect improvement and less than 1 reflect harm. OR = odds ratio; CAS = Child Assessment Schedule; CBCL = Child Behavior Checklist. From "Impact of legal intervention on sexually abused children" by D. Runyan, M. Everson, G. Edelsohn, W. Hunter, & M. Coulter, 1988, *Journal of Pediatrics, 50,* p. 651. Copyright 1988 by the Mosby Yearbook, Inc. Reprinted by permission.

prison. We perceived that the juvenile courts appear to have become more contentious and more like the criminal court in recent times. We speculated that this has occurred in part because many defense attorneys use the juvenile courts to assess the evidence available to the state in criminal proceedings. We were unable to assess whether the criminal court will have the same or an opposite effect on the child witness.

The use of categorical improvement and ORs is not conventional in mental health studies but is an attractive method of presenting estimates of the degree of effect associated with a dichotomous variable. However, the small sample size limited the number of control variables that could be entered into the models. Although socioeconomic status was not placed in any of the above models, we found that the estimated verbal IQ from the Peabody Picture Vocabulary Test strongly covaried with social class and thus that variable was included.

We were unable to pursue the foster-care study effectively with the data collected for this study. As we proceeded, it became clear that the time lapse between contacting the parents to obtain informed consent and placement of a child was too short to allow data collection prior to the child's placement. Nearly two-thirds of the children to be removed from the home were already removed prior to enrollment in the study. The children who were subsequently placed in foster care had significantly higher baseline CAS scores (55 vs. 42) than did children left in their homes; it was not possible to determine whether the distress was a reflection of the acute impact of placement or a differential use of placement for more distressed children. Future work to clarify this relationship will probably have to be done within a social service agency in which preplacement testing is regarded as a necessary adjunct to careful protective service practice.

THE IMPACT OF MATERNAL SUPPORT

Early in the study, we were confronted by a mother who stated her ambivalence about supporting her daughter; she saw the daughter as "the other woman." The issue of maternal support for the victim became even more salient when another subject, age 5, testified in court about abuse perpetrated by a maternal boyfriend while her mother actively shook her head, indicating her disbelief during most of the testimony. Our observer thought the obvious maternal disbelief troubled the child, although she was able to complete her testimony.

Faller (1984) and others (Adams-Tucker, 1982; Lyon & Kouloum-pos-Lenares, 1987) have previously examined maternal support. The percentage of sexual abuse victims judged to have supportive mothers ranged from 27% to 56%, and it was noted that support varied in predictable ways related to the intensity of the maternal relationship to the perpetrator, age of the child, and gender. Specifically, younger male children were observed to receive the most support. Because the mental health literature is so suggestive that social support in general is an important determinant of well-being, we decided to examine the impact of support or its absence on both the children and the outcomes of the case using our longitudinal data (Everson, Hunter, Runyan, Edelsohn, & Coulter, 1989).

With the development of the Parental Reaction to Incest Disclo-sure Scale (PRIDS), Everson, Hunter, and I attempted to assess: (1) the general emotional support offered to the child by the mother, (2) whether clear statements of belief in the child had been made, and (3) whether the mother's actions toward the alleged perpetrator demon-strated belief in the child. A scale of +5 to −5 was created summing scores for each of the above categories of support, and mothers were then classified as supportive, ambivalent, or hostile. Eighty-four children in the North Carolina sexual abuse study were included in this analysis; 38 ratings were assigned retrospectively as the children had already been enrolled in the study prior to the development of this instrument. To examine whether ratings were comparable by retrospective record review and prospective assignment, we blindly assigned retrospective ratings to children who were rated prospectively as to maternal support by the original interviewer. The two methods produced virtually the same ratings (r = 0.96) and were considered interchangeable.

In our analysis of maternal support, gender and age of the victim were not significantly associated with maternal support although the mean scores for support by gender and age did differ in the directions suggested by prior research. Our data showed that perpetrator admissions were significantly associated with increased support of the child. Also, there were significant differences in the level of support offered children who were subsequently removed from the home and placed in foster care compared to children who stayed in their home; children placed with relatives received an intermediate level of maternal support.

There were significant relationships between maternal support and CAS total pathology, depression, and self-image scores. The low maternal support group had significantly higher scores in each of these areas, indicating greater distress. The CBCL scores were also higher for the low support group but not significantly so.

An analysis of the impact of the maternal-support score on the decision to place a child in foster care revealed that it was the single most important factor to predict placement (Hunter, Coulter, Runyan, & Everson, 1990). Nearly 40% of the variance in placement decisions could be explained by the maternal support variable. This variable was far more important than family, child, or abuse characteristics.

CONCLUSIONS

The conduct of valid research in a child protective service environment is complex. The data sought by researchers may touch on areas having legal implications for the subjects, interviewers, and investigators. Beyond the usual difficulties involved in asking children and adults about acts and behaviors that are emotionally charged, consenting to research participation may result in families and victims revealing information that is of direct interest to the courts or social service providers, thus challenging the usual precepts of subject confidentiality. Nevertheless, complex and difficult decisions are being made daily about the lives of maltreated children and part of the function of research is to provide data that can better guide the process of intervention. Ways must be found to conduct research in an appropriate and sensitive manner if we are ever to improve the intervention process.

Although our initial study demonstrated wide variation in the use of foster care among social service agencies and the apparent chaotic nature of social service intervention, our work examining foster-care placement among sexually abused children indicated that maternal support was associated with the decision. In regard to our initial study, it is important to note that measure of cooperation with social services and support of the child were not contained in the North Carolina central registry data. Because maternal support is such an important factor related to child functioning, the implications of our later findings are that the apparent chaotic nature of social service intervention may be more rational and just than the early study implied.

Many have worried that the process of intervention itself may be more destructive than the harm inflicted on children in many cases of physical or sexual abuse. The data to date do not support this concern. In the studies of foster care I found no evidence that the children in foster care were worse off because of their placement. Among the sexually abused children studied subsequently, there were high levels of mental health distress at the time they came to societal attention. Over time the distress appeared to moderate significantly. In all of my work to date, I have found few children who appear worse after intervention.

I have not been the only observer concerned with the impact of foster care (Widom, 1991). The data on the impact of foster care are unclear. Foster care is a "black box" in which too many place a misguided trust. Even the objectives for foster care are not commonly shared. Is foster care to be protective or therapeutic? As we struggled to understand foster care we found many who believed that short-term foster care, providing respite and incentive for change to natural families, was the ideal. Clearly, more often than not, foster care is a much longer experience for the children and may actually impede or excuse the natural family from involvement in services. Early questions that we wrestled with in the designs of our studies still remain: If foster care is therapeutic, how long must foster care be experienced before its effects can be measured? Is foster care a treatment for the parents or for the children? No pronounced positive or negative effects of foster care have been uncovered in either my work involving all forms of maltreatment or in my work on sexually abused children. Understanding the impact of foster care will require much more restricted samples of children, with careful examinations of both the home in which the child has been placed and the home from which the child was removed. Foster-care research must be comparative to the natural home and restrictive in terms of studying children with similar patterns of difficulties and family dynamics. Despite the lack of clarity on these issues, I have been reassured by the absence of an overall effect for foster care in any of our work; a simple answer as to whether foster care does more good than harm is not likely, and a foster home may be quite appropriate for many children.

The courts appear to modify the degree or speed of resolution of child victim distress. We have raised a concern that delays in criminal court proceedings slow recovery. A surprising finding was that testimony in juvenile court appeared to speed the resolution of anxiety for the children who testify. Although we have some difficulty arguing that this observation represents more than simple regression to the mean, the actual level of anxiety for the testifiers (M = 4.08) at the end of the study was lower than the mean level of anxiety recorded for the nontestifiers (M = 5.10) at the conclusion of the study. That the testifiers might pass the nontestifiers and actually have lower scores suggests that regression to the mean is not the strongest explanation. As of yet, my collaborators and I are unable to address the impact of criminal court testimony on sexually abused children. Too few of our subjects were involved in this activity to produce any meaningful comparisons. We feel that the juvenile court is a significantly different environment from the criminal court and that it is likely that the impact of the criminal courts is quite different.

Simple analyses of the impact of the courts are attractive, but the actual circumstances of the process vary so widely that it will be difficult to explain much of the variance. As a part of our sexual abuse study in North Carolina, we sent observers into many courtrooms for a qualitative assessment (King, Hunter, & Runyan, 1988). The variations in children's experiences between individual cases were great, which suggests that many generalizations may be meaningless. Further efforts will need to be made, both with large samples in quantitative analysis and in smaller qualitative studies, to describe patterns within the court process and to observe the impact on the child. Studies of the courts and the impact of the courts on children must proceed with full recognition that criminal court testimony among sexually abused children is a relatively infrequent event in many jurisdictions. Large sample sizes will be necessary to allow further inquiry in this area. Sample selection from prosecutors' offices or other selection criteria that increase the number of children experiencing court will be necessary research adjuncts. Future work in this area will be increasingly complex and require both significant financial support and a commitment from courts and social service agencies to encourage and support it.

Maternal support has emerged as a significant issue in its own right. Little is known about the determinants of maternal support for the child victim. We know little about the mothers' histories of abuse and often overlook the complex and variable constructions of families. The relative importance of maternal mental health, emotional ties to the perpetrator, financial ties to the perpetrator, and the characteristics of the attachment between parent–child in the capacity of the non-perpetrating parent are fruitful areas for further research. Future intervention strategies may need to include ways of facilitating the process of the mother developing empathy and support for her child victims and sufficient emotional and financial strength to make independent decisions about the truth and implications of child sexual abuse.

I have seen the awareness of the potential for harm by the courts increase since the beginning of this work and note that many jurisdictions have gone to great lengths to make children comfortable. I am optimistic about the capacity of societal agencies charged with intervening to improve their practice. I have been reassured in part by the interest my own work has generated among social service providers both in my own state of North Carolina and elsewhere.

ACKNOWLEDGMENTS

Current colleagues and collaborators (Mark Everson, PhD, Wanda Hunter, MPH, and Nancy King, JD) and earlier colleagues (Martha Coulter, DPH, Gail Edelsohn, MD, MSPH, and Carolyn Gould, MD) shared the conceptualization and conduct of the studies reviewed here. Without their involvement, the work would not have been completed. The conduct of the research was supported by the Robert Wood Johnson and Edna McConnell Clark Foundation, the National Center on Child Abuse and Neglect (Grant No. 90-CA-0921), and the National Institute of Justice (Grant No. 85-IJ-Cx-0066).

REFERENCES

Achenbach, T., & Edelbrock, C. (1983). *Manual for the Child Behavior Checklist and the Revised Child Behavior Profile.* Burlington, VT: University of Vermont.

Adams-Tucker, C. (1982). Proximate effects of sexual abuse in childhood: A report of 28 children. *American Journal of Psychiatry, 139,* 1252–1256.

Everson, M., Hunter, W., Runyan, D., Edelsohn, G., & Coulter, M. (1989).

Maternal support following exposure of incest. *American Journal of Orthopsychiatry, 59,* 197–207.

Faller, K. (1984, May). *Sexual abuse by caretakers.* Paper presented at the National Conference of Family Violence Researchers, Durham, New Hampshire.

Finkelhor, D., & Browne, A. (1985). The traumatic impacts of child sexual abuse: A conceptualization. *American Journal of Orthopsychiatry, 55,* 530–541.

Fletcher, R., Fletcher, S., & Wagner, E. (1988). *Clinical epidemiology* (2nd ed.). Baltimore, MD: Williams & Wilkins.

Hodges, K. (1985). *Manual for the child assessment schedule (CAS).* Columbia, MO: University of Missouri—Columbia.

Hunter, W., Coulter, M., Runyan, D., & Everson, M. (1990). Determinants of placement for sexually abused children. *Child Abuse and Neglect, 14,* 407–417.

King, N. M. P., Hunter, W., & Runyan, D. (1988). Going to court: The experience of child victims of intrafamilial sexual abuse. *Journal of Health Politics, Policy, and Law, 13,* 705–721.

Kleinbaum, D., Kupper, L., & Morgenstern, H. (1981). *Epidemiologic research.* Belmont, CA: Lifetime Learning Publications.

Lyon, E., & Kouloumpos-Lenares, K. (1987). Clinician and state social worker: Collaborative skills for child sexual abuse. *Child Welfare, 67,* 517–527.

Newberger, E. (1987). Prosecution: A problematic approach to child abuse. *Journal of Interpersonal Violence, 2,* 112–117.

Pfouhl, S. (1977). The discovery of child abuse. *Social Problems, 24,* 310–323.

Runyan, D., Everson, M., Edelsohn, G., Hunter, W., Coulter, M. (1988). Impact of legal intervention on sexually abused children. *Journal of Pediatrics, 113,* 647–653.

Runyan, D., & Gould, C. (1985a). Foster care for child maltreatment: Impact on delinquent behavior. *Pediatrics, 75,* 562–568.

Runyan, D., & Gould, C. (1985b). Foster care for child maltreatment II: Impact on delinquent behavior. *Pediatrics, 76,* 841–847.

Runyan, D., Gould, C., Trost, D., & Loda, A. (1981). Determinants of foster care for the maltreated child. *American Journal of Public Health, 71,* 706–711.

Whitcomb, D., Shapiro, E., & Stellwagen, L. (1985). *When the victim is a child.* Washington, DC: National Institute of Justice.

Widom, C. S. (1991). Foster care and adult criminal behavior. *American Journal of Orthopsychiatry, 61,* 195–209.

12

Hearing and Testing Children's Evidence

Rhona H. Flin
Robert Gordon University

In the last 10 years the subject of children's testimony has developed from a minority academic interest to a topic that is receiving nationwide media attention. In many countries psychologists are at the forefront of research investigations into the emotional and cognitive demands facing children who witness crimes both as bystanders and as victims. This chapter discusses the problems that children can encounter when they are required to give evidence in a criminal trial. The focus of this chapter is on children's testimony within the context of the British legal systems. However, research relevant to children's court experiences generally will be discussed. Recent attempts to reform the rules of evidence governing child witnesses will be examined in order to assess the extent to which they offer psychologically sound solutions for preserving children's evidence without jeopardizing the rights of the accused.

THE BRITISH LEGAL SYSTEMS

In Britain there are two separate legal systems with different rules of evidence and procedures—Scot's law applies in Scotland, while English law applies in England, Wales, and Northern Ireland. (Southern Ireland [Eire] has its own legal system, and has recently reviewed its procedures for hearing children's evidence in sexual abuse cases; see Irish Law

Reform Commission, 1990.) The Scottish and English legal systems are accusatorial in nature with an adversarial trial procedure, in common with the courts of Eire, Australia, Canada, and the United States but unlike most of the countries of mainland Europe where a more inquisitorial approach is favored. There is a growing interest in the legal procedures used by different countries to hear and test children's evidence, and reports from two international conferences on this subject offer fascinating insight into the alternative techniques used to tackle the same fundamental problems of child witnesses' competence, credibility, and welfare (Spencer, Nicholson, Flin, & Bull, 1990; Loesel & Bender, in press). It should be said that the accusatorial systems compare rather unfavorably to those of a more inquisitorial persuasion in terms of their sensitivity to the needs of child witnesses. Before discussing the psychological research into children's evidence, the relevant legal rules of the Scottish and English systems will be outlined. (For a full description, see Spencer & Flin, 1990.)

Scot's Law

In Scotland there is no lower age limit for hearing children's evidence. A child of any age is legally competent to give evidence, provided the trial judge is satisfied, by appropriate questioning of the child, that he or she can give evidence intelligibly and can understand the difference between truth and falsehood. Younger children are admonished to tell the truth while older children (usually from 12 to 14 years of age) will be asked to take the oath or to affirm to tell the truth. There are no special rules regarding the corroboration of children's testimony—in Scotland the testimony of every witness, child or adult, must be corroborated. Until very recently there have been no special procedural rules for hearing children's evidence, and they could be examined and cross-examined in the same way as an adult witness.

In response to an increasingly vocal lobby from professionals working with child victims, the Scottish Law Commission began in 1987 to consider the procedures employed for hearing children's evidence. The Commission published a discussion paper in June 1988, followed by a detailed list of recommendations for legal reform (1990). To date the report has resulted in the issue of a practice direction to judges recommending a number of practical measures to make court procedures less formal and intimidating; for example, removal of wigs and gowns, allowing the child to sit outside the witness box, permitting the presence of a supporting adult, better waiting facilities (see Nicholson & Murray, 1992, for a copy of this practice direction). The other major innovation included in the Law Reform (Miscellaneous

Provisions) (Scotland) Act 1990, was the provision for live videolink systems that enable judges to allow children to give their evidence via a closed-circuit television link from an adjacent room. This has recently been introduced on a pilot-basis and the first case was successfully prosecuted using the videolink to present the child's evidence in April of 1992. A similar videolink system has been evaluated by psychologists in England (Davies & Noon, 1991), who concluded that it "facilitates the giving of evidence by children, who were happier, more fluent, and less likely to give inconsistent testimony" (p. 75).

English Law

The English rules for hearing children's evidence were strongly criticized during the '80s following a series of spectacularly unsuccessful prosecutions of child sexual abuse. As in Scotland, child witnesses could be treated in the courtroom in the same fashion as adult witnesses, and the problems of appearing in court and confronting the accused were clearly hampering the prosecution of cases involving child victims. However, there was also a major restriction that effectively prevented younger children's evidence from being heard at all in England. This was the result of an appeal judgment for an incest case in 1958 (Wallwork 42 Cr. App. R. 153), in which Lord Goddard condemned the practice of calling young children to give evidence. His remarks gave rise to a rule that children under 6 years of age should not be called to give evidence. In practice, English prosecutors tended to avoid calling children as witnesses under the age of 8. One English lawyer described these rules as reading like "a child molester charter" (Spencer, 1987).

Continued professional and media pressure for reform has now produced a number of significant changes. Since 1989, videolink systems have been installed on an experimental basis in 21 Crown Courts for child witnesses under 14 years of age in cases of sexual assault or violence (see Davies & Noon, 1991 for an evaluation of the pilot study). When the Criminal Justice Act 1991 comes into force in October 1992, the age limit will be raised to 17 years for sex cases. The requirement that children's unsworn evidence should be corroborated has been abolished. But if the case concerns a sexual offense and there is no corroboration, the judge will still be required to warn the jury of the risk of convicting on the basis of uncorroborated evidence (this requirement applies to adult complainants as well as to children). The case law stating that children below the age of 7 or 8 were incompetent and could not therefore be admitted as witnesses has now been superseded by the admission of 3- and 4-year-olds to give evidence.

Although some of the reforms implemented to date are commend-able, there is still a feeling that more innovative techniques are required. Many professionals would like to see the introduction of videotaped depositions where the child's evidence would be taken and tested in advance of trial (with an opportunity for questions from the defense), and these examinations would be videorecorded and played at the trial in place of the child's evidence. This was the basis of the scheme proposed by Judge Pigot's advisory group, which considered the possible applications of videorecording children's evidence (Pigot Committee, 1989). In Scotland videotaped evidence is not admitted at present but this looks likely to change in the near future. In England the Criminal Justice Act 1991 permits the admission of videotaped interviews with child witnesses in place of the examination-in-chief but only on the strict condition that the child attends court for a live cross-examination (Home Office, 1992). This is a half-baked measure that fails to demonstrate a proper understanding of the difficulties facing child witnesses (see Spencer, 1992). The remainder of this chapter considers the specific problems encountered by children who have to testify in criminal courts and the extent to which innovative practices will actually improve the present situation.

SOURCES OF STRESS

Psychologists, social workers, and doctors have been arguing since the early 1980s that for many child victims giving evidence in criminal trials is unacceptably traumatic, however, it is only recently that this problem has been acknowledged and addressed by the most senior members of the legal profession. Lord Mackay (Lord Chancellor and Minister of the Crown, who is responsible for the English legal system), recently stated:

> Today there is growing recognition by all those involved that, where a child has suffered or is witness to a serious, violent or sexual attack, to appear in court, seeing the perpetrator again, and facing cross-examination can cause anguish, may often be terrifying, and can sometimes have traumatic effects. Unnecessary stress in such a situation cannot be in the interests of the unfortunate children involved and it certainly does nothing to further the interests of justice. (Mackay, 1990, p. 1)

Although legal reform of the present system for hearing children's evidence is overdue and extremely welcome, it is important that proposed changes to legal rules or court procedures are based on a proper understanding of the factors that cause anxiety and trauma. Data on the sources of stress for child witnesses can be drawn from witnesses' anecdotal accounts, professional opinions, and research surveys of child witnesses. From a review of this literature (Spencer & Flin, 1990) the main sources of stress for child witnesses appear to be:

1. Long delays before the trial.
2. Lack of legal knowledge.
3. Courtroom environment.
4. Confronting the accused.
5. Being examined and cross-examined.

These stressors are discussed in turn with reference to the relative merits of hearing children's evidence using a videolink system or videotaped interviews compared with the conventional procedures.

Long Delays before the Trial

Child witnesses can wait many months and in some cases even years between witnessing or being the victim of a crime and being examined in court. Two surveys conducted in Scotland showed that child witnesses (bystanders and victims) wait around 6 months on average for their evidence to be tested in court (Flin, Davies, & Tarrant, 1988; Flin, Bull, Boon, & Knox, 1992). Davies and Noon (1991) found that child sexual abuse victims are faced with an average delay of 10 1/2 months before their cases reached court and delays are generally regarded as a problem for child victims (Plotnikoff, 1990). Adler (1987), in a study of English rape cases, reported that a "delay of around eight months is average, but some women may have to wait for as long as a year and a half before being called upon to appear in court" (p. 50). In a recent American study of child sexual abuse cases, Goodman et al. (in press) found that the average delay between disclosure of abuse to authorities and the trial was 9 months (4.6 months from the disclosure to the preliminary hearing).

American (Goodman et al., in press; Whitcomb, 1990), Canadian (Sas et al., 1991), and Scottish (Flin et al., 1988) studies have indicated that such long delays can create anxiety for child witnesses and, in the case of victims, may hamper therapeutic interventions (Glaser & Spencer, 1990). But the emotional distress resulting from this waiting period may not be the only problem—a recent study (see Flin, Boon, Knox, & Bull, in press) suggests that the memories of younger children may be disproportionately affected by long delays compared to those of older children and adults.

There has been very little research on the effects of long delays on children's memory, with the exception of psychiatric case histories of child victims' long-term memories for traumatic events (Pynoos & Nader, 1988; Terr, 1988) and psychological experiments measuring children's memories for witnessed events after several years (Goodman, Rudy, Bottoms, & Aman, 1991; Hudson & Fivush, 1991). In order to explore this question, Flin et al. (in press) designed an experimental study to measure the effects of a 5-month delay on the recall ability of subjects ages 5–6 years (n = 68), 9–10 years (n = 65), and adults (n = 43). All subjects witnessed a brief argument between three female adults that occurred during a routine talk on hygiene. Each age group observed a separate enactment of the same sequence of events while attending school or college. Subjects within each age level were randomly allocated to one of three treatment groups; two of these groups were interviewed both 1 day after the event (using two slightly different interview methods) and again 5 months later. The third group was only interviewed after a 5-month delay interval. The results showed that while there were no differences in overall accuracy levels when the groups were interviewed after 1 day, age affected accuracy following the 5-month delay. The adult group did not show a reduction in overall accuracy but the 6-year-olds and the 9-year-olds did, with the reduction in performance being greatest for the 6-year-olds. The younger children seemed to lose more detail over time; that is, their memory deficit was characterized by omission errors. Inaccuracy scores (commission errors) were generally low, and for the adults and the 6-year-olds did not change over the 5-month delay. The 9-year-olds gave slightly more inaccurate responses at the 5-month interview than at the immediate test.

These data are derived from a preliminary investigation of this issue and require replication; however, they do concur with the findings of cognitive development researchers who have recently argued that younger children forget information at a faster rate than do older children (Brainerd, Reyna, Howe, & Kingma, 1991). And, perhaps more unusually, they also agree with British legal opinion, which states that young children's memories are particularly sensitive to the passage of time.

> It is now widely accepted that children including very young children, can be as reliable in their recollection of events as adults. However, it also seems to be generally accepted that a child's capacity for recall, especially on points of detail, may deteriorate more rapidly over time than would that of an adult. (Scottish Law Commission, 1990, p. 3)

One marked evidential weakness of children is that their power of recall or recollection fades more rapidly than that of adults. Thus lengthy delays in the hearings, which are regrettably inherent in our present system, are likely to impair the quality of their oral testimony and undermine its credibility. Oral evidence which is widely regarded as the cornerstone of our system of criminal justice loses its validity when young children in court are trying to recall events which may have happened at least 12 months before. (Pigot, 1990, p. 211)

Judge Pigot is a senior English judge who chaired the Home Office advisory group that recommended that early videorecorded interviews (usually conducted by police or social workers) should be admissible as evidence and that instead of the child being examined and cross-examined at the trial, such questioning should take place at a preliminary hearing that would also be videorecorded and played to the court. As mentioned earlier, despite the eminent sense of this proposal, only the early interview can be admitted in place of live evidence; the child is still be required to attend the trial to be cross-examined usually via the videolink (Criminal Justice Act, 1991). This means that the child will still have the anxiety of waiting months for the trial, and if the child is young, the delay may well have a significantly detrimental effect on his or her memory. Although this practice is likely to enhance the defense, it is unlikely to be in the interests of the child or the prosecution. Accepting the recordings of the initial interview is a welcome step in the right direction, but there appear to be two good reasons (emotional stress and memory fade) for cross-examining a young child's evidence at the earliest opportunity and making a videotape of the proceedings. The videolink system does nothing to solve the problems of these pretrial delays and in this respect will not compensate for the weaknesses of the new legislation.

Lack of Legal Knowledge

Do you know what a procurator fiscal is? This was one of the questions we asked Scottish children and adults in a study of legal knowledge. A "procurator fiscal" is the public prosecutor in Scotland, but very few of the children and a surprisingly small percentage of adults were able to correctly describe the job of this important legal official. The study was prompted by our preliminary experiences attending criminal trials involving child witnesses when we discovered not only that children and their parents had a limited knowledge of how the legal system operated, but also that as researchers our own knowledge was distinctly superficial. To assess levels of legal knowledge, a sample of 90 children (ages 6, 8, and 10) and 15 adults were asked questions about 20 terms related to criminal proceedings. The results of the survey showed that (1) there is a clear increase in the amount of legal knowledge with age; (2) children show not only ignorance but also misunderstanding; (3) children sometimes claim to know the meaning of a word but when tested give an erroneous answer; and (4) adults do possess a perfect understanding of basic legal terms and procedures (Flin, Stevenson, & Davies, 1989).

This problem is not peculiar to Scottish children; similar findings illustrating how little children know about their own legal systems have been reported in California (Saywitz, Jaenicke, & Camparo, 1991), Tennessee (Warren-Leubecker, Tate, Hinton, & Ozbek, 1989), and Australia (Cashmore & Bussey, 1990). Sas (1991) encountered the same problem for Canadian child witnesses and cites a 10-year-old girl who defined a subpoena as "a male's private part." These results confirmed anecdotal and research reports from professionals working in the criminal courts, indicating that one major difficulty for child witnesses was their lack of knowledge and a consequent fear of the unknown (e.g., Flin et al., 1988; Whitcomb, Shapiro, & Stellwagen, 1985). In fact, Saywitz (1989) found that American children with experience as witnesses demonstrated even less accurate and less complete knowledge of the legal system than age mates without legal experience: "A subjective reading of their responses indicated that they were more confused" (p. 153).

By 1990, attempts had been made in many jurisdictions to give children the requisite knowledge and confidence to enable them to cope with their participation in a very unfamiliar procedure. In Scotland a special leaflet "Going to Court" is given to child witnesses to explain in simple words and colored illustrations what will take place during a trial; children may also be shown around an empty courtroom before the trial to familiarize them with the courtroom setting.

Even more sophisticated procedures are used in some parts of North America. For example, the national Children's Advocacy Center in Alabama uses a "Court Prep Group" to conduct group sessions with child victims that involve both court preparation and anxiety-reduction techniques (Sisterman-Keeney, Amacher, & Kastanakis, 1992). In Ontario, Canada, Sas (1991) has developed a model of intervention that includes assessment, role playing, and stress-reduction techniques as well as familiarizing children with court procedures. Sas has just completed an evaluation of 144 child witnesses who participated in this program and concluded that "the Child Witness Project's court preparation served to mitigate the negative effects of a documented major stressor, length of time in the criminal justice system, and resulted in better adjustment in some of the psychological measures of fear, increased knowledge of court, and better performance (i.e., testimony) by child witnesses as rated by crown attorneys" (Dezwirek-Sas, 1992).

Children who are asked to testify in criminal cases, either as victims or as bystanders, should be provided with whatever knowledge and support they require to enable them to cope with a potentially traumatic experience. More research is needed to evaluate and refine such programs and to make teaching materials available in a variety of suitable media. If children's evidence is to be videotaped or transmitted by videolink, specialist preparation will still be required to explain the significance of these techniques to the child. It is also important that appropriate training be given to those professionals charged with preparing children for court. Many defense lawyers are now aware of such developments and may imply that the child's evidence has been coached or contaminated during the preparation. (For this reason some programs are now labeled "orientation" rather than "preparation" to emphasize that the child is being enabled or empowered rather than rehearsed.) Anecdotal reports certainly indicate that appropriate preparation helps many children and in some cases improves the quality or quantity of the child's evidence. Paradoxically, the evidence of a well-prepared child who is not demonstrably anxious in the witness box may have less impact on the jury than that of a child who becomes visibly upset or incoherent. Perhaps there is a concomitant need to prepare the juries who judge the credibility of children's evidence as well as the children who testify. (See Luus & Wells, 1992, for a recent study of adults' judgments of the credibility of children's testimony.)

Courtroom Environment

Many adult witnesses find that attending court is a daunting and unfamiliar experience. Witnesses may have to wait for several hours before they are called to give evidence and waiting facilities can be overcrowded and unsuitable for small children. Child witnesses who have had to wait at court for hours before testifying may be too bored or too tired to give competent evidence by the time they reach the witness box.

Criminal courts are deliberately designed to emphasize the majesty of the law, and the layout of most courtrooms is more likely to increase rather than assuage the anxiety of nervous witnesses. Surveys of professionals who work with child witnesses have confirmed that the courtroom environment can itself be a source of stress for children. Apart from confronting the defendant (discussed later), the main problems appear to be the dimensions of the room, the elevation of the judge, the isolation of the witness box, the wearing of wigs and gowns, poor acoustics, and the large audience of strangers (Flin, 1991; Whitcomb et al., 1985). In Scotland, it is now acceptable for lawyers to remove their wigs and gowns, and for the judge to come off the bench and sit with the child at the lawyers' table in the well of the court. However, the child is still in a large and unfamiliar room and in a jury trial (juries of 15 members in Scotland, 12 in England); even though the trial can be closed to the public when a child gives evidence, there still may be as many as 30 strangers present to listen to the child's evidence.

Until recently, children could be required to enter the courtroom alone, without the support of a parent of friend, which for small children makes the whole procedure even more intimidating (Flin et al., 1988; Whitcomb et al., 1985). Now in many jurisdictions, including Scotland, a support person is permitted to sit with the child in court while he or she is giving evidence. Allowing a small child to be accompanied by a trusted adult may have benefits not only in terms of the child's emotional state but also with respect to the quality of the evidence, because reducing the child's anxiety may increase the child's fluency and facilitate memory recall. However, very little empirical research has been conducted on the effects of stress at the time of recall on memory performance. Moston (1992), who has conducted a number of experiments on the effects of peer support on children's eyewitness recall, points out that while providing support can enhance recall under certain conditions, considerable care must be taken to ensure the suitability (neutrality) of the support person. In an intrafamilial abuse case, for example, it might be better to use a professional support person (e.g., a guardian ad litem or a victim support assistant) rather than an "uninvolved" family member. Clearly, more research is needed on the effects of a supporting adult's presence on the child's testimony and on the appropriate advice that should be given to those performing this role. Nevertheless, if children are required to give evidence in open court, they should be given the option of having a supporter present.

If the child's evidence can be videotaped, there is no need for the child to visit the courthouse. The examinations could be conducted in a suitable environment such as a purposely built child-interview room, of the type used by specialist police and social work teams or by child psychologists. When the live videolink system is used, the child still has to come to the courthouse and wait to be examined in an interview room equipped with a television camera. At present there is insufficient evidence on the operation of the videolink system to know whether these "courthouse" factors still constitute a significant source of stress for children.

Confronting the Accused

In accusatorial systems, witnesses are generally required to give their evidence in the presence of the defendant. There is no constitutional right of confrontation in Britain (unlike in the United States) (see Whitcomb, 1990, 1992), but confrontation is still an accepted practice in criminal trials. For many victims, children and adults, this can be one of the most disturbing aspects of giving evidence.

> How can anyone expect a young girl to describe things that happened to her when the person she is most frightened of stands and watches? (mother of an 8-year-old victim in a rape trial) (*Scotland on Sunday*, 1989, p. 2)

> A little girl of 11 experienced a total breakdown when she was asked to point out the man who attacked her—the following day, the court was informed that psychiatric treatment had to be arranged for her. (Adler, 1987, p. 51, describing a rape trial at the Old Bailey in London)

Although lawyers may believe that confrontation is by its very nature truth enhancing, the psychological reality is that for child witnesses it can be totally counterproductive, resulting in little or no evidence presented to the court (Spencer & Flin, 1990). Goodman et al. (in press) in their study of child abuse victims in court, found that "the children who were most upset about testifying in front of the defendant had a more difficult time in answering the prosecutors' questions" (p. 90). It is now widely recognized that confrontation is a primary stress factor for many child victims (Sas et al., 1991; Whitcomb, 1990) and that for both humane and evidential reasons, child witnesses should not have to come face to face with the accused. One way this problem has been tackled in Britain (since 1987) has been to introduce screens that shield the child from the gaze of the accused. Although these screens have proved helpful in a number of cases, they have not been used in any consistent fashion and are officially regarded as a stop-gap measure, with the videolink system preferred as a longer-term solution (Morgan & Plotnikoff, 1990).

In Scotland, there was, until recently, an additional difficulty because witnesses could be asked to identify the accused in court. For example, in one case, a child managed to give her evidence from behind a screen but became very upset when the screen was removed in order to permit the required identification. The new Law Reform (Scotland) Act 1990 now allows prior evidence of identification to be admitted for children who testify via live videolinks (section 58). This makes a great deal of sense because in Scotland, children do not have to confront the accused at an identification parade—all witnesses view lineups through one-way screens. Moreover, even preschool children can make identifications from behind these screens: "After the horrific rape, the little victim [aged 4] and a young boy who had been with her were asked to view a unique identification parade with Garvock on it. Because the children couldn't read or understand numbers, each person on the parade was identified by a picture of a beach ball, an apple, a cat, a house, a bird and an umbrella, instead of numerals. The children picked out Garvock, the man with the beach ball" (*Scottish Daily Record*, 1990, p. 7). Garvock, a former minister, was later found guilty and given a 10-year jail sentence after the little girl gave evidence at his trial.

Both the videolink system and the admission of videotaped evidence remove this problem of direct confrontation, although it is still possible for the defendant to observe the child indirectly via a TV monitor or through a one-way mirror. If these video options are not implemented in all courts, it would seem advisable for screens or some other device to be provided for children who do not wish to see the defendant.

Being Examined and Cross-Examined

The final factor to be considered is the impact of the adversarial method used by lawyers to present and test a witness's evidence during the trial. In a typical Scottish trial, where the child is normally the prosecution witness, he or she will first be subjected to an examination-in-chief (direct examination) to present the prosecution's case; then he or she will be cross-examined by the defense lawyer who will try to damage the prosecution's case by demonstrating the unreliability or weakness of the child's evidence. The prosecution lawyer may then conduct a reexamination to reestablish its case. Many adults, including police witnesses, find the business of being examined in court both stressful and confusing. Even experienced professionals appearing as expert witnesses are given special training to enable them to present their evidence to the courts more coherently and without undue anxiety (see Carson, 1990).

There is now growing concern that the standard adversarial examination is not the best way to hear or test children's evidence (see

Spencer & Flin, 1990). Eileen Vizard, a child psychiatrist, has said, "As an experienced expert witness, I can confirm that there is not the slightest chance of a traumatised sexually abused child surviving cross-examination by a experienced barrister. That is not to be unduly critical of lawyers but simply to state plain common sense" (*Independent*, 1987). It is not only the cross-examination that is problematic; there have also been cases in which children have been unable to complete the direct examination by the prosecution. The main difficulties seem to concern (1) the formality of the interview procedures, (2) the unfamiliarity of the language, (3) the challenging nature of the cross-examination, and (4) the time taken to conduct the examinations in serious trials.

Although the live videolink system and the admission of videotaped interviews certainly alleviate a number of known stress factors for child witnesses, they still require the child to be cross-examined by opposing lawyers in the presence of a judge. We need to know exactly what happens during this adversarial process, how children react to the experience, and how it affects their ability to recall and recount the events witnessed. These are extremely difficult questions to address empirically due to both evidential and ethical constraints. However, the issues are important and the first psychological investigations of child witnesses testifying in criminal courts in the United States and in Scotland have recently been completed.

Goodman et al. (in press) studied a sample of 218 child assault victims referred to district attorneys' offices in the Denver area between 1985 and 1987. The researchers' principal objective was to assess the emotional effects of testifying in court for child victims. As part of this investigation, researchers recorded interview and observational data on 40 children testifying at preliminary hearings, 8 children at competence hearings, and 17 children who testified at trial. The data were recorded by researchers who watched the child testifying and recorded their observations on a series of specially designed rating scales. In Scotland, another team of psychologists tracked 212 children cited (by the procurator fiscal's office in Aberdeen) to give evidence in the criminal courts between 1986 and 1987 and recorded observations of 22 children giving evidence at trial (Flin et al., 1988). This was followed by a larger study of 1,800 child witnesses cited for trials in Glasgow between 1988–1989, which included observations of 89 children testifying, using a Scottish version of Goodman et al.'s (1991) Courtroom Observation Scale (Flin et al., 1992). The following discussion draws on results from these studies as well as other writing and research on the suitability of the adversarial process when the witness is a child.

First, the formality of the examination procedure is likely to be strange and potentially threatening for a child who has never been interviewed in this way before. Carson (1990), advising experts, explains:

> [Witnesses] stand at a distance from and have to project their voices to listeners over a distance that is likely to be most unusual in their daily lives. They are required to begin by using very strange language (the oath or affirmation), to answer questions from one person whilst addressing another. (They must answer to the judge even though the questions come from a lawyer.) And they are expected to answer questions crafted (or at least they should be) to elicit particular answers and not give away other information. (p. 6)

Since children may also be examined in this fashion, the opportunities for building rapport or relaxing the child remain limited, especially if the child has to stand in the witness box. Although it is possible in some jurisdictions for judges to permit the use of innovative practices to support the child or make the proceedings less formal, these practices appear to be implemented with some inconsistency.

Morgan and Plotnikoff (1990) in an English study of child victims observed a number of cases that went to court and reported:

> A wide variety of procedures are now available [e.g., removal of wigs and gowns, seating arrangements, screens, victims support] which may ameliorate stress for the child witness and facilitate the giving of testimony, but the way in which they are used is fairly haphazard. There appears to be little shared information and experience among courts about the treatment of child witnesses. (p. 192)

Similarly, Goodman et al. (in press) reported that in Denver while some practices were more regularly adopted, such as permitting the victim assistant or nonoffending parent to remain in the courtroom, other techniques such as videolink or screening the defendant were used relatively infrequently. Flin et al. (1992) concluded that the adoption of special measures (e.g., screens, removal of gowns) was sporadic in Glasgow. So, although attempts can be made to reduce formality in the courtroom, this is not always done. Although children are still required to testify in open court, it should be possible to reduce the degree of formality without threatening the rights of the accused. As mentioned previously, Scottish judges have recently been issued a practice direction regarding the use of such measures so that child witnesses may be treated in court in a more consistent and supportive fashion.

Second, both the vocabulary and the grammatical constructions used in court are likely to be at best unfamiliar to a young child and at worst totally incomprehensible. Legal terminology (e.g., Your Honour, my Lord, learned friend, allegation, objection, counsel, the accused) serves to accentuate the formality of the proceedings but may baffle a child who typically has a very restricted knowledge of legal jargon. Lawyers who have limited experience in dealing with small children may also have difficulty in wording their questions in a form comprehensible to a young child. This can be as true of judges assessing competence, of prosecutors conducting an examination-in-chief, and of defense agents cross-examining. In cases of sexual abuse it may be especially important to understand and use the child's language rather than advocates' euphemisms: Goodman and Aman (1990) found that preschool children often pointed to their hands, arms, or feet when asked to indicate their "private parts."

It is not only vocabulary that can be problematic; children may fail to understand the style or phraseology of the questions posed. Courtroom lawyers use a highly controlled style of interviewing and in cross-examination leading questions are permitted. Not only are these interviewing techniques difficult for children to comprehend, but they also maximize the chances of contaminating the child's memory.

Brennan and Brennan (1988) studied the language used during the cross-examination of child witnesses in Australian courts and concluded:

> It is clear that in a courtroom there is a mismatch between the language of the lawyers and the language capacities of the children. As the questions become more courtroom specific and more combative, as under cross-examination, the less likely it is that children will be able to hear the language of the question and the less likely it is that they will be able to respond in a meaningful and truthful way. (p. 41)

From an analysis of 26 transcripts, Brennan and Brennan identified 13 "strange aspects" of lawyers' courtroom language including multifaceted questions, unclear or confused expressions, use of negatives, and repetitions of previous responses. Goodman et al. (1991) rated the age appropriateness of the language used to examine child victims and found that while most questioning was regarded as reasonably age appropriate, defense attorneys used more age-inappropriate wording of their questions than did prosecutors. Flin et al. (1992) also found that while 88% of direct examinations were carried out using vocabulary rated as "virtually all age appropriate," only 58% of cross-examinations fell into this category. These are preliminary observations, and they mainly serve to demonstrate how much further research is required. The Brennans' pioneering research provides a good example of how transcripts of lawyer–child witness dialogues can be used to test children's comprehension of typical legal questioning.

All other professionals who communicate with children as part of their job are given appropriate and, in some occupations, lengthy training. It seem surprising that those responsible for eliciting and assessing children's evidence (lawyers and judges) receive no relevant training whatsoever. It is hoped that this situation will change. The Irish Law Commission (1989) recently stated that a lawyer involved in a sexual abuse case "requires skills and faces demands which go beyond purely legal ones. . . . The lawyer needs to understand the language of children and to be able to communicate with children, not in the esoteric language of the law, but in the language appropriate to the particular stage of the child's development" (p. 195).

A third potential stress factor associated with cross-examination is its inherently challenging nature, which is designed to test the witness's credibility. Brennan and Brennan (1988) argued that "under conditions of cross-examination the child is placed in an adversarial and stressful situation which tests the resilience of even the most resourceful of adults" (p. 91). Experienced defense lawyers have an armory of interrogative tricks at their disposal to control the witness's responses to cross-examination. Carson (1990) presents an illuminating description of techniques (such as pinning out, focusing on peripheral issues, interrupting, and making suggestive remarks) that lawyers use when cross-examining expert witnesses. He describes "pinning out" as follows:

> The object is, by a series of preliminary questions, to fix the witness—as if by pins to a board—into a position from which she or he cannot move when the critical question—directed at the heart—eventually comes. Witnesses are often caught because the preliminary questions can appear to be so innocent, indeed complimentary to them. Also the questions can be framed so that only one answer is really possible. (p. 34)

Although these strategies may be invaluable when cross-examining hostile adults, unhelpful experts, and awkward defendants, it is debatable whether cross-examination is the most suitable technique for testing a child victim's account of a sexual assault. Some psychiatrists have complained that cross-examination need not be aggressive to be harmful:

Children can be discredited much more readily through a process of engaging their trust in the initial cross-examination, and then implanting suggestions about their capacity to tell lies in their minds later. All this can be done in a pleasant, charming way, by a skilled defence counsel, who does not want to alienate the jury. (Vizard, 1989, p. 30)

There are many anecdotal reports that children find the cross-examination to be distressing or that they "clam up" and refuse to speak (Spencer & Flin, 1990). However, given the heterogeneity of cases, defense attorneys, and child witnesses, as well as the relatively small numbers of trials studied, it is very difficult to judge the precise impact of cross-examination on memory or emotional state from the observational studies. Neither Goodman et al. (in press) nor Flin et al. (1992) reported major differences in children's demeanor between direct and cross-examinations. In both studies, about 50% of the children observed at trials were rated as being "tense" or "showing some distress." It should be remembered that child witnesses can be reporting extremely embarrassing or traumatic events such as a rape, a traffic fatality, or a murder and that simply being asked to remember and to relate the incident in open court may in itself be upsetting.

The final aspect of the trial that has been mentioned as a potential stress factor is the length of time it can take to conduct the examinations, especially if the offenses are serious or there are multiple accused. In the notorious McMartin trial in California, one child was on the witness stand for 16 days (Crewdson, 1988). The observational studies found that examinations tended to last for less than an hour in most cases. Goodman et al. (in press) measured the time spent on the stand by child sexual abuse victims. In preliminary hearings this ranged from 4 to 90 minutes (average 27 minutes), in competence examinations 4 to 21 minutes (average 10 minutes), and in trials 13 to 270 minutes (average 69 minutes). Flin et al. (1992) reported that examinations-in-chief lasted from 3 to 92 minutes (average 16 minutes), the cross-examinations lasted from 1 to 59 minutes (average 10 minutes), and reexaminations lasted from 1 to 18 minutes (average 4 minutes). (Many of these were bystander witnesses and not all children were subjected to all three examinations.) What is possibly just as important as the length of the formal examinations is the time the child has to wait at the courthouse before giving evidence and the number of interruptions or adjournments that occur during their testimony. Observing child victims in England giving evidence via the videolink system, Davies and Noon (1991) found that examinations-in-chief lasted from 2 to 88 minutes (average 18 minutes), cross-examinations lasted from 2 to 95 minutes (average 25 minutes), and reexaminations ranged from 1 to 42 minutes (average 6 minutes). There is thus some indication that cross-examinations may take longer with the videolink system, but these are preliminary findings.

CONCLUSION

Although the videolink system takes the child out of the courtroom, he or she is still subjected to pretrial delays, a visit to the courthouse, and the normal legal process of formal interviewing, potentially inappropriate language, and cross-examination by lawyers who are not specially trained to interview children. In fact, one judge recently suggested that English lawyers were cross-examining more aggressively through the videolink than in open court (see Spencer & Flin, 1990). Some lawyers do not see any of this as problematic: "It sometimes seems to me that rule number one of the lawyer's manual of human psychology is that memory improves with the passage of time, and rule number two is that stress improves recall" (Spencer, 1990). The videotape options, which include a pretrial hearing, tackle the problems of delay and the courthouse environment, but even these do not fully address all the potential weaknesses of adversarial examinations.

Only in the most enlightened proposals is it suggested that a specialist child examiner could, if necessary, question the child on behalf of both parties. (Judge Pigot's committee recommended this in 1989, but the representative of the bar dissented.) The very idea of relinquishing control of the cross-examination of child witnesses would disturb most defense lawyers. Spencer explains that it is part of the folklore of the English Bar that the foreign lawyers at the Nuremberg trials were much impressed by the Anglo-American method of cross-examination, thinking it superior to their own methods of getting at the truth.

> Indeed, English lawyers are so proud of this story that they have sometimes used it an an argument against proposals to change the rules of evidence for child witnesses. It is strange that they should do so. Apart from the point that techniques suitable for extracting the truth from major Nazi war criminals might seem a little excessive where children are concerned, the Anglo-American method of cross-examination in fact provoked mixed reactions from lawyers from other systems. (Spencer & Flin, 1990, p. 222)

These other legal systems that tend to be inquisitorial in nature are prepared to make greater use of hearsay evidence and expert witnesses or court-appointed child examiners in order to keep child witnesses out of criminal courtrooms (see Spencer et al., 1990; Loesel & Bender, in press). Now that the single European market has arrived, we may also be able to trade innovative methods for hearing and testing children's evidence with our continental neighbors.

REFERENCES

Adler, Z. (1987). *Rape on trial*. London: Routledge.

Brainerd, C., Reyna, V., Howe, M., & Kingma, J. (1991). Development of forgetting and reminiscence. *Monographs of the Society for Research in Child Development, 55* (3–4, Serial No. 222).

Brennan, M., & Brennan, R. (1988). *Strange language*. Wagga Wagga, Australia: Riverina Literacy Centre.

Carson, D. (1990). *Professionals and the courts: A handbook for expert witnesses*. Birmingham, England: Venture Press.

Cashmore, J., & Bussey, K. (1990). Children's conceptions of the witness role. In J. Spencer, G. Nicholson, R. Flin, & R. Bull (Eds.), *Children's evidence in legal proceedings* (pp. 177–188). Cambridge, England: University Law Faculty.

Crewdson, J. (1988). *By silence betrayed*. Boston: Little, Brown.

Davies, G., & Noon, E. (1991). *An evaluation of the live link for child witnesses* (Report to the Home Office). London: Home Office.

Dezwirek-Sas, L. (1992). Empowering child witnesses for sexual abuse prosecutions. In H. Dent & R. Flin (Eds.), *Children as witnesses* (pp. 181–200). Chichester, England: Wiley.

Flin, R. (1991). Implications of the law for the child. In K. Murray & D. Gough (Eds.), *Intervening in child sexual abuse* (pp. 122–128). Edinburgh, Scotland: Scottish Academic Press.

Flin, R., Boon, J., Knox, A., & Bull, R. (in press). The effects of a five-month delay on children's and adults' eyewitness memory. *British Journal of Psychology*.

Flin, R., Bull, R., Boon, J., & Knox, A. (1992). Children in the witness box. In H. Dent & R. Flin (Eds.), *Children as witnesses* (pp. 167–180). Chichester, England: Wiley.

Flin, R., Davies, G., & Tarrant, A. (1988). *The child witness* (Report to the Scottish Home and Health Department). Edinburgh, Scotland.

Flin, R., Stevenson, Y., & Davies, G. (1989). Children's knowledge of legal proceedings. *British Journal of Psychology, 80*, 285–297.

Glaser, D., & Spencer, J. (1990). Sentencing, children's evidence and children's trauma. *Criminal Law Review*, 371–382.

Goodman, G. S., & Aman, C. J. (1990). Children's use of anatomically detailed dolls to recount an event. *Child Development, 61*, 1859–1871.

Goodman, G. S., Rudy, L., Bottoms, B. L., & Aman, C. J. (1991). Children's concerns and memory. In R. Fivush & J. Hudson (Eds.), *Knowing and remembering in young children*. New York: Cambridge University Press.

Goodman, G. S., Taub, E., Jones, D., England, P., Port, P., Rudy, L., & Prado, L. (in press). Emotional effects of criminal court testimony on child sexual assault victims. *Monograph of the Society for Research in Child Development.*

Home Office (1992). *Memorandum of good practice on video recorded interviews with child witnesses for criminal proceeding.* London: Her Majesty's Stationery Office.

Hudson, J., & Fivush, R. (1991). As time goes by: Sixth graders remember a kindergarten experience. *Applied Cognitive Psychology, 5,* 347–360.

Irish Law Reform Commission. (1989). *Consultation paper on child sexual abuse.* Dublin, Ireland: Author.

Irish Law Reform Commission. (1990). *Report on child sexual abuse.* Dublin, Ireland: Author.

Loesel, F., & Bender, D. (Eds.). (in press). *Psychology and law facing the nineties.* Amsterdam: Swets & Zeitlinger.

Luus, E., & Well, G. (1992). The perceived credibility of child eyewitnesses. In H. Dent & R. Flin (Eds.), *Children as witnesses* (pp. 73–92). Chichester, England: Wiley.

Mackay, J. (1990). Opening address to the International Conference on Children's Evidence. In J. Spencer, G. Nicholson, R. Flin, & R. Bull (Eds.), *Children's evidence in legal proceedings* (pp. 1–6). Cambridge, England: Cambridge University Law Faculty.

Morgan, J., & Plotnikoff, J. (1990). Children as victims of crime: Procedures at court. In J. Spencer, G. Nicholson, R. Flin, & R. Bull (Eds.), *Children's evidence in legal proceedings* (pp. 189–192). Cambridge, England: Cambridge University Law Faculty.

Moston, S. (1992). Social support and children's eyewitness testimony. In H. Dent & R. Flin (Eds.), *Children as witnesses* (pp. 33–46). Chichester, England: Wiley.

Nicholson, G., & Murray, K. (1992). The child witness in Scotland. In H. Dent & R. Flin (Eds.), *Children as witnesses* (pp. 131–150). Chichester, England: Wiley.

Pigot, T. (1990). Women and children first. In J. Spencer, G. Nicholson, R. Flin, & R. Bull (Eds.), *Children's evidence in legal proceedings* (pp. 210–214). Cambridge, England: Cambridge University Law Faculty.

Pigot Committee. (1989). *Report of the Home Office Advisory Group on Video Evidence.* London: Home Office.

Plotnikoff, J. (1990). Delay in child abuse prosecutions. *Criminal Law Review,* 645–647.

Pynoos, R., & Nader, K. (1988). Children's memory and proximity to violence. *Journal of American Child and Adolescent Psychiatry, 27,* 236–241.

Sas, L. (1991). *Reducing the system-induced trauma for child sexual abuse victims through court preparation, assessment and follow-up.* Ontario: London Family Court Clinic.

Saywitz, K. (1989). Children's conception of the legal system. In S. Ceci, D. Ross, & M. Toglia (Eds.), *Perspectives on children's testimony.* New York: Springer-Verlag.

Saywitz, K., Jaenicke, C., & Camparo, L. (1991). Children's knowledge of legal terminology. *Law and Human Behavior, 14*, 526–536.

Scotland on Sunday. (1989, December 24). Young girl's court ordeal. P. 2.

Scottish Daily Record. (1990, November 27). Beast swore to God he didn't touch her. P. 7.

Scottish Law Commission. (1990). *Report on the evidence of children and other potentially vulnerable witnesses* (SLC 125). Edinburgh, Scotland: Her Majesty's Stationery Office.

Sisterman-Keeney, K., Amacher, E., & Kastanakis, J. (1992). The court-prep group: A vital part of the court process. In H. Dent & R. Flin (Eds.), *Children as witnesses* (pp. 201–210). Chichester, England: Wiley.

Spencer, J. (1987, October 3). Child abuse: The first steps to justice. *The Times,* p. 8.

Spencer, J. (1990). Children's evidence in legal proceedings in England. In J. Spencer, G. Nicholson, R. Flin, & R. Bull (Eds.), *Children's evidence in legal proceedings* (pp. 113–125). Cambridge, England: Cambridge University Law Faculty.

Spencer, J. (1992). Reforming the law on children's evidence in England. In H. Dent & R. Flin (Eds.), *Children as witnesses* (pp. 113--130). Chichester, England: Wiley.

Spencer, J., & Flin, R. (1990). *The evidence of children.* London: Blackstone.

Spencer, J., Nicholson, G., Flin, R., & Bull, R. (Eds.). (1990). *Children's evidence in legal proceedings.* Cambridge, England: Cambridge University Law Faculty.

Terr, L. (1988). What happens to early memories of trauma? *Journal of American Child and Adolescent Psychiatry, 27*, 96–104.

Vizard, E. (1989). *Videorecorded evidence and the implications for the child.* Paper 2 submitted to the Pigot Committee.

Wallwork, 42 Cr. App. R. 153. (1958).

Warren-Leubecker, A., Tate, C., Hinton, I., & Ozbek, N. (1989). What do children know about the legal system and when do they know it? In S. Ceci, D. Ross, & M. Toglia (Eds.), *Perspectives on children's testimony* (pp. 158–183). New York: Springer-Verlag.

Whitcomb, D. (1990). When the victim is a child: Past hope, current reality and future prospect of legal reform in the United States. In J. Spencer, G. Nicholson, R. Flin, & R. Bull (Eds.), *Children's evidence in legal proceedings* (pp. 133–146). Cambridge, England: Cambridge University Law Faculty.

Whitcomb, D. (1992). *When the victim is a child* (2nd ed.). Washington, DC: National Institute of Justice.

Whitcomb, D., Shapiro, C., & Stellwagen, E. (1985). *When the victim is a child.* Washington, DC: National Institute of Justice.

13

Effects of Context on the Accuracy and Suggestibility of Child Witnesses

Jennifer Marie Batterman-Faunce
State University of New York at Buffalo

Gail S. Goodman
University of California at Davis

U ntil recently, children were infrequent visitors to the courtroom. In those rare cases when children were called to testify, their statements were distrusted and could not be admitted without corroboration. Laws virtually excluding child witnesses from the courtroom began to change as society focused on the plight of child victims of sexual assault. Children began to enter the legal system as witnesses in ever-increasing numbers as society fought to protect children from further victimization (Goodman, 1984; Whitcomb, 1992). Presently, new adaptations—some with profound legal implications— are being instituted to facilitate child testimony and to prevent further victimization by the court process itself. For example, laws requiring the corroboration of child statements have, for the most part, been dropped, hearsay exceptions have become more liberal, and innovative techniques such as closed-circuit testimony, children's courtrooms, videotaped testimony, and the use of screens and special lighting have been developed (Bulkley, 1985; Myers, 1987). Although children are now testifying more frequently and are at times doing so using modified courtroom practices, both their statements and the modifications used to obtain their testimony are controversial.

This controversy arises in large part because the legal community is charged with the responsibility of protecting the rights of both child witnesses and alleged abusers. This task is complicated by questions regarding a child witness's competence, accuracy, and suggestibility. Recent modifications in courtroom techniques such as use of closed-circuit testimony are assumed to ease the trauma of open court and promote accurate and reliable testimony. Until recently, these assumptions, however, have not been empirically validated. Additionally, there are concerns that some of the modifications accommodating child witnesses may compromise the constitutional rights of defendants to face-to-face confrontation with their accusers, as specified in the Sixth Amendment, and prejudice a jury, abrogating defendants' rights to a fair trial (Goodman, Levine, & Melton, 1992; Perry & Wrightsman, 1991; Wilson, 1989).

In the present chapter, we discuss research relevant to children's testimony and courtroom modifications. We also present findings from some of the first empirical research to examine effects of innovative courtroom techniques on children's testimony and to evaluate jurors' attitudes toward such techniques.

CONTEXT AND CHILD TESTIMONY

For a child to be considered competent to testify as a witness, the law specifies that the child must "possess certain characteristics, including the capacity to observe, sufficient intelligence, adequate memory, the ability to communicate, an awareness of the difference between truth and falsehood, and an appreciation of the obligation to tell the truth" (Myers, 1987, p. 54). It has become quite important to the establishment of the child witness's competence and credibility to discern the memory limits and abilities of children and to establish their relative suggestibility. These efforts are particularly salient since widespread belief and early research labeled children as deficient in their memory abilities (Goodman, 1984; Otis, 1924; Stern, 1910; Whipple, 1913).

Social scientists have thus become intimately involved with the legal process in discovering the abilities and suggestibility of child witnesses at various ages and stages of development. Social scientists have also been concerned with situational influences on children's testimony. The research literature shows that the task of understanding children's testimony is not simple in large part because age is only one of many factors to be considered in the evaluation of witness accuracy (Baxter, 1990; Goodman & Schwartz-Kenney, 1992; Myers, 1987; Spencer & Flin, 1990). Recent research on cognitive development stresses the importance of situational influences on children's cognitive abilities (Donaldson, 1979; Fischer & Bullock, 1984). This view maintains that a child's expectations of and familiarity with a given situation influence the way the situation is interpreted and recalled (Donaldson, 1979; Nelson, 1986). Similarly, the manner in which a situation is described to a child will have an effect on the way he or she conceptualizes it (Donaldson, 1979). Conditions of testing are also influential in how a child performs (e.g., Fischer & Bullock, 1984; Price & Goodman, 1990; Vygotsky, 1978). In other words, children's abilities interact with the context in which those abilities are assessed.

Fischer and Bullock (1984) criticize traditional theories of cognitive development on the grounds that the interaction of a child's mind with his or her physical and interpersonal environments has been neglected. Instead, they propose the following:

> The child is seen as always acting in some particular context that supports his or her behavior to varying degrees. One result of this focus is that concepts of ability, capacity, and competence are radically altered. They are no longer fixed characteristics of a child but emergent characteristics of a child in a context. (p. 131)

Child accuracy and suggestibility can therefore be conceptualized as context dependent rather than as absolute abilities determined solely by cognitive maturity. Such a view has important implications for research on the ability of children to give accurate and reliable testimony in court or during a forensic interview. If children's statements reflect an interaction with interpersonal and physical contexts, then their testimony might be facilitated or impaired by the courtroom or interview environment.

CHILDREN'S MEMORY AND SUGGESTIBILITY

Human memory is generally conceptualized as being comprised of three main processes: encoding, storage, and retrieval (see, e.g., Anderson, 1990; Kail, 1990). Each of these processes affects the task of retelling an experience or witnessed event, and each process can result in reliability and accuracy or introduction of unreliability and inaccuracy. Rather than providing an exact replica of an event, human memory is best described as a reconstruction process whereby approximations of actual events are created, stored, and reported (Bartlett, 1932). However, the gist and central details of salient events are often retrieved with considerable accuracy by adults and children (Brewer, 1990; Nelson, 1986).

Psychologists' conception of human memory is based mainly on laboratory studies of memory for words, stories, and the like. Many researchers are moving away from laboratory experiments in favor of more ecologically valid designs in their studies of child witness memory abilities. These efforts are in part a reaction to evidence that data collected in less ecologically valid studies are limited in their applications to legal contexts (Goodman, Rudy, Bottoms, & Aman, 1990; Spencer & Flin, 1990; Yuille, 1988). Recent findings indicate that "the ability to remember information is a function of not only memory capacity, but also of prior knowledge, mnemonic techniques, contextual cues, motivation, and emotional state" (Spencer & Flin, 1990, p. 239). Thus, the situational variables differentiating laboratory and forensic settings may be intrinsically involved in memory performance.

The general research paradigm employed in much of the current child testimony and memory work involves a staged event or interaction that the child observes or experiences. Memory for the event is then tested via questioning that may immediately follow the event or may occur after a delay up to as much as 6 years later (see Fivush, Chapter 1, this volume; Goodman, Wilson, Hazan, & Reed, 1989). The postevent interview may involve free-recall questions, specific (often leading) or misleading questions, and recognition tasks (especially photo identification or lineup tasks).

Free Recall

Recall memory is often described as the most complex form of memory because it involves retrieval of previously observed or experienced events with very few prompts (Anderson, 1990; Kail, 1990). It is also a type of memory frequently demanded by legal contexts (Myers, 1987). This type of questioning generally elicits the most consistent age differences, with younger children reporting less information than older children or adults (Goodman & Reed, 1986; Marin, Holmes, Guth, & Kovac, 1979; Leippe, Romanczyk, & Manion, 1991; Spencer & Flin, 1990). However, although some have found that young children's free recall is less accurate than that of their older counterparts (Davies, Tarrant, & Flin, 1989), many others have found that the information young children divulge is quite accurate although incomplete (e.g., Goodman, Aman, & Hirschman, 1987; Goodman & Reed, 1986; Marin et al., 1979; Nelson, 1986) and may at times be even more accurate than information given by older children and adults (Marin et al., 1979).

Children's ability to recall information is one matter; children's willingness to do so is yet another. Like children's ability to recall information, children's willingness to divulge information does not necessarily increase with age. In fact, interesting reverse developmental trends occur.

The types of information about which child victim–witnesses must testify in court may be highly sensitive, traumatic, or embarrassing. In a recent study of children's memories for a physical examination that either involved or did not involve genital touch, Saywitz, Goodman, Nicholas, and Moan (1991) found that older children questioned about a nongenital examination reported significantly more information than did younger children. However, older children performed as poorly as younger children on free-recall questions concerning the genital examination, suggesting that memory abilities alone did not account for the results. Embarrassment also played a role. Similarly, reverse age trends in the willingness to reveal information were reported by Bottoms, Goodman, Schwartz-Kenney, Sachsenmaier, and Thomas (1990). They found that older children were less likely than younger children to disclose transgressions by their mothers. Thus, emotional and situational variables may outweigh simple developmental changes in free-recall capacity. It stands to reason that children may be more or less willing to report sensitive information depending on the context in which they are interviewed.

Specific Questions

An intermediate form of memory is required in the answering of specific questions. To answer such questions, children are required to retrieve and communicate an answer they have stored in memory (as in free recall) but are prompted by the content of the questions. This type of questioning is frequently used with child victims of sexual abuse because their spontaneous free recall may be cursory. However, in a court of law such questions may be considered as "leading" in nature.

In response to specific questions about central actions and salient experiences, children's testimony has been found to be more accurate than early research findings indicated. It should be added that what is best remembered is what is central to the child, not what is central to the adult (King & Yuille, 1987). There is additional evidence that children remember better what they themselves have experienced via participation as opposed to what they remember via observation (Baker-Ward, Hess, & Flannagan, 1990; Tobey & Goodman, in press).

Nevertheless, young children asked specific questions are at times less accurate than are older children and adults (Brigham, VanVerst, & Bothwell, 1986; Davies et al., 1989; Goodman, Bottoms, Schwartz-Kenney, & Rudy, 1991; Leippe et al., 1991; Spencer & Flin, 1990), especially when nonsalient, ambiguous, and peripheral information is queried. Goodman and Reed (1986), however, found that children as young as 6 are able to answer specific questions about as well as adults, a finding consistent with results reported by Marin et al. (1979). Age differences in witnesses' ability to answer specific questions can be expected to vary depending on such factors as the type of information queried and the difficulty of the language employed. For example, children have difficulty answering questions about time, height, weight, and age (Brigham et al., 1986; Rudy & Goodman, 1991; Saywitz et al., 1991) as well as questions couched in complex language such as the "legalese" often used in court (Brennan & Brennan, 1988; Carter, 1992).

The above conclusions are based, however, primarily on studies that did not include questions concerning physical or sexual abuse (e.g., "Did he touch your bottom?"). Recent studies including such questions generally find that under normal conditions of questioning, children are unlikely to commit commission errors to abuse-related questions (e.g., Rudy & Goodman, 1991; Saywitz et al., 1991; Tobey & Goodman, in press), although the error rate increases when preschoolers are tested (Goodman & Aman, 1991) and when age inappropriate language is employed (Carter, 1992). These findings suggest that the responses of children to specific questions concerning central, personally relevant, and abusive events may be particularly—although not always—accurate.

Suggestibility of Children's Reports

In addition to the practice of asking children specific questions, interviewers, prosecutors, and defense attorneys have—inadvertently or not—made frequent use of misleading questions. One primary concern in asking misleading questions is whether a child's answers will be influenced by such questioning. The belief that children are suggestible has discouraged the courts from allowing children's testimony for fear that children fill in gaps of memory with the suggestions of others. However, since the turn-of-the-century when children's suggestibility was documented, evidence has accumulated verifying that adults are at times also likely to change their reports as a result of misleading questioning (Gudjonsson & Clark, 1986; Loftus & Davies, 1984; Loftus, 1974; Loftus & Palmer, 1974; Smith & Ellsworth, 1987).

Studies that target the suggestibility of children for real-life events have produced mixed results, with some emphasizing children's resistance to suggestion (Brigham et al., 1986; Marin et al., 1979; Rudy & Goodman, 1991) while others have delineated the increased suggestibility of young, particularly preschool-aged, children (Ceci & Leichtman, 1992; Clark-Stewart, Thompson, & Lepore, 1989; Goodman & Reed, 1986). Researchers are exploring reasons for this variability by further investigating the conditions and situational variables that lead to increased suggestibility.

In empirical studies, young children are found to be more influenced by leading questions when (1) asked for descriptions of unfamiliar people rather than events (Goodman, Hirschman, Hepps, & Rudy, 1991), (2) pressed for additional details (Dent, 1990), (3) asked about an event for which they have uncertain and incomplete memory, such as may occur after a long delay (Goodman et al., 1989), (4) questioned under intimidating conditions (Goodman, Bottoms, Schwartz-Kenney, & Rudy, 1991), (5) questioned by someone of authority (Ceci, Ross, & Toglia, 1987; Tobey & Goodman, in press), and (6) when instilled with a negative stereotype about someone and then questioned with misleading suggestions over many (e.g., 12) weeks (Ceci & Leichtman, 1992).

However, age alone is an imperfect index of suggestibility. For example, Warren, Hulse-Trotter, and Tubbs (1991) found that the initial strength of a memory trace is related more strongly than age to suggestibility. When "memory impairment" (a form of suggestibility) is studied, forgetting rates have also been found to be more important than age per se (Howe, 1991). However, with increasing age, memory abilities often improve, leading to greater resistance to suggestion.

As was true for studies of children's responses to specific questions, studies of children's responses to misleading questions have mainly concerned suggestibility for details and actions that are not directly related to abuse allegations. Studies investigating children's suggestibility when children are asked such questions as "He took your clothes off, didn't he?" show that children evidence substantial resistance to such questions. Again, however, especially in young children, such resistance is context dependent. When young children (e.g., 3-year-olds) are questioned in an intimidating atmosphere, their suggestibility to abuse-related questions increases (Goodman, Bottoms, et al., 1991). Individual differences in suggestibility can also be strong, especially at young ages. Thus, again, one cannot rely on age alone in evaluating children's potential as witnesses.

Instead, researchers such as Gudjonsson and Clark (1986) discuss suggestibility as a function of a dynamic relation between a person, the environment, and significant individuals within that environment. This view is in contrast to the view that suggestibility is a stable age-related or personality trait. According to Gudjonsson and Clark's (1986) model, there are three important antecedents to a suggestible response: uncertainty, interpersonal trust, and expectations. An adult or child witness is expected to be more suggestible when uncertain of the facts due to poor memory for details, lack of information about the interrogative situation, and ambiguous questions. Additionally, Gudjonsson and Clark (1986) postulate that to yield to suggestions, one must perceive that the interviewer intends to be genuine rather than misleading. A suspicious attitude toward an interviewer is believed to increase resistance to suggestion, at least in adults. They further postulate a link between uncertainty and interpersonal trust, where heightened uncertainty combined with trust in the questioner will lead to responses more influenced by suggestive questioning.

To the extent that children's suggestibility is not inherent in the child but results instead from an interaction between children's minds and the contexts in which they are questioned, it should be possible to heighten children's resistance to suggestion. Fortunately, several researchers have been interested in ways to decrease children's susceptibility to misleading questions or to obtain reports from children without the use of leading questions (see Geiselman, Saywitz, & Bornstein, Chapter 4, this volume; Saywitz & Snyder, Chapter 6, this volume). Warren et al. (1991) found that warning child witnesses that questions were tricky or difficult significantly reduced the effect of misleading questions across all age groups tested. Even so, 7-year-old children were still found to be more negatively affected by misleading questioning than were 12-year-olds or adults. Goodman and colleagues (Goodman, Bottoms, et al., 1991) report that a warm, supportive environment also served to decrease young children's suggestibility, negating the age differences in suggestibility generally reported for preschool children.

As the legal community begins to reevaluate the procedures used to elicit reports from children, researchers are being called on to specify conditions under which children in general are most accurate and least suggestible, as well as which particular children profit from certain interview techniques and testimony settings. Although more research is needed, it is clear that contextual factors play an important role in reducing or increasing children's suggestibility.

Recognition Memory

Recognition is described as one of the most basic forms of memory, since it simply requires that an object be identified as something seen previously (Anderson, 1990; Kail, 1990). In general, recognition improves as children mature. For example, Myers and Perlmutter (1978) report that 2-year-old children were correct in their recognitions 81% of the time, whereas 4-year-olds were correct 92% of the time. However, age differences are not found on all recognition tasks. The prototypical recognition task in forensic interviews or court testimony concerns person identification, for example, identification of a culprit in a photo lineup or a defendant in court.

Few studies have investigated children's ability to identify familiar persons; this is unfortunate because identification of familiar as opposed to unfamiliar persons is more likely to be at issue in child abuse cases. To date, virtually all studies concern recognition of unfamiliar adults. For example, Brigham et al. (1986) found that 4th-grade children performed significantly worse on a photo lineup task of an unfamiliar person than did older, 8th- and 11th-grade children. Moreover, children appear to be more prone than adults to false identification of briefly seen strangers on photo lineup tasks (Parker & Carranza, 1989); however, practice trials in which children are trained not to make false identifications can help alleviate such errors (Goodman, Bottoms et al., 1991). Despite such age-related findings, some researchers fail to uncover age effects on person-identification tasks (Davies et al., 1989), and others find that children actually perform better than adults (Goodman & Reed, 1986), perhaps again implicating situational variables or complex interactions of age with task demands.

Memory for Stressful Events

Given that children often testify about traumatic events, it is important to consider how well children can remember a stressful incident. Although some psychologists have proposed that stress hinders accurate memory (e.g., Loftus, 1979), a more current view is that core features of highly emotional events are remembered especially well, although memory for peripheral details may at times be adversely affected (e.g., Christianson, 1992). Findings from several studies of children's memory for stressful events are consistent with this more current conclusion. For example, Warren and Startwood (in press) report that children who were more upset about the space shuttle Challenger disaster retained the event in greater detail than children who were less upset. Steward (1992) found that compared to children who were less distressed during painful medical procedures, children who were more upset reported a greater amount of information and more accurate information at a 6-month interview. These results are consistent with earlier studies by Goodman and her colleagues (Goodman, Hepps, & Reed, 1986; Goodman, Hirschman, Hepps, & Rudy, 1991) showing that distress was associated with children's more complete recall and greater resistance to suggestion (but see Peters, 1991). It is important to note that such findings do not imply that children's reports of stressful events are completely accurate. In studies of children's memories for horrifying events such as sniper attacks on schools, kidnappings, and homicides of loved ones, both accuracies and inaccuracies have been noted (e.g., Pynoos & Eth, 1984; Terr, 1991).

Of considerable recent interest is the topic of "repressed memory." Can memory for a traumatic event, such as child sexual abuse or witnessing a murder, be inaccessible to consciousness for years, only to vividly reemerge later? Some authorities point to adults' and children's suggestibility as the basis for repressed memory reports (Loftus, 1992), but there is growing evidence that incidents of childhood sexual abuse can be temporarily or even permanently forgotten. Briere and Conte (in press) interviewed 450 women and men who reported a history of child sexual victimization. Over 50% of the sample stated that they had experienced periods of partial to total amnesia for the abuse they experienced at some point in their childhood. Linda Williams (1992) interviewed women who, as children, were treated at a hospital emergency room for alleged sexual abuse. Approximately 38% of the women evidenced no memory for the emergency room visit or for the sexual assault. Williams provides some fascinating case examples to support the view that repressed memories for traumatic events can exist, especially when the victim was under 5 years of age at the time of the assault. At this point in time, perhaps the most balanced view is that repressed memory can occur, but that false reports of early traumas are made at times too.

Retrieval in memory of a stressful event may depend in part on the contextual cues (e.g., reminders) available at the time of recall, especially if the victim was young when the traumatic event took place and many years have elapsed since it occurred. In addition, a supportive emotional context may be necessary for a child to be willing to recount, and possibly relive, a traumatic incident. However, even if a child is initially willing to describe what happened—testifying about a highly stressful event in the context of an intimidating court appearance—this, in the end, can be an emotionally overwhelming experience for a vulnerable child witness.

Summary

The literature upholds the idea that children, under certain conditions, can be competent, credible, and accurate sources of information concerning events they have experienced. Generally, children's abilities to both remember and recount events is found to increase with age. However, several studies indicate that the abilities of children may depend on other situational variables. These variables include the kinds of questions used, the interpersonal context of the interview, and the information a child has concerning what is expected. It can be concluded that although generally accurate, children (like adults) are sensitive to the interpersonal environment in which they are questioned, and that the situational variables have an impact on the veracity of the testimony they ultimately relate. Future efforts to improve the accuracy and reliability of the information children give in legal contexts may mean altering the circumstances under which they testify.

EFFECTS OF COURTROOM INTIMIDATION AND TRAUMA ON THE CHILD WITNESS

Testifying in court can be an intimidating experience for anyone, regardless of age. For a child, however, there may be additional factors that make testifying in court particularly frightening. The legal system expects witnesses to "undergo multiple interviews and court appearances, expects testimony to be detailed and articulate, and provides opportunity for a cross-examination that may confuse even the most sophisticated of witnesses" (Perry & Wrightsman, 1991, p. 133). Each of these elements, in addition to a general lack of sound knowledge of and experience with legal procedures, long pretrial waiting periods, frequent postponements and continuances, and the formality of the courtroom, may pose serious complications for the introduction of a child as a key witness (Goodman et al., in press; Melton et al., 1992; Saywitz, 1989). These elements may additionally serve to exacerbate a child's stress and trauma.

Although many have discussed the potential harm to the child witness, still others have suggested that testifying in court may be cathartic for some children, giving them a sense of competence and control (Berliner & Barbieri, 1984; Whitcomb, 1981). Pynoos and Eth (1984), in their study of child witnesses to homicide, suggested that involvement in the legal system can serve as a coping strategy, helping children to come to the aid of a deceased loved one through their courtroom testimony. Researchers have begun to investigate the question of whether children suffer additional trauma or benefit as a result of testifying in court. To date, however, the empirical evidence is still relatively scant.

Early research efforts suggested that children who testify in court are adversely affected by the experience. However, these early studies were fraught with methodological difficulties, making sound conclusions difficult. Gibbens and Prince (1963) found that children who testified in court showed greater psychological disturbance than those who did not. However, those children who testified in court were also the victims of more serious abuse and tended to come from more disturbed families, making comparisons between the groups questionable. DeFrancis (1969) found that involvement in court proceedings created considerable stress and tension for children. However, this study confounds involvement in the legal process with the aftereffects of victimization, as it does not contain a comparison group.

Goodman et al. (in press) attempted to clarify whether testifying in court is traumatic or cathartic for child victims in a study of children involved as victim–witnesses in child sexual abuse prosecutions. In their interviews of children who testified in sexual abuse cases as well as children whose testimony was not necessary, they found that children were generally fearful of the courtroom and apprehensive about testifying. After testifying, some children reported that the experience had not been as aversive as they had anticipated; others maintained that the experience was as bad or worse than they had expected. Goodman et al. (in press) report that, on the whole, "the short-term effects were traumatic rather than cathartic." They further found that children's trauma was exacerbated when children had to testify multiple times, when they lacked maternal support at the time of disclosure, when there was an absence of corroborating evidence, and, to a lesser extent, when the defendant was a close relative. They concluded that "continued involvement as a witness can at least temporarily interfere with children's improvement" (Goodman et al., in press), a conclusion shared by others (DeFrancis, 1969; Gibbens & Prince, 1963; Perry & Wrightsman, 1991; Spencer & Flin, 1990; but see Runyan, Chapter 11, this volume).

Child witnesses in sexual abuse cases not only must overcome the intimidation of the courtroom setting, they must also relate highly personal, often traumatic experiences in the presence of the accused. Because many abusers are familiar or even related to the child victim and may have threatened or intimidated the child, facing the defendant may be particularly intimidating and frightening for child witnesses. Current legal debate revolves around the requirement of a child to face the defendant in open court. This debate has been intensified by the recent use of alternative courtroom procedures and mechanisms that eliminate this face-to-face contact, such as the placement of screens or the use of closed-circuit testimony (*Coy v. Iowa*, 1988; *Craig v. Maryland*, 1990).

The general belief that children are particularly distressed by the presence of the defendant in the courtroom has received some support. Children interviewed just before testifying were found to be anxious about facing the defendant and fearful of incurring retribution for their testimony (Goodman et al., in press; Spencer & Flin, 1990). Those children who were particularly anxious when testifying in the presence of the defendant had more negative views of the entire experience following testimony (Goodman et al., in press). Spencer and Flin (1990) report that children interviewed before testifying feared that the accused would make threats, faces, or even attack them during their testimony. Goodman et al. (in press) further found that:

> Fear of the defendant was a common response. A number of children stated that they were so frightened they tried not to look at the defendant. One young adolescent said, "I was scared. I didn't look at him. If I would have looked at him, I would have freaked." Other children complained that seeing the defendant "brought the memory all back again." Instead of fear, some children felt anger at seeing the defendant and/or the defendant's behavior. . . . Finally, some children expressed mixed emotions. These children tended to express the desire to see the defendant convicted but were frightened at the thought of testifying. One such child commented . . . "In some ways, I wish he was there so I can show him I'm going to put him in jail. In some ways I don't. He'll make me scared and give dirty looks."

Although testifying face to face with the accused in open court can induce stress in child witnesses, it is important to emphasize that adverse reactions to testifying in criminal court are not found in all children. Moreover, some children who do not have their day in court feel disenfranchised and wish they could have taken the stand (Goodman et al., in press).

Effect of Stress on Children's Reports

Although the emotional state and comfort of child witnesses in the courtroom are of concern, it is particularly important that the testimony children give is accurate, reliable, and complete. Several researchers are investigating the effects on children's testimony of the stress incurred by confrontation, which is typically required in the legal process. Generally, these researchers stage some sort of event or crime and then evaluate the accuracy of children's reports when children participate in mock legal procedures or interviews that mimic aspects of legal procedures. These studies investigate children's ability to relate accurate reports under stressful and intimidating circumstances, when exposed to what Peters (1991) calls "confrontational stress."

Dent (1977) and Dent and Stephenson (1979) were the first to demonstrate experimentally that children performed significantly better when they did not have to face a live defendant. In their study, children had to identify a person from a live lineup or were allowed to identify the defendant from photographs. Those children who were asked to identify a suspect from a live lineup demonstrated considerable fear, embarrassment, and nervousness. Additionally, those in the live-lineup condition made fewer correct identifications.

In a more recent study, Bussey, Lee, and Ross (1991; Bussey, Lee, & Grimbeek, Chapter 7, this volume) found that young (i.e., 3- to 5-year-old) children are less likely to report a transgression in the presence of the defendant, but they also found that the reports of older (i.e., 9-year-old) children were not affected by such confrontation. Even so, Bussey et al. (1991) found that the older children expressed discomfort at disclosing the incident in front of the defendant. This study suggests that young children have particular difficulty relating transgressions under conditions of direct confrontation, such as that required by traditional court settings.

Similarly, Peters (1990) also found that intimidation has a negative effect on children's reports. After witnessing a staged robbery, children were either interviewed alone or in the presence of the thief. When the thief was present, the accuracy and amount of information the children offered severely declined. Compared to those interviewed in the presence of the thief, five times as many of those interviewed in the thief-absent condition related what they had witnessed. Like Dent's (1977) and Bussey et al.'s (1991) findings, this study suggests that the amount and kind of information children willingly relate vary with the situational conditions under which the child is questioned.

Hill and Hill (1987) conducted an experiment to evaluate whether children's recall differs with forensic setting, hypothesizing that children questioned in a regular courtroom would recall less information and less accurate information than when questioned in a smaller, more intimate setting. Their results supported the hypothesis; when compared to children interviewed in a smaller setting, children in a courtroom setting tended to recall fewer central items in free recall and to respond with noncommittal "I don't know" or "I don't remember" answers more frequently. In this study, children had not been in any way victimized by the defendant; hence, for real child victims, the effects of intimidation would probably be even more salient. It seems likely that child witnesses will show greater accuracy in a more supportive environment.

Summary

It has been argued that "the specific reactions of a particular child witness depend in large measure upon the personality of the child, the nature of the trial, the way in which the child witness and courtroom personnel have been prepared, and the procedures allowed by the trial court" (Perry & Wrightsman, 1991, p. 138). Even so, most agree that the experience of testifying in open court is often stressful. The evidence regarding the veracity and reliability of children's testimony under such stressful and intimidating circumstances suggests careful consideration of alternative courtroom techniques. Evidence concerning the ability of children to give clear, accurate, and uninfluenced accounts of their experience, suggests that under certain conditions, children can be valuable witnesses. However, one can reasonably question how often the courts currently provide those conditions.

PROCEDURES AND MODIFICATIONS DESIGNED TO REDUCE TRAUMA OF CHILD WITNESSES

Although children have a right to be protected from further victimization, defendants also have a right to a fair trial. Unfortunately, some of the courtroom practices that accommodate child witnesses may violate the constitutional rights of defendants. Our constitution allows the accused face-to-face confrontation with his or her accuser. The Sixth Amendment states in part that "in all criminal prosecutions, the accused shall enjoy the right . . . to be confronted with the witnesses against him . . . ." Traditionally, this has been the basis for the presence of the defendant in open court and the often vigorous cross-examination of the prosecution's witnesses. The purpose of such practices is to ensure that only reliable testimony is admitted into the court record by providing the defendant the opportunity to question the witness via cross-examination by the defense attorney and by providing the jury with the opportunity to observe the witness' demeanor during such questioning in the presence of the accused. These are, however, the very practices many claim could be traumatic for child witnesses (e.g., Goodman, Levine, et al., 1991; Pynoos & Eth, 1984).

The interpretation of the confrontation clause is problematic in cases involving child victims. One current controversy surrounds the necessity for the child witness to be physically present in the courtroom. Can defendants' rights be upheld if the child testifies via closed circuit or videotaped testimony? The U. S. Supreme Court has been called upon to outline the specific circumstances under which a defendant's right to face-to-face confrontation can be outweighed by a child's need for protection and the court's need to maintain the truth-seeking function of a trial. Previous state court decisions generally relied on a literal interpretation of the confrontation clause, mandating that procedures limiting the face-to-face meeting are in violation of the Sixth Amendment (e.g., *Herbert v. Superior Court*, 1981; Marchese, 1990). Some of the more innovative measures used to protect child witnesses, such as the placement of screens between the defendant and the witness or the removal of the child from the courtroom, as in cases involving closed-circuit or videotaped testimony, might be interpreted by some to be in direct violation of such a literal interpretation. Although recent U. S. Supreme Court decisions (e.g., *Craig v. Maryland*, 1990) reflect a willingness of the justices to loosen the restrictions of the confrontation clause, the decisions also encourage conservative use of such alterations in court procedures. Some state supreme courts (e.g., Pennsylvania's) have decided that their state constitutions require face-to-face confrontation, regardless of the federal constitutionality of modified procedures. These recent decisions clearly reflect controversy regarding balancing the rights of child witnesses and alleged abusers. As of yet, many of these decisions rest on scant empirical evidence.

Current questions regarding the constitutionality of protective measures that compromise a defendant's Sixth Amendment rights, in conjunction with continuing skepticism regarding the veracity and integrity of child testimony, make the continued use of innovative protective measures such as closed-circuit testimony uncertain. Many have argued instead for the use of less drastic modifications to accommodate child witnesses, such as reducing the number of pretrial interviews; educating child witnesses about standard court personnel and procedures; providing specially trained support personnel to accompany child witnesses through court procedures; allowing special exceptions to laws restricting hearsay testimony and leading questions; and creating child-friendly courtroom environments. Although these modifications may be helpful to some children in reducing their potential trauma, such modifications still require the child witness to face an alleged abuser in open court. It is this experience of physical, face-to-face confrontation that may be particularly stressful for many young children and against which closed-circuit technology safeguards.

Closed-Circuit Courtrooms

In 1988, the U. S. Supreme Court ruled against laws that give blanket approval for the use of physical screens and special lighting designed to shield alleged child sexual abuse victims from the defendant (*Coy v. Iowa*, 1988). In that U. S. Supreme Court decision, Justice Scalia voiced concern that the very use of protective mechanisms in court may enhance the jury's view that the defendant is, in fact, guilty. Part of this concern is that the presumption of innocence may be undercut by the notion that the defendant must be guilty if the use of such modifications is necessary to elicit a child witness' testimony. The court ruled that the Sixth Amendment rights of the defendant were violated, noting that face-to-face confrontation helps ensure the veracity of testimony by making it more difficult to fabricate. Justice Scalia, writing for the majority, said:

> The State can hardly gainsay the profound effect upon a witness of standing in the presence of the person the witness accuses, since that is the very phenomenon it relies upon to establish the potential "trauma" that allegedly justified the extraordinary procedure in the present case. That face-to-face presence may, unfortunately, upset the truthful rape victim or abused child; but by the same token it may confound and undo the false accuser, or reveal the child coached by a malevolent adult. It is a truism that constitutional protections have costs. (p. 2802)

Thus, the Supreme Court restricted the broadband use of protective measures in child sexual abuse cases but did not eliminate any possibility of their use. Instead, the Court emphasized the need to establish potential trauma to the victim before waiving the face-to-face confrontational rights of the defendant.

In its decision in *Craig v. Maryland* (1990), the U. S. Supreme Court upheld the use of closed-circuit testimony when a particularized determination of its necessity is made, maintaining that the confrontational rights assured by the Constitution are not absolute in their requirement of a face-to-face encounter. The Court upheld the use of closed-circuit simultaneous broadcasting procedures, charging that the Constitution allows for exceptions to the confrontation clause in cases where a child victim may be traumatized by testifying in open court in the presence of the defendant such that the accuracy and completeness of his or her testimony would be adversely affected. Justice O'Connor wrote the majority opinion:

> The Confrontation Clause does not guarantee criminal defendants an absolute right to a face-to-face meeting with the witnesses against

them at trial. The Clause's central purpose, to ensure the reliability of the evidence against a defendant by subjecting it to rigorous testing in an adversary proceeding before the trier of fact, is served by the combined effects of the elements of confrontation: physical presence, oath, cross-examination, and observation of demeanor by the trier of fact. Although face-to-face confrontation forms the core of the Clause's values, it is not an indispensable element of the confrontation right. (p. 673)

In the *Craig* case, the conditions of physical presence, oath, cross-examination, and observation of demeanor by triers of fact were satisfied. Specifically, the child, prosecutor, and defense counsel moved to another room where the child was questioned and cross-examined. The defendant, judge, and jury remained in the courtroom and were able to view the child's testimony via an one-way, closed-circuit television. Using such technology, the child was unable to see the defendant, although the defendant was able to observe the child. Of particular importance, and unlike the procedure used in the *Coy v. Iowa* case, there was an individualized finding that the child witness would suffer undue trauma from direct confrontation, satisfying the Court's requirement of a particularized finding of trauma. This more recent ruling allows children to testify via closed-circuit technology when, and only when, an a priori determination is made that they would be unduly traumatized by the experience of testifying before the defendant so much so that their testimony would be adversely affected. The specifics of what constitutes such undue trauma are still undecided and may necessitate a marriage between the legal and psychological communities (Goodman et al., 1991). More appeals cases involving closed-circuit and videotaped testimony are likely until the Court adopts a more detailed policy.

To date, empirical evidence concerning the effects of closed-circuit technology on the statements and reports of children is virtually nonexistent. One of the few empirical studies to examine the effects of closed-circuit and videotape technology in the courtroom examined the reactions and decisions that jurors make when presented with child testimony via these alternative methods (Swim, Borgida, & McCoy, 1991). Subjects in the study were placed in either a videotaped-deposition condition, where they viewed child testimony presented via videotaped deposition, or a "live" condition in which they saw the child's "live" testimony. However, all subjects were presented with a videotaped trial. Thus, subjects in the videotaped deposition saw a videotape of a videotaped deposition, whereas those in the "live" condition saw a videotape of a child testifying in open court. Swim et al. (1991) found that the predeliberation verdicts of mock jurors who had seen the testimony presented as a videotaped deposition were less likely to find the defendant guilty on the most severe charge. They additionally found that videotaped testimony was more likely to increase the jurors' certainty that the defendant was guilty of the lesser charges. Although this study makes an important contribution by beginning to evaluate the effects of child testimony given via alternative methods, further research is needed, especially given Swim et al.'s (1991) operationalized distinction between the presentation of the videotaped and "live" testimony, because the latter was also presented on videotape.

RECENT FINDINGS ON EFFECTS OF INNOVATIVE PRACTICES ON CHILDREN'S TESTIMONY

What are the effects of innovative techniques on children's courtroom testimony? As mentioned above, Goodman et al. (in press) examined the emotional effects on child sexual assault victims of testifying in criminal court. As part of that study, the researchers were also able to evaluate relations between certain innovative courtroom practices and children's performance.

In the study, researchers observed 4- to 17-year-old children testify in actual child sexual abuse prosecutions in Colorado, either at preliminary hearings (n = 39) or at trials (n = 17). Use of innovative courtroom procedures was noted, as was the children's behavior while testifying and the attorneys' behavior toward the children. The researchers also made judgments about the children's credibility.

A few innovative techniques were used frequently, but many others were rarely employed. The most common technique was to have a victim advocate in court with the children as a support person, which occurred in 80% of the preliminary hearings and 94% of the trials. Permitting a child's parent or other loved one to remain in court was less frequent but still occurred in 46% of the preliminary hearings and 29% of the trials. Although a loved one or support person was at times present, only one child was permitted to testify while sitting on the lap of a loved one or support person, and this occurred at a preliminary hearing. In 45% of the preliminary hearings observed, the courtroom was cleared of spectators; however, the courtroom was cleared in only 6% of the trials. Children at times were able to take a toy to the stand for comfort or use a prop (e.g., an anatomically detailed doll) to help them testify. This occurred more often at trial than at preliminary hearings. Children took a toy to the stand in 11% of the preliminary hearings and

30% of the trials; children used props as testimony aids in 11% of the preliminary hearings and 53% of the trials.

Although laws permitting closed-circuit and videotaped testimony existed at the time of the study, these techniques were rarely used. Only one child testified over closed-circuit television, and this was permitted at a preliminary hearing, not a trial. No children testified via videotape. Another option for avoiding face-to-face confrontation is to have the defendant sit out of view of the child. This occurred in only 8% of the preliminary hearings and 12% of the trials. However, the study took place before the *Craig v. Maryland* U.S. Supreme Court decision; it is possible that the use of closed-circuit television technology has increased since the decision was reached.

A few of the innovative techniques were employed frequently enough that it was possible to evaluate relations between their use and the children's performance (see Table 13.1). At preliminary hearings, these techniques included presence of a parent/loved one, presence of a victim advocate, and clearing the courtroom of spectators. As can be seen in Table 13.1, children appeared less frightened of the defendant

TABLE 13.1. Significant Correlations between Use of Innovative Courtroom Techniques and Children's Testimony

	Preliminary hearing		
	Parent/loved one present	Victim advocate present	Court cleared
Fear of defendant	−0.39	0.34	
Inconsistent peripheral details	−0.35		
Credible witness	0.34		
Recanted ID of perpetrator		−0.38	
Recanted main actions		−0.37	
Crying			−0.33

	Trial		
	Parent/loved one present	Taking a toy to the stand	Use of props
Answered prosecutor's questions	0.48		
Use of leading questions		−0.67	
Inconsistent peripheral details		0.57	0.63
Child's speech faltering			0.57
Cooperative with defense attorney			0.48
Defense attorney supportive			0.50

when a parent or loved one remained in the courtroom. Compared to children without such support, children whose parent or loved one was permitted to remain in court provided less inconsistent testimony regarding peripheral details during cross-examination by defense attorneys. These children were also rated as more credible witnesses. Presence of the victim advocate was associated with the children appearing more frightened. One possible interpretation of this relation is that victim advocates were more likely to accompany children to the stand when the children were already frightened, but the victim advocate's presence may have been less helpful in calming the children's fears than the presence of parents would have been. Nevertheless, the presence of the victim advocate was associated with the child being less likely to recant the identity of the perpetrator and less likely to recant the perpetrator's main actions, at least during defense questioning.

Finally, clearing the courtroom was associated with children being less likely to cry during defense questioning.

Because the use of innovative techniques differed somewhat at preliminary hearings and trials, Goodman's research team could not examine the same set of variables for the trials. However, they were able to examine the trials for associations between children's performance and presence of the parent/loved one, use of toy props, and taking a toy to the stand.

Again, presence of a parent or loved one had beneficial effects for the children. When a parent or loved one stayed with the child, the child was able to answer a larger number of the prosecutor's questions. Use of toy props was associated with a variety of effects. Children were more likely to use props if their speech was faltering. Defense attorneys' demeanor toward the children was more supportive if the children used a prop, and children who used props were more cooperative with defense attorneys. The children also were more likely to provide inconsistent testimony concerning peripheral detail.

Finally, taking a toy to the stand for comfort was associated with prosecutors asking fewer leading questions and with the children providing more inconsistent testimony concerning peripheral details.

In general, these findings indicate that the presence of a support person, particularly the child's parent or loved one, is associated with beneficial effects on children's testimony. This finding nicely complements results of laboratory experiments indicating beneficial effects of social support on children's testimony (e.g., Goodman, Bottoms et al., 1991; Moston, 1987). Clearing the courtroom, another means of making the situation less intimidating, was also associated with benefits for children in that they cried less. However, the use of props, either as testimony aids or as a means to comfort the children, resulted in mixed findings. The primary deficit was that their use was associated with greater inconsistencies about peripheral details.

The findings of this study should be interpreted cautiously given their correlational nature. For example, it is possible that props were used when children were already having considerable trouble testifying and that the props themselves were not responsible for resulting inconsistencies. Further research is clearly needed to determine the effects of innovative practices on children's performance. Moreover, because certain techniques were rarely if ever used, researchers may need to rely on laboratory simulations to examine certain innovative practices, such as the effects of closed-circuit television, on children's testimony.

RECENT FINDINGS ON LAYPERSONS' ATTITUDES ABOUT INNOVATIVE TECHNIQUES

One important role of the adversary system is to maintain perceptions of fairness. If the courts use techniques that are perceived as biased and unfair, faith in the legal system might be quickly lost. Therefore, studies are also needed of laypersons' attitudes toward innovative courtroom techniques. Do people view techniques to protect children as fair?

We are currently examining this question in a large study involving hundreds of mock jurors drawn from the community (see Goodman et al., 1992). Results to date are based on over 700 community respondents. These respondents viewed 8-year-old children testifying in a series of mock trials held at the Buffalo City courts. The children testified about a standardized event (i.e., making a movie with a man) that they experienced approximately 2 to 3 weeks earlier. Half of the children testified in open court in a "regular trial" condition, in which typical adversarial procedures were employed. These children testified from the witness stand and were placed under direct and cross-examination by actor attorneys while at least 12 mock jurors and the "defendant" observed. In contrast, the other children testified in a closed-circuit condition, in which they testified via one-way closed-circuit television from a room adjoining the courtroom. Each attorney entered the room to question the child; the defendant and jurors remained in the courtroom. Regardless of the experimental condition, the mock jurors then completed a battery of questionnaires. In the questionnaires, mock jurors were asked how strongly they would advocate the following courtroom techniques: a child testifying live in court, a child testifying on videotape, a child testifying via two-way closed-circuit television, a child testifying via one-way closed-circuit television, and a child questioned by a neutral party, such as a social worker or psychologist rather than by attorneys. Results are shown in Table 13.2.

As can be seen, mock jurors were not of one opinion; ratings varied across the full range of the 6-point scale. However, of the various techniques mentioned on the questionnaire, mock jurors overall were more negative about traditional courtroom appearances for children than about any of the other options mentioned. Respondents were more likely to advocate use of videotaped testimony, one-way closed-circuit television, or interviews by a neutral party. However, these results varied somewhat depending on the type of trial the mock jurors viewed. Jurors who viewed children testify via closed-circuit television were less likely to advocate live testimony, $r = .34$, $n = 703$, $p < .001$, and somewhat more likely to advocate use of

TABLE 13.2. Percentage of Respondents Advocating/Not Advocating Use of Traditional and Innovative Practices for Children in Court

	1	2	3	4	5	6
	Not advocate					Advocate
Overall ($n = 707$)						
1. Testimony live in court	32	19	12	13	13	12
2. Testimony on videotape	11	11	12	19	20	27
3. Testimony via 2-way TV	11	11	12	21	26	19
4. Testimony via 1-way TV	9	9	10	18	24	30
5. Testimony elicited by neutral party	17	13	11	15	18	25
Regular Trials ($n = 356$)						
1. Testimony live in court	17	19	11	19	18	12
2. Testimony on videotape	12	12	16	19	19	27
3. Testimony via 2-way TV	11	11	16	26	26	19
4. Testimony via 1-way TV	11	12	12	21	22	21
5. Testimony elicited by neutral party	18	13	13	19	24	25
Closed Circuit Trials ($n = 351$)						
1. Testimony live in court	48	19	12	7	7	7
2. Testimony on videotape	9	10	9	19	21	33
3. Testimony via 2-way TV	11	11	9	17	26	26
4. Testimony via 1-way TV	6	5	8	16	26	40
5. Testimony elicited by neutral party	15	14	9	17	17	27

one-way closed-circuit television, $r = .24$, $n = 701$, $p < .001$, than jurors who viewed children testifying in regular trials.

Further research is needed to determine the replicability of our findings. Nevertheless, these results suggest that most laypersons are not strongly opposed to innovative courtroom techniques, and many would even advocate their use in cases involving child witnesses. Overall, these findings lend support to the U. S. Supreme Court's decision to permit closed-circuit testimony at trials when vulnerable children testify.

CONCLUSION

The American legal system was designed with the testimony of adult witnesses in mind. The recent rise in child sexual abuse cases has challenged this adult system not only to accept and accurately interpret the testimony of child witnesses, but to adapt to their special needs. There are numerous questions about the ability of children to provide accurate, credible, and complete testimony. One question concerns the contexts that best support accurate and complete reports. Research on the effects of situational variables on children's statements has revealed children's sensitivity to the interpersonal and emotional contexts in which they are questioned. More specifically, intimidation and "confrontational stress" appear to have an adverse effect on child testimony (Bussey, Lee, & Grimbeck, Chapter 7, this volume; Goodman et al., 1991; Hill & Hill, 1987; Peters, 1990), whereas social support, including the presence of a parent or loved one in court and shielding the child witness from onlookers, appears to have beneficial effects for children (Goodman, Bottoms, et al., 1991; Goodman et al., in press; Moston, 1987).

The research described in this chapter addresses the current controversy of allowing children to testify through the use of innovative courtroom techniques. At present, legal discussion continues as to the need for such modifications, and future rulings by the courts are expected. One important consideration for the courts is whether innovative techniques are perceived as fair. Although further research is needed, it appears from our survey that many laypersons support protective measures for child witnesses.

Because children have become frequent visitors to the witness stand, research that promotes the most accurate and complete testimony and that promotes the fairness of trials is increasingly important.

ACKNOWLEDGMENT

Writing of this chapter was funded in part by grants to Gail S. Goodman from the National Center on Child Abuse and Neglect and the Baldy Center for Law and Social Policy at the State University of New York at Buffalo. We thank Ann E. Tobey, Holly Orcutt, Sherry F. Thomas, Cheryl Shapiro, Greg Clark, David Barringer, Kathleen Cavanaugh, Cathy Saint John, and Toby Sachsenmaier for their assistance.

REFERENCES

Anderson, J. (1990). *Cognitive psychology and its implications.* New York: W.H. Freeman.

Baker-Ward, L., Hess, T. M., & Flannagan, D. A. (1990). The effects of involvement on children's memory for events. *Cognitive Development, 5,* 55–69.

Bartlett, F. (1932). *Remembering.* Cambridge, England: Cambridge University Press.

Baxter, J. S. (1990). The suggestibility of child witnesses: A review. *Applied Cognitive Psychology, 4,* 393–407.

Berliner, L., & Barbieri, M. K. (1984). The testimony of the child victim of sexual assault. *Journal of Social Issues, 40,* 125–138.

Bottoms, B. L., Goodman, G. S., Schwartz-Kenney, B., Sachsenmaier, T., & Thomas, S. (1990, March). *Keeping secrets: Implications for children's testimony.* Paper presented at the American Psychology and Law Meetings, Williamsburg, VA.

Brennan, M., & Brennan, R. E. (1988). *Strange language.* Waga Waga, Australia: Riverina Murray Institute.

Brewer, W. (1990). Memory for randomly sampled autobiographical events. In U. Neisser & E. Winograd (Eds.), *Remembering reconsidered: Ecological and traditional approaches to the study of memory* (pp. 21–90). Cambridge, MA: Cambridge University Press.

Briere, J., & Conte, J. (in press). Self-reported amnesia for abuse in adults molested as children. *Journal of Traumatic Stress.*

Brigham, J. C., Van Verst, M., Bothwell, R. K. (1986). Accuracy of children's eyewitness identifications in a field setting. *Basic and Applied Social Psychology, 7,* 295–306.

Bulkley, J. (1985). *Innovations in the prosecution of child sexual abuse.* Washington, DC: American Bar Association.

Bussey, K., Lee, K., & Ross, C. (1991, April). Factors influencing children's lying and truthfulness. In M. DeSimone & M. Toglia (Chairs), *Lying and truthfulness among young children: Implications for their participation in legal proceedings.* Symposium presented at the Society for Research in Child Development, Seattle, WA.

Carter, C. (1992). *The effects of linguistic complexity and social support on children's reports*. Unpublished doctoral dissertation, State University of New York at Buffalo, Buffalo.

Ceci, S. J., & Leichtman, M. (1992, March). Group distortion effects in preschoolers' reports. In D. Peters (Chair), *Issues related to the witness child*. Symposium presented at the American Psychology and Law Biennial Meeting, San Diego, CA.

Ceci, S. J., Ross, D., & Toglia, M. (1987). Suggestibility of children's memory: Psycholegal implications. *Journal of Experimental Psychology: General, 116,* 38–49.

Christianson, S. A. (1992). Emotional stress and eyewitness memory: A critical review. *Psychological Bulletin, 112,* 284-309.

Clarke-Stewart, A., Thompson, W., & Lepore, S. (1989, April). *Manipulating children's interpretations through interrogation*. Paper presented at the Society for Research in Child Development Convention, Kansas City, MO.

Coy v. Iowa, 108 S. Ct. 2798 (1988).

Craig v. Maryland, 110 S. Ct 834 (1990).

Davies, G., Tarrant, A., & Flin, R. (1989). Close encounters of the witness kind: Children's memory for a simulated health inspection. *British Journal of Psychology, 80,* 415–429.

DeFrancis, V. (1969). *Protecting the child victim of sex crimes committed by adults*. Denver, CO: American Humane Association.

Dent, H. (1977). Stress as a factor influencing person recognition in identification parades. *Bulletin of British Psychological Society, 30,* 339-340.

Dent, H. (1990). Interviewing. In J. Doris (Ed.), *Suggestibility of children's recollections* (pp. 138–146). Washington, DC: American Psychological Association.

Dent, H., & Stephenson, G. (1979). An experimental study of the effectiveness of different techniques of questioning child witnesses. *British Journal of Social and Clinical Psychology, 18,* 41–51.

Donaldson, M. (1979). *Children's minds*. New York: W. W. Norton.

Fischer, K., & Bullock, D. (1984). Cognitive development in school-age children: Conclusions and new directions. In W. Collins (Ed.), *Development during middle childhood: The years from six to twelve* (pp. 70–146). Washington, DC: National Academy Press.

Gibbens, T., & Prince, J. (1963). *Child victims of sex crimes*. London: Institute for the Study and Treatment of Delinquency.

Goodman, G. S. (1984). Children's testimony in historical perspective. *Journal of Social Issues, 40,* 9–31.

Goodman, G. S., & Aman, C. (1991). Children's use of anatomically detailed dolls to recount an event. *Child Development, 61,* 1859–1971.

Goodman, G. S., Aman, C., & Hirschman, J. (1987). Child sexual and physical abuse: Children's testimony. In S. Ceci, M. Toglia, & D. Ross (Eds.), *Children's eyewitness memory* (pp. 1–23). New York: Springer-Verlag.

Goodman, G. S., Bottoms, B. L., Schwartz-Kenney, B., & Rudy, L. (1991).

Children's testimony about a stressful event: Improving children's reports. *Journal of Narrative and Life History, 7,* 69–99.

Goodman, G. S., Hepps, D., & Reed, R. S. (1986). The child victim's testimony. In A. Haralambie (Ed.), *New issues for child advocates.* Phoenix, AZ: Arizona Council of Attorneys for Children.

Goodman, G. S., Hirschman, J., Hepps, D., & Rudy, L. (1991). Children's memory for stressful events. *Merrill-Palmer Quarterly, 37,* 109–158.

Goodman, G. S., Levine, M., & Melton, G. B. (1992). The best evidence produces the best law. *Law and Human Behavior, 16,* 244–251.

Goodman, G. S., Levine, M., Melton, G. B., & Ogden, D. W. (1991). Child witnesses and the confrontation clause: The American Psychological Association Brief in *Maryland v. Craig. Law and Human Behavior, 15,* 13–29.

Goodman, G. S., & Reed, R. (1986). Age differences in eyewitness testimony. *Law and Human Behavior, 10,* 317–332.

Goodman, G. S., Rudy, L., Bottoms, B. L., & Aman, C. (1990). Children's concerns and memory: Issues of ecological validity in the study of children's eyewitness testimony. In R. Fivush & J. A. Hudson (Eds.), *Knowing and remembering in young children* (pp. 249–284). New York, NY: Cambridge University Press.

Goodman, G. S., Sachsenmaier, T., Batterman-Faunce, J., Tobey, A., Thomas, S., Orcutt, H., & Schwartz-Kenney, B. (1992, August). Impact of innovative court procedures on children's testimony. In B. L. Bottoms & M. Levine (Chairs), *The actual and perceived competency of child witnesses.* Symposium presented at the American Psychological Association Convention, Washington, D.C.

Goodman, G. S., & Schwartz-Kenney, B. (1992). Why knowing a child's age is not enough: Effects of cognitive, social, and emotional factors on children's testimony. In R. Flin & H. Dent (Eds.), *Children as witnesses* (pp. 15–32). London: Wiley.

Goodman, G. S., Taub, E., Jones, D., England, P., Port, L., Rudy, L., Prado, L. (in press). Emotional effects of criminal court testimony on child sexual assault victims. *Monographs of the Society for Research in Child Development.*

Goodman, G. S., Wilson, M., Hazan, C., & Reed, R. (1989, April). *Children's testimony nearly four years after an event.* Paper presented at the Eastern Psychological Association Convention, Boston, MA.

Gudjonsson, G. H., & Clark, N. K. (1986). Suggestibility in police interrogation: A social psychological model. *Social Behavior, 1,* 83–104.

Herbert v. Superior Court, 117 Cal. App. 3d 611, 172 Cal. Rptr. 850 (1981).

Hill, P., & Hill, S. (1987). Videotaping children's testimony: An empirical view. *Michigan Law Review, 85,* 809–833.

Howe, M.L. (1991). Misleading children's story recall: Forgetting and reminiscence of the facts. *Developmental Psychology, 27,* 746–762.

Idaho v. Wright, 110 S.Ct. 3139 (1990).

Kail, R. (1990). *The development of memory in children* (3rd ed.). New York: W.H. Freeman.

King, M., & Yuille, J. (1987). Suggestibility and the child witness. In S. Ceci, M.

Toglia, & D. Ross (Eds.), *Children's eyewitness memory* (pp. 24–35). New York: Springer-Verlag.

Leippe, M., Romanczyk, A., & Manion, A. (1991). Eyewitness memory for a touching experience: Accuracy differences between child and adult witnesses. *Journal of Applied Psychology, 76*, 367–379.

Loftus, E. F. (1974). Reconstructing memory: The incredible eyewitness. *Psychology Today, 8*, 116–118.

Loftus, E. F. (1979). *Eyewitness testimony.* Cambridge, MA: Harvard University Press.

Loftus, E. F. (1992, August). *The reality of repressed memories.* Paper presented at the American Psychological Association Convention, Washington, D.C.

Loftus, E. F., & Davies, G. M. (1984). Distortions in the memory of children. *Journal of Social Issues, 40*, 51–67.

Loftus, E., & Palmer, J. (1974). Reconstruction of automobile destruction: An example of the interaction between language and memory. *Journal of Verbal Learning and Verbal Behavior, 13*, 585–589.

Marchese, C. L. (1990). Child victims of sexual abuse: Balancing a child's trauma against the defendant's confrontation rights—*Coy v. Iowa. Journal of Contemporary Health Law and Policy, 6*, 411–435.

Marin, B. V., Holmes, D. L., Guth, M., & Kovac, P. (1979). The potential of children as eyewitnesses. *Law and Human Behavior, 3*, 295–306.

Melton, G., Berliner, L., Limber, S., Jacobs, J. E., Oberlander, L. B., Yamamoto, M. (1992). *Preparing sexually abused children for testimony: Children's perceptions of the legal process* (Grant No. 90-CA-1274). Final report to the National Center on Child Abuse and Neglect, Washington, DC.

Moston, S. (1987, September). *The effects of the provision of social support in child interviews.* Paper presented at the British Psychological Association Annual Conference, York, England.

Myers, J. (1987). *Child witness law and practice.* New York: Wiley.

Myers, N., & Perlmutter, M. (1978). Memory in the years from two to five. In P. A. Ornstein (Ed.), *Memory development in children* (pp. 191–218). Hillsdale, NJ: Erlbaum.

Nelson, K. (1986). *Event knowledge.* Hillsdale, NJ: Erlbaum

Otis, M. (1924). A study of suggestibility in children. *Archives of Psychology, 11*, 5–108.

Parker, J., & Carranza, L. (1989). Eyewitness testimony of children in target-present and target-absent lineups. *Law and Human Behavior, 13*, 133–150.

Perry, N. W., & Wrightsman, L. S. (1991). *The child witness.* Newbury Park, CA: Sage.

Peters, D. (1991). Confrontational stress and children's testimony: Some experimental findings. In J. Doris (Ed.), *The suggestibility of children's recollections* (pp. 60–76). Washington, DC: American Psychological Association.

Price, D. W. W., & Goodman, G. S. (1990). Visiting the wizard: Children's memory of a recurring event. *Child Development, 61*, 664–680.

Pynoos, R., & Eth, S. (1984). The child as witness to homicide. *Journal of Social Issues, 40,* 87–108.

Rudy, L., & Goodman, G. S. (1991). Effects of participation on children's reports: Implications for children's testimony. *Developmental Psychology, 27,* 527–538.

Saywitz, K. (1989). Children's conceptions of the legal system: "Court is a place to play basketball." In S. Ceci, D. Ross, & M. Toglia (Eds.), *Perspectives on children's testimony* (pp. 131–157). New York: Springer- Verlag.

Saywitz, K., Goodman, G. S., Nicholas, E., & Moan, S. (1991). Children's memories of a physical examination involving genital touch: Implications for reports of child sexual abuse. *Journal of Consulting and Clinical Psychology, 59,* 682–691.

Smith, V. L., & Ellsworth, P. C. (1987). The social psychology of eyewitness accuracy: Misleading questions and communication expertise. *Journal of Applied Psychology, 72,* 294–300.

Spencer, J., & Flin, R. (1990). *The evidence of children: The law and the psychology.* London: Blackstone Press.

Stern, W. (1910). Abstracts of lectures on the psychology of testimony and on the study of individuality. *American Journal of Psychology, 21,* 270–282.

Steward, M. (1992). Preliminary findings from the University of California–Davis, Child Memory Study. *The Advisor, 5,* 11–13.

Swim, J., Borgida, E., & McCoy K. (1991, August). Children's videotaped testimony and jury decision making. In A. Brown (Chair), *Child witnesses and children's testimony.* Annual meeting of the American Psychological Association, San Francisco, CA.

Terr, L. (1991). *Too scared to cry.* New York: Harper & Row.

Tobey, A., & Goodman, G. S. (in press). Children's eyewitness memory: Effects of participation and forensic content. *Child Abuse & Neglect.*

U. S. Constitution, Amendment VI.

Vygotsky, L. S. (1978). *Mind in society: The development of higher psychological processes.* Cambridge, MA: Harvard University Press. (Original work published 1934)

Warren, A., Hulse-Trotter, K., & Tubbs, E. C. (1991). Inducing resistance to suggestibility in children. *Law and Human Behavior, 15,* 273–285.

Warren, A., & Startwood, J.N. (in press). Developmental issues in flashbulb memory research: Children recall the Challenger event. In E. Winograd & U. Neisser (Eds.), *Affect and accuracy in recall: The problem of flashbulb memories.* New York: Cambridge University Press.

Whipple, G. (1913). Psychology of testimony and report. *Psychological Bulletin, 10,* 264–268.

Whitcomb, D. (1981). Assisting child victims in the courts: The practical side of legislative reform. *Response, 9,* 9–12.

Whitcomb, D. (1992). *When the victim is a child* (2nd ed.). Washington, DC: Department of Justice.

Williams, L. M. (1992). Adult memories of childhood abuse: Preliminary findings from a longitudinal study. *The Advisor, 5,* 19-21.

Wilson, C. E. (1989). Criminal procedure—Presumed guilty: The use of videotaped and closed-circuit televised testimony in child sex abuse prosecutions and the defendant's right to confrontation—*Coy v. Iowa*. *Campbell Law Review, 11*, 381–396.

Yuille, J. (1988). The systematic assessment of children's testimony. *Canadian Psychology, 29*, 247–262.

Index